# Contents

GW01314336

# Introduction

The research for this book evolved organically because the initial intention was to prepare a piece of work to mark the 50th Anniversary of The Hills Cricket Club and to update the *History of Cricket in Fingal* which the late Joe Clinton had presented to the Skerries Historical Society in April 1994. The early stages of the work provided the basis for a Nostalgia Evening at The Hills CC. Later, a tribute event for the Fingal Cricket League was held at The Hills, and there was a sense that something of a more permanent nature should be attempted so that the place of cricket in the sporting heritage of Fingal would be recorded for posterity.

This was an opportune time to undertake some research and to do some writing. General articles on the Fingal Cricket League were drafted, and then follow-up chapters on individual clubs were written. It appeared that the material would rest on the laptop and never see the light of day, and I mentioned to Barry Chambers of Cricket Europe that I had been writing some bits and pieces, but they were probably only of very localised interest. Barry very kindly uploaded the different articles, and he was very complimentary, so this provided the impetus to keep going.

In the words of a famous Irish storyteller, "things rested so", until there was a chance encounter with Alan Little of Merrion Cricket Club who offered to assist if I wished to turn the various articles into a book. I am very grateful to Alan for the patience which he has shown during the past few months with all the edits that have been done, and I know that he has been particularly impressed with the emphasis on the Oxford comma.

When the chapters were written, they were complete with endnotes, but for practical reasons, it was decided to dispense with them. If, however, any person wishes to check out a reference, this can be readily accommodated. The aim of the project was to tell the story of Fingal cricket in a general sense, and for that reason, the chapters on the various clubs are of necessity synoptic. Originally, each chapter was written on a stand-alone basis, with the result that there was a certain amount of repetition when the chapters were combined in book form, and insofar as was possible, much of the repetition has been eliminated.

## Acknowledgments

I wish to acknowledge with gratitude the tremendous amount of support, encouragement, and information which I received from very many people, and I apologise in advance if I have omitted any person from the following list:

Peter Agnew, John Andrews, John Archer, Roland Bradley, the Byrne Family (Maureen, Martin, and Paddy) who gave me access to the Minutes of the Fingal Cricket League Committee, Gillian Byrne, Fergus Carroll, Barry Chambers, Joe Clinton (RIP) and Mary Clinton, Seamus Clinton (RIP) and Margaret Clinton, Ray Daly, Derek Dockrell, Joe Doherty, P. J. Doolan, Matt Dwyer, Michael Dwyer, William Dwyer, John Elder, Martin Everard, Bill Felton, Dick Forrest, Jim Garry, Michael Gavin, Malachy Gavin, Kathleen Gavin, Jim Glennon, Brian Gilmore, Seán Hoare, Albert Harper, Jim Hawkins, Paschal Henchy, Alan Hughes, Eddie Lewis, Tommy Geraghty, George Kitteringham, Bernadette Marks, Joey and Angela Mooney, Declan Moore, John, Anna and Jody Morgan, the family of Thomas Mc Grane who gave me access to some of the Fingal League Archives, Audrey Rooney-Murphy, Anne Murphy, Tom Murphy (RIP), Joe Murphy, Kevin Murray, David O'Connor, Maurice O'Keeffe, Brian O'Sullivan, Donal O'Sullivan, Murray Power, John M. Pryor, Liam Rooney, Oona Roycroft, Martin Russell, Michael Sharp (RIP) and Mary Sharp, Stella Downes, Avril and Eddie Scanlan, Matt Sheridan, Ger Siggins, Philip Smith, Rodney Smythe, Brian Stirling, Bill Stuart, Bobby Swarbrigg, Ian Talbot, Heatley Tector, Peter Thew, Henry Tighe, Deryck Vincent, David Williams, and John Wills.

I am hugely indebted to Joe Curtis who has provided the majority of the photographs which appear throughout the text. He has been incredibly generous with his time, his photographic expertise, and his knowledge of local history. Margaret Curtis is included in this note of gratitude because she was always very welcoming and hospitable when I intruded on the Curtis household.

My wife, Marie, continued to be a model of tolerance and forbearance while all this research was being undertaken, and I am very grateful to her for her love and support over the years. My sons, Pat and James, my daughter-in-law, Carla, have all been very supportive on an ongoing basis, and Alex, our lovely grandson, has brought much joy and happiness into all our lives. This book is dedicated to them.

### Fingall: Ancient and Modern

The ancient district of Fingall comprised of the major part of County Dublin which lies north of the River Tolka. The *Annals of the Four Masters* refer to the Rivers Tolka and Delvin as being its northern and southern boundaries and suggest that its western boundary runs from a "small hill west of Finglas". In *Fair Fingall*, Patrick Archer suggested that this small hill is close to Cappagh Hospital. From Ballybough on the Tolka to Knocknaggin at the mouth of the Delvin, Fingall was 32km in length, and its greatest width – from Rush to Knockineek – was 20km.

The name Fingall is derived from the Gaelic, *Fine Gall*, (pronounced "finna gall") and originally meant the tribe of foreigners. This was the name given to a force of Danish invaders who settled in the area along the coast in the 9$^{th}$ century, but in time, the name, Fingall, came to mean the strip of land which these people occupied, and as the invaders conquered more and more land, the district was extended, and Fingall came to mean the territory of foreigners or of strangers. Fingall continued to be a distinct district until 1210 A.D. when King John assigned it to the County of Dublin. About the close of the 16$^{th}$ century, the name, Fingall, ceased to be used officially, but it remained in use among the people because it was seen as being indicative of their origins as a distinctive community, and the people of the area continued to be known as Fingallians. As part of the process of Anglicisation, the spelling of the name changed to Fingal, and this spelling of the name can still be seen in the Fingal Gaelic Football league and the Fingal Cricket League.

## Fingal

The county of Fingal was established on 1 January 1994. It covers an area of 448 square km and extends from the River Liffey and the city boundary to Balbriggan. The Fingal region includes Castleknock, Clonsilla, Blanchardstown, Mulhuddart, Swords, Skerries, Malahide, Rush, Lusk, Donabate, Balbriggan, Portmarnock, Howth, Sutton, and a large rural area to the north and west of the county.

## Fingal Cricket League

The teams involved in the league were mostly within a 10 to 15 km radius of Balbriggan. Cricket wasn't played in Swords, although a team from Technicon, a factory in Swords played intermittently in the Fingal League. Malahide is very much part of Fingal, but Malahide CC only played in the Fingal League for one season as far as can be ascertained. Using the old Dublin to Belfast road as a guide, Knockbrack, Ring Commons, Balrothery and the Man-O'-War Cricket Clubs were on the west of the road; Balbriggan was in the middle, with Skerries, Rush and The Hills being on the east. The Cricket Leinster website lists 10 teams as being in the Fingal area, but it was beyond the scope of this research to include clubs such as Castleknock, Lucan, Swords and Tyrrelstown which have been established in the very recent past.

# Chapter 1: Cricket in Fingal, 1825-1925

## Early Days, 1825-1890

The earliest references to cricket in the Fingal area are contained in the diaries of Mrs Taylor of Ardgillan when she mentions cricket in Hampton (Balbriggan) and in Rush (Kenure) in the 1820s. This is what was colloquially called "Big House" cricket where the gentry of an area played games against each other during the day and then had a tea-party and dance after the game. Hampton was again the venue when cricket was revived in Balbriggan in 1844, and on 15 July 1844, Balbriggan beat Rathmines by an innings and 38 runs.

By the early 1860s, the focus had shifted from the Big Houses to the formation of cricket clubs, although members of the gentry were centrally involved in these enterprises, and continued to provide the playing facilities, the equipment, and the players. Malahide Cricket Club was founded in 1861 and Balbriggan Cricket Club was re-established on 12 May 1863. In 1863 also, there is a reference to a team from Balcunnin playing against White Hart, and in 1865, Balbriggan played Drogheda, home and away.

In the 1870s, there are very few reports of games, but in the ones which are reported, the influence of the gentry continued to be very much in evidence. When Co. Meath played Malahide, the Hon. Mr Talbot "contributed 18 by steady play and held possession of his wicket to the last." The reply for Co. Meath was led by the Hon. Mr R. Plunket who scored 20, not out. The result of this game was Malahide 55, Co. Meath, 54. The Hussey family of Westown House did not confine their cricketing activities to playing for Westown House, they also featured for Navan. In the game against Co. Louth in August 1872, Navan did not have a great start because the team was two players short (the two Mr Husseys), for the first innings but the situation was retrieved in the second innings when the Husseys arrived, and young Mr Hussey scored 32 runs. His father, Malachi was not as fortunate. He scored a duck.

By the mid-1870s, it was recognised by the mainstream Nationalist paper, *The Freeman's Journal* that cricket which had been considered elitist was now recognised as "being good" for members of the general populace. In the words of a contributor to the *Freeman's Journal* 1875:

> Country gentlemen should unite and form clubs in their county. These clubs should not be exclusively composed of gentlemen. The best men, whether gentlemen or otherwise should be found and got to play matches.

The leader writer of the *Freeman's Journal* weighed in with his comments regarding cricket on 26 April 1875:

> It is only yesterday, comparatively speaking that the Ancient British recreation spread to Ireland, where it was at first rather unpopularised by the notion that it was altogether an aristocratic business and therefore a thing to merit the aversion of Demos. But people soon recognise what is good for themselves; speedily the healthful and enjoyable amusement began to supersede the rough and sometimes dangerous pastimes which had previously made the joy of popular leisure. At present, it is no exaggeration to say, cricket is known and played all over the island. We may take it for granted that the youth of the "next series" will establish it permanently.

Members of the gentry such as Hamilton of Hampton, Filgate of Lowtherstone Lodge, Woods of Milverton Hall, Woods of Whitestown, and Hussey of Westown House played their part in fostering cricket, and the tenant farmers, farm labourers and small farmers who lived in the vicinity of the landed gentry were also very involved in playing cricket. If the "Big House" team was short of players, the gardeners, the farm labourers, or tenant farmers were recruited to make up the side. They tended to be bowlers, fielders, and late-order batsmen because it was important that the gentlemen batted first.

By the early 1880s, there was evidence of the democratisation of the sport in Fingal. There were names on the scorecards other than members of the gentry. Knockbrack CC was founded in 1880, and there were new teams in Skerries (Skerries Excelsior), Balbriggan, Garristown, Naul and Balscadden. At this stage, there was evidence of sensitivities arising from the Land War, and when Mr Hussey made the facilities at Westown available for Naul CC, a reporter was taken very severely to task by a letter-writer for confusing Naul CC and Westown, and salt was rubbed into the wound because the paper also reported the score incorrectly:

> In your issue of this day there appears a report of a cricket match played between Westown Naul CC and Matt CC. Same report is incorrect, no club whatsoever being in Westown. The game was between Naul CC and Matt on the ground of A. S. Hussey, Westown kindly given for the occasion. When stumps were drawn, Naul had scored 41 for their second innings for the loss of 5 wickets. Your report states they were all out for 40. (Signed:) Thomas Duff.

Why did it matter that the name of the club was reported incorrectly? Apart from the obvious comment regarding the importance of accuracy, the Duffs were Nationalists, and although they were grateful for the use of the ground, they did not wish to be associated too closely with the gentry. Despite these reservations, Mr Hussey played for Naul CC in the following season, and he featured prominently in a game against Inchicore Catholic Club when he contributed 65 runs. Another person, J. Ennis, also got runs (27 not out) for Naul CC, and his son, J. T. ("The Squire") Ennis was to be very influential in ensuring the preservation of cricket in Fingal.

## Why did Cricket Survive in Fingal? 1890-1925

Sports historians and various commentators have provided many reasons for cricket's decline from being a mainstream sport in Ireland in the 1870s to its status as a minority sport in the early 20th Century. It is beyond the scope of this study to analyse the causes for this phenomenon, but it is necessary to outline them briefly so that a context can be provided for an account of cricket in Fingal. One of the consequences of the Land Wars of the early 1880s was to drive a further wedge in the already difficult relationship between landlords and tenants with the result that landlords were not inclined to engage in sporting activities with their tenants when violent actions were occurring on a regular basis. The Gaelic Revival of the early 1890s with its emphasis on all things Irish and its castigation of English games and goods meant that there was plenty of ammunition (no pun intended) for those who perceived cricket as being the most quintessentially English of all field sports, and Irish-Irelanders were quick to vent their spleen on cricket and cricketers.

It is dangerous to generalise, and Paul Rouse suggests that the complexities of life in rural Ireland meant that different factors were at work in different areas, and that it is not always possible to ascribe neat divisions in sport to a particular reason. This was undoubtedly the case in Fingal (and Meath) towards the end of the 19th Century and the beginning of the 20th Century, and while cricket was dying in parts of the country, it was thriving in these two areas. To ascertain the reasons these regions appeared to be swimming against the tide, it is necessary to examine the factors which contributed to the development of cricket in Fingal during this period.

There were large-landed estates in Fingal such as those of Holmpatrick in Skerries and Talbot in Malahide, but the pattern of land ownership in Fingal differed from that which existed in the rest of Ireland. Due to the various Land Acts, many of the tenant farmers were enabled to buy-out their holdings, with the result that there was not the same level of dependence on the gentry for the promotion of cricket. The farmers who were able to give access to a field for cricket couldn't be without the field for the season so the only fields that could be given over were used for grazing purposes. From a cricketing perspective, it was always preferable to be given a field which had sheep grazing on it because the grass tended to be shorter. A consequence of the animals grazing on the field was that one of the first jobs on the day of a game was to clear the field of excrement.

It is not being suggested that Fingal was an egalitarian Utopia, and that relationships between landowners and farm-labourers were always harmonious, but at a general level, it appears that there was a level of tolerant co-existence with the gentry leading totally separate lives to the rest of the community. Cricket was an area of activity where there was a connection between the gentry and their tenants although it was reported that at some games, the gentry took their refreshments in different quarters to their workers.

The availability of the rail network was of crucial importance because it provided flexibility and choice in terms of fixtures for teams and it is no coincidence that clubs were founded in Malahide, Skerries, Balbriggan and Rush. The train timetables tended to dictate the starting and finishing times of games. For example, the members of the Civil Service 2nd XI were advised to meet at Amiens Street Station at 1.30 p.m. for a game against Balbriggan which was scheduled to commence at 3.00. Corduff's wonderful trip to Dublin to play against St James CC, which involved some cricket, and lots of singing and dancing was curtailed by the "unwelcome train time."

Among the other factors which contributed to the growth of cricket in Fingal was the involvement of the visitors to Skerries and Rush who rented houses in these towns during the summer. The Holmpatrick cricket team was comprised of members of the sizeable Anglican population in Skerries, summer residents and visitors to the area. Balbriggan had developed as a major manufacturing centre with the result that there was a constant influx of migrant workers from England to the town.

Due to a lack of league structures and a resistance among some people to the concept of competitions, clubs arranged games by placing advertisements in the local newspapers, indicating available dates or preferences in terms of travel. For example, the Emmet Cricket Club in Skerries expressed a desire for "a few more fixtures with country clubs." The other means of obtaining fixtures was to issue a public challenge.

On the evidence of the reports in the local newspapers, there were at least twenty-eight cricket clubs in Fingal during the period 1897 to 1910. Many of these clubs could more correctly be called teams because they were simply groups of like-minded individuals who came together to play cricket and had been given access to a field by a friendly landowner. The fields which were used could change from season to season, or even during a season, and finding a field in which to play was a constant problem.

Between 1910 and 1913, there are very few reports of cricket being played in Fingal. Whether this was due to less cricket being played or if there was pressure on space due to publicity being given to other sports or other events is not clear. In 1913, Ring Commons CC indicated in April that it was open for challenges for the coming season. Knockbrack continued to play cricket, and Gormanstown CC made a comeback after being absent for some years. There was some cricket being played during the war, because on 29 August 1915, Lieutenant M. F. Healy thought it strange that people in Skerries preferred playing cricket and golf to fighting in the war. From 1913 until 1925, the only report in the local press is a reference to a schoolboys' game which was played in Rush in 1920.

Local, national, and international events were predominant during the next twelve years or so, with minimal attention being given to the reporting of cricket. The Farm Labourers' Strike, the 1916 Rising, the War of Independence and the Civil War caused attitudes to harden regarding anything to do with England, and cricket was adjudged by cultural nationalists to be the most English of all sports, a source of fraternisation with the enemy and the cause of emasculation of the virile Irish people. Politically and socially, it was not expedient to be involved in cricket during troubled times, but the regard for cricket in Fingal ran very deep, and traditionally, Fingallians are "possessed of an independent spirit." They did not appreciate being dictated to by cultural nationalists or others regarding the games that they might or might not play.

The re-birth of cricket in Fingal commenced in 1925 with the re-organisation of Skerries CC and Knockbrack, but the most important development was the announcement in October 1926 that North County Dublin cricket clubs intended to form a league and were confident of having the league "in full working order before the opening of the next season". Having taken all other factors into account, the greatest single factor in the preservation of cricket in Fingal was the establishment of the Fingal League.

Ardgillan, circa 1900 (Photo courtesy of Joe Curtis)

Hampton Hall, courtesy of Joe Curtis

Winter Lodge (Woods Family)

Milverton Hall (Photo courtesy of Joe Curtis)

Circa 1925

Lowtherstone Lodge, Home of the Filgate Family  (Photo courtesy of Joe Curtis)

Westown House in a derelict state (Photo courtesy of Joe Curtis)

Whitestown House

# Chapter 2: The Fingal League, 1926-2012

## The Establishment of The Fingal League, 1926-1930

It took some time after the War of Independence and the Civil War for cricket clubs to be re-formed in Fingal because emotions were still very raw regarding the playing of this most English of games. In July 1925, Skerries Cricket Club was re-organised, and Knockbrack CC also re-commenced its cricketing activities. In 1926, there were cricket teams in Balbriggan, Ring Commons, Knightstown, Skerries and Knockbrack, but fixtures for the most part were still being arranged as challenges rather than there being any official structures in place.

There are conflicting accounts regarding when the Fingal League was actually established. At the Fingal Cricket League's First Annual Dance in 1931, Mr J. T. Ennis gave a brief account of the history of the League, and he stated that it started in Ring Commons in 1926 with two clubs. Skerries was definitely one of the clubs because it was reported in 1928 that Skerries had won the League three years in a row, so this suggests that there was some form of competitive structure in place in 1926. A report in the *Drogheda Independent* of 23 October 1926 refers to an imminent meeting of North County Dublin Cricket Clubs with a view to forming a league. It also indicated that the promoters of the concept were "confident of having the league in full working order before the opening of the next season." A committee was formed, and it met in Ring Commons Schoolhouse on 13 March to make some additions to the rules with the named officers being Adhamh Mac an Bhaird (Secretary) and John Mc Dermott (Treasurer). There is absolutely no doubt that the Fingal League was fully operational in 1927 because detailed reports of games were furnished to the *Drogheda Independent*. The teams which competed in the Fingal League in 1927 were Skerries, Knockbrack, Macraidh (Knockbrack Second XI), Ballymadun, Knightstown, Black Hills, and Ring Commons. The first fixtures were played on Sunday, 15 May 1927 and the final game was played on 18 September 1927.

At a meeting of Skerries Cricket Club on 26 September 1927, a motion was adopted thanking Adam Ward, League Secretary "for his very efficient and satisfactory services... and the able manner in which he had handled many difficult problems, but the club also put on record its commendation for all the clubs who had taken part in the League on "the splendid sporting spirit which dominated throughout the season".

J. T. Ennis continued as President, but a new Secretary (John Purfield) and treasurer (J. W. Rooney) were elected at the AGM on 18 March 1928. The number of teams had increased to ten, with the three new teams Barnageeragh, Baldwinstown and Balrothery joining the seven teams which had played in 1927. It was now necessary to create two divisions, and there was a play-off between the two teams which finished top of their sections. The final was played at Michael White's field in Ring Commons on 2 September 1928 between Skerries and Barnageeragh. The scores were Skerries 29, Barnageeragh 21.

In 1929, the number of teams had increased to fifteen. There were no defections from the previous year and the new teams were Balbriggan, Naul Hill, Skerries B, Balcunnin and Curkeen. Again, the league was divided into two sections, and by the end of the season, most of the teams in Division A had played 12 games, and the teams in Division B had played 14 games.

During this incident-packed season, there were two other developments which are worthy of mention. The Knockbrack Club indicated its intention to sponsor the purchase of a cup which would be presented to the winners of the Fingal League, and it was anticipated that Knockbrack's name would be inscribed on the cup when it was placed on exhibition, but the cup was not bought until early in 1930 so Knockbrack's name was not inscribed on the Cup as the first winners. In addition to Fingal League games, challenge matches were still being organised. Baldwinstown was due to play Ballymadun on 6 October for £5 a side and to avoid any allegations of bias, neutral umpires were appointed.

**A Period of Growth, 1930-1940**

At the AGM in 1930, there was a wave of optimism with representatives of twenty-five clubs present which if it had translated into teams entered in the Fingal League would have constituted an increase of ten teams in comparison with the 1929 season. The officers, President (J. T. Ennis), Secretary (J. A. Purfield), Treasurer (W. Rooney), were re-elected, and P. J. Daly was elected Vice-President, but by the commencement of the season, only 19 teams had entered the League. The new teams were Portrane Psychiatric Hospital, the British Legion, and Man-O'-War. Balcunnin and Knockbrack contested the 1930 final, and the official score was 40 runs each but the *Drogheda Independent's* Correspondent, and at least another 100 people in the ground had the score at 41 to Knockbrack Second XI and 40 to Balcunnin, but the marker's decision was final, and the replay was fixed for the following Sunday.

The replay was also played at Balbriggan, and in typical Fingal fashion, the bowlers were on top. Knockbrack Second XI had the honour of being the first team to have its name inscribed on the Fingal Challenge Cup.

At the AGM in March 1931, there were twenty-five clubs represented, and the existing officers were re-elected. The playing regulations were amended, and a decision was taken to play two innings per side in the semi-finals and finals. Ring Commons CC also convened its AGM in March, but the meeting was abandoned because it was decided to have cricket practice due to the day being so fine.  When the fixtures for the season were announced, seventeen teams had entered for the league. The new teams were Baldwinstown Second XI and Rush, with the Black Hills, the British Legion and Balcunnin dropping out of the League. Balcunnin however competed in the cup competition which was played later in the season. Rush also entered the Leinster League, and two years later under the captaincy of Simon Hoare won the Leinster Junior Cup. Ballymadun and Skerries contested the Fingal League Final, and this resulted in a very easy win for Skerries.

The Management Committee then decided to organise "the Fingal Cricket Championship" which would be played as a knock-out tournament during the month of September. The final was played at Balbriggan on 27 September between Portrane and Baldwinstown. Unfortunately, it is not possible to give a definitive answer regarding the name of the winning team because two separate reports in the *Drogheda Independent* gave conflicting accounts.

For the 1932 season, P. J. Daly replaced Mr J. T. Ennis as President, the other officers remained in place, and Balbriggan CC proposed the formation of an Umpires' Association. There was general approval for this proposal and the issue was to be addressed more fully at a special delegate meeting on 24 April. This meeting was held, and the sixteen teams for the new season were arranged in Divisions A, B and C, but there was no reference to the formation of an Umpires' Association. Balcunnin re-entered the league, and a very late entry was received from Black Hills CC. This application was granted even though the first round of matches had been played.

It was obvious from early in the season that Balcunnin CC was going to be a force to be reckoned with, and the heading, "Bowling Feats at Balcunnin" in the *Drogheda Independent* of 23 July 1932 was a sign of things to come. The report referred to "one of the most marvellous bowling feats ever accomplished in the history of Fingal Cricket League". Balcunnin batted first and scored a total of 13 runs. There is then an unfortunate typographical error because the report states that it looked as if Balcunnin would have an easy victory. Even by Fingal standards, a score of 13 in the first innings should not have made any team favourites to win. By a process of elimination and by checking the teams which played in that division, the report should have stated Balbriggan. The Balbriggan reply foundered very quickly because "Murphy and Hoare found form, and it was amazing to see wicket after wicket fall in quick succession and finally to see the visitors dismissed with the incredibly low score of three runs."

The 1932 Fingal League Final was played between Balcunnin and Portrane on 11 September. Portrane was ahead after the first innings had been completed (48 runs to 36), but Balcunnin scored 80 in the second innings (S. Hoare, 23, B. Monks 25*), and Portrane only scored 47 in reply. This was Balcunnin's first time to win the Fingal Cup, and in the words of the *Drogheda Independent*, Balcunnin "played cricket in style and ran out easy winners." For the 1933 season, there were seventeen teams affiliated, with Garristown entering a team for the first time. The final between Balcunnin and Ring Commons was played at Balbriggan, and Balcunnin won by an innings.

In the 1934 season, the number of affiliated teams had fallen to thirteen with Curkeen, Knightstown, Skerries, Balcunnin and Baldwinstown Second XI opting out, and a second team from Naul joining up. It was decided to regionalise the League into two sections, East, and West Fingal, with the winner of each section playing a deciding game for the Fingal Challenge Cup. Oldtown and Portrane contested the final, with Portrane winning by two wickets.

In 1935, there were ten teams affiliated, and while the teams fluctuated from one season to the next, the league structure enabled teams to re-join if their circumstances changed whereas in the era of challenge matches, it was very difficult for a team to re-establish itself once it had opted out. Naul won the Fingal Challenge Cup for the first time by beating the Black Hills in the final. Naul scored 33 runs in the first innings, and in reply, the Black Hills scored 27. In the second innings, Naul scored 47, and with 15 minutes left to play, the Black Hills lost 6 wickets for 8 runs.

In 1936, there were still ten teams affiliated, but there were significant changes in the membership of the Fingal League. Garristown, Man-O'-War, and Balbriggan did not affiliate, but Portrane and Naul Hill had re-entered, and the new teams were Blanchardstown and Clonsilla. Rush did not enter the Fingal League for a number of seasons, because it was involved in the Leinster League, but Portrane, which also had joined the Leinster League played both Fingal League and Leinster League cricket. The final of the Fingal Cricket League was between the Black Hills and Balrothery, and the Black Hills won a low-scoring game (38 runs to 16 runs), with Hoare taking 6 wickets for 9 runs, and J. Murphy taking 4 wickets for 3 runs.

Information on the 1937 season is in scarce supply. The most noteworthy elements were the continuation of Portrane in the Leinster League and the Fingal League despite the loss of a number of prominent players. Skerries made a return to Fingal League cricket and G. L. McGowan, Secretary of the Fingal League, was elected TD in the 1937 General Election. The Fingal League Championship was won by Balrothery.

The 1938 season was a memorable one because it took three games between Portrane and Balrothery to decide the eventual winners of the Championship. Balrothery and Portrane also contested the 1939 final. The game was nearly as exciting as the previous year's encounters, with Balrothery winning by 4 runs.

## Ups and Downs, 1940-1960

At the AGM in 1940, the main officers were re-elected, and ten teams were represented at the meeting. The policy of dividing the league into two divisions continued because this facilitated the playing of a final. Balrothery maintained its dominance of Fingal cricket by beating the Black Hills in the final by 10 runs, the final score being 76 runs to 66 runs. In 1941, the same two teams contested the final, but on this occasion the result was reversed. The other noteworthy event in this season was the withdrawal of Portrane from the League due to the outbreak of foot and mouth disease.

The Fingal League structures regarding fixture-making facilitated the return of Naul Hill to cricket after a lapse of several years. The teams represented at the AGM in 1942 were Balrothery, Rush, Black Hills, Tubbergregan, Oldtown, Naul Hill, Ring Commons, Knockbrack, Baldwinstown, Ballymadun, Portrane and Balbriggan. Clonard also played in the league during this season. In 1942, the league was again divided into two sections, mainly due to transport difficulties during the Emergency. Tubbergregan beat Walshestown in the League final on a score of 69 to 29. In 1943, there were ten teams entered for the Championship, but teams had difficulties in fulfilling fixtures due it is assumed to transport issues. For example, on 16 May 1943, Oldtown and Portrane failed to travel to Ring Commons and Black Hills. Despite these difficulties, the Fingal League continued to promote a knock-out cup and the championship. Balrothery was back in the Fingal Challenge Cup Final again in 1943 but was well-beaten by Portrane.

Balrothery CC was the dominant force in Fingal Cricket during the period 1944 to 1946, winning the Challenge Cup in each of those years. The 1946 Final was not played until 1947 because Tubbergregan indicated that it would not fulfil a fixture that was scheduled for so late in the season (27 October). The game should have been played a month ago, but "harvesting operations had delayed the holding of the game." Farming matters intervened again at the start of the 1947 season with the AGM having to be postponed due to the large number of members engaged in the tillage drive. At this AGM, Mr Joe Boyce stepped down as President due to ill-health, and he was succeeded by Mr P. J. Daly. The 1946 final was eventually played on 29 June 1947 and resulted in a facile win for Balrothery who scored 53 runs against Tubbergregan who only scored 15 runs having "collapsed before the splendid bowling of Russell and Mooney." The 1947 Final between Walshestown and Knockbrack resulted in a first Fingal Challenge Cup win for Walshestown. Balrothery CC beat Knockbrack handsomely in 1948 in the final on a score of 133 runs to 21. Simon Hoare (40) was the main contributor to the Balrothery score.

At different times during the twenty years which are under review, the phrases, Fingal League Challenge Cup and Cup, are used to denote different competitions. From very early on in the life of the Fingal League, there were two sections and at one stage, three sections. This facilitated play-offs and a final. However, in order to maintain interest, a knock-out competition was also organised, but it was only played on an intermittent basis until an actual cup was purchased in 1962. For example, there is a reference at the 1949 AGM to the 1948 Final between Balrothery and Walshestown having been postponed, and re-fixed for the first day of the new season. Walshestown won the Challenge Cup in 1949 and it was won by Balrothery the following year.

There was evidence that Leinster League competitions were taking precedence over Fingal League games because in his report on the 1951 season, the Secretary of the Fingal League, Eddie Dunne, stated that the season had been a very bad one for the League with only four teams competing for the Fingal Cup, and the final between Portrane and Knockbrack not being played due to unforeseen difficulties.

In 1952, Eddie Dunne appealed to the old established clubs to re-affiliate with the league. In this category, he listed Skerries, Rush, Naul, Oldtown, and perhaps Malahide, and he indicated that teams from the three holiday camps,

Mosney, Red Island and Mr Gents would be welcome. This appeal constituted a change of policy and a change of approach because in an earlier era, Skerries had been castigated for playing people who were not "true Fingallians". This appeal was very fruitful, and there was a perception that Balrothery's successes in Leinster and in the Irish Junior Cup the previous year had provoked a revival of interest in Fingal Cricket circles. In addition to the Fingal Championship, the cup competition was also revived, and entries were received from Balrothery, Knockbrack, Portrane, Walshestown, Malahide, Naul, Skerries and Drogheda.

The surge of optimism continued into the 1953 season, and it was hoped to have thirteen teams playing in the league. The final between Walshestown and Portrane was played at Cottrellstown, and Walshestown won on a score of 18 runs to 11 runs. A new name, Cottrellstown, was added to the list of Fingal Cup winners in 1954 when Walshestown was defeated in the final. Cottrellstown played in the 1955 Final but lost to Balrothery on a score of 26 to 22 runs.

By 1956, the earlier enthusiasm had dissipated, and a special meeting was convened in late November to review the state of Fingal League cricket. There had been a big "falling-off" in the number of affiliated clubs, and cricket was deemed to be in decline in North County Dublin. Some members argued that the Fingal League should be dissolved, but the majority viewpoint was in favour of persevering. As an aside to this development, Eddie Dunne resigned as Secretary and was replaced by Thomas McGrane. Another meeting was to be held in February 1957 and every effort was to be made to get more clubs in Fingal to join the League.

The revival campaign was unsuccessful in the short-term, because only five teams affiliated for the 1957 season, and half-way through the season, Cottrellstown withdrew from the League due to "a shortage of players or a lack of interest." This was a body blow for the Fingal League, and it meant that "after some 35 years in West Fingal, cricket gets a rest." There was now a pattern developing of finals being postponed, and the 1958 Final was played in June 1959, and it resulted in a win for Knockbrack. Knockbrack retained the cup in 1960 by defeating Portrane at the Ballast Pit Grounds, Skerries.

In 1961, there were only four teams affiliated to the League and the one positive development was that Ring Commons CC re-formed. In 1962, Balbriggan re-formed with the result that the seven teams in the Fingal League were Man-O'-War, Balbriggan, Skerries, Ring Commons, Knockbrack, Balrothery and the Black Hills. Gerry Byrne was Chairman of the League and the other officers remained unchanged. It was now decided to put the second competition on a more formal footing and to purchase a cup. Balrothery CC was the first winners of this cup, and earlier in the season, had also won the Fingal Championship.

The minutes and annual reports for the 1962 to 1964 seasons were made available in 2019 by the Byrne Family, and they make fascinating reading because they provide an in-depth perspective on the work of the Fingal League Committee. For example, one of the founder member clubs was suspended for not being up to date with the Rules (sic) of Cricket, and there was a very detailed discussion regarding what constituted eligibility to play Fingal League Cricket. In the end, it was decided not to amend the existing rule.

The position regarding eligibility to play in Fingal cricket continued to exercise the members of the Fingal League Committee, and the rule was amended to read – " a person residing a week in one place was eligible to play in Fingal League". This rule was tested to the limit at various stages with teams importing professional cricketers from clubs outside the Fingal League to play Fingal League games. On the cricketing front, ten teams played in the Fingal League during the 1964 season and Knockbrack won the League and Cup double for the second year in succession.

For the next few seasons, issues regarding grounds dominated. In the 1965 season, Rush was in the difficult position of having to play all its games away due to the loss of its beautiful ground at Kenure. In 1965, Skerries CC hoped to play its games at Holmpatrick.

Man-O'-War and Knockbrack joined the Leinster League in 1963 and 1964 respectively, and Fingal League sides were very successful in Leinster cricket during this decade, winning a total of ten trophies. Irrespective of successes in Leinster, it was vitally important for Fingal League clubs to win their own competitions. Balrothery won the Fingal League and Cup double in 1965, and it won the League again in 1967. From 1966 to 1971 inclusive, Man-O'-War won the Fingal Challenge Cup every year and won the Perpetual Challenge Cup (The League) in 1966, 1969 and 1970. Balbriggan CC won the Leinster Junior Cup in 1967 and had an even more successful year in 1968 when it won the Leinster Junior League and the Fingal League for the first time by beating Man-O'-War in the final.

The teams playing in the Fingal League in 1969 were Knockbrack, Black Hills, Balbriggan, Rush, Balrothery, and Man-O'-War. This year was a landmark year for Rush CC because it opened its new ground at Kenure Park on 20 July 1969. Members of the Black Hills CC who had been playing Leinster League cricket for Balrothery decided to enter a team in the Leinster League in 1970. Permission was obtained from the Wentges' Family to play at *The Vineyard*, and The Hills CC was established at a meeting in the Holmpatrick Hotel, Skerries in October 1969.

In 1970, there were six Fingal League teams, Balrothery, Man-O'-War, Knockbrack, Balbriggan, Rush, and The Hills, playing in Leinster League cricket, and during this decade, 36 trophies were won. The Fingal League added a B League to its list of competitions, and Gerry Byrne sponsored a cup to be competed for by youth teams in Fingal.

Successes in Leinster League competitions were no guarantee of success at Fingal League level, and in 1971 while The Hills started on its long unbeaten run in Leinster cricket when it won the Junior League and Cup, Man-O'-War CC continued to be the most successful club in Fingal Competitions. In 1971, Man-O'-War won the Fingal Cup for the sixth successive year by beating Balrothery on a score of 121 to 51. Man-O'-War had three fathers and their sons on their team, Murphys (Tom and John), Sheridans (Tom and son, Dermot), and Morgans (Tom and John, his son). John Morgan (39) was top scorer for Man-O'-War, with valuable contributions from Anthony Rooney (20) and Val Farrell (20).

Balrothery won the Fingal League Cup for the 23rd time by beating The Hills, and the enthusiasm for the game was demonstrated by the group of children who marched around the field chanting "2, 4, 6, 8, we will beat you out the gate." This game was Fingal cricket at its best. Balrothery bowled 78 overs while The Hills made its way cautiously to 114. The top scorers for The Hills were Hugh Cowling (26), Jimmy Byrne (19) and John Archer (17) while the best bowlers for Balrothery were Bunny Casey (4 for 36), Kit Mooney (3 for 11) and Tommy Mooney (3 for 33). Balrothery conceded 26 extras in the field. There was a successful appeal against the light after one ball, and play resumed on the Sunday. The opening partnership of Neil Carpenter (43) and John (Ranger) Mooney (60*) put on 100 exactly, and John Mooney was joined at the crease by his uncle, Kit who had also been a member of the Balrothery team which beat The Black Hills in the final of 1944. The winning shot was a 6 by John Mooney.

In 1972, Balrothery also ended Man-O'-War's run of successes in the Fingal Championship in 1972 when it won the cup by a margin of 8 wickets. Man-O'-War lost its first four wickets for 7 runs, and John Murphy (43*) and Dermot Sheridan (10) were the only batsmen to reach double figures. Kit Mooney took 7 wickets for 18 runs off 16 overs, with the first 8 overs being maidens. In reply, John Mooney (43*) and Joe Russell (21) brought the score to

60, and then Kit Mooney (13*) with his nephew, John, achieved the target score. In 1973, The Hills' run of successes at Leinster League continued but the icing on the cake was winning the Fingal Challenge Cup for the first time under its new name. The Man-O'-War won the Fingal Championship Cup for the 7th time, shared the Senior 2 League with Clontarf, and Balrothery won the Senior 3 League.

In the Fingal League in 1974, The Hills won the first of its five in a row victories in the Championship, while Balbriggan and Man-O'-War shared the Perpetual Challenge Cup. On 28 September 1974, Christy Russell, one of the legendary Fingal cricketers, collapsed and died while he was playing for Balbriggan. In his later years, he wasn't in good health and the family had asked clubs in the area not to be asking him to play. On the day that he died, he had borrowed cricket gear to play for Balbriggan in a game against the Man-O'-War. He drove a ball through the covers and ran a single. When he arrived at the non-striker's end, he started to lean on his bat, and just as Tom Murphy came in to bowl, Christy collapsed in front of Tom Dwyer, the umpire, and died of a heart attack. Balbriggan CC presented a trophy in his memory, and until the demise of the Fingal League, the Christy Russell Trophy was the prize for winning a T20 competition.

At this stage, each of the Fingal League clubs which played in Leinster League cricket had reasonable security of tenure, and as a result, it was possible to spend time and effort on improving the pitches and the outfields. As the Fingal teams moved up the grades and played games against the more established clubs in Dublin, there was also pressure on the Fingal clubs to improve their ancillary facilities. Knockbrack opened a new pavilion in 1973, "a fine building" that had "ample dining space" and provided "a clear view of the playing field for indoor spectators." The Hills opened a new pavilion in 1977 and Rush built a pavilion in 1980.

Every year from 1975 to 1979 inclusive, Man-O'-War won the Challenge Cup, and this run of victories was interrupted by The Hills in 1980. Between 1975 and 1980, Fingal League teams won 15 Leinster League trophies, with the high points being The Hills winning the Senior 2 League in 1977 and each of The Hills' three teams winning their leagues in 1978.

In the 1980s, applications from Fingal League clubs for senior status in Leinster cricket occupied a lot of time and energy, but this did not distract from the efforts which the Fingal clubs made with regard to winning the Fingal League trophies because bragging rights continued to be very important. In many respects, the competition became more intense because when The Hills CC was eventually granted senior status, it now became even more important to show that some of the other Fingal clubs were as deserving, if not more deserving of senior status than The Hills. The late Tom Murphy of the Man- O'-War described with great relish a Fingal Cup Final between Man-O'-War and The Hills, which was played at The Vineyard sometime after The Hills had been granted senior status, and it was attended by the "great and good of the Leinster Cricket Union." He got runs, took wickets, and was named Man-of-the Match which in the circumstances gave him considerable pleasure because a "junior club" had beaten a "senior club".

While there was no diminution of effort in the Fingal League games, the involvement of the Fingal clubs in multiple competitions under the auspices of the Leinster Cricket Union had an impact on coverage in the local newspapers and less prominence was given to Fingal League games. As a consequence, it will only be possible to provide random details of the games which took place over the next thirty years or so.

## Fingal League Cricket in the 1980s

In Fingal, there has consistently been a respect for cricket as part of the social and cultural heritage of the region, and anniversaries of particular events were invariably marked by a commemorative celebration. In late September 1980, an event was held in Balrothery to mark the 50th Anniversary of Fingal League Cricket. This description of the event as the 50th Anniversary is not accurate because Fingal League competitions had commenced in 1926, and 1980 was the 50th Anniversary of the purchase of the Fingal Perpetual Challenge Cup. The various Fingal League trophies were presented by Brian Southam (Chair) and Seamus Clinton, and those who collected trophies were Tom Murphy, Michael Murphy (Man-O'-War), Michael Dwyer (The Hills), Albert Harper (Balbriggan), John White (Ring Commons) and Tom Mooney (Balrothery). The event was organised by Martin Russell and the Master of Ceremonies was Tom McGrane (Knockbrack) which was fitting because his club had the longest record of continuous involvement in Fingal League Cricket.

In the early 1980s, the seven teams in the Fingal League were Ring Commons, Man-O'-War, Knockbrack, Rush, The Hills, Balrothery, and Balbriggan. Karl Johnston of the *Irish Press* group and later of the *Irish Times* was a great advocate for Fingal cricket and he likened the passion for the game which existed in Fingal to the passion for rugby which existed in his native Limerick among working-class people as distinct from the stereotypical descriptions of both games as being the preserve of the middle-classes. Johnston referred to the great players of bygone days whose deeds made them legends in Fingal, and he named three in particular – Simon Hoare, a superb all-rounder, Kit Mooney, "a most feared bowler" who was still taking wickets in his "twilight days" and Christy Russell who died while playing the game that he graced for so many years.

Some of the games of the 1980s produced feats that were still being talked about many years later and the first of those games was the 1981 Fingal Championship Cup Final which contained all the ingredients which have typified Fingal cricket since its early days. The Hills batted first and in characteristic Fingal style, only managed to score 54 runs. Man-O'-War, to its acute embarrassment chased the score, but could not surpass it, and the game ended in a tie, with Martin Byrne being awarded Man-of-the-Match for taking 3 wickets in the last over. The following week, Martin Byrne was Man-of-the-Match again as The Hills emerged as winners.

In the 1984 Final between Balrothery and Man-O'-War, Man-O'-War batted first and scored 134 runs for 9 wickets, with Joey Mooney bowling 25 overs and taking 6 wickets for 46 runs. In reply Balrothery scored 51 runs all-out, with Joe ("Big Bird") Murphy taking 9 wickets for 16 runs. 7 of these wickets were clean bowled, there was one LBW, and one batsman was caught by Michael Murphy off the bowling of Joe Murphy. The "not-out" batsman was P. Nolan, and the only other batsman whose wicket was not taken by Joe Murphy, was Joey Mooney, later to be Joe Murphy's brother-in-law, who was run-out.

The 1985 Final between Man-O'-War and Balrothery had an historical significance because the two clubs amalgamated after this game to form North County CC, and the intention of the new club was to obtain senior status for Leinster League cricket. From a Fingal League perspective, they were going to retain their individual identities and to maintain two separate grounds, The Nevitt and the Matt. The first game was rained-off, so the players and supporters played games of "twenty-five" for the afternoon. When the game was played, Balrothery was bowled out for 61 runs, with Liam Rooney taking 7 wickets for 24 runs, Christy Garry taking 2 for 20 and Joe Murphy's figures were 1 wicket for 3 runs in 2 overs.

Man-O'-War contested the 1986 Fingal Championship Cup Final, and on that occasion, Balbriggan provided the opposition. Man-O'-War was captained by Thomas Garry, and other key players were Tom Murphy Snr, Joe Murphy, Liam Rooney, and there was a possibility that Michael Murphy who was playing senior cricket with Malahide would line out with Man-O'-War. Balbriggan was captained by Patrick Hickey, and there were three Guildeas – Frank and Alan, his son, and Brendan, his nephew. That was another of the quintessential Fingal finals, with superb bowling and fielding, and a low score. Man-O'-War batted first and made 56 runs in 37.2 overs, with only 2 batsmen getting into double figures (Joe Murphy 15, Liam Rooney 10). The bowling honours were taken by Albert Harper (5 for 22 in 19 overs) and Patrick Hickey (4 for 21 in 18.2 overs). In chasing this score, Balbriggan scored 57 runs, but lost 8 wickets. Albert Harper scored 14 runs, David Harper scored 14*, Paddy Donnelly was 7*, and Paddy hit the winning two runs. Liam Rooney took 5 wickets for 25 in 24 overs, Joe Murphy took 2 for 25 in 19 overs and Tom Murphy took 1 for 3 runs in 7 overs. Albert Harper was Man of the Match, and the award was presented in absentia because the game had to be continued on Thursday evening and Albert was working.

Man-O'-War was back on the winning trail in 1987 and reached the final again in 1988 where the opposition was provided by Balrothery. Balrothery batted first and accumulated a score of 164 for 9, with impressive contributions from John Andrews (49), Paul Mooney (26), Tommy Mooney (22) and Noel Hickey (15*). The wickets were taken by Thomas Murphy (3 for 35), Paul Martin (2 for 46) and Joe Murphy (1 for 32). In reply, Michael Murphy (66) and Thomas Garry (56) got the lion's share of the runs, and Man-O'-War had retained the Fingal Cricket Championship Cup by a margin of 5 wickets. In terms of marking achievements, Gerry Byrne, President of the Fingal League, made a special presentation to 14-year-old Paddy Martin, the North County cricketer, who had taken 10 wickets in a game against Malahide.

At the start of the 1989 season, John Andrews, the Balrothery Captain, decided to transfer to the Hills CC because he wanted to test his batting skills against the bowlers in Leinster senior cricket. The Fingal Challenge Cup was won by Rush in 1989, and The Hills won the Fingal Championship Cup, but Man-O'-War continued to bring silverware to the Nevitt when it won the Christy Russell Cup by beating Balbriggan. Man-O'-War batted first, and Michael Murphy (59) and Anthony Rooney (27) provided a solid start. Alan Rooney scored 12, and Joe Murphy provided the impetus to the innings by scoring an unbeaten 43 in 5 overs to bring Man-O'-War up to a score of 145 for 4 in 20 overs. Albert Harper (6) and Alan Guildea (5) were out early, but Patrick Hickey (86*) and Colm Reilly (26) with a 106- run stand brought Balbriggan back into the game. Balbriggan needed 6 runs in the last over for a win, but Ivan Harper was run out and Tom Colgan clean bowled. Patrick Hickey ran a single and was left becalmed at the non-striker's end which meant that Balbriggan finished 2 runs short of a victory.

## Fingal League Cricket in the 1990s

Man-O'-War won the Fingal Perpetual Challenge Cup and the Championship Cup in 1990, but 1991 belonged to Rush CC. Alf Masood was playing Fingal League cricket with Rush, and Man-O'-War employed Gary Wood, the Malahide professional to counteract the presence of Masood, but in the final, Brendan Wilde (42) was the star on a day when Rush had other key performers such as Dara Armstrong who took 5 catches behind the wicket and Paul Carthy and Michael Donnelly who each took 2 wickets. Rush beat Man-O'-War again on the following Thursday to win the Fingal League double for the first time.

On 1 September 1991, Brian Southam, who had been Chairman of the Fingal League and a leading administrator with Man-O'-War and North County, died suddenly, and the club decided to present a trophy to the Fingal League to commemorate his memory. 1992 was the first year of the Brian Southam Cup, and it was the prize for a T20 competition for second teams of the Leinster League clubs and clubs such as Portrane and Drogheda Ramblers who just played Fingal cricket. Rush's Second XI was the first winners of the Brian Southam Cup in 1992, and it was won by The Hills Second XI in 1993.

With The Hills and North County playing Leinster Senior Cricket and Rush applying for senior league status, Balbriggan CC was another Fingal club on an upwards curve, and it played Balrothery in the final of the Fingal Championship Cup in 1992. Balrothery batted first, and the main contributors to its score of 102 were Joey Mooney (32), Peter Gregg (11), Noel Hickey (13) and John White (25*). Albert Harper took 3 wickets for 32, Terry Byrne took 2 for 19, Cliff Harper took 1 for 19, but Tommy Power was the star bowler with 4 wickets for 17 runs. Balbriggan struggled against the "fiery" bowling of Joey Mooney but stuck to the task and with runs for Colm Reilly (20), Terry Byrne (23) and Patrick Hoare (24) managed to win by 2 wickets in a "gripping finish." Balbriggan had also won the Whelan Cup in 1992, and it was successful in developing its ancillary facilities when its new clubhouse which had cost £20,000 was completed in March 1990 and opened officially on 18 September 1992 by Mr Ray Burke, T. D.

Gerry Byrne, President of the Fingal League, and long-time administrator at The Hills CC died on 6 March 1993, and it was an appropriate tribute to a wonderful supporter of Fingal cricket that his club was the dominant one in Fingal competitions in 1993 when it won 4 Fingal trophies. In the Christy Russell final, The Hills scored 153 runs with the main batsmen being Seán Hoare (45), Matt Dwyer (27*) and John Archer (18). Balbriggan only scored 89 in reply. In the Fingal Championship Final, The Hills played Rush who won the toss and batted first. Alf Masood was caught by John Archer in the first over, and Rush collapsed to 32 for 5. The fightback was led by Cyril McGee (37) and Dara Armstrong (19), and Rush finished on 112 runs. Martin Byrne, a son of Gerry Byrne, took 4 wickets for 39, and Matt Dwyer, the leading bowler in Leinster Senior League, took 4 wickets for 26. At 20 for 4, The Hills was in trouble, but it was rescued by Declan Moore (54), a future Irish senior international, Seán Hoare (10), Matt Dwyer (7), and Martin Byrne (10*), with Martin Byrne and Noel Harper steering The Hills home.

Ben Finnegan, a leading Fingal League cricketer, died in October 1993. He had played with Tubbergregan in the Fingal League, and then he emigrated to Scotland where he played First Class cricket with Arbroath CC and Meagle CC. He returned to Ireland in 1978, settled in Knockbrack and was the vice-president of Knockbrack CC at the time of his death. A trophy was donated to the Fingal League and for a number of years, a game was played each year for the Ben Finnegan Cup.

In the mid-1990s, the clubs in Fingal were fielding multiple teams (men and women) in the Leinster League competitions, and there was a major increase in the amount of youth cricket being played by boys and girls. There were also schools' fixtures to be accommodated, and this proliferation of fixtures caused severe pressure on the grounds. It rendered fixture-making in the Fingal League almost impossible because it was very difficult to find days on which all teams were free, or grounds were available. Fingal League teams had become much more cosmopolitan in composition, and while the players were committed to their teams, there was not the emotional attachment of earlier generations to the Fingal League. Allied to this, employment patterns had also changed and with more people working away from Fingal, it was difficult to schedule games during the week. Mrs Maureen Byrne, in writing to the Executive of the Fingal League to thank the officers for their kindness and sympathy after the death of her husband, Gerry in 1993, expressed the wish "that the Fingal League would always continue and prosper". In April 1994, Joe Clinton gave a talk entitled "A History of Cricket in Fingal" to the members of the Skerries Historical Society, and he was acutely aware that interest in Fingal League cricket was dissipating, and he urged the Fingal clubs to continue supporting Fingal League cricket.

In all the years of Fingal League cricket, no century had been scored in a final until 1994 when John Andrews scored 139 runs in the game against Rush. Mark Clinton scored 61 runs, and The Hills finished 119 runs ahead of Rush for whom Michael Donnelly scored 59 and John Scanlan scored 49 runs. At the end of the 1994 season, Rush was granted senior status by the Leinster Senior League, and with three senior clubs in Fingal, their priorities were changing because it was essential for the clubs to retain this much-valued and much-sought after senior status.

In 1995, the seven clubs in Fingal League competitions were Balbriggan, Rush, The Hills, Man-O'-War, Balrothery, Knockbrack and Dundalk Crusaders. There were five teams in the A League – The Hills 1, Rush 1, Balrothery 1, Man-O'-War 1 and Balbriggan 1. Regulations were amended to take account of The Hills and Rush being senior teams, whereas Man-O'-War and Balrothery as separate entities were not deemed to have senior status. Rush and The Hills were obliged to star nineteen players who would not be eligible for the 2nd Division League or the Brian Southam Cup. Man-O'-War and Balrothery were obliged to star eight players for the Fingal A League. The teams in the Second Division were Rush Second XI, The Hills Second XI, Balbriggan Second XI, North County, Knockbrack, and Dundalk. The honours for the season were evenly divided with Man-O'-War winning the Fingal League Championship and the Christy Russell Cup, Rush winning the Cup, The Hills Second XI winning the Brian Southam Cup, and Knockbrack winning the B League.

1996 was the last year that Balrothery played at the Matt, and work commenced to source a new ground in the same locality. In that season, Man-O'-War and Balrothery remained separate entities for the Fingal A League, but its second team was an amalgam of players from both clubs and played under the North County banner. The Hills' Firsts added the Fingal A League to the Leinster Senior Cup and the Wiggins Teape League victories, Rush won the Championship Cup and the Christy Russell Cup, while The Hills' Second XI won the Brian Southam Cup and the B League.

In 1997, Dundalk Crusaders left the Fingal League, but Portrane re-joined the League after an absence of many years. Man-O'-War and Balrothery used their individual names but played together as one team which meant that there were only six teams in total playing in Fingal League competitions. Knockbrack won the Brian Southam Cup, Man-O'-War/Balrothery Second XI won the B League, and The Hills won the other three competitions.

In 1998, North County had sourced a site for its new ground at Inch, Balrothery, and raised between £15,000 and £20,000 at an auction which was compered by Micheál Ó'Muircheartaigh. Knockbrack hosted the Ben Finnegan Cup game in which Malahide was expected to provide the opposition, but it was unable to fulfil this commitment due to a clash with a cup game in the Leinster League, and North County stepped into the breach. Knockbrack batted first and scored 137 for 5 off 40 overs; Patsy Harford was the top-scorer with 38 runs. There were other valuable contributions from Martin Moore (24), Raymond Peters (17), and Niall Callaghan (14). Thomas Garry took 3 wickets for 10 runs, and Thomas Rooney took 2 for 20. Due to rain, the target for North County was reduced to 103, and this was achieved with 3 runs being scored off the last ball by Seán Casey. Thomas Garry was Man of the Match because he added 41 runs to the 3 wickets, he had taken in the first innings. Shane Garry scored 20 runs, Tommy Plant got 19 and Terry Richardson scored 11. The great Seán Moore took 3 wickets for 6 runs. In the Fingal League competitions, Man-O'-War/Balrothery won the Christy Russell Cup, while The Hills won all the other competitions.

The Fingal League Committee for the 1999 season was President – Jack Harper, Secretary/Treasurer-Thomas McGrane, and other committee members were Joe Murphy (Man-O'-War/Balrothery, Thomas Murphy (Balbriggan), Gerry Monks (Rush), Patrick Hoare (The Hills), Patsy Harford (Knockbrack), and Paschal Henchy (Portrane). In a review of the 1998 season by the Fingal League Committee, there is a reference to "mishaps on and off the field of play", but it does not specify what these mishaps were. It appeared that there were differences regarding the playing regulations because for the 1999 season, the playing regulations for each competition were given in detail, and in practically every instance, they were compatible with the Leinster Cricket Union's regulations, or the regulations used for the Irish Senior Cup. For example, the playing regulations for the Fingal Championship were the same as the regulations for the Irish Senior Cup, with the only exception being the regulation regarding the 30 yards circle. The A League games consisted of 40 overs per side; the highest score won the match and if the runs and wickets were equal, the highest score after 20 overs won the game. The regulations for the Brian Southam Cup and the Christy Russell Cup were the same as the ones used in the Alan Murray Cup. There were still six clubs playing in the competitions, with four teams (The Hills 1, Rush 2, Man-O'-War /Balrothery 1 and Balbriggan) playing in the A Division.

The big news at the start of the 1999 season was the transfer from Malahide to North County of Dara Armstrong (the outstanding wicket keeper in Leinster) and Conor, his brother. North County had also recruited Craig Fittler, an Australian, as its overseas player, and with the players having been training from January, the club hoped to compete for honours during the new season as distinct from hoping to avoid relegation. Man-O'-War/Balrothery's strength in depth enabled the club to win three of the 4 adult competitions while The Hills won the Christy Russell Cup.

**The 2000s**

In 2000, there was an increase in the number of teams for the first time in years, with Ring Commons CC returning to the fold. There were four teams in the A Division (the Hills 1, Rush 1, Man-O'-War/Balrothery 1 and Balbriggan 1), while there were seven teams in the B Division. There are only two reports available for Fingal League games during this season because the Leinster League games were now completely dominant in terms of coverage. The 1999 Brian Southam Cup Final was not played until 2000, and Man-O'-War/Balrothery played Knockbrack. Thomas Garry's innings of 68 runs plus runs from Des Casey (21) and Terry Richardson (24*) left Knockbrack facing a target of 155 runs to win in 20 overs. Knockbrack managed to score 104, with Chris Lindsay (35), John McGarry (20), Martin Moore (17), Andrew Moore (17) being the main contributors to Knockbrack's score. In the other competitions, Man-O'-War/Balrothery won the League and the Championship while Rush won the Christy Russell Cup.

The Ben Finnegan Cup game was played between Knockbrack and Portrane, with Knockbrack managing to score 119 for 8 in 30 overs despite being 11 runs for 3 wickets at one stage. Barry Grimes scored 61 runs and Dermot Coyle ended on 28*. The wicket takers for Portrane were R. Shivmangal (2 for 45), I. Haq (4 for 57), and P. Henchy (2 for 16). Portrane lost 2 quick wickets, but D. Neville (69) and I. Haq (21) ensured that Portrane reached its target with 15 balls to spare. Martin Moore took 2 wickets for 6 off 8 overs, but he was the only Knockbrack bowler who could look back on his display with any degree of satisfaction.

By 2001, it was obvious that the Fingal League in its existing format had run its course and needed to keep pace with developments in cricket. The cricketing scene in Fingal had undergone a huge change since the 1990s, with three of the teams, (The Hills, Rush, and North County) fielding professional players, and the importance ascribed to the Fingal competitions was lessening year by year. Despite the difficulties in getting fixtures fulfilled, the Executive of the Fingal League continued to organise an ambitious playing programme. There were five competitions for adults, and one competition for juveniles, but it was only necessary for bad weather to impact on the Leinster League programme for the Fingal League games to become collateral damage.

A survey was undertaken in 2001 to ascertain the thoughts of the seven clubs with regard to the continuation of the Fingal League. Based on the results of the survey, the Fingal League Committee produced a paper to address the loss of interest in its competitions. Among the proposals were that the Senior 1 teams (The Hills, North County and Rush) would play in the Fingal Championship only, and not play in the Cup. Other proposals included playing the competitions as 20 overs Leagues, with all games being played on the same day. It also recommended banning all "professional" players from the League. From that year onwards, all Fingal League cricket consisted of 20 overs per side games, and while this reflected a new reality, the unique character of Fingal League cricket was lost.

Notwithstanding the travails of the Fingal Cricket League, cricket was thriving in Fingal. The *Fingal Independent*, a subsidiary of the *Drogheda Independent* had consistently given wonderful coverage to cricket, and a trawl of its data base for the period 2000 to 2006 showed that the paper contained 2,122 references to cricket matches, cricket personalities, cricket club fund-raising events, award nights, coaching courses, and other cricket-related issues. By way of contrast, there are only 8 references to Fingal League cricket during the same period, and only one of those related to a game. This game was the opening game of the Fingal League for the 2005 season between The Hills and North County. North County made 220 for 6 in 20 overs, with runs for Strydom (66), Conor Armstrong (66), and Dara Armstrong (62). In reply, The Hills scored 176 with runs for Joseph Clinton (37) and Barry Archer (32, retired hurt). There is a comment in this report which would have appalled all Fingal cricketers when it is mentioned that having played this game, the two clubs would be ready "for the competition proper" which was a reference to playing in the Alan Murray Cup at the weekend. There was never an instance of a game between Fingal clubs being seen as preparation for any other game because all games were contested fiercely, without any quarter being asked for or given.

The other references to the Fingal League in the *Fingal Independent* during this period are of the nostalgic variety remembering when Balrothery won the Middle League and the Minor Cup, and the Murphys playing for

Walshetown in 1953. There are photographs of legendary Fingal League cricketers such as Billy Tolan, Joe Clinton, Billy Beggs, Thomas McGrane, Kit Lindsay, Michael Marsh, Johnny Gill, and Bill Stuart; there is also a wonderful photo of a great Balrothery team of the 1980s which featured Aidan Pollis, John ("The Ranger") Mooney, David Powell, Phil Mooney, Joey Mooney, Cathal Hickey, James ("Bisto") Mooney, Thomas Barker, Noel Hickey, Joe Russell, John Collins, and Tommy ("Chink") Mooney.

While the same value might not have been placed on Fingal League cricket in the 2000s, the tradition of honouring and celebrating legends of Fingal League cricket was not allowed to lapse. In October 2006, Tommy Geraghty, Treasurer of Balbriggan CC, made a special presentation to Jack Harper, the President of both Balbriggan, and the Fingal League. Tommy referred to Jack as "Mister Cricket" and thanked him for the work that he had done in inspiring people to play cricket and in preparing magnificent pitches on which to play. When Thomas McGrane was 80 years of age, members of the Fingal League clubs joined together to honour a man who had done so much to coordinate Fingal League cricket in his role as Secretary/Treasurer of the League. In voicing their appreciation for Thomas's work, the clubs wanted to ensure that he was aware of their gratitude to him for the contribution which he had made to the community and to cricket and not to be waiting for a graveside oration to express those sentiments.

Between 2007 and 2012, there are only nine references to the Fingal League and cricket, with the same blend as the early years of the century. There are reports on Cottrellstown and Portrane winning Fingal championships in a bygone era and an obituary of John Reynolds, an outstanding cricketer and umpire. Of the more modern pieces of news, there is an account of Jody Morgan, father of Eoin Morgan, being elected President of the Connacht Cricket Union, and photographs and reports of Ring Commons' new ground being opened in 2012.

Each year in the Leinster Cricket Union Handbook, details were given of the five Fingal League adult competitions, and the Youth Competition, which was sponsored by the family of Gerry Byrne, but it was a real struggle to fit the games into a crowded fixture list. In 2010, there were only four clubs playing Fingal League cricket, and they were The Hills, Rush, North County and Balbriggan. The Fingal League competitions continued to be played until 2011, and the administrators and players who had strong family connections with the League, maintained their commitment to Fingal cricket, but on a general level, it was obvious that it was no longer possible to organise games when clubs were fielding multiple teams in the Leinster Cricket Union's competitions.

In 2012, fixtures were made for the season on 7 February. Present at that meeting were Seamus Clinton (President), Thomas McGrane (Secretary/Treasurer), Albert Harper, Joe Murphy, Gerry Monks, and Johnny White. The last meeting of Fingal Cricket League was held on 18 July 2012, and Thomas McGrane indicated that he would be stepping down at the end of the season. Unfortunately, Thomas became ill, and the fixtures for 2012 were not played. In March 2020, The Hills CC hosted a Fingal League Tribute Evening, and this event was attended by people from the existing clubs and clubs which had long gone out of existence. Specific tributes were paid to Tom Murphy Senior, and Thomas McGrane for their commitment to ensuring that Fingal League cricket remained an important, integral element of Fingal's sporting heritage.

The Fingal League was of its time. It preserved the much-loved game, it nurtured and developed it over practically ninety years, and a debt of gratitude is owed to the officers and players of the Fingal League who have contributed so much to the sporting and social history of Fingal, Leinster, and Ireland.

# Appendix A

## Fingal League Teams (1926-2012)

- Knockbrack
- Macraidh (Knockbrack Seconds)
- Skerries
- Ballymadun
- Knightstown
- Ring Commons
- Black Hills (which was later shortened to The Hills)
- Barnageera
- Balrothery
- Baldwinstown (3 teams added in 1928)
- Naul Hill
- Curkeen
- Skerries B (1930)
- Balcunnin
- Balbriggan (teams added on 1929, and no team gone yet)
- Man-O'-War
- Dalahasey
- Oldtown
- Portrane Hospital
- British Legion (teams added in 1930)
- Rush (1931)
- Baldwinstown Seconds (1931)
- Garristown (1933)
- Naul (Down to 10 teams in 1935)
- Blanchardstown
- Clonsilla (1936)
- Mulhuddart
- Clonard
- Hedgestown
- Tubbergregan
- Walshestown
- Bohill
- Beau Hill (listed as playing, but this may have been confusion with Bohill)
- Bettystown
- Drogheda YMCA

- Malahide (played in 1952, but never got involved in Fingal League Cricket to any great extent)
- Cottrellstown
- Technicon (in League in 1990, could have been there prior to that)
- Dundalk Crusaders
- Drogheda Ramblers
- Winter Lodge (1962) attended Fingal League meetings, but there is no record of team playing in competitions. It seems that they only played friendly games
- North County
- Second Teams of Rush, Balbriggan, The Hills, Man-O'-War/Balrothery, North County

# Appendix B (Part One)

# Fingal League Winners, 1926-1961

| Date | Fingal A League | Cship (Cup) (1962) | C. Russell (1975) |
|---|---|---|---|
| 1926 | Skerries | | |
| 1927 | Skerries | | |
| 1928 | Skerries | | |
| 1929 | Knockbrack | | |
| 1930 | Knockbrack2 | | |
| 1931 | Skerries | | |
| 1932 | Balcunnin | | |
| 1933 | Balcunnin | | |
| 1934 | Portrane | | |
| 1935 | Naul | | |
| 1936 | The Hills | | |
| 1937 | Balrothery | | |
| 1938 | Portrane | | |
| 1939 | Balrothery | | |
| 1940 | Balrothery | | |
| 1941 | The Hills | | |
| 1942 | Tubbergregan | | |
| 1943 | Portrane | | |
| 1944 | Balrothery | | |
| 1945 | Balrothery | | |
| 1946 | Balrothery | | |
| 1947 | Walshestown | | |
| 1948 | Balrothery | | |
| 1949 | Walshestown | | |
| 1950 | Balrothery | | |
| 1951 | Portrane | | |
| 1952 | Walshestown | | |
| 1953 | Walshestown | | |
| 1954 | Cottrelstown | | |
| 1955 | Balrothery | | |
| 1956 | Knockbrack | | |
| 1957 | Portrane | | |
| 1958 | Knockbrack | | |
| 1959 | Knockbrack | | |
| 1960 | Knockbrack | | |
| 1961 | Knockbrack | | |

# Appendix B (Part Two)

# Fingal League Winners, 1962-2011 (A)

| Date | Fingal A League | Cship (Cup) (1962) | C. Russell (1975) |
|---|---|---|---|
| 1962 | Balrothery | Balrothery | |
| 1963 | Knockbrack | Knockbrack | |
| 1964 | Knockbrack | Knockbrack | |
| 1965 | Balrothery | Balrothery | |
| 1966 | Man-O'-War | Man-O'-War | |
| 1967 | Balrothery | Man-O'-War | |
| 1968 | Balbriggan | Man-O'-War | |
| 1969 | Man-O'-War | Man-O'-War | |
| 1970 | Man-O'-War | Man-O'-War | |
| 1971 | Balrothery | Man-O'-War | |
| 1972 | Man-O'-War | Balrothery | |
| 1973 | The Hills | Man-O'-War | |
| 1974 | MOW/Balbriggan | The Hills | |
| 1975 | Man-O'-War | The Hills | Man-O'-War |
| 1976 | Man-O'-War | The Hills | Man-O'-War |
| 1977 | Man-O'-War | The Hills | Man-O'-War |
| 1978 | Man-O'-War | The Hills | The Hills |
| 1979 | Man-O'-War | Man-O'-War | Balrothery |
| 1980 | The Hills | The Hills | Man-O'-War |
| 1981 | Man-O'-War | The Hills | Man-O'-War |
| 1982 | Man-O'-War | Balrothery | Man-O'-War |
| 1983 | Man-O'-War | Balrothery | Man-O'-War |
| 1984 | Man-O'-War | Man-O'-War | Balrothery |
| 1985 | Man-O'-War | Man-O'-War | Man-O'-War |
| 1986 | Rush | Balbriggan | The Hills |
| 1987 | Man-O'-War | Man-O'-War | Balrothery |
| 1988 | Man-O'-War | Man-O'-War | Man-O'-War |
| 1989 | Rush | The Hills | Man-O'-War |
| 1990 | Man-O'-War | Man-O'-War | Balbriggan |
| 1991 | Rush | Rush | Balbriggan/MOW |
| 1992 | Rush | Balbriggan | Rush |
| 1993 | The Hills | The Hills | The Hills |
| 1994 | The Hills 1 | The Hills 1 | The Hills 2 |
| 1995 | MOW1 | Rush 1 | MOW1 |
| 1996 | The Hills 1 | Rush 1 | Rush 1 |
| 1997 | The Hills 1 | The Hills 1 | The Hills 1 |
| 1998 | The Hills 1 | The Hills 1 | MOW/Br |
| 1999 | MOW/Br1 | MOW/Br | The Hills 1 |
| 2000 | MOW/Br1 | MOW/Br | Rush 1 |
| 2001 | The Hills | The Hills 1 | MOW/Br1 |
| 2002 | Balbriggan | The Hills 1 | MOW/Br2 |
| 2003 | MOW/Br1 | The Hills 1 | MOW/Br1 |
| 2004 | MOW/Br1 | Balbriggan | MOW/Br1 |
| 2005 | MOW/Br1 | MOW/Br | MOW/Br1 |
| 2006 | Rush 2 | The Hills 1 | MOW/Br1 |
| 2007 | Not played | Not played | N. County |
| 2008 | Not played | Rush | Rush |
| 2009 | Not played | The Hills | N. County |
| 2010 | N. County | Balbriggan | The Hills |
| 2011 | N. County 2 | N. County | The Hills |

# Appendix B (Part Two)

# Fingal League Winners, 1962-2011 (B)

| Date | B. Southam (1992) | B League | G. Byrne (1971) |
|------|-------------------|----------|-----------------|
| 1962 | | | |
| 1963 | | | |
| 1964 | | | |
| 1965 | | | |
| 1966 | | Ring Commons | |
| 1967 | | | |
| 1968 | | | |
| 1969 | | | |
| 1970 | | | |
| 1971 | | The Hills | Man-O'-War |
| 1972 | | The Hills | Man-O'-War |
| 1973 | | | The Hills |
| 1974 | | | Rush |
| 1975 | | | Man-O'-War |
| 1976 | | | |
| 1977 | | The Hills | |
| 1978 | | The Hills | The Hills |
| 1979 | | Ring Commons | |
| 1980 | | Balbriggan | The Hills |
| 1981 | | | The Hills |
| 1982 | | | The Hills |
| 1983 | | The Hills | |
| 1984 | | | |
| 1985 | | | |
| 1986 | | | Rush |
| 1987 | | | |
| 1988 | | | The Hills |
| 1989 | | The Hills | The Hills |
| 1990 | | The Hills | The Hills |
| 1991 | | | The Hills |
| 1992 | Rush 2 | | Rush |
| 1993 | The Hills 2 | | The Hills |
| 1994 | Rush 2 | Rush2 W/O | The Hills |
| 1995 | The Hills 2 | Knockbrack | N. County |
| 1996 | The Hills 2 | The Hills 2 | N. County |
| 1997 | Knockbrack | MOW/Br2 | The Hills |
| 1998 | The Hills 3 | The Hills 3 | The Hills |
| 1999 | MOW/Br2 | MOW/Br2 | N. County |
| 2000 | MOW/Br2 | Knockbrack | The Hills |
| 2001 | Rush 2 | Knockbrack | N. County |
| 2002 | MOW/Br3 | MOW/Br3 | Rush |
| 2003 | Rush 3 | Rush 3 | N. County |
| 2004 | MOW/Br3 | The Hills 3 | The Hills |
| 2005 | MOW/Br3 | MOW/Br3 | Rush |
| 2006 | Rush 3 | Rush 3 | N. County |
| 2007 | Rush | Not played | N. County |
| 2008 | N. County | Not played | N. County |
| 2009 | N. County | Not played | Rush |
| 2010 | N. County | Balbriggan | The Hills |
| 2011 | N. County | B/Briggan2 | Rush |

# Appendix C

## Winners of Cup Competition prior to 1962

| Year | Winners | Runners-up |
|------|---------|-----------|
| 1931 | Baldwinstown | Portrane |
| 1941 | Rush | Balrothery |
| 1942 | Balrothery v Blackhills  (result not known) | |
| 1943 | Portrane | Tubbergregan |
| 1947 | Walshestown | Knockbrack |
| 1948 | Balrothery | Walshestown |
| 1949 | Walshestown | Balrothery |
| 1950 | Walshestown | Clonard |
| 1952 | Walshestown | Skerries |
| | | |

These are the details of a cup competition which was played intermittently until 1962 when it was put on a formal footing and a cup entitled the Championship Cup was purchased.

# Appendix D

## Some Officers of Fingal Cricket League, 1926-2012

| President | Chairman | Secretary | Treasurer |
|---|---|---|---|
| J. T. Ennis | | Adam Ward | Joe Mc Dermott |
| P. J. Daly | P. J. Daly | John Purfield | J. W. Rooney |
| Joe Boyce | Gerry Byrne | E. G. Deignan | W. Rooney |
| George  McNally | | G. L. McGowan | J. Hagan |
| Eddie Dunne | | J. A. Martin | J. Hagan |
| Gerry Byrne | | Eddie Dunne | T. Murphy |
| Thomas McGrane | | T. Murphy | S. O'Donnell |
| Jack Harper | | S. Clinton | W. Donnelly |
| | | M. O'Connor | J. Clinton |
| | | P. Casey | S. Clinton |
| | | P. Martin | T. McGrane |
| | Brian Southam | A. Harper | |
| Seamus Clinton (2008) | Albert Harper | T. McGrane | |

Thomas McGrane at 80

Gerry Monks making presentation to Coach of Oman

## Tom Murphy

## Seamus Clinton

## Joe Clinton

## Gerry Byrne

Fingal Cricket History

Albert Harper, Jack Harper, Franco Guildea

Seán Hoare and Matt Dwyer

*Figure 1, Billy Tolan, last game*

## Martin Russell and Paddy Byrne

Paschal Henchy and Michael Dwyer

## Paschal Henchy and Michael Dwyer

## Joe Murphy

## Jody Morgan

# Chapter 3: Some Characteristics of Fingal Cricket

## Cricket Equipment and Clothing

In the early days of cricket in Fingal, equipment tended to be managed on a communal basis because very few batters had their own bats or leg guards. In terms of clothing, the most important element was the white shirt, but on occasion, if a player wished to have a white trousers, he might cut down a pair of painter's overalls. Odlum's flour bags were also recycled as cricket trousers.

## Transport

With most of the games against "country clubs", the Fingal cricketer invariably cycled to games.

## Catering

A drink during the innings break, and then the home club provided a half-keg of beer at the end of the game. When that was gone, the cricketer had to cycle home. In many instances, the "teas" were provided in private homes because there were no clubhouses.

## Pitches

The farmers who were able to give access to a field for cricket couldn't be without the field for the season so the only fields that could be given over were used for grazing purposes. Paddy Byrne's description of his first visit to *The Vineyard* (home of The Hills CC) emphasised the depth of the cattle hooves. If a field was given over, a strip 22 yards by 10 feet was prepared and rolled during the week prior to a game.

## Quality of Pitches

With the preparation of pitches not being given the time required, the ball often behaved in a very inconsistent manner after it was bowled. Grass on the outfields tended to be very long and this meant that to score runs, the batsmen were forced to hit the ball in the air with the obvious risk of being caught. With everything is favour of the bowlers, scores tended to be very low, and games did not last for long. In order to lengthen the games, the Fingal League ordained that games be played as two innings per side.

**Brilliant Bowlers**

While the bowlers were adept at making the most of the favourable circumstances which obtained in many of the grounds in Fingal, Fingal acquired a reputation for producing magnificent bowlers. In that category were Simon Hoare, Kit Mooney, Christy Russell, and Tom Murphy of the earlier period, but it important to state that these bowlers also took many wickets on the "better" pitches in Dublin. Even with the improvements in the quality of pitches, Fingal continued to produce wonderful bowlers, and here we list Seán Moore, Tommy Mooney, Ray Kelly, Paddy Byrne, Martin Byrne, Liam Archer, Noel Harper, Matt Dwyer, Joe Murphy, Joey Mooney, Paul Mooney, Paddy Martin, John Mooney, Liam Rooney, Joseph Clinton, Luke Clinton, Albert Harper, Duane Harper, Paddy Martin, and Eddie Richardson. Their quality is borne out by the number of Fingal League cricketers who have won the Oulton Cup for Senior 2 bowlers, and then the O'Grady Cup when the Fingal League clubs attained senior status.

Analysis of the Leinster League's individual awards shows the extent to which Fingal League cricketers tended to dominate.

**Oulton Cup (Best Bowler in Senior 2)** - Bear in mind that some Fingal League teams only played in Leinster from the 1950s onwards:

1971  Ray Kelly – Malahide (but a native of Balbriggan, and played for Balbriggan and The Hills)

1973  Tom Murphy, Man-O'-War

1975  John Murphy, Man-O'-War (son of Tom)

1977  Liam Archer, The Hills CC

1978  Paddy Byrne, The Hills CC

1980  Martin Byrne, The Hills CC

1981  Liam Rooney, Man-O'-War

1982  Matt Dwyer, The Hills CC

1983  Liam Rooney, Man-O'-War

1984  Liam Rooney, Man-O'-War

1989  Joe Murphy, Man -O-War (son of Tom)

1995  Joseph Clinton, The Hills CC

1997  Luke Clinton, The Hills CC

1998  Martin Byrne, The Hills CC

1999  Pat Bennett, The Hills CC

2005  Joe Murphy, North County

2010  Duane Harper, Balbriggan

17 Fingal League winners between 1971 and 2018 – 36% of the winners.

**O'Grady Cup (Best Bowler in Senior 1)** – The Hills only in Senior Cricket from 1983

1985  Martin Byrne, The Hills CC

1990  Matt Dwyer, The Hills CC

1991  Matt Dwyer, The Hills CC

1993  Matt Dwyer, The Hills CC

1994  Matt Dwyer, The Hills CC

1996  Matt Dwyer, The Hills CC

2005  Paddy Martin, North County

2006  John Mooney, North County

2011  Eddie Richardson, North County

2013  Eddie Richardson, North County

2015  Eddie Richardson, North County

(Overseas players with Fingal League clubs have also won award, but they have been excluded.)

11 out of 35, 31%

**Batsmen**

There were very few distinguished batsmen at Fingal League level. The major exception in this regard was Michael Murphy, and it is arguable that Michael played at Senior 2 for too long in terms of his development as a batsman. In modern times, with improvements in coaching methods and pitches, the balance has been redressed and in the category of excellent Fingal batsmen, we can number Declan Moore, Barry Archer, Eoin Morgan, Paul Mooney, John Mooney, Conor Armstrong, Mark Clinton, and Eddie Richardson.

**Bookman Cup Winners (Best Batsman in Senior 2)**

1948 and 1952 Paddy Neville (Malahide, but played Fingal League with Portrane)

1982 and 1983 Michael Murphy (Man-O'-War)

1987 and 1989  Michael Murphy (North County)

1992 and 1993  Michael Donnelly (Rush)

2001 and 2006  Michael Murphy (North County)

2018            Harry Archer (The Hills)

**Marchant Cup (Best Batsman in Senior 1)**

Excluding overseas players who played for Fingal clubs and those players who became naturalised, the only Fingal League players to win the Marchant Cup are Conor Armstrong in 2005 and Eddie Richardson in 2016. While he was playing for Malahide CC, P. A. Neville won the Marchant Cup on 3 occasions, 1956, 1960, 1963.

**Samuels Cup (Best All-rounder in Senior 1)** - Fingal League cricketers have featured here, usually because of a strong contribution from the bowling linked with competent batting.

1996  Matt Dwyer

1997  Dara Armstrong

2013  Eddie Richardson

2014  Eddie Richardson

2017  Eddie Richardson

**Fielders and Wicket Keepers**

In addition to having very good bowlers, Fingal League sides were also renowned for their fielding abilities. Many of the cricketers were very fine Gaelic footballers. Seán Pender referred to The Hills as being "out on their own" for the quality of their fielding. He added the comment that it was alleged that The Hills practised "their fielding by attempting to catch the low-flying Milverton swallows."

**Awards for Fielding (Cricket Leinster, it became the Solomons Cup in 1999)**

1985  Matt Dwyer

1991  Patrick Hoare

2002  Conor Armstrong

2005  Barry Archer

2021 Tomás Rooney-Murphy (Tom Murphy's grandson)

**Awards for Wicket Keeping in Leinster (Hopkins Cup)**

Allied to the quality of the fielding, there was a succession of very good wicketkeepers, starting with the James (The Squire) Ennis, a graduate of Trinity College, who played with the Gentlemen of Ireland, and stood up to all bowlers. Other distinguished wicketkeepers were Mick Gosson, Paddy Martin, Michael Dwyer, Dara Armstrong, Fintan Mc Allister and Jamie Grassi.

1985  Michael Dwyer

1995, 1996, 1997, 1998, 2000, 2001, 2003, 2006, 2010 – Dara Armstrong

2016, 2017 Jamie Grassi

**Umpiring**

Umpiring in the Fingal League required a range of skills, diplomacy being the top of the list, followed by an ability to count to six. On one occasion, a very senior cricketer shared his assessment of an umpire's performance by giving a running commentary to the spectators, and his final damning verdict was that the umpire couldn't even count to six. When an umpire complained that he had been insulted by a leading bowler, the matter was referred to the Executive of the Fingal League – the insult was redefined as an incident, and the minutes recorded that the meeting ended "in harmony". For many Fingal League games, each side provided an umpire, and this made for some very interesting situations. There was a very famous umpire who batted for his team in the first innings, and then donned the white coat because in his own words, "he would be of greater benefit to the team with the coat on." One of the most intriguing justifications for a decision was the umpire who explained that he had given the batsman out because he was trying to get to the 7.30 p.m. Mass at Dublin Airport.

**Scorers**

Even scorers weren't exempt from criticism. In the 1930, Balcunnin and Knockbrack Seconds contested the final, and the official score was 40 runs each but the *Drogheda Independent's* Correspondent, and at least another 100 people in the ground had the score at 41 to Knockbrack Seconds and 40 to Balcunnin. The marker's decision was final, and the replay was fixed for the following Sunday.

There was a unique system of scoring at some games, with the obvious opportunities for plenty of discussion and debate. It was two runs for a ball hit into the long grass, four runs into the longer grass, and six if a ball went over the hedge without hitting a briar. Given the length of the grass, one fielder was delegated to watch the batsmen running between the wickets, and to declare the ball lost as soon as the batsmen had run 6. This was to ensure that the batsmen didn't keep running while the search for the ball continued.

**Regulations regarding Eligibility of Players:**

The residential issue was a perennial problem because there were many people who rented houses in Skerries and Rush for the summer. Some of these summer residents played cricket, and it was a bone of contention whether they should be allowed to play in the Fingal League. The Executive of the League addressed the matter in 1962, and the eventual ruling provided scope for lots of chicanery. A person had to reside in Fingal for a week, but allowance was made for someone who was living 3 miles over the Meath Border. Clubs were very vigilant regarding other teams using "hired guns", "people on holidays" or people who just walked into the ground having seen it from the plane or the train. When Rush signed Alf Masood, another Fingal club imported a professional from a neighbouring club for the Fingal Cup final. Eventually, professional cricketers were barred from playing in the Fingal League, but this introduced lots of other queries, with the first one being how is a professional defined? Is it a person being paid to play cricket or is it just the person brought in for the season who is the officially designated overseas player.? The Celtic Tiger phenomenon made this regulation impossible to implement as more people came to Ireland from South- East Asia, South Africa, and Australia to work here, and some of these people were assisted with accommodation and/or work so that they would play with a club in Fingal.

### Nicks and Caught Behind

Nicks and Caught behind were never an issue because life was too short to be lumbered with the name of not walking. If you got a nick, you put the bat under your arm immediately and if you were a bit tardy to react, there might be some vocal encouragement.

### LBW

The late Billy Tolan who played cricket for 64 years, top score 49*, the possessor of two bats – a blocking bat and a hitting bat- was a scrupulously fair umpire, but he couldn't stand incessant appealing. In one game, the fielder at deep square leg appealed every time that the ball hit the pads, and Billy was too much of a gentleman to say anything. He got his chance in the second innings when our appealing friend came to bat. "May I have 2, please, Billy? "Will you be wanting it from here or from square leg?"

### Front Foot No Ball

The front foot no ball law again featured Billy Tolan and Joe Clinton. Joe referred to Billy's query as a 20-mile question because that is the distance that was covered in the car while this matter was being debated, and this included pulling the car into the side of the road and using the road markings to show where the front foot could land.

### Wides

On wides, there were two schools of thought. One definition was that wides were only called if a ball hit a cow in the next field. However, Seamus Clinton mentioned that that he could not get the great Simon Hoare to aim for outside the off stump because Simon had a holy horror of being called for a wide, especially in the second innings, when the law concerning wides might be implemented very strictly.

### Run-Outs

On a glorious occasion at The Hills, on a very tight call, the batsman was given run out, and he continued to run out through the gate and half-way up the hill outside the ground. He then shouted back into the umpire "how much further past the stumps do I have to be to be in?"

### Hospitality

The hospitality in the Fingal Clubs is legendary. Over the years, the Fingal clubs have provided feeds of potatoes, roast beef, beautiful salads, scones with jam and cream. Not only have they competed on the field of play, but they have also competed regarding which club provided the "best teas".

**Family ties**

The contribution which particular families made to their clubs and to cricket in general cannot be overstated. In addition to playing cricket, they were also very involved in the administration of the clubs, and invariably looked after the grounds. The names of the families will become more obvious when the stories of individual clubs are chronicled. In some instances, such as in the case of the Clintons, they provided the playing field.

Matt Dwyer

Martin Byrne

Paddy Byrne

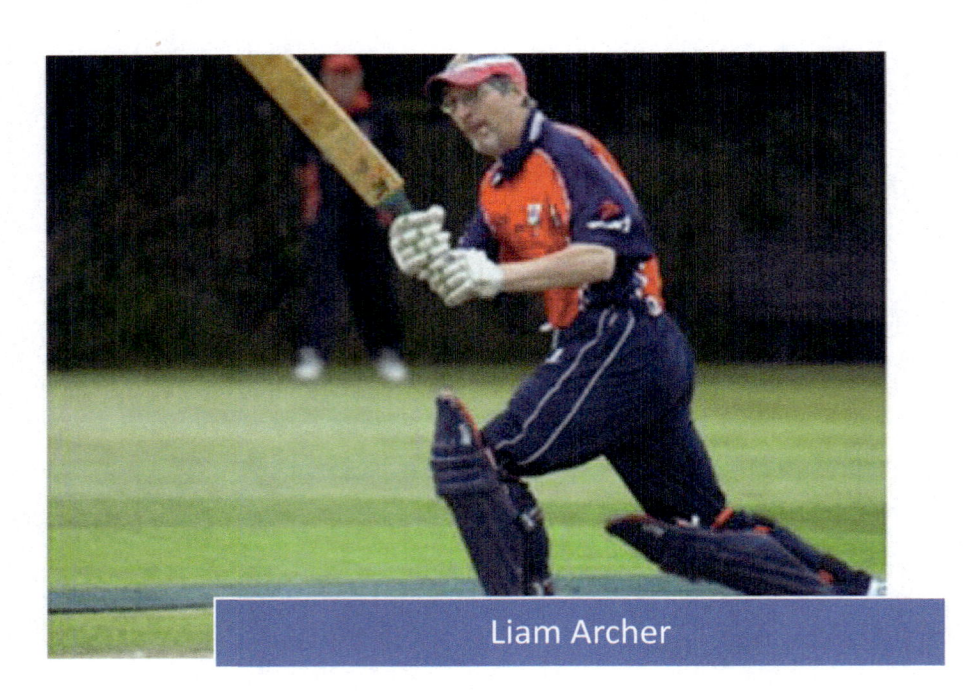

Liam Archer

Joey Mooney

Tommy Mooney

Liam Rooney

Kit Mooney and Seán Moore

Tom Murphy

John Murphy

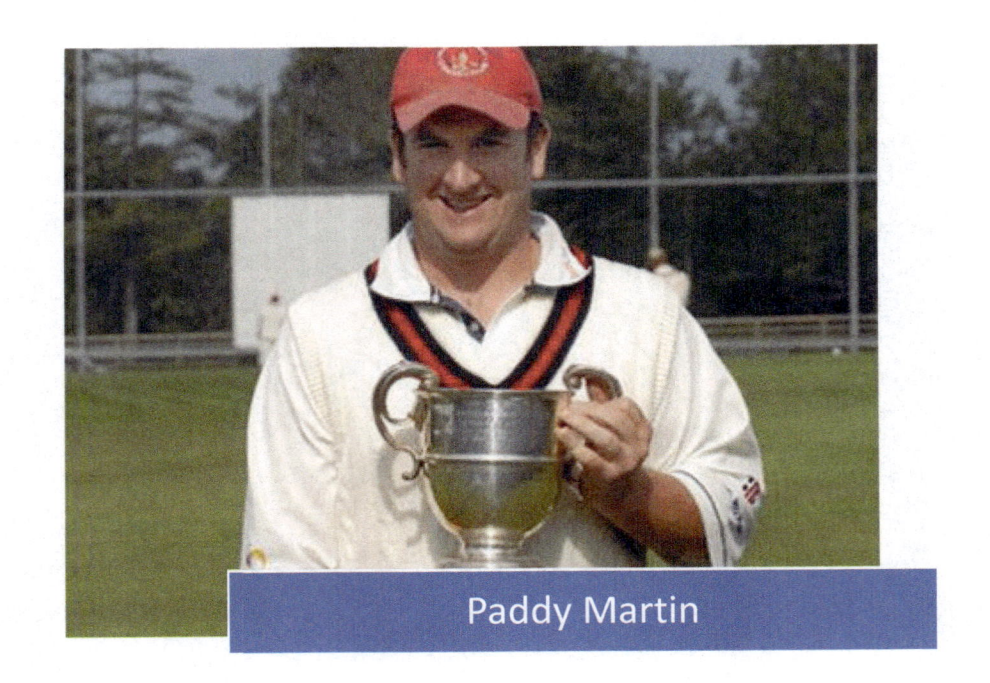

Paddy Martin

Joe Murphy

Simon Hoare

Luke Clinton

Eddie Richardson

Joseph Clinton

Noel Harper

Albert Harper

Duane Harper

Eoin Morgan

Michael Donnelly

Conor Armstrong

Declan Moore

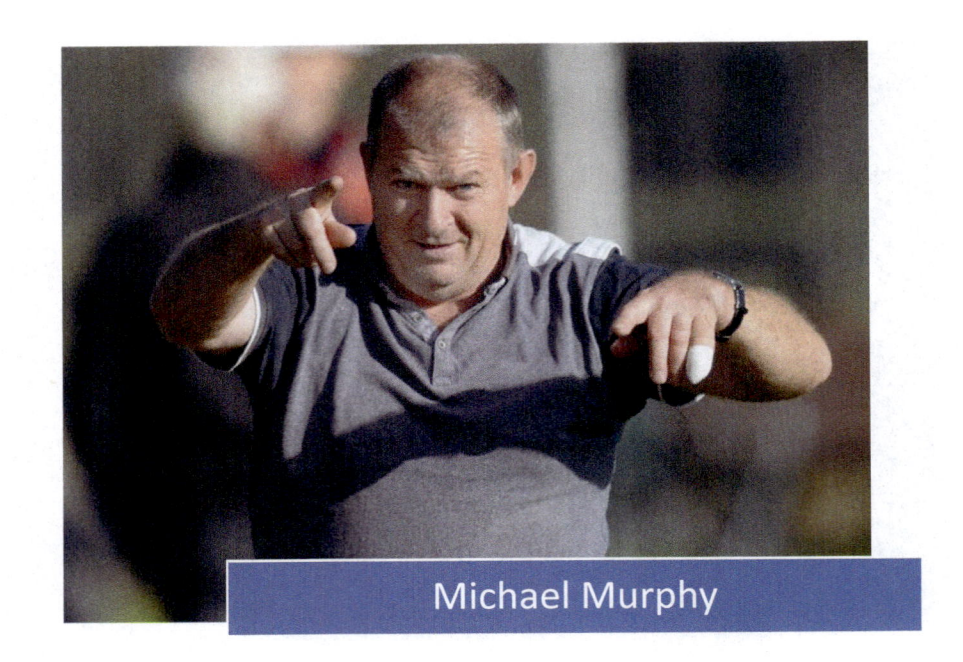

Michael Murphy

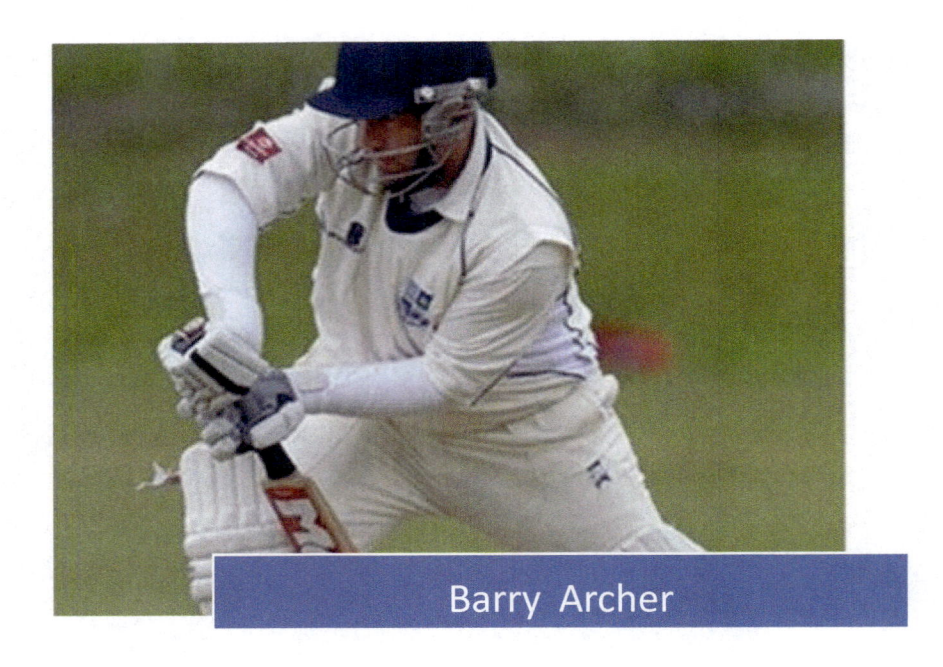

Barry Archer

Paul Mooney

John Mooney

John Andrews

Mark Clinton

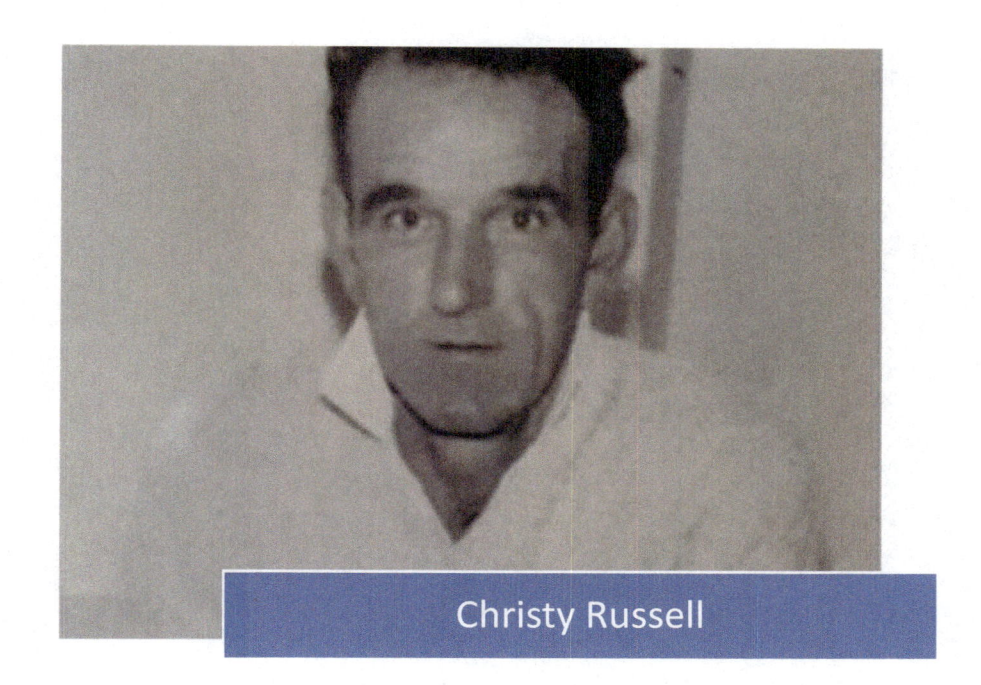

Christy Russell

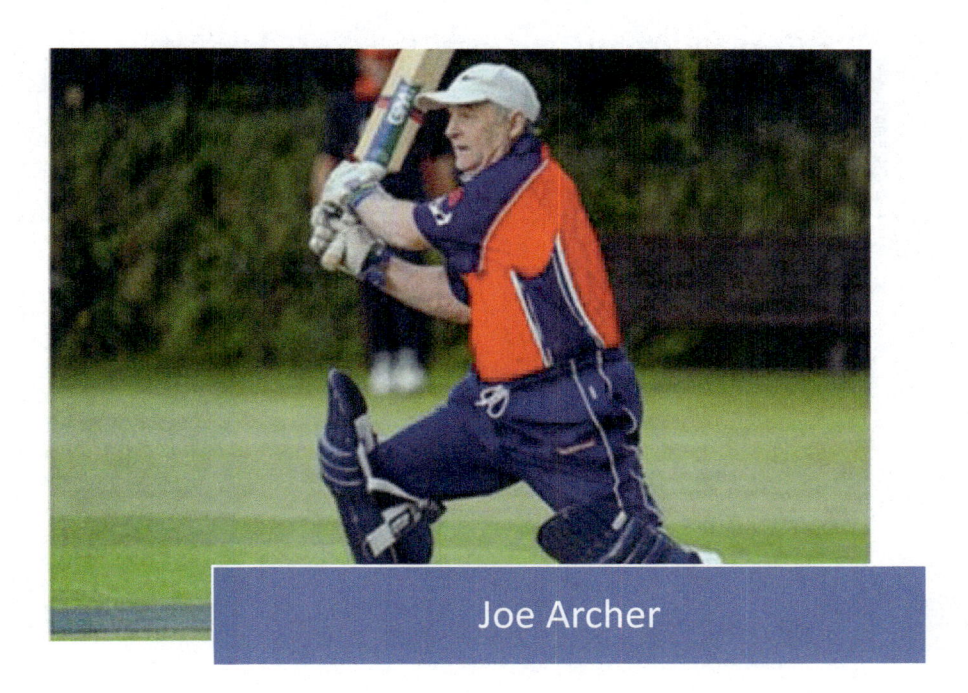

Joe Archer

John Morgan

Matt Sheridan

Seán Hoare

Patrick Byrne

John Archer

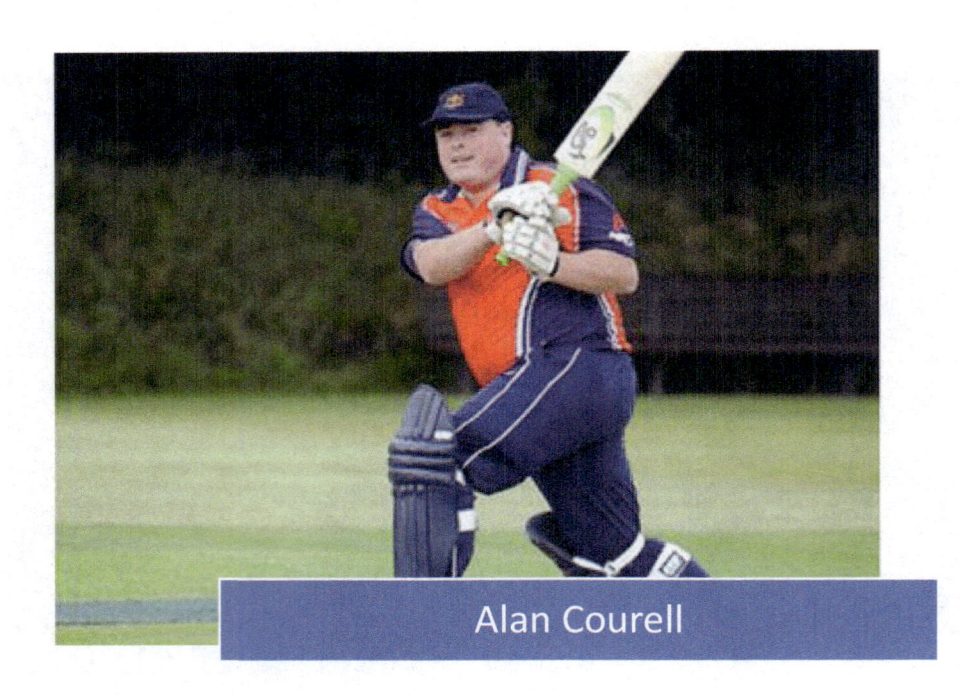

Alan Courell

Mark Dwyer

Cormac McLoughlin-Gavin

Dara Armstrong

Michael Dwyer

Fintan McAllister

Jamie Grassi

Stephen Doheny

Neil Rock

Ian O'Herlihy

Mark Donegan

Matt Dwyer Fielding

Eddie Richardson Fielding

Joe Connolly

Martin Russell

John Andrews

Michael Dwyer

Siobhán McBennett

Angela Mooney

George Kitteringham

Andrew Mooney

# Chapter 4: Development of a Corporate Fingal Identity

The Fingal League has always had a very strong corporate identity, and this was nurtured over the years by the involvement of the Fingal League selections in representative games. It was very important for Fingal League cricketers to test their prowess against "senior cricketers" because for much of the period under review, players in the Fingal League were deemed to be "junior cricketers". In 1934, a Fingal League selection played a Meath selection for a trophy sponsored by G. L. McGowan, solicitor. A return game was played in Somerville Cricket Club in 1936 between Deanhill and a Fingal League selection. Deanhill was dismissed for 40 runs with Hoare and Murphy taking the bowling honours, but the Fingal League team was dismissed for 31, with Morgan 13* and Mooney 12 being the chief contributors to the score. As a postscript to this report, the correspondent expressed the hope that there would be more of these games in the coming season "as it would do much to revive the declining interest in Meath cricket."

The Fingal League Selection's next outing was in 1939 and the game in aid of the Skerries New Church against Pembroke First XI was advertised as "The Event of the Season". There were two separate reports on this game in the *Drogheda Independent,* with one headline reading "County Cricket at Skerries", the other headline was more emphatic – "Fingal win well – Pembroke 1st XI Outclassed." The Fingal team was drawn principally from Skerries, Balrothery, Portrane and Knockbrack while the Pembroke team contained two internationals. Fingal batted first, and scored 90 runs, with P. Neville contributing 20 of this score. Pembroke "never mastered the bowling of A. Quinn and C. Mooney and were all out for 29". The game was sponsored by G. L. McGowan, and the report ended with a plea to have regular games of cricket in Skerries because of "the immense popularity of this pastime in the district."

The next major outing for the Fingal Selection was on 15 August 1943 when a Phoenix Selection played at the Clonard Grounds, Balbriggan. The Phoenix team contained such illustrious cricketers as J. C. Boucher, F. M. Quinn, P. J. Quinn, K. J. Quinn, G. J. Quinn (Irish Internationals), and the game which was described as one of the best games seen in North County Dublin for many years was witnessed by a very large crowd. The fielding of the Fingal side was "admirable", and the bowlers (Mooney, Russell, Murphy, and Hoare) were in their best form." Hoare took 5 wickets for 0 runs, and Phoenix ended on a score of

59. The Fingal Selection made 62 for the loss of 7 wickets, with Jim Coleman scoring 10 and Joe Caprani scored 19*.

The Fingal League team was again in action in 1944 when on 5 August, it played against a Meath Selection. The result was a win for Fingal League on a score of 106 runs to 73. The main contributors to the Fingal League's score were Christy Russell (30) and Tom Murphy (15). The League team's other outing in 1944 was against Phoenix, and the Fingal League emerged victorious by 10 runs. The top scorers for Fingal were E. Moore, J. Neville, and T. Murphy, with C. Russell and J. Neville being the outstanding bowlers.

In 1946, the Leinster Cricket Club sponsored a Festival week at Rathmines, and a Fingal Selection was invited to play against Leinster 3rds. The report on this game mentioned that the Fingal selection "looked very clean and neat in their whites which was very necessary for this big occasion." Fingal scored 171 for 6 declared, the opening pair of P. O'Brien and T. Murphy contributed 46 to the total. Leinster scored 66 in reply because the Fingal attack and fielding were "too good."

There were two representative games in 1947. In the first of them, the Fingal League played the Meath League, and the result was a win for Fingal on a score of 77 to 43. In the second game, the Fingal League played a Leinster selection at the Market Green, Balbriggan on 24 August. The home side scored 79, with K. Murphy, C. Russell, and J. McGrane being the main contributors to the total. Leinster was all out for 43 due to the "splendid attack of C. Mooney, C. Russell, S. Hoare and J. Murphy supported by very keen fielding."

The tradition of Fingal League selections playing games was maintained during the 1963 and 1964 seasons with fixtures being arranged with Carlow CC and Bray CC. In 1963, a Fingal League selection travelled to Carlow, and had a convincing win over the home side on a score of 157 to 44 runs. The report in the *Nationalist and Leinster Times* referred to the team being accompanied by a "host of friends and well-wishers to give moral and active support". In an era before the Internet, the people back in Fingal were kept informed by the supporters releasing "innumerable carrier pigeons to take home the news of their safe arrival to villages all over North County Dublin." The opening partnership of V. Casey and T. Murphy put on 79 for the first wicket, and B. Casey contributed 37 to the Fingal score. The main bowlers were Mooney (4 for 11), Murphy (5 for 15) and Fanning (1 for 18). Unfortunately, for reasons unspecified, Carlow did not travel to Fingal for the game in 1964, and the first instinct of some members of the Fingal League Committee was not to fulfil the away fixture, but wiser counsel prevailed, and it was decided to play the game. In terms of priorities, it was agreed to order 6 dozen stout, 5 dozen ale and 5 dozen minerals, and to ask the clubs to make an all-out effort to sell tickets for the bus to Carlow.

Until 1974, the Fingal League's games were classified as exhibitions and not necessarily taken too seriously by the senior players in the opposition, but in 1974 the Fingal League players were provided with the opportunity to test their cricketing skills against senior players when the Leinster Cricket Union invited a Fingal League selection to play in the Alan Murray (T20) Competition. This development was on an experimental basis in 1974 and a combined CYMS/ Civil Service team was also invited to play in the competition. In its first game, the Fingal League Selection played YMCA and scored 70 runs in its innings with John Morgan having the top score of 24 runs. YMCA reached its target for the loss of 7 wickets, and Seán Moore took 3 wickets for 15 runs. In the second game, the Fingal League played Pembroke, and it appears that the game was decided on wickets lost because according to the *Irish Times*, both teams scored 70 runs, but the Fingal League was 70, all out, whereas Pembroke's score was 70 for 9. Anthony Rooney was top scorer with 17 runs, and Tom Murphy took 3 wickets for 11 runs. In its third game, the Fingal League played Merrion on 18 June at Anglesea Road. Merrion batted first and scored 109 runs for the loss of 6 wickets. In reply, the Fingal League scored 78 runs for the loss of 8 wickets, with Tommy Mooney (26) being the main contributor to the total.

Although the Fingal League did not win any of its games, it acquitted itself well enough to justify the continuation of the experiment for the following season. In 1974, cricketers from the Man-O'-War had played for the Fingal League, but in 1975, Man-O'-War played in the Alan Murray Competition in its own right, and the players on the Fingal League Selection were from The Hills, Balrothery, Rush and Knockbrack. The Fingal League was again in the same section as YMCA, and on this occasion, the report in the *Irish Times* read, "YMCA suffered a shock 21 runs defeat in the Leinster 20 overs mid-week competition". Liam Archer was the star performer on the night, with a top score of 34 runs, and he also took 4 wickets for 13 runs. The final scores were Fingal League, 99 for 8; YMCA, 78 all out. In the final, the Fingal League played Pembroke who had won this trophy 5 times, and in its innings, the Fingal League scored 74 runs, with the top scorers being Liam Archer (16), John Archer (13) and Tommy Mooney (12). In quintessential Fingal fashion, the bowlers came to the rescue, and Pembroke's final score was 63 runs for 7 wickets. The bowling heroes on the night were Martin Byrne (3 for 14), Paddy Byrne (2 for 13) and Tommy Mooney (2 for 21).

The Fingal League reached the final again in 1976 and played against Malahide. Malahide batted first and had scored 32 runs for 2 wickets in 9 overs, then it collapsed to 43 for 9 after 14 overs and ended up on 57 runs. Seán Moore took 4 wickets for 17, Paddy Byrne took 3 for 23 and the bowling was backed up by "keen work in the field". There were some anxious moments during the reply, but Matt Sheridan (26*) and S. Neville (11*) steadied the Fingal nerves, and the margin of victory was 5 wickets. The Fingal League was scheduled to play Donemana on 25 September 1976 in the final of the All-Ireland Beckett Cup, but it appears that this game fell foul of the weather and was never played.

The drive for three in a row was ended by Clontarf when it won a tense game at Rush. In previous years when Fingal won a game, it was described as a surprise, but the development of the team over the three years was such that Clontarf's win was described as "the biggest upset". Clontarf scored 98 runs, and the Fingal League's final tally was 94 for 7. Sean Moore was again the most successful bowler, with 3 wickets for 14 runs, and the top scorers were N. Harper (15), J. Neville (13*) and L. Archer (13).

The Fingal League Selection had one further outing in this season when it played a Senior 2 League XI at Rush in September 1977. The visitors batted first and scored 135 for 9 wickets after 45 overs. The best bowlers for Fingal were Paddy Byrne (4 for 39 runs, off 15 overs), Tommy Mooney (3 for 34 off 14 overs) and Martin Byrne (2 for 33 off 13 overs). In reply, Fingal had a steady start, but then lost 4 wickets for 7 runs. Liam Archer (22) and John Neville (20) ensured that a collapse was averted, and Matt Sheridan (29*) whose innings included 2 sixes, finished off the game with his customary aplomb. The *Drogheda Independent's* comment on this victory was that "the strength of Final Cricket was demonstrated again."

From 1978 onwards, the ambitions of individual clubs began to change, and there were less clubs available from which to select the Fingal League teams. The Hills played in the competition in 1978, Man-O'-War continued as an individual entity and the Fingal League Selection was no longer as strong at the teams which had represented the League in previous years. Having said that, the Fingal League selection reached the semi-final of the Alan Murray Cup in 1979, but lost to Leinster, the eventual winners of the trophy. In 1980, The Hills, Man-O'-War and Rush played in the competition so the number of players available for selection by the League was reduced even further.  There are reports of a Fingal League selection playing in the Alan Murray competition until 1988 at least when a Fingal League team lost to Clontarf at Knockbrack,  but after that date, there are no further references to a Fingal League Selection playing in the Alan Murray Cup.

The involvement of a Fingal League Selection over a fifteen- year period in the Alan Murray Cup brought benefits to both the Fingal League and to the Leinster Cricket Union. For the individual players, there was an opportunity to play against senior cricketers, and to assess whether their own ambitions to play senior cricket were realistic or unrealistic. Given that games between Fingal clubs were often ultra-competitive, it was of value for players from the different clubs to play with as distinct from against each other. For the clubs, there was an opportunity to compare the facilities which they encountered at the senior clubs, and to decide on the improvements which were necessary at their own clubs if they were to attain senior status. For cricket in Leinster, it invigorated the competition because of the passion and commitment with which the Fingal team played, and it showed that it was possible to defend small scores with superb bowling and fielding. For the Fingal Cricket League as a body corporate, it was an important vehicle for maintaining the concept of Fingal identity within the wider cricket community.

## THE EVENT OF THE SEASON !

# CRICKET

# Pembroke 1st XI. v. Fingal

# League Selected

# AT SKERRIES

## ON SUNDAY, 27th AUGUST, 1939

(Postponed from August 20th owing to inclemency of the weather).

At 3 p.m. sharp.

Cricket—Phoenix 1st XI will meet Fingal League XI at Phoenix Park on Sunday next at 11.30 a.m. Fingal League XI will be as follows:—C. J. Mooney (Balrothery C.C.) capt.; S. M. Hoare (Balrothery C.C.); C. F. Russell (Balrothery C.C.); J. K. Mooney (Balrothery C.C.); P. P. O'Brien (Tubbergregan C.C.); M. P. Gossan (Skerries C.C.); P. Neville (Portrane C.C.); J. Neville (Portrane C.C.); J. Caprani (Portrane C.C.); K. Murphy (Walshestown C.C.); J. A. Martin (Rush C.C.); 12th man, A. J. McDonnell (Skerries C.C.).

Drogheda Independent, 14 June 1944

Back Row: Billy Tolan, James Byrne, Dick Byrne, Gerry Byrne, John Mooney.
Front Row:      Kit Mooney, Simon Hoare, Jim Coleman.      October 1991

GL McGowan &
Louis Derham
1970

# Cricket

## FINGAL LEAGUE SIDE BEAT PEMBROKE

The Fingal League side carved ou. a nice bit of cricket history for themselves when in only their second year in the competition, they became the first junior side to take possession of the Alan Murray Cup when they defeated five-times winners Pembroke in the fnal of Leinster mid-week 20 overs League at Sydney Parade last night.

Fingal League Sel. 74 (L. Archer 16. J. Archer 13. T. Mooney 12: J. Byrne 2 for 7. R. Moulton 2 for 18, A. Parker 2 for 22): Pembroke 63 for 7 (G. Mellon 32 n.o., R. Moulton 9. M. Moriarty 6 n.o.; M. Byrne 3 for 14. P. Byrne 2 for 13, T. Mooney 2 for 21).

COUNTY CHAMPIONSHIP

IT, 11 September 1975

# Fingal League win 20-overs title

Good bowling by Sean Moore and Pat Byrne supplemented by a match-winning innings from Matt Sheridan gave the Fingal League a second successive Leinster mid-week 20 overs title when they defeated league winners Malahide by five wickets in the final at Malahide last night.

Batting first, Malahide looked comfortable enough when they reached 32 for two after nine overs but a dramatic slump followed with the scoreboard reading 43 for nine after 14 overs before Les O'Shea and Barry Gilmore in a brave last wicket stand carried the score to a still meagre 57.

The medium pace attack of Moore (4 for 17 in six overs) and Byrne (3 for 23) backed up by keen work in the field was the key to the winners' success.

But they also had some anxious moments as they began their reply, losing four wickets for 16 runs after 12 overs to the Malahide pace attack of Alan Hughes and Doug Goodwin.

At Malahide: MALAHIDE 57 (D Martin 13, G. O'Brien 11; S. Moore 4 for 17, P. Byrne 3 for 23); FINGAL LEAGUE 58 for 5 (M. Sheridan n.o. 26, S. Neville n.o. 11; A. Hughes 3 for 10, D. Godowin 1 for 4). Fingal League won by 5 wickets.

Watford — Hertfordshire SH — Eire Og

IT 8 September 1976

## *Cricket*

## BECKETT CUP FINAL

The Fingal League, winners of the Alan Murray Cup, and Donemana, winners of the Mid-Ulster Cup, meeting in the final of the all-Ireland Beckett Cup at Malahide, today. The match, starting at one o'clock, wil be staged over 50 overs.

IT, 25 September 1976

# FINGAL LEAGUE BEAT CITY MEN

Drogheda Independent, 16 September 1977

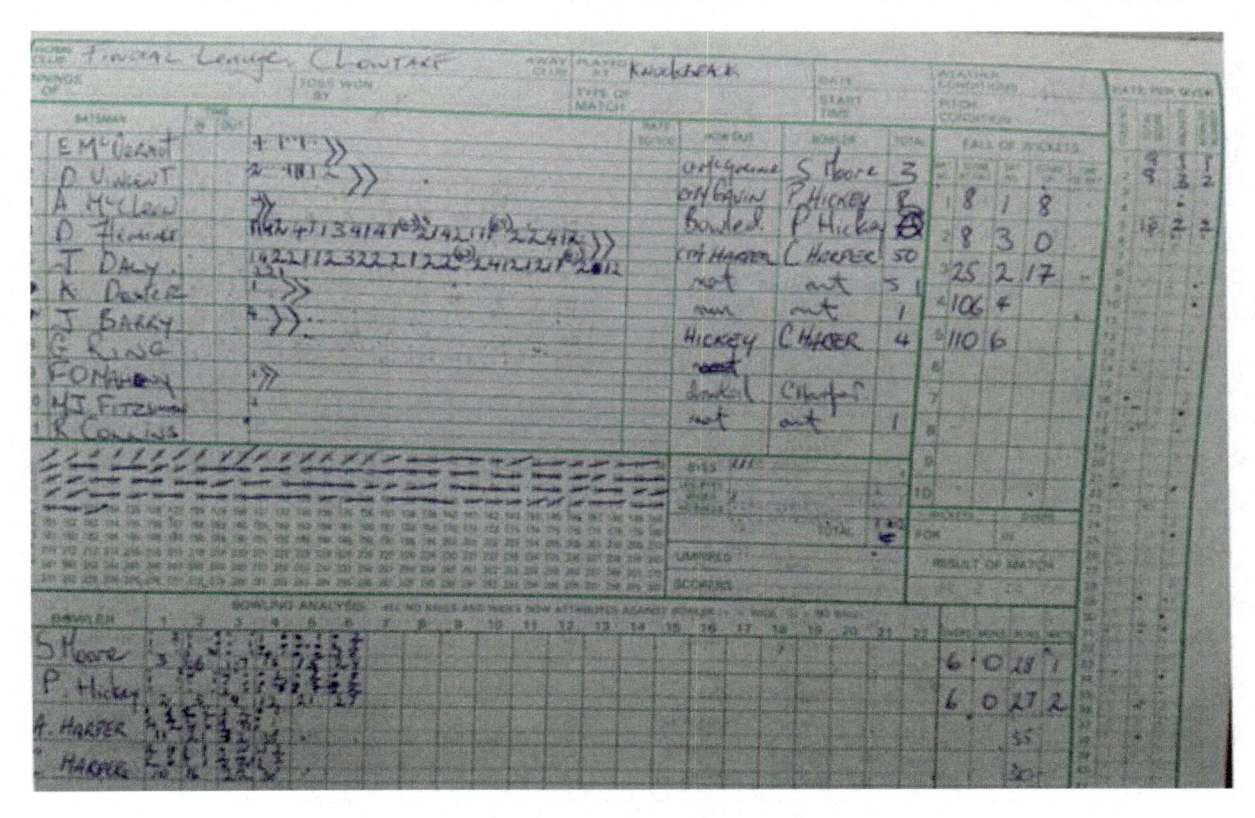

*Fingal Selection v Clontarf, 24 May 1988*

# Chapter 5: Cricket in Knockbrack

Knockbrack is in the Electoral Division of Hollywood, in the Civil Parish of Hollywood, in the Barony of Balrothery West, in the County of Dublin. The LCU Handbook gave the following directions to the cricket club: "Near Balrothery, 2nd left after Murtagh's Pub on the Balbriggan Road."

## Early Days, 1880-1924

Knockbrack Cricket Club was founded in 1880, but the first available reference to cricket in the area is not to a game, but to an athletics' meeting in 1883 at which one of the events was throwing a cricket ball. It was won by P. Reynolds with a throw of 105 yards, second was F. Kernan with a throw of 100 yards, and in third place was T. Ludden who threw the ball 99 yards, 2 feet and 2 inches. This was the sixth annual meeting which was held at Kitchenstown, and despite the "threatening appearance of the morning meteorologically", there were "fully five thousand spectators present, with the proceedings being "characterised by order and decorum throughout".

On 20 October 1884, Knockbrack played Naul in a closely contested game, and the result was a victory for Knockbrack with a "few runs and two wickets to spare". The reporter was impressed with the bowling of Messrs Purfield and Dillon, while Messrs J. Gilsenan, J. Bissett and J. Purfield "batted cautiously and displayed admirable judgement and patience at the wickets".' fielding was very good, the batting of Messrs J. Duff, J. Ennis, and P. Rielly (sic) was "creditable", but "the peculiar slow bowling took no effect". The final score after two innings per side was Knockbrack 60 runs and Naul, 57. At its AGM in 1885, the previous season was deemed to have been very successful, and the following officers were elected: J. Rock (Captain), C. Gilsenan (Treasurer), P. Gilsenan (Secretary), and T. Lindsay, A. Sherwin, P. Donnelly, E. Lindsay, J. Dillon, and J. Purfield (Committee members). There are only three other games for which reports were submitted between 1885 and 1903. In May 1885, Knockbrack beat Naul on a score of 54 runs to 50; in July 1886, Knockbrack beat Ashbourne by 36 runs (110 runs to 74) and in October 1886, Naul beat Knockbrack by 7 runs (48 to 41).

The *Drogheda Independent* has consistently given wonderful coverage to cricket in Fingal and in Meath, with score cards, accounts of games and exchanges of views between club secretaries being published in considerable detail. This archival material demonstrates very clearly the widespread popularity of cricket in these two areas, and it is also a rich source for the social history of this era. On 26 July 1903, Knockbrack played the Grallagh at Knockbrack, and the result was a comprehensive victory for the Grallagh on a score of 89 runs to 18, with extras (6) being the highest scorer for Knockbrack. In the return game, Knockbrack gained revenge for the previous defeat when it won on a score of 23 runs to 19. There was an obvious tension between the two clubs because the Secretary of Knockbrack mentioned that this was "a much easier win for Knockbrack than readers of last week's *Independent* would anticipate." It was difficult to ascertain the reason for this comment unless it was reaction to the note from the Secretary of the Grallagh to the effect that the club was "ready to receive a challenge from Meath or Dublin". On the first week in September 1903, Knockbrack played Garristown at Knockbrack and won on a score of 64 runs to 32, with the biggest contributions with the bat coming from McDermott (24) and Durnan (15), and Durnan also took 5 wickets. The game between Knockbrack and Oldtown which was played on 27 September resulted in a narrow win for Knockbrack on a score of 43 to 38 runs, with Fitzpatrick scoring 17*.

There was also an edge between Knockbrack and Corduff which manifested itself when the Secretary of Knockbrack published his review of the season's activities:

> For their season Knockbrack played twelve matches – winning eight and losing four. Their record does not seem so good as that of Corduff; but unlike Corduff, Knockbrack refused no challenge from clubs that were likely to beat them.

There was no possibility that this aspersion was going to be left unchallenged, and the Corduff Secretary took aim at two clubs - Knock CC for suggesting that his club picked and chose the teams against which they played and Knockbrack for several reasons:

> Corduff has played and defeated better teams than they ever were and would not have refused to play (and be sure to defeat them), only on the grounds that we were certain they were inclined to pick a local team whom we have defeated but are very much inclined for rising rows.

The Secretary of Knockbrack rose to the bait, and not only did he repeat the allegation regarding Corduff handpicking its opponents, but he also alleged that it was guilty of importing "guest" players for some games:

The fact is patent that Corduff refused to play Knockbrack and also Grallagh. The same excuse is hardly applicable to the two teams. With reference to the charge of picking the local team, of whom they are afraid, we can state a fact they are not able to do, viz., that we had not a picked man playing with us for the season.

The 1903 season ended on that sour note, and based on that exchange of views, it was unlikely that Corduff and Knockbrack would be playing against each other for the foreseeable future.

The 1904 season started with many of the players involved in a different code. Knockbrack played Dunshaughlin in a hurling match, and there is a significant overlap between the players on the hurling team and the members of the cricket club. Knockbrack had not played hurling before, and the odds were "a pound to a shilling on Dunshaughlin" (20 to 1 in new money). The game was drawn on a score of 5 points to Knockbrack and 1 goal and 2 points for Dunshaughlin. This result was attributed to "the redoubtable Jack McNally, who was ably supported by his brother, Matt, John Rock, Ned Lindsay and the two Macs from Kitchenstown, Johnnie Mac, in particular, doing yeoman service in the goal, in fact his 'puck out' was worth going several miles to see."

On the cricketing front, there are references to seven games that Knockbrack played during this season, and by all accounts, the games were models of harmony. On 19 June Knockbrack beat St Dominick's on a score of 63 runs to 50 in a "most pleasant and friendly game". On 10 July, Knockbrack played Emmet CC in Skerries and won by 64 runs. During the same month, there were victories over Balbriggan (49 runs to 29), and Curraha (25 runs to 21). The return game between Knockbrack and Skerries Emmet was played on 8 August and resulted in another victory for Knockbrack (54 runs to 44). The Skerries Band was singled out for praise because of the "really first-class programme of music which they contributed on that occasion."

Knockbrack commenced the new season with an "easy" victory over Man-O'-War (57 runs to 32) and advertised its forthcoming game against Skerries Emmet as a festive occasion because there was going to be a Tug-O-War between "two celebrated teams" and a band in attendance. The ensuing cricket match resulted in an "easy win" for Knockbrack (57 runs to 33 runs). The return game was played in Skerries on 9 July and the period of détente and harmony came to an end as was evidenced by the report which was submitted to the *Drogheda Independent* by P. Fitzpatrick, Hon. Secretary of Knockbrack:

This match was played on the grounds of the latter, on Sunday last, 9th inst., and would undoubtedly result (sic) in an easy win for the visitors, but for the excited element that prevailed amongst the spectators, when the home team had but one wicket to fall by over-ruling the umpire's decision and refusing to let their last man bat. Score: Knockbrack, 35, Skerries, 21 and 1 wicket to fall.

Without an overarching authority to arbitrate on these disagreements, letters to the paper were the only means by which clubs could present their interpretation of events, with the result that diplomatic relations between clubs might be strained for a considerable period. This was the major contribution which the Fingal League made when it was established because now matters could be discussed, and even if there were disagreements, the clubs would continue to play against each other. The game between Knockbrack and Ratoath was the final game of the 1905 season for which there was a report available, and the result was an "easy win" (the words of Mr Fitzpatrick, Secretary of Knockbrack) on a score of 50 runs to 28.

From 1906 to 1925, there are very few references in the local press to cricket being played by Knockbrack. In 1907, the club indicated that it was open to accept challenges to play friendly matches for the season, and the only game for which there is a report was against Curraha which Knockbrack won by "a few runs". The next games for which it was possible to access reports were against Gormanstown which were played in September 1913. The first game resulted in a win for Gormanstown on a score of 50 runs to 26, and there was a more detailed report on the return game which was played on the grounds of Lord Gormanston, "kindly lent for the occasion to Nockbrack (sic)." Gormanstown batted first and scored 31 runs, "principally contributed by T. Reilly (8*) and Vincent Purfield (8). Knockbrack scored 17 runs, "thanks to the splendid batting of P. Hughes", but the bowling of Reynolds of Balbriggan for the home club was unplayable".

The lack of references to cricket in Fingal during this period is puzzling because between 1906 and 1914, the *Drogheda Independent* published 333 reports on cricket, but they were mostly concerned with cricket in Meath. One possible explanation is that preference was given to competitive games in the Meath League as distinct from challenge matches which were being played in Fingal. Cricket was also competing with Gaelic games for players and publishing space, and the close association in some minds between cricket, the gentry, and the R. I. C. may have contributed to the lack of cricket/reports on cricket in

Fingal. The classification of cricket as a foreign game exercised the minds of the members of the Meath GAA County Board in its meeting in June 1905, and Mr P. Daly, who at a later stage was to become a leading figure in Fingal cricket did not mince his words when he referred to the Ban as an example of Coercion:

> It was Coercion on the part of the Central Council to pass a byelaw preventing the playing of cricket by men that played cricket before the Gaelic Association was started.... If that order came from the Tories, they would try to hound them out of Ireland and would denounce them in all the Nationalist papers in Ireland.

That was Mr Daly's perspective in 1905, but by 1913, the criticisms of cricket and cricketers had become more vitriolic in some quarters. In a lengthy article entitled "Language and Pastimes, Seaghan Mac na Midhe, a contributor to the *Drogheda Independent* gave vent to a whole series of insults/ prejudices. He referred to "shoneen colleges where the sons of the graziers and squireens get a smattering of French and a full course in English pastimes and come back ignorant of the fact that we have pastimes of our own second to none on the face of the globe". In an either-or argument, he did not see that it was possible to play cricket and football:

> Our games are played all the year round, and the population is too sparse to allow of a cricket club and a football club in the same parish. Hence the national pastimes have practically wiped-out *foreign* games, even though the latter were frequently subsidised by the local magnate and made attractive by the half-barrel. The two games are in open competition, and it is only natural that sentiment should play some part in the fight. A few still cling to the bat and barrel but they are of the kind that would not reflect great credit upon a Gaelic Association.

This association between cricket and Englishness was reiterated the following month by James Quigley, who also availed of the opportunity to belittle cricket as a game:

> No other nation ever did, or ever will play such a foolish game. The English themselves are ridiculing it to death.... Irish cricket is funnier than the Connacht French Lord Ashbourne had to tell about. There are many things that we might usefully learn from the English but leave them their cricket and their soccer.

In justifying the exclusion of members of the R. I. C. from the G. A. A., P. Ua Uaithne contended that cricket was a more appropriate game for them:

We should regard the G. A. A. as the voluntary army of Ireland, and the effort to get policemen into it should be resisted by all means. Let the police learn cricket, or hockey or golf or some other such Dublin Castle game. They are not wanted in Irish Ireland.

With some upholders of public opinion maintaining such extreme views on cricket, it is scarcely credible that cricket began to be played again in Fingal after the events of the period from 1913 to 1922.

### Knockbrack CC, 1925-1980

In July 1925, Skerries Cricket Club was re-organised, and Knockbrack CC also re-commenced its cricketing activities in 1925. The two clubs met at Knockbrack on 6 September, and a scorecard was appended to the report, but the scores do not tally. It appears that Knockbrack scored 50 runs and in reply, Skerries got 58 runs for the loss of 8 wickets.

In 1926, there were cricket teams in Balbriggan, Ring Commons, Knightstown, Skerries and Knockbrack, but fixtures for the most part were still being arranged as challenges as distinct from there being any official structures in place. There was some form of competition in place in 1926, and based on circumstantial evidence, the second team was Knockbrack. This was the commencement of Knockbrack's involvement in Fingal League cricket, and until the club left cricket at the end of the 2003 season, it was the most loyal of all clubs to the Fingal League. Whatever queries there were about the 1926 season, there is no doubt that the Fingal League was fully operational in 1927 because detailed reports of games were furnished to the *Drogheda Independent*. The first fixtures were played on Sunday, 15 May 1927 and the final game was played on 18 September 1927 between Knockbrack and Skerries, which Skerries won on a score of 125 runs to 63 for Knockbrack. The final commendation from Mr Duff was for the "two independent umpires whose tact and appreciation carried the appreciation of both sides." The prize for winning the league was a cheque for the purchase of a cricket set.

By 1929, the number of teams in the League had increased to fifteen, and the reports on the games are further enlightening examples of sports journalism in a bygone era. When Balbriggan played Knockbrack, the game is disposed of in a single sentence - Balbriggan 52 and Knockbrack 29, but there is then a lyrical account of Knockbrack:

The playing pitch is most picturesquely situated on a level plain near the summit of the famous Hill of Knockbrack. From the eminence a panoramic view of great beauty may be obtained. At the foot of the Hill is a lovely valley, whilst in the distance the Dublin mountains, Howth, Ireland's Eye, Lambay and the sea glimmering beneath a cloudless summer's sky being prominent features in a delightful picture which was never seen to better advantage than on Sunday last... People who rave about Warrenpoint, Killarney and other beauty spots further afield should visit Knockbrack and see for themselves the delightful scenery that we have at our very doors.

Skerries' reign as champions was ended when they lost the semi-final to Knockbrack, and in terms of hyperbole, the reporter again excelled himself. The game was played at Balbriggan on a crease that that was laid 24 years earlier by the late Terence O'Neill and Patrick Cumiskey and was reckoned to be "one of the finest in Ireland and "still in perfect order." The correspondent then waxed eloquently on the quality of the cricket. He deemed the game to have been "the finest exhibition of cricket ever witnessed in Fingal, with the game being "up to Test standard, with the fielders and bowlers winning the day." After these comments, it is astonishing to read that Knockbrack only scored 14 runs, with Ennis (6) being the only one to make anything worthwhile. A score of 14 would appear in most circumstances to render the result a foregone conclusion, but not in Fingal. Skerries was dismissed for 13 runs, and Knockbrack went on to play Baldwinstown in the final.

The final was played in Balbriggan on Sunday, 15 September in front of a "large gathering". The fielding and bowling of both sides were deemed to have been "perfect". Rock was singled out for special mention due to "two brilliant left-handed catches" in the slips. For Knockbrack, Hughes and Rooney bowled in their "usual capable manner", and for Baldwinstown, the bowling of Clarke and Rooney was "perfect". With bowling and fielding of such a high standard, it is reasonable to assume that the scores would be low, and the final result was Knockbrack, 24 runs and Baldwinstown, 16. Knockbrack indicated its intention to sponsor the purchase of a cup which would be presented to the winners of the Fingal League, and it was anticipated that Knockbrack's name would be inscribed on the cup when it was placed on exhibition. However, the cup was not bought until early in 1930 so Knockbrack's name was not inscribed on the Cup as the first winners.

With a valuable trophy for the Fingal League winners, and a continuing increase in the number of teams, the 1930 season was awaited eagerly. Knockbrack fielded two teams, Knockbrack 1 and Knockbrack Seconds (An

Macraidh), and it was obvious from early in the season that both teams were genuine contenders for the Fingal League Championship Cup. In one of the first games of the season, Knockbrack 1 beat Balbriggan on a score of 41 all out to 42 for 5 wickets in a game which commenced late due to a procession at the Church. The report deemed Knockbrack to have been excellent all-round, and it paid tribute to the quality of Knockbrack's fielding.

One of Knockbrack's next games was at Knightstown, and it adjusted very well to the conditions even though it had only played once before on a mat. In its score of 93, the main contributors for Knockbrack were T. Moore (19), P. Moore (18), J. Casey (16), C. Lindsay (10) and J. Moore, Jnr (8). For Knightstown, E. Moore took 4 wickets and C. Gilsenan took 5. The batsmen who contributed most to Knightstown's total of 74 runs were V. Gallen (16), D. Connor (8), W. Rickard (8), E. Moore (7) and J. Connor (7), father of David O'Connor, past President of Cricket Ireland. J. Moore took 5 wickets, J. Murphy took 2, and was deemed unlucky not to have taken more wickets because his "bowling was very deadly".

In the meantime, Knockbrack Second XI was also going well, and on 20 July, it beat Balrothery on a score of 60 runs to 26 runs. The main batsman for Knockbrack was J. Kierans (21), and there were useful contributions from P. Corr (7) and J. Moore, Jnr, (6). By 16 August, the two Knockbrack teams were topping their sections of the league, and the local derby was going to have a major bearing on the destination of the trophy. At that point, Knockbrack First XI had won 8 games out of a possible 10, and the Second XI had won 7 games out of 9. In a preview of the game, it was suggested that "it was an open secret that the second team is going to give their elders a surprise." The big needle game was played on 17 August, and the Second XI was "superior to their elders in every department". Knockbrack 1 batted first and scored 45 runs with Farrell and Ennis being the only batsmen to make any scores. The Second XI appeared to have everything under control, but with four runs required and three wickets in hand, they lost 2 wickets for no runs. Rooney's bowling was "deadly", and the main batsman for the Second XI was McGrane. The final score was 54 runs to 45, and the Second XI had earned the right to play Balcunnin in the final on 24 August.

The final was played at Balbriggan, and although the game was of "moderate quality" and had "no brilliant batting as most of the score was made through the medium of byes", it was not without incident. At the end of the game, the official marker gave the score as 40 runs each, but "at least 100 [people]" had the score Knockbrack Seconds 41, Balcunnin 40.

The replay was also played at Balbriggan, and in typical Fingal fashion, the bowlers were on top. Knockbrack batted first and lost the first 4 wickets for 7 runs. The final score for Knockbrack was 23 runs, with Johnny Murphy taking 6 wickets and Simon Hoare taking 4 wickets. Nine Balcunnin wickets fell for 14 runs, but the last pair, Tommy Power and John Hoare, brought the score to 22 when Jem Murphy took a miraculous one-handed catch off his own bowling to leave Knockbrack Seconds the winners by one run. Knockbrack Seconds had the honour of being the first team to have its name inscribed on the Fingal Challenge Cup. This was the end of a wonderful season for the Fingal League with interest in cricket at an all-time high, the finances of the League in a flourishing position, and an expectation that that there would be a big increase in the number of teams for the next season.

Knockbrack CC's community involvement has always been significant, and it is noticeable that the Second XI appeared to be a club within a club because it organised a dance in Naul Hall on 30 November, admission was 1s, dancing was from 8 to 2, and there was bus serving Skerries, Lusk, Balrothery and Balbriggan to bring patrons to this event. The Second XI organised another dance on 25 January and held its own Annual Meeting on 16 February 1931.

For the next number of years, Knockbrack CC was competitive, but it did not win another Fingal League trophy until the 1950s. For example, in 1933, it finished joint top of Division B, but lost the play-off to Oldtown. Despite the lack of success on the playing field, the club continued to make a huge contribution to life in the community with events being organised on a regular basis. On 20 January 1935, it organised a Whist Drive and a Dance. The top score in the Whist Drive was £5, cards were 2s 6d each, and admission to the dance for non-players was 1s 3d. Music on the evening was provided by the Tolan's Band.

Moving into 1940, Knockbrack beat Ballymadun on a score of 52 runs to 46. The principal scorers for Knockbrack were J. Byrne (18), C. Lindsay (9) and J. Murphy (6), J. Murphy took 5 wickets for 20 runs and J. Byrne took 4 wickets for 18. In the return fixture at Ballymadun, Knockbrack won by 2 runs on a score of 30 runs to 28. The best batsmen for Knockbrack were J. Murphy (12), C. McGrane (11*) and the best bowlers were J. Moore, 6 wickets for 6 runs, and J. Murphy, 3 for 19. With this result, Knockbrack qualified to play the Black Hills in the final of Division B. Black Hills won a game that "was well-contested", a "fine sporting spirit prevailed, and "some fine catches were made by the fielders on both sides while sound judgment and a thorough knowledge of the game was much in evidence". Knockbrack lost 5 wickets for 15 runs, but the sixth wicket partnership brought to the total to 26. However, when it seemed that victory was assured for Knockbrack, it lost all its wickets and ended on 34 runs, 2 runs short of the Black Hills' total.

Cricket continued in Fingal during the Emergency and the view was expressed that "notwithstanding the amount of difficulties confronting the Fingal cricket this season, a very high standard of cricket has been witnessed since the season opened." Knockbrack played Balrothery on 1 June 1941 but lost on a score of 43 runs to 31, with J. Maguire (12) making the top score for Knockbrack. The community involvement also continued, and Knockbrack joined forces with Ring Commons CC to hold a Ceilidh and Old-Time Waltz in the Town Hall, Balbriggan on 26 January 1941, dancing was from 9 to 1, admission was 1s 6d and the music was provided by Jack Ryan's Band. The next dance was at the end of the cricket season, and the advertisement started with the words, "Hello! A Dance you are sure to enjoy!" The same band, the same price, the same venue, but now a slow waltz had been added to the old-time waltz.

At its AGM in 1942, there were familiar names among the officers – the President was P. Moore, P. Corr was Captain, the Vice-Captain was M. Brogan, J. Casey was Treasurer, O. C. Lindsay, and Committee was comprised of C. McGrane, J. McNally and G. McNally. A significant note was appended to the end of the report – "a vote of thanks was also passed to Mr Michael Reilly for the use of his ground for many years." For the 1942 season, the Fingal League was divided into two divisions because of transport difficulties, and Knockbrack was placed in the West Division along with Naul Hill, Ballymadun and Tubbergregan. Transport continued to be an issue during the 1943 season, and although Knockbrack fulfilled its fixtures, it was noted on one weekend that Oldtown and Portrane failed to travel to Ring Commons and Black Hills respectively.

There was little of note from a Knockbrack perspective for the next two seasons, except that its rivalry with near neighbours, Tubbergregan, began to assume epic proportions. When Knockbrack journeyed to Tubbergregan for one of the first games of the 1946 season, it won the toss and elected to field. P. O'Brien and T. Tiernan opened the batting to the bowling of J. Magrane (sic) and M. Ayres. The report mentioned both batsmen giving chances, but they were still there on 23 runs when O'Brien had a "strange hit to leg for 2 which hopped across three fields – the actual playing field, the corner of a second and well into the third one"! Based on this report, it seems that Mr. O'Brien may have had reason to be aggrieved to be only given two runs for a shot that ended up two fields away from the cricket ground. He was bowled by Ayres when the score was 25, and then the rain came to end play for the day. The game was replayed on 23 June at Tubbergregan, and Knockbrack won by 6 runs on a score of 43 to 37 runs. The stars on this occasion for Knockbrack were M. Ayres, the ex-Walshestown player, who took 6 wickets for 21 runs, and C. Lindsay (15) and C. McGrane (13) who got the lion's share of the runs.

The return game was played at the "celebrated Hill of Knockbrack" in "lovely sunshine and a refreshing air" in front of a very large crowd of spectators. In the words of the reporter, the visitors had all the luck, "while Knockbrack could do nothing right, even their fielding failed, which is usually their strongest point". Knockbrack won the toss, elected to field, and the "visitors tail wagged very well to make the fine score of 49". Knockbrack had a bad start, never looked like winning and were all out for 35, "of which John Maguire (10*) and J. Byrne (7) were the best batsmen". This result meant that the two teams would have to meet again in "a test match for division honours".

The test match was played in "brilliant sunshine" at Balbriggan on 25 August. Knockbrack won the toss and elected to field first. Tubbergregan lost its first six batsmen for 7 runs, but "the tail wagged very well", and the last four batsmen brought the score up to 32 runs. The main contributors were P. Ennis (9), T. Tiernan (6) and T. Moore (6). The main bowlers for Knockbrack were J. McGrane, 4 wickets for 9 runs, and M. Ayres, 3 wickets for 13 runs. The reporter was critical of the decision not to allow Ayres to continue bowling. In chasing this "moderate score". Knockbrack had 21 runs for the loss of 3 wickets, but the other wickets fell for 7 runs to leave Knockbrack all out on 28 runs. The turning point of the match came towards the end when M. Kiernan of Tubber "caught a lightning catch, hit by J. Byrne". The top scorers for Knockbrack were C. Lindsay (10) and T. McGrane (6), and the best bowlers for Tubber were M. Morgan, 5 for 12 and P. Ennis, 4 for 4.

Having been beaten in the semi-final in 1946, Knockbrack went one better in 1947 when it reached the final and played against Walshestown at the Market Green, Balbriggan. On the day, Knockbrack was well-beaten and only one batsman, M. Ayres (17) got runs of any consequence with extras (7) being the next highest contributor to a total of 34 runs. Walshestown's final score was 94 runs, with significant scores from J. McNally (25), J. Murphy (19) and extras (19). Knockbrack was back in the final in 1948, and this time it was against the mighty Balrothery. There was another unfortunate batting collapse and Knockbrack only managed to score 21 runs. Balrothery had batted first and in a "very polished display", its stars were Simon Hoare (40), John Mooney (20) and Val Farrell (17).

In the early 1950s, cricket in Fingal was at a low ebb, with only four teams competing for the Fingal Cup. It is always an indication of problems if an organisation does not manage to get its competitions completed during the current year, and in 1951, "due to unforeseen difficulties", the final between Knockbrack and Portrane was not played. The final was played eventually in Skerries on 25 May 1952, and for the third time in five years, Knockbrack was beaten in a final. The game was played "in brilliant sunshine", Knockbrack lost early wickets and by the fall of the fifth wicket, had only scored 26 runs, and most of these runs had been byes. The other batsmen came and went rapidly, and Knockbrack's total was 36 runs all out. Portrane set about its task methodically, but with 8 wickets down, it needed four runs to win. Three more runs were scored when another wicket fell, but the last pair managed to obtain not just the necessary single "but one extra for good measure" to leave Portrane the winners on 38 runs.

Knockbrack's commendable community involvement continued apace. In August 1952, it organised a Fancy-Dress Ball in the Grand Hotel, Malahide and admission was 5s. There was another dance in the Grand Hotel on 12 October 1952 and there was a Ceilidh in the Town Hall, Balbriggan on 17 October with admission, 3s 6d. Whist Drives were another popular fund-raiser and "there was a fairly large gathering" in the Town Hall, Balbriggan on 28 March 1954 for the Whist Drive which was sponsored by the Knockbrack Cricket Club.

In 1956, in addition to playing Fingal League cricket, Knockbrack decided to enter the Dunsany Cup Competition which was for teams in Meath or on Dublin/Meath border. It was drawn against Addinstown in the first round, and on winning the toss, Knockbrack elected to field first. Addinstown was dismissed for 27 runs, but Knockbrack was dismissed for 12 runs, with E. Shaw taking 7 wickets for 6 runs, and P. Browne taking 3 wickets for 6. After many years of endeavour, Knockbrack eventually won the Fingal Championship Cup in 1956. This information has been derived from the Fingal League Archives rather than a first-hand account from the local newspapers.

Cricket in Fingal was in such a parlous state in 1956 that a meeting was held with a view to winding-up the League, but the majority perspective was that every effort should be made to ensure its continuation. At this meeting,

Eddie Dunne, the long-serving Secretary, resigned and he was replaced by Thomas McGrane of Knockbrack who was to give a lifetime of service to cricket in Fingal. In addition to taking on this post, Thomas was also Secretary of Knockbrack CC.

Knockbrack played Mounthanover in the Dunsany Cup in 1957, but the first game was rain-affected, and later results showed that Mounthanover played in the semi-final so it can be inferred that Knockbrack was beaten in the replayed game. Knockbrack played Portrane in the final of the Fingal League at Kenure Park, Rush. Portrane batted first and was dismissed for 43 runs. In the words of the report, "at this stage an easy win for Knockbrack was anticipated", but superb bowling by J. Neville, J. Young and O. Meenan put paid to that prediction and Knockbrack was dismissed for 33 runs, with its best batsmen being S. Moore (10) and Kit Lindsay (9).

For the second time in this decade, the championships were not completed during the season, and the 1958 final was not played until June 1959, with Knockbrack and Portrane in opposition. Knockbrack won by 11 runs on a score of 59 to 48, with Seán Moore of Knockbrack taking 4 wickets for 4 runs. Knockbrack retained the Championship in 1959 and it also played in the Dunsany Cup competition, but this competition had an unsatisfactory ending because the team on the bottom of the league conceded the points of their games with Knockbrack and Addinstown, and this meant that Addinstown retained the Cup. The 1959 Fingal final was not played until 1960, and Knockbrack completed its three in a row by beating Portrane on a score of 97 runs to 68. The same two teams were due to play the 1960 final in May 1961, but Portrane withdrew from the League for an unspecified reason to leave Knockbrack winning its four in a row in an unsatisfactory manner. In place of a final, Knockbrack played a challenge game against Ring Commons which had only recently re-formed after a lapse of 20 years. Knockbrack scored 56 runs, and Ring Commons declared when it had scored 56 runs, with only 2 wickets down.

In 1962, Balbriggan re-formed with the result that the seven teams in the Fingal League were Ring Commons, Balbriggan, Skerries, the Black Hills, Man-O'-War, Balrothery and Knockbrack. It was now decided to put the second competition on a more formal footing and to purchase a cup. Balrothery CC beat Knockbrack to be the first winners of this cup, and earlier in the season, it also ended Knockbrack's quest for five in a row when it won the Fingal Championship.

The revival of cricket in Fingal gathered pace and in 1963, there were ten teams in the area – Man-O'-War, Portrane, Knockbrack, Balrothery, Skerries,

Black Hills, Naul, Rush, Ring Commons and Balbriggan. The Fingal Championship final was played at the Nevitt between Balrothery, the holders, and Knockbrack. The game was attended by over two hundred spectators, and Balrothery batting first was in trouble immediately against the "fiery bowling attack of Seán Donnelly who took 5 wickets for 10 runs, and Seán Moore who captured 4 for 11." John Mooney (11) was the only batsman to reach double figures and Balrothery was dismissed for 36 runs. In reply, Knockbrack did not fare much better, and it lost 6 wickets for 7 runs, but the seventh wicket partnership of 17 runs between George McNally (3) and Thomas McGrane (15) brought Knockbrack back into the game. The eighth wicket fell when the score was 31 and the ninth wicket fell at 32 runs. The last man in, Noel Masterson, joined Seán Donnelly at the wicket with 5 runs needed for victory. The first delivery struck Donnelly on the knee, and he went down injured, but he recovered sufficiently to carry on, and with Masterson, hit the required runs in singles to give Knockbrack victory by one wicket. "The two players were chaired off the field by their supporters and there was sustained applause for the gallant losers". Two of the Balrothery bowlers, Bunny Casey and Jemmie Bissett were singled out for honourable mention because Casey's figures were 27 overs bowled, 15 maidens and 3 wickets for 19 runs, while Bissett took 5 wickets for 12 runs in the 17 overs that he bowled. Knockbrack celebrated the victory in Naul that evening, and the celebrations were continued a fortnight later at a second social event, again in Naul. To round off a wonderful season for Knockbrack, it also won the Fingal League, and further celebrations were held in Naul in February 1964.

Knockbrack won the Fingal double again in 1964. It beat the Black Hills by one run with eight wickets in hand to win the Fingal Cricket Cup with E. Moore (13) being the main contributor to the score. In the play-off for the Championship, Knockbrack beat Man-O'-War on a score of 105 runs to 37. The turning point of this game was the "brilliant catch" by Eamonn Moore to dismiss James Murphy, and shortly after, Tom Murphy was "well-caught" by Thomas McGrane. The other members of the Man-O'-War team offered "no resistance" to the bowling of Seán Moore and G. McNally and they were all out for 37.

In the 1964 season Knockbrack entered the Leinster Cricket League, and although the secretary referred to the club having only had "limited success" in its first season in the League, it had still done sufficiently well to be promoted from the Minor League to the Junior League for the 1965 season. In many respects, at this stage, the club was back to the "good old days" of the late 1920s and early 1930s, and because it had such an increase in membership, it decided to enter a second team in the Fingal League in addition to having a team in the Leinster League.

1964 was the last year in which Knockbrack won any title at Fingal League level until the early 1990s, but it was very successful in Leinster League competitions. In 1965, it won the Leinster Junior Cup by beating Leinster CC at the Civil Service Grounds. Knockbrack batted first and scored 70 runs and then bowled Leinster out for 49 runs. The Knockbrack squad on this auspicious occasion was Sean and Eamonn Moore (the *Drogheda Independent* said Morris), Noel Masterson, John Fanning, George McNally, Tom Hunt, Eddie, Chris and Loughlin Lindsay, Tom McGrane, and Seán Donnelly. This season, in addition to a Social at Naul Hall in August, the club organised its First Annual Dinner Dance at the Holmpatrick House Hotel.

The club continued to develop and in 1966, it moved to its "newly-acquired grounds". It intended to play in the Leinster Minor and Junior Leagues, and to fulfil its engagements in the Fingal League. At Leinster level, it had another successful season because the Leinster Junior League and Cup were retained, and it finished runners-up in the Fingal Championship. In 1968, Knockbrack played in the Intermediate and Minor Leinster competitions, and in the Fingal League and Championship, but it was some time before it won another title. In July 1968, Knockbrack played a friendly game against Cooke Selection, Belfast and rounded off the day with a social at Naul Hall.

In April 1973, Knockbrack opened the season with a friendly against Balrothery, and this game coincided with the opening of a new pavilion which had "ample dining space" and provided "a clear view of the playing field for indoor spectators. In 1975, Knockbrack won the Intermediate B League for the first time when it played 13 games, won 10 of them, drew 1, lost 2 and finished with 80%. The team which came second was 13 percentage points behind Knockbrack. Wonderful bowling feats are often highlighted in the reports of games, and one of these examples came in 1976 in a game versus Mullingar at Mount Murray when Seán Moore took 6 wickets for 10 runs, and Mullingar was bowled out for 40 runs. In 1977, the Intermediate A League was won, and another Knockbrack bowler, Seán Donnelly, received special mention in the *Evening Herald's* review of Junior Cricket for "being virtually unplayable" by taking 9 wickets for 11 runs when Knockbrack played Leinster IV at Knockbrack.

Knockbrack retained the Intermediate A League and reached the final of the Whelan Cup in 1978 when it played against Man-O'-War in a Fingal derby. It scored 61 runs in its 20 overs with Tom Murphy taking 3 wickets for 7 runs, and

Albert Harper taking 2 wickets for 16. Man-O'-War got the required score for the loss of 3 wickets, and the main contributor to its score was Jody Morgan, father of Eoin, with 17*. In 1979, Knockbrack won the Middle Cup by beating Leinster at Rush, and thus qualified for the Irish Junior Cup competition for the following year. Unfortunately, Ballyarton from Derry was too strong on the day, and it won by 6 wickets with Knockbrack being dismissed for 44 runs.

Prior to this, Knockbrack celebrated its 100th anniversary season by hosting a game between a Leinster Cricket Union Selection and a Knockbrack XI. The players on the Leinster side were M. McDevitt, D. Goodwin, J. Caprani, S. Oakes, S. Mitchell, J. B. Bunworth, N. Grier, R. Waters. D. Robinson, F. Malin, and N. Seale. There are very few details available regarding the actual cricket, but the wonderful singsong after the game is still remembered fondly over 40 years later by one of the players on the Knockbrack Selection. There was another pleasant function at the end of the season which marked the 50th Anniversary of the Fingal Cup, and Knockbrack had the unique distinction of having competed in the Fingal League competitions every year since the inception of the League in 1926.

It is beyond the scope of this chapter to review the final twenty-three years of Knockbrack CC's existence other than to give a summary of events during that period. In 1984, Knockbrack won the Intermediate Cup, and in 1987, Knockbrack and Ring Commons CC amalgamated to form KBRC. The team was captained by Thomas Bertram and strengthened by the return of George McNally who had played senior cricket with Malahide. This amalgamation produced instant success and in the first year, KBRC won the Intermediate B League and the Second XI won the Junior B League. In the final of the Middle Cup, KBRC played Balbriggan and won on a score of 137 to 136. This year also, KBRC played Dundalk Crusaders in the final of the George McNally Cup. Appropriately, George McNally Jnr, scored 100*, and the opening pair scored over 200 runs before a wicket was lost. KBRC ended up on 247 runs in 40 overs, and although the Crusaders made their highest ever 40 overs score, 176, they were never in with a chance of winning the game. Knockbrack's arrangement with Ring Commons ended at the end of the 1989 season, and the two clubs again became separate entities.

In the early 1990s, Knockbrack had an informal arrangement with Dundalk CC, and this produced instant dividends in terms of player numbers and trophies won. In 1992, Knockbrack 1 won the Leinster Intermediate C League and the Second XI finished as runners-up in the Junior League. Among the Dundalk players was Dr Hamid Ali Khan who was described as a "colossus in the side [because he] consistently produced match-winning contributions with both bat and ball". Bob Shackleton was another Dundalk player singled out for praise, and there was a reference to the "terrific century" which he had scored in Greystones which according to the *Drogheda Argus* was the first for the club in 112 years. This assertion is open to correction because it already has been noted that George McNally had scored at least two centuries prior to Bob Shackleton's achievement, albeit if one of the centuries was for KBRC as distinct from Knockbrack.

The following season, Knockbrack clinched the Intermediate A League when it secured the draw against Malahide which it required to win the title. Knockbrack batted first in difficult conditions and made 142 for 9 in 45 overs, with the openers, Jimmy McQuillan (20) and Patsy Harford (25) putting on 45 runs for the first wicket. There was then a collapse in which 5 wickets were lost for 30 runs, but Hamid Ali Khan came to the rescue with 61*, again according to the *Argus*, "displaying his exceptional talent". He also picked up 2 wickets and with Paddy O'Connor taking 4 wickets, Malahide was restricted to 102 runs for 6 wickets down. To round off a wonderful season for the club, Knockbrack Seconds won the Junior A League.

In the 1994 season, the club was able to field three teams in the Leinster Leagues, but it was the Second XI which took pride of place. On its route to the final of the Junior Cup, Knockbrack Seconds beat North Kildare on a score of 216 runs to 39. The architects of this big win were two members of the Dundalk contingent, Jimmy McQuillan (106*) and Neil O'Callaghan who took 7 wickets for 19 runs. The *Argus* referred to McQuillan's feat as being the second player in the club to score a century, but the validity of this assertion is open to correction. Knockbrack played Leinster in Rathmines in the Junior Cup Final in what was the club's first appearance in the Final since 1965. If the team required a boost in confidence, it was provided by the preview which was published in the *Argus*. The team had a "powerful batting line-up" with Mc Quillan having scored 500 runs for the season at an average of 74, and his opening partner, Eddie Lindsay had scored over 300 runs at an average of 50. The middle-order batsmen, Shackleton, O'Callaghan, and Carson, were "equally strong," and O'Boyle "has the knack of saving his best innings for tight situations." The bowlers, Seán Moore, O'Callaghan, Rooney, Barry Grimes, Stephen Rushe and Mc Quillan "rarely give much away", and "the team's ground fielding is second to none". In addition to all this talent, Colman Rushe was a "top-class keeper who has pulled off some breath-taking stops this season along with many excellent catches", and John Carson possessed "one of the longest throws in Leinster cricket".

In the final Leinster won the toss and batted first on a "superb wicket". They were restricted to 143 runs for 6 wickets by the bowling of Seán Moore and Neil O'Callaghan. Despite having lots of other bowlers, Moore and O'Callaghan bowled unchanged throughout the innings, and "they hardly bowled a bad ball between them." Seán Moore ended up with figures of 2 for 66 in 25 overs, and O'Callaghan's figures were 3 for 73 runs. Carson excelled in the field, and he was responsible for a key run-out. In reply, McQuillan (62) and Eddie Lindsay (32*) put on 84 runs for the first wicket, and although 3 quick wickets were lost, Carson removed any doubts regarding the eventual winners with an "ice-cool innings full of class". The winning runs were hit by Eddie Lindsay, and the victory "was celebrated well into the night by the team and the army of supporters who had travelled to the final". To finish off a perfect season, the Second XI completed the double by winning the Junior A League.

After the highs of the 1994 season, the following season was somewhat fallow in terms of title successes, but a Fingal League trophy was won for the first time in years when Knockbrack annexed the B League title. In 1996, Knockbrack played Pembroke IV in the final of the Whelan Cup, and restricted Pembroke to 131 for 4, with Seán Moore taking 2 wickets for 14 runs. In reply, Knockbrack reached the required target for the loss of only two wickets. Chris Lindsay scored 71* and Jim McQuillan scored 40 runs. Knockbrack also won the Minor Cup, and it was the focus of a wonderful documentary which was written by Conor O'Callaghan, a Knockbrack member, and broadcast on RTE radio on 25 October 1996.

In 1997, Knockbrack won the Brian Southam Cup, a T20 competition which was established in memory of a much-loved member of the Man-O'-War CC who had died suddenly in 1992. It also played against Mullingar in the final of the Leinster Intermediate Cup but fell 43 runs short of Mullingar's total of 177 runs. The following season, Knockbrack won the Intermediate and the Junior B Leagues, and a review of the cricketing year on the *Argus* mentioned the batting of Chris Lindsay who got 35 runs in the local derby against North County, and Sean Moore Senior and Junior and Dermot Keelan as "being explosive with the ball." Unfortunately, in its list of the players who had played for the Firsts, it only gave seven -names – Jimmy McQuillan, Neil Callaghan, Hamid Khan, Riaan Vorster, Bob Shackleton, Paddy Connor, and Martin Moore (Capt). At a celebratory event in early 1999, the *Argus* published a photograph of three club stalwarts, Thomas McGrane, Martin Russell and Eamonn Moore who had marked the book for many years after his retirement as a player.

In 1999, Mullingar played Knockbrack at Belgee, and during the game, Mullingar broke several club records. A second wicket unbeaten partnership between Woody O'Neill (156*) and Sammy Murphy (117*) put on 295 runs, and in the words of the *Westmeath Examiner*, "the pair inflicted such a devastating onslaught on the Knockbrack bowling that one nearly felt sorry for them". Undaunted, Knockbrack set about the huge target in style, and the opening batsman who is not named, but was possibly George McNally, hit 14 off the first over. That was as good as it got for Knockbrack, and it was finally dismissed for 130 after 36.4 overs.

By 2000, interest in the Fingal League competitions had waned to such an extent that the Executive issued a questionnaire to ascertain the steps which might be taken to arrest the decline. Knockbrack continued to support the League's competitions, and it won the Fingal B League in 2000 and 2001. It also played in Leinster until 2003, but before the start of the new season, it has lost access to its ground, and after 123 years, Knockbrack CC ceased to exist.

Knockbrack CC was a quintessential Fingal cricket club, with dogged batsmen, canny bowlers, and eager fielders. Its players were willing to fight for every run and to ensure that every run that the opposition got was hard-earned. Its hospitality was legendary, and it was contended by many that its teas were the best in Leinster. Its loyalty to the Fingal League was unequalled and it was the only club that during its existence played Fingal cricket every year from 1926. Among its membership were some wonderful characters whose approach to cricket and to life in general provided the basis for hundreds of anecdotes. In Thomas McGrane, it had a wonderful administrator, and the debt which cricket in Fingal and Leinster owes to him is incalculable. The entire cricketing community in Leinster was diminished by the loss of Knockbrack CC, and it is only fitting that the huge contribution which the club made to cricket and to social life in the community are honoured and recorded.

Knockbrack Scene and Map

# KNOCKBRACK CRICKET CLUB - FINAL LEAGUE WINNERS 1930

Back L/R John Hamiton.Pat Moore.John Cole.Martin Moore.Niall Casey.John(Dot) Fanning.PeterWhite
Seated: Michael Gavin.Lawrence Flynn.Raymond Peters.JohnMelia.Mark White
Front Declan Moore.  Chris Lindsay          KNOCKBRACK  RING COMMONS ( K.B.R.C.)

Thomas McGrane and Martin Russell

Eddie Lindsay

## Malachy Gavin

Malachy Gavin

## Michael Gavin and Patsy Harford

## Seán Moore

## Martin Moore

# Chapter 6: Cricket in Skerries

## 1882-1925

The proximity of Skerries to Dublin and the availability of the railway network were key factors in the development of Skerries as a holiday destination, and from the 1880s onwards, some people from Dublin either rented houses for lengthy periods during the summer or if they had the necessary financial resources, purchased a holiday home in Skerries. The confluence of these factors meant that there were people residing in the town on a temporary basis for whom cricket was their sport of choice.

The first specific reference to cricket in Skerries was a game between the exotically named Skerries Excelsior and Balscadden which was played at Balscadden on 31 July 1882 and resulted in a win for Balscadden by 31 runs. The next game for which there was a report took place the following year between Skerries Excelsior and Stamullen CC, and it resulted in a win for Stamullen by 35 runs. There were no further references to cricket in Skerries until August 1888 when Skerries played against a team called the North City which had not played any cricket up to that date due to the death of one of its members. The result was a win by four runs for the North City team, and the visitors (North City) "were entertained in a most hospitable manner at the Hamilton Arms Hotel". Later in the same month, Skerries Visitors XI had a fixture against Drogheda which was played at Bettystown.

By 1889, the concept of seaside cricket appeared to have taken hold, and the Skerries Visitors entertained the Sutton Visitors on Wednesday, 28 August, and according to the report, the crease "was excellent, being situated above the town on a vantage ground, giving a glorious view from the Mourne Mountains to Lambay". The game was played on a one-innings per side basis and Skerries visitors won on a score of 131 runs to 82. Among the players on the Sutton team were G. Casey and P. Manders who also played with Malahide while Mr J. Blood on the Skerries team was to become a very active participant in the sporting life in the town during the summer. The return game was played at Sutton on 7 September, and there was a significant level of continuity in the teams which represented Skerries, with eight people playing on both occasions. Skerries won a two-innings per side game, due chiefly to the Considine brothers who took 10 wickets each, and the batting of Cordner who scored 27 runs. Representing Sutton on this occasion was the famous T. J. S. Casey who had played for Ireland and had the honour of scoring the first century for two clubs

(Malahide and Trinity). The anonymous reporter for the Sport was very impressed to see that "the renowned T. J. S. Casey had been caught in the vortex of seaside cricket". Seemingly, Mr Casey had reason to be aggrieved because his first innings was summarily halted by his "own umpire" who gave him out LBW and this was a decision with which everybody except Mr Casey concurred.

The following season, the seaside cricket continued, and Skerries Visitors played Laytown, with the result being a win for Laytown who scored twice as many runs as Skerries. The importance of the railway network has already been mentioned, and the report on this game ended with a note of appreciation for the station-master's co-operation:

> As usual the Railway company stopped the 8.10 p.m. train to take up the Skerries cricket team. The Company always kindly stopped trains at Laytown to take up or set down cricket teams at the request of the Hon. Sec. of the Laytown Cricket Club, Mr Thos. J. A. Wall.

In 1891, Skerries CC played 5 games, won 4 and lost 1. Most of the people that had played on the team in the 1880s were still playing, and this level of continuity was commendable for a team of seasonal residents. At the end of that season, the averages were published in the *Freeman's Journal*, and Tom Considine was the leading player with a total of 87 runs in 5 innings, with one not out, which gave him an average of 17.2. The next highest was C. E. Ireland who scored 60 runs in 7 innings, with two not outs, and an average of 12. The leading bowlers were Tom Considine (31 wickets) and C. E. Ireland (25). The last report for the team called Skerries CC was of a game against the B Company, Army Service Corps which was played at Lusk and resulted in a win for Skerries on a score of 75 runs to 32.

From this point onwards, the cricket teams in Skerries have specific names which reflected their political, social, or religious affiliations. While cricket was played by all classes, it also appeared to have been very important for people to play with those with whom there was a perceived social compatibility, whether that was in relation to religious affiliations, political beliefs, or employment status. During this period there were seven cricket clubs in the Holmpatrick and Skerries districts, and they were Holmpatrick CC, Emmet CC, Workmen's CC, Crescent CC, The Shamrocks CC, Balcunnin CC and Arondales, Ballykea.

The Workmen's Cricket Club, Skerries appears to have been in existence for just three years, 1899 to 1901 inclusive. During this period, it played most of its games in Fingal or Meath. In 1901, the Workmen's CC lost to Naul CC on 30 June, and also lost the return game which was played at Naul on 4 August. There are no further references to the Workmen's CC in the local papers from that date onwards, but some of its players transferred their allegiance to other clubs in the area.

A team called Arondales, Ballykea played cricket during the 1904 and 1905 seasons. In 1904, Ballykea played Man-O'-War at Ballykea and won handsomely. It featured in a local derby against Skerries Emmet in May 1905 but was beaten comfortably by the Skerries team.

Many of the clubs of this era could more correctly be called teams rather than clubs because they were simply groups of like-minded individuals who came together to play cricket, but Holmpatrick CC applied to have the club registered under the *Registration of Clubs, Ireland Act 1904*. The first application was made to the Balbriggan Petty Sessions in February 1905 and renewed in 1906, 1907 and 1908. The report on the proceedings gave details of the facilities at the club, and its reason for applying for registration. The only building on the grounds was a "wooden shed with a corrugated iron roof without any furniture in it". D. I. Routledge believed that within the meaning of *The Act*, Holmpatrick CC should not be called a club at all. He expressed the view that the premises were unsuitable but that it would only be open for a few months of the year. The Chairman, Mr W. St Leger Woods, thought that club was under the impression that a licence was necessary because it was intended to get in a few dozen of beer for the "entertainment of their friends at a cricket match". It was never intended to sell liquor, and on that basis, the State would not oppose the club being registered.

The Holmpatrick cricket team was comprised of members of the sizeable Anglican population in the district, summer residents and visitors to the area. In the game against Pembroke in 1900, only one player, Edward Bailey (later Secretary of Skerries Golf Club) lived full-time in Skerries. The Holmpatrick team which played against Balbriggan in 1901 contained two residents of Skerries, (Rev. R. W. Shegog, the Rector, and Edward Bailey, the other nine players as far as can be ascertained from a search of the 1901 Census appeared to have had their main residences in Dublin.

In the team which played Malahide on 24 June 1905, there are only two players (Shegog and Bailey) whose names appear on the 1901 Census as being resident in Holmpatrick. Even within a season, there is a significant turnover of players and when Holmpatrick played Emmet CC on 1 July 1905, only six of the players from the previous week featured in this game. In the games against Pembroke Wanderers on 13 July 1907 and against Richmond on 3 August 1907, only two players (Wellington Shegog, Club Secretary and son of the Rector, and F. Milligan) played in both games. Over a period of three seasons, only one player (W. Shegog), played in the games which have been analysed. On 10 July 1909, Holmpatrick CC played Drumcondra, and the final score was Drumcondra 69, Holmpatrick CC 11 runs. There is no overlap between the team which played Drumcondra in 1909 and the team which played in 1907. The team sheet only gave initials for the forenames of the players, but it appears, based on the available evidence that only one of the players (W. J. McClenaghan) was resident in Holmpatrick or Skerries on a full-time basis. He was a solicitor and acted for the club when the licence was being renewed in 1907. The *Irish Times* of 24 July 1909 contained a reference to the cricketer "being well provided for by the Holmpatrick Club", and that is the final reference to cricket at Holmpatrick CC.

Reasons for the disappearance of Holmpatrick CC from the cricketing calendar can only be based on conjecture. The opening of Skerries Golf Club in 1906 is one possible reason because many of the leading players (the Shegogs and Mr Bailey) became involved very heavily in the activities of the golf club. By 1910, many of the teams from Dublin which had played against Holmpatrick were playing junior and minor league cricket, and this had an obvious impact on the willingness of teams to play friendlies. Also, for a team to function efficiently, it is essential to have a committed nucleus of players available for all games. Holmpatrick CC with its blend of local players and visitors struggled to have any form of continuity in its team selections. In the period between 1900 and 1909, based on the team sheets which were published, it appears that over sixty players played with Holmpatrick CC. This turnover of players makes it very difficult for a team to continue especially if the locally based players who were the backbone of the club had other commitments.

The full name for the club was the Holmpatrick Cricket and Tennis Club, but it did not confine its activities to sport. It was very involved in the community and concerts were an integral element of its annual programme. According to the *Drogheda Argus and Leinster Journal*, the concert in 1904 promised to be "a very great success" because its "admirable programme" included the names of several very prominent Metropolitan artistes". A concert was held in the Recreation Hall on 4 August, and it was deemed to be "most enjoyable". Some of the names which featured on the team sheets were seen to good effect, and the female members of the club such as Miss Ina Shegog, Mrs Briscoe, Miss Dunham and Miss Blood-Smyth made very valuable contributions to the successful staging of the concerts. After the concert, the floor was cleared, and "the free of movement were able to indulge in the practice of Terpsichorean art to their hearts' content." The success of the concerts which were staged between 1904 and 1908 is illustrated by the provision of a special train at 12.15 p.m. to enable concert-goers to return to Dublin.

In 1904, there is a reference to a team called Crescent CC, Skerries which indicated that it was available to play matches against junior teams from July to the end of September, and it appeared to have access to a ground because it was willing to play games in Skerries or away, but no further details are available regarding this team.

By way of contrast with Holmpatrick CC, the members of Emmet CC were Catholic, nationalists and permanent residents of the town. Emmet CC played some away games in the Phoenix Park, but most of its games were against "country clubs" because for the Fingal cricketer, the modus operandi was to cycle to the game, use communal playing equipment, have a drink during the innings break, drain a half-keg of beer dry at the end of a game, and cycle home.

In addition to the differences already identified between the two clubs, Holmpatrick CC had security of tenure, the Emmet Cricket Club did not, but it depended on the goodwill of landowners for access to a field. For example, in a report on a game against Oldtown, the landowner, Mr William Healy was thanked for giving the field for the occasion. At its AGM in 1904, there is a reference to the handicap of operating without "a proper ground", and the main reason given was the fact that land in Skerries was very valuable. The landlord (Lord Holmpatrick) was seen as the chief obstacle to procuring a field and the passing of the recent Land Act had exacerbated the situation because it had estranged "the sympathy of Lord Holmpatrick, or to be more accurate of his trustees."

Details of fixtures for the Emmet CC are available from 1899 onwards. Between 1899 and 1902, games were played against Gormanstown, Tredagh CC, Naul and Knockbrack. There is a photograph extant of the Skerries team from the 1902 season but there are no reports for the 1902 and 1903 seasons. The impression is given from the 1904 AGM that this meeting constituted an attempt to revive cricket in Skerries:

The proceedings made it pretty evident that cricket is in by no means a moribund state in Skerries, indeed it is the intention of the club to prove that the very reverse is the case.

The Emmet CC made strenuous efforts during the 1904 season to ensure that the game survived. The initial fixture list consisted of eight games, but the club managed to arrange at least five additional fixtures, and to turn the games into major social events. For example, after the game versus Garristown, "there were songs rendered by both teams suitable for the occasion". St Patrick's Brass and Reed Band was present at two of the games on 10 July 1904, and 24 July 1904. In a report on the game on 10 July 1904, the Knockbrack correspondent was fulsome in his praise of the hospitality received and "the inspiriting strains of the Skerries Brass and Reed Band contributed not a little to make the visit a thoroughly enjoyable one". Presumably the enjoyment was enhanced for the correspondent by Knockbrack winning by 61 runs.

Many of the members of Emmet CC being nationalists did not prevent them from being excoriated in 1905 by "Fir Bolg" in the *Drogheda Independent*, and his comments were reflective of an attitude among Irish-Irelanders to those who played cricket:

> It is with sorrow he has recently noticed that honoured name (Emmet) appended to a club organised for the express purpose of fostering seoininism in Ireland. The writer refers to a cricket club named after Robert Emmet. Cricket is a foreign game and men who play such have no right to use the name of dead patriots as titles for their clubs…. (I) might hazard the opinion that the name of the club be changed to a more appropriate one. Or better why not change the game. We are long enough under the laws of the foreigner. Must we be under their intellectual genius as well?

Emmet CC did not become involved in this exchange of views, other than to continue to use the name and to play cricket. Inspection of the team-sheets for the game on 14 May 1905, the next game versus Gormanstown on 21 May 1905 and the game versus Holmpatrick CC on 1 July at Holmpatrick's ground demonstrated a continuity in team selection which was lacking for the Holmpatrick CC. Emmet CC won the local derby by 36 runs, and a noteworthy feature of this game was that the Holmpatrick team included the Rector, Mr Shegog and his two sons.

While the games were promoted as family events, it did not follow that the cricket was uncompetitive. A great premium was placed on the accurate reporting of the results, and the practice was for the Secretary of one of the teams to submit the results to the *Drogheda Independent*. On 15 July 1905, a report of a game between Knockbrack and Emmet CC mentioned that Knockbrack would have had an "easy win", but for "the excited element that prevailed amongst the spectators when the home team had but one wicket to fall by over-ruling the umpire's decision and refusing to let the last man bat. Score: Knockbrack: 35; Skerries 21 and one wicket to fall. The Secretary of the Emmet CC, Mr M. Armstrong, may have decided against responding to the Irish-Ireland critics, but he was not going to allow a perceived inaccurate report to go unchallenged:

> I wish to remind the honorary secretary that he was absolutely wrong in his report. The match was broken off through a wrong decision of the umpire. Therefore, the score stood: Knockbrack, all out: 35 runs; Skerries, 2 wickets to fall, 21 runs. I fail to see where an easy win could be judged on either side.

Notwithstanding this contretemps, the Emmet's season continued unabated, with games against Corduff, Avoca, Myra, and the return fixture against Holmpatrick CC.

Emmet CC was again involved in cricket in 1906 and 1907 but there is a paucity of information regarding fixtures and results. However, there is no reason to doubt that games were played during these seasons, and in 1908, Michael Armstrong, Secretary, announced that the "club is once again in the ranks and are open for fixtures for the following season". There is a lyrical account of a game between Emmet CC and Mullafin which Mullafin won by 14 runs, but the "rivals displayed great skill in all its intricacies, good batting, bowling and fielding being the order of the day". In addition to the wonderful cricket, there was wonderful music:

> That famous musical body, the Skerries Brass Band was in attendance, ... and it is no exaggeration to say that it held all those who were fortunate in being listeners fairly spellbound by the splendid manner in which it discoursed all the latest selections and also those stirring National airs so dear to the hearts of all lovers of our own green Isle."

The report ended by declaring that the bandsmen and cricketers were a "credit to the stirring seaside town."

The auguries for the 1909 season were very positive. A strong committee was appointed, many new members were enrolled, "the popular Johnny Duff" was appointed captain, and the "worthy coadjutor to him" was Willie McLoughlin, "the genial veteran of the bat". There was still a warm glow resulting from the previous year's encounter with Mullafin; the Press and the different clubs were thanked for their "courtesy and kindness", and it was hoped that future visits to Skerries by invited clubs would "contribute to the friendly feelings of the past". Unfortunately, the Emmet CC's hopes for the season do not appear to have been realised, and there are no further reports on cricket in Skerries in 1909. In the period from 1910 to 1924, out of two hundred and eighty nine references to cricket in the *Drogheda Independent*, there is only one mention of cricket in Skerries, and that was a criticism of the men of Skerries who preferred to play cricket and golf rather than join the British Army.

In the absence of evidence, it is only possible to engage in conjecture regarding the fate of Emmet CC during the period 1909 to 1925. There was agitation during 1911 regarding rents and the sale of the Holmpatrick estate. Relations between farm labourers and landowners were particularly strained during the farm labourers' strike in 1913 when an ultimatum was given to the farm labourers to leave the union or be dismissed; a tomb belonging to the Woods' family was desecrated and cattle were released on to the road. In October 1914, the Skerries Branch of the Town Tenants' League organised a protest meeting to condemn evictions, the increased demands for rent and charges for seaweed by Lord Holmpatrick and his agents. Some of people on the platform such as Wm Healy, Wm McLoughlin, P. Grimes, and Walter Collins had also been involved in playing cricket with the Emmet CC and the Black Hills.

### Skerries Cricket Club, 1925-1969

Skerries Cricket Club was re-organised at a meeting on 4 July 1925. There were forty people present, and Richard Mc Loughlin, nephew of William McLoughlin became acting Secretary. An emphasis was placed on the inclusive nature of the club, and each sports club in Skerries was adjudged to have "added materially to the progress of sport in this progressive seaside resort." Evidence of games played by this team in 1925 has been difficult to access, but the other clubs in the area around this time were Knockbrack, Ring Commons CC and Balbriggan. The two clubs met at Knockbrack on 6 September, and the *Meath Herald* in addition to giving the scores, published a detailed account of the journey from Skerries to Knockbrack:

Skerries team journeyed to Knockbrack via Balbriggan on Sunday, 6th inst., for their fixture with Knockbrack. Mr Paddy Duff supplying the charabanc and arriving up in time enabling the match to start promptly at 3 o'clock – quite a lot of enthusiasm was displayed, and the visiting team was heartily received especially as the event had been looked forward to on account of the fact that Knockbrack had yet to receive its first defeat.

A scorecard is appended to the report, but unfortunately, the scores do not tally. It appears that Knockbrack scored 50 runs and in reply, Skerries got 58 runs for the loss of 8 wickets. There was also cricket played in Skerries in 1926 because a person from Dunboyne was charged with using a commercial vehicle for "char-a-banc purposes". He had brought seven passengers to play cricket in Skerries and the solicitor for the defendant argued that the man just wanted to see the game. The passengers accompanied him, but he had not received any payment for this service.

For clubs such as Skerries CC which left cricket for a period and re-formed, the whole process of arranging challenge games was time-consuming and difficult because other clubs already had regular fixtures in place which meant that new fixtures could not be accommodated too readily. There is no doubt that the establishment of the Fingal League was the major contributory factor in the preservation of cricket in the area because structures were put in place for fixture-making, and teams could opt in and out of cricket depending on their circumstances each season.

The Fingal League was fully operational in 1927, and Skerries played Knockbrack in the final. The Secretary of Skerries Cricket Club, James Duff, submitted a very detailed account of this game to the *Drogheda Independent*. Given that "history is written by the victors" and allowing for elements of hyperbole in Mr Duff's report, it provides the reader with an example of the manner in which sporting occasions were reported during a bygone age. We are told that there were over 1,000 spectators at the final in Skerries. A cocoanut matting provided "a perfect pitch", Knockbrack had "numerous followers", and among the attendance were "those whose chances had been vanquished by the contestants." Knockbrack batted first and J. Ennis who played with a "delightful straight bat" had a "splendid innings" of 33 which included 13 boundaries. "The applause from the field emphasised the appreciation of the spectators of his excellent batting skill." The main contributor to the Skerries' response was D. Moran "who by drives, cuts and slips made the handsome and useful score of 61 runs." Crawford made 18 runs, and Skerries won on a score of 125 runs to 63 for Knockbrack. The final commendation from Mr Duff was for the "two independent umpires whose tact and appreciation carried the appreciation of both sides."

Skerries won the Fingal League and received a cheque to buy a cricket set. Knockbrack came second and Ballymadun was in third place. The victory for Skerries was not greeted with universal acclaim because of the prevalence of "outsiders on the team." According to the Secretary of the League, "Knockbrack and Ballymadun are to be congratulated as they played in a clean and sportsmanlike manner and had no one on their teams but Fingallians."

At the AGM of Skerries Cricket Club in 1927, it was decided to enter one team in the Fingal League and the Firsts would play in the Dublin League. In 1928, there were ten teams in the Fingal League, and the new teams were Barnageeragh, Balrothery and Baldwinstown. Skerries retained the League title by beating Barnageeragh on a score of 29 runs to 21.

By 1929, Skerries CC had two teams in the Fingal League, but its quest for four in a row was stymied by Knockbrack. According to the report in the *Drogheda Independent*, the game between Skerries and Knockbrack was "the finest exhibition of cricket ever witnessed in Fingal.... The game was up to Test match standard." It comes as something of a surprise to read that Knockbrack scored 14 runs but managed to defend this score with Skerries losing its last man when the score was 13.

Skerries CC was involved in a "unique situation" according to the *Drogheda Independent* of 14 June 1930 when "Baldwinstown received "a walk over" in a Fingal Cricket League match on Tuesday. Baldwinstown's eleven arrived for the match in an 1.0. C. omnibus, and the captain of Skerries CC refused to allow his players to take the pitch against "strike-breakers". The outcome of this dispute was awaited with interest, and based on the league tables, it appears that the game was voided, with no points being awarded. Skerries CC won the Fingal League in 1931 when it beat Ballymadun in the final on a score of 78 to 30.

Skerries CC continued to play Fingal League cricket in 1932 and 1933, but in 1934, the team dropped out of the Fingal League and did not play in 1935 or 1936. However, in 1936, Mr J. Duff requested that the Health Board erect a pavilion and sanitary conveniences at the Sports Park so that the ground could be used for cricket and football. During the subsequent discussion, it was revealed that the park had become a dumping ground and was not yielding any revenue to the Health Board. It was decided to refer the matter to the County Engineer so that a report might be prepared. Skerries CC was back in Fingal League cricket in 1937, but the person writing in the *Skerries News* was a little bit late with his story because he only heard that Skerries CC was back in cricket in 1938: "we are pleased to hear that the cricket team has been revived and have (sic) entered the Fingal League".

An illustration of the extent to which cricket was mainstream in Skerries is shown by the fact that a challenge match was played between a Fingal Selection and Pembroke 1st XI in aid of the New Church Building Fund on 27 August 1939 :

> Sunday last's game was sponsored by Mr G. L. McGowan, solicitor, an ardent cricketer, and all-round sportsman himself who infuses some of his own tremendous enthusiasm into every venture he touches…. Why not keep on? With no tennis facilities at Skerries and a pitch, which though not yet groomed to perfection, would respond well to good treatment, Skerries would benefit from and keenly appreciate a series of good weekly matches in the season. No one is more competent to promote these successfully than Mr G. L. McGowan so here's throwing out the suggestion.

In 1940, there are ten teams in Fingal League and Skerries are still there, but they are not in evidence in 1941, 1942 or 1943. Skerries CC was back in Fingal Cricket in 1944, and M. Gosson and A. J. Mc Donnell from Skerries CC are mentioned as being on a Fingal League panel which played Phoenix on 17 June 1944. In addition to league cricket, friendly games were also organised during this period, and one of the most hotly contested in terms of bragging rights, was between Skerries Cricket Club and Skerries Rugby Club. In June 1944, Skerries Cricket Club won by 14 runs in a game played in the Park on a score of 75 runs to 61.

Skerries CC played again in the Fingal League in 1945 and there is a report on a game versus Walshestown which Skerries won on a score of 68 to 29. The players who played well for Skerries were M. Gosson (31) and R. Byrne (11*), and the best for Walshestown was Tom Murphy (12). The same teams met in the semi-final of the league, but on this occasion, Walshestown won with Tom and Kevin Murphy starring.

The major development in 1946 was that Skerries played in Leinster League cricket in addition to the Fingal League. In its first game in the Leinster

League, Skerries beat Clontarf in front of a "very large attendance". The best players for Skerries were J. Curry, M. Gosson and G. Walsh while Caprani and Dexter were best for Clontarf.  It appeared that Skerries' first year in Leinster League cricket was going to be very successful, but in a complete reversal of an earlier result, Skerries lost the cup final to Clontarf 3rds on a score of 145 to 45.

Skerries CC was in the Leinster League again in 1947, and it is noticeable that players from other Fingal League clubs played Leinster League cricket with Skerries. Just as the Rush team contained cricketers from other Fingal clubs, players gravitated to Skerries for Leinster League games because playing against established clubs in Dublin provided an opportunity for Fingal cricketers to encounter better facilities and to play on better pitches.

While 1947 was a quiet year, in 1948, things went awry again. The *Drogheda Independent* gave an indication in its issue of 22 May that the cricket club was in bother. The report started positively enough:

> Skerries Cricket Club, another of our splendid institutions, is still very much to the forefront. They defeated James's Gate at the Iveagh Grounds last Saturday…. We are in grave doubt about the Recreation Park being ready for next Saturday's important game. The local sports clubs are complaining that the delay in re-sodding the ground is retarding a big programme of sporting events. It is time that the Council authorities used proper vision and foresight.

Matters came to a head in June 1948 when Skerries CC was forced to withdraw from the Leinster Cricket League, nor did it play in the Fingal League owing to a lack of ground facilities. The reporter didn't spare the Council:

> The club which has been an institution for many years, has had the bottom knocked out of its activities this year. The same fate has befallen other clubs here – Hockey, Gaelic, Rugby, Soccer – no ground. The Co. Dublin Commissioner should earnestly tackle this irritating problem of a playing field and remedy this state of affairs without delay.

Richard Mc Loughlin kept up the pressure regarding the lack of sports facilities in Skerries. He sympathised with Skerries Harps GAA club in having to play all their games away, and he contacted the Land Commission in 1946 and again in 1948. Other than a formal reply, no action was taken. He urged the Land Commission to acquire sites for sports fields, and he reported that a committee had been appointed in Skerries to "press forward for the remedying of this grievance." The situation with regard to playing facilities in Skerries was addressed by the Dublin County Council in December 1948, but it was simply decided to advertise the park for letting whereas the clubs in the town were looking for the park to be sold, and a bigger park provided.

Skerries Cricket Club played in the Fingal League in 1949 and used the Recreation Park for their matches. Its first game of the new season was against Knockbrack on Sunday, 29 May 1949, and Skerries lost on a score of 36 runs to 19, but the reporter was reasonably optimistic about the team's prospects for the season: "The Skerries XI is quite new to league cricket but will be able to produce a good side before the end of the current season. Moles had top score for Skerries."

In 1950, a reporter was under the impression that Skerries CC was a new club:

> The newly formed clubs will mostly be led by well-known players: Skerries by D. Cashell of Holmpatrick, and Bettystown by B. Hardy of Dundalk and ex-Laytown. A Skerries newcomer, Kevin McArdle, is reported to be the find of the season.

There was a move away from the Recreation Park, and Skerries CC intended to play its home games at Red Island Holiday Camp.

1951 was a very difficult year for cricket in Fingal with only four teams competing for the Challenge Cup. The Honorary Secretary of the Fingal League, Eddie Dunne, hoped that "old, established clubs" such as Skerries, Rush, Naul, Oldtown and perhaps, Malahide would take part in the League in the following season. His words bore fruit because Skerries CC returned to the Fingal League in 1952 and competed very successfully until losing the final to Walshestown. As an indication of its place in mainstream society, the cricket club commenced the 1953 season by organising a dance at Red Island. From 1954 to 1958, Skerries CC was missing from Fingal League Cricket, but the club was re-organised in 1959, with many of the old stalwarts such as Eddie Dunne, Paddy Hughes, Basil Costello and Willie Beggs still involved. The club had also acquired use of a ground belonging to the De La Salle school.

In 1960, the club was on the crest of the wave. Its first annual dance at the Holmpatrick Hotel was "an outstanding success", and it had been given access to a different ground, the Ballast Pit. The club intended to play in the Leinster League, (if possible), the Fingal League and the Meath League, and it had a credit balance of £18. Between 1961 and 1965, nothing untoward appeared to have happened, although there must have been a level of uncertainty regarding plans for the 1965 season because the club was late with its application to play in the Fingal League. However, its entry was accepted, and the team was now playing its home games at Holmpatrick.

In addition to league cricket, friendly games involving the boys' clubs that came over from England to stay at Gents' Camp were arranged on an ad-hoc basis. There was also the annual festival match between the local side and a Visitors team, and they competed for a trophy called *The Young at Hearts* Cup. In 1961, the Visitors' team was captained by Paddy Quinn of Phoenix, an Irish international cricketer, but the local team captained by Paddy Hughes won on a score of 86 runs to 82. In 1966, the Chairman, Mr Fethersonhaugh, reported that the club had secured a ground from Messrs Roadstone for the season. The ground when developed should make one of the "best pitches" in the county. "The late Richard Mc Loughlin, the father of cricket in the town always had the Ballast Pit in mind and was the first to secure it from GNR so it is good to see his wish come true and also to see two of his grandchildren playing for the club". Again, there was an aspiration to enter the Leinster League in addition to playing Fingal League cricket. In 1966 in the annual challenge, the Visitors batted first, and made 22 runs. Jim Walsh took 6 wickets for 5 runs, and Skerries passed the score for the loss of 2 wickets.

In 1967, the never-say-die attitude of the Committee was very much in evidence, and its first annual dinner dance at the Windmill in August was so successful, that it was intended to hold another dinner dance at Christmas. The Visitors were victorious in the annual challenge game and were presented with the trophy at a function in the Windmill.

The use of the Ballast Pit as a cricket ground was short-lived because the issue of a suitable place to play cricket reared its head again in 1967. The Honorary Secretary, Mrs Hirrell, asked the "cricket-minded" people in the town to come forward to help the club in its quest for a pitch, because the club was playing on a public park which was too dangerous to play on when there were children present. In 1968, Skerries played its first game of the season against Knockbrack, but the writing was on the wall for the club. "The Skerries club has always been very popular, but membership has fallen off somewhat in recent years." A special appeal was made to anyone interested to come along and attend at the park on Tuesday evenings.

At the AGM of the Fingal League in 1969, Eddie Dunne of Skerries was elected to the committee, but there is no reference to Fingal League cricket being played in Skerries in 1969, and the constant struggle to obtain a ground appears to have taken its toll on the members, especially when there were opportunities to play cricket at neighbouring clubs.

Being without a permanent base meant that there was no elaborate winding-up process, Skerries Cricket Club just ceased to exist. For well over seventy years, people in each generation had sought to ensure that cricket survived in Skerries, with the contribution of Skerries' people to the Fingal League cricket being especially commendable. At the start of the 20th century, cricket in Skerries reflected a stratified society, but as the century unfolded, cricket served a valuable function in breaking down divisions and uniting people of different creeds. In the late 1960s, with clubs in the hinterland of Skerries thriving, and recurring difficulties in obtaining a suitable ground, it was an opportune time to leave the stage and pass on the torch to other clubs in the area.

Back Row: Joe Herbert, Louis Flanagan, H Armstrong, John Duff, John J Duff, Pat May.
Front Row: W. McLoughlin, John Duff, Jack Derham, Joe Morris, Patrick Coleman, Edward Duff.

Emmet CC

# Holmpatrick CC, 1905

## Irish Times - Tuesday 27 June 1905

**MALAHIDE V. HOLMPATRICK (SKERRIES).**

This match was played at Skerries on Saturday, and resulted in a win for the visitors by four wickets. Score :—

### HOLMPATRICK.

| | | | |
|---|---|---|---|
| H. Alexander b. A. Adams | 9 | E. Bailey c. Campion b. C. Adams | 4 |
| J. Coyle c. A. Adams b. Bradley | 5 | J. Anderson b. C. Adams | 3 |
| R. Carey not out | 23 | J. Cosgrove b. C. Sneyd | 2 |
| J. Milligan b. A. Adams | 1 | P. Coyne b. C. Sneyd | 4 |
| W. Cartley b. C. Adams | 15 | W. Shegog b. C. Adams | 4 |
| G. Cluffe b. C. Adams | 0 | Extras | 11 |
| | | Total | 81 |

### MALAHIDE.

| | | | |
|---|---|---|---|
| D. Campion b. Alexander | 2 | H. Holton b. Coyle | 12 |
| D. Bradley b. Shegog | 10 | C. Sneyd not out | 15 |
| L. Archbold c. and b. Alexander | 2 | A. Adams b. Shegog | 9 |
| C. Adams c. Carey b. Coyle | 20 | J. Jackson not out | 1 |
| | | Extras | 13 |
| | | Total (6 wkts.) | 84 |

Did not bat—W. S. Sneyd, J. Riordan, T. Bailey.

## Richard Wellington Shegog, 1886-1917

In sacred and loving memory of
Richard Wellington Shegog
Captain R.A.M.C
who died of wounds received in action
whilst attending the wounded near Ypres
1st August 1917 Aged 31 years
Faithful unto death

*Front Row L to R* Fran Grimes, W. Beggs, Mick Moles, P. Murray
*Centre* Paddy Hughes  *Back Row L to R* Frank Glennon, P. Curry, Bobby Beggs,
J. Walsh, R. O'Connor, John Joe Duff

Medal won by Frank Glennon; photograph presented by Jim Glennon (former T. D.)

## Grounds

- Healy's Field, 1904
- Recreation Park
- Red Island, 1950
- De La Salle School Ground, 1959
- Holmpatrick, 1965
- Ballast Pit, 1960; 1965
- Recreation Park

## Bobby Beggs (*Evening Herald*, 24 September 1976)

'I remember one Fingal Cricket League final when we played Knockbrack. We had them out for 13; but they bowled us out for 12."

So much for Fingal League Cricket and Bobby Beggs' somewhat undistinguished career at the game, but he adds, "I was on the same cricket team as Ernie Crawford, once gave the great Jimmy Boucher a "sickener" and broke windows with a ball in Balbriggan Street. One game I did not play was soccer.

# Red Island, 1949

Red Island Skerries Co. Dublin.

# Chapter 7: Cricket in Garristown

**Note:** Garristown is a village in North-East Fingal; Baldwinstown is a townland in the Garristown Electoral District; Ballymadun is a townland in the Garristown Electoral District. At one stage, all three districts fielded cricket teams; in time, these teams consolidated into one team and the name of the team was then derived from the location of the cricket field.

## Early Days

Garristown CC played at least five games during the 1881 season. *The Freeman's Journal* of 28 June 1881 contained a report of a game between Garristown and Ashbourne which was played at Garristown. Garristown won by 2 runs and 6 wickets to fall, and those who received honourable mention were Wogan, O'Brien and Carroll whose "bowling proved destructive for the visitors." The fielding of both sides was deemed to be excellent. The scores were Ashbourne, 11 runs and 24 runs; Garristown, 21 and 15 for 5 wickets. In the fixtures for August 1881, Garristown has a game listed against Clonavy, and played Bellewstown on 15 August. This game was won by Bellewstown, with Mr Flannigan starring with the ball for Bellewstown and Mr R. Wogan batting well for Garristown. Garristown had a return game against Oldtown on 22 August at Baldwinstown, and the name of the Garristown team is listed as Faughabhallagh CC, Garristown.

## Identity

The name Faughabhallagh, is a significant statement of identity because even though cricket had its origins in England, some clubs adopted names deliberately to show where their loyalties lay. Gormanstown CC is another example of the naming dichotomy because this team's home ground was at Gormanston Castle, but the cricket team insisted on calling itself Gormanstown, presumably because it did not wish to be associated too closely with Lord Gormanston, a leading member of the gentry.

For the 1882 season, there are results of two cricket matches played by Garristown, and a reference to a return game, although the result of the return game is not given in the newspapers. Confusingly, the Garristown teams are listed with two different names, Garristown Reds, and Garristown Faughaballagh. The Garristown Reds played Oldtown on 3 July 1882 and won convincingly because the fielding of the Garristown team was "too much" for the visitors. On 10 October 1882, Garristown Faughballagh lost to Oldtown in a game played at Oldtown. There may have been two different teams in

Garristown, or the reports to the papers may have been submitted by a different person because there was another instance of that occurring when Balbriggan played Ring Commons and one paper gave the name of the team as Briarland, while the other used the name, Ring CC.

From 1884, the names, Reds and Faughabhallagh, were dispensed with, and the team was appearing on the newspapers as Garristown CC. Ballymadun CC was active as well, and it played against Garristown on 11 August 1884. Unfortunately, a premature ending to the local derby provoked Mr R. Finegan to write to the *Freeman's Journal* and complain about the "less than handsome" behaviour of Garristown. He stated that the teams had agreed to play until 7.00 p.m., but Garristown was leading by 45 runs to 31 at the end of the first innings and refused to play on. In the same season, Garristown played Ratoath, and this game was less contentious. Messrs Wogan and Cahill scored 26 and 20 respectively, and Garristown accumulated 78 runs in total for the first innings. According to the report, Ratoath made "a very poor stand, having all been disposed of for the small score of 8 runs, which caused a follow-on." It played better in the second innings, and scored 54 runs, but was beaten by an innings and 11 runs. There are no further reports on games for the 1880s, and reports on cricket in the 1890s are also very scarce. There are only three references to cricket being played in the area between 1884 and 1899. On 28 May 1893, Ballymadun beat Curraha very easily; on 13 June 1897, Ring Common CC beat Garristown by 20 runs, and on 13 August 1899, Naul CC beat Garristown by an innings and 53 runs.

From 1900 to 1905, there is a big increase in coverage of cricket, and the *Drogheda Independent's* reports give a fine insight into the sporting and cultural values of that era. In addition to being a sport, cricket is also a social activity, and this is emphasised consistently in instances where detailed accounts are submitted to the newspapers. The report which Mr J. Moore, Honorary Secretary of Garristown, wrote on the game versus Blanchardstown is an example of the balance between cricket as a sport and cricket as a social and cultural activity. The game was played at Garristown on 19 August 1900, and the Blanchardstown Brass Band played a "splendid march to the field of battle", after some "refreshments had been taken". The visitors batted first and were all out for 38 runs. Garristown scored 46 runs and won by 8 runs. Both teams then "spent a very enjoyable evening in singing and dancing." Other games which Garristown played during 1900 were against Macetown, Naul, Duleek (home and away). Mr Moore did not spare Duleek in his report on the game at Duleek. They made a "very bad stay against the bowling of J. Andrews and J.

Donnelly, and "were all riddled for 14 runs". Possibly due to this victory, he reported that "the visitors spent a very enjoyable evening".

During this period, the lack of a transport infrastructure meant that of necessity, most of Garristown's games were against teams on the Dublin/Meath border. In 1901, Garristown played home and away games against Duleek, Ratoath, Blanchardstown, Emmet CC, and Kentstown. Duleek was beaten twice, and in his report on the away game against Duleek, Mr Moore mentioned four players, M Hollywood (20), A. Moore (16), T. Hollywood (15), A. Moore (11), and he referred to the team returning home with "an honourable victory" after partaking of the usual refreshments. Some of the reports are replete with imagery and hyperbole, and the two reports on the Kentstown games contain examples of this literary style. For the game played at Kentstown, the emphasis is on housing images. Kentstown batted first and some of its batters "were evicted" by the fine bowling of Brown and Andrews "before they could make anything in trying to save the little house". The imagery continued with a reference to Kentstown managing "to keep the roof up" until 68 runs had been scored. Garristown's reply was 55, and Tully and Hogan were the bowlers for Kentstown "that left roofless cabins with the Garristown men". Mr Moore's account of the return game has less imagery, but nevertheless contained flourishes. Kentstown batted first, and the "splendid bowling of J Brown and J Andrews" made scoring "impossible for the Kentstown men with Kentstown ending up on a score of 14 runs. The "fine" bowling of J. Donnelly and E. Hogan made life difficult for Garristown, but they "managed to keep the roof till their score reached 41". J. Donnelly, the Garristown captain, received honourable mention for "his activity on the field and a well-played 20 not out".

Garristown's programme for the 1902 season was broadly similar to that of 1901. There were games against Blanchardstown, Mullafin, Ratoath, and a trip to the Phoenix Park to play Castleknock. Ballymadun also featured in the reports for this season, and played against Corbalton, home and away. The game in Corbalton was won by Corbalton, but the "visitors were most hospitably entertained, and after a very enjoyable evening of singing and dancing, the visitors returned home well pleased with their day's outing." In the return game, Corbalton scored 22 runs and was "trundled out by the bowling of Brown and Finnegan". That was as good as it got for Ballymadun, because it "succumbed to the bowling of Tancred and Reilly" and only scored 8 runs."

There is a dearth of reports for Garristown for the 1903 season, and the only detailed account is of the game against Moorpark at Moorpark which resulted in a win for the home team. Bill Gargan and John Finnegan were the main contributors to the Moorpark victory which was "witnessed by a large crowd of spectators from all parts of the country". After the game, "the remainder of the evening was spent in a most enjoyable dance with sweet music. The visitors returned home about 9.30 p.m. well pleased with their day's outing."

Ballymadun played in the 1903 season, and there are accounts of games against Priestown and Ratoath, both of which Ballymadun lost. The score in the Priestown game was 29 runs to 25, and Ratoath won on a score of 40 runs to 17. In 1903, C. Brown, Secretary of the Grallagh CC issued a challenge to any team from Meath or Dublin, and this provoked the Secretary of Knockbrack CC to add a comment to his match report for the game between Knockbrack and the Grallagh. The result of the game was 23 runs to 19, but the significant element of the report was the comment that Knockbrack "had a much easier win,... than readers of last week's *Independent* would anticipate". In an overview of the season, the Grallagh CC reported that it had played 14 games, winning 12 and losing 2. The captain was W. Brunkard, who handled the team "in a masterly manner", and the club was given access to a field by Mr G. Wilson. Its best batsmen during the season were R. Tierney, P. Durnan and J. Corbally, while the bowling honours went to M. Durnan, T. Tiernan and J. Whyte.

For the 1904 season, Garristown CC indicated its intention to commence the season with a practice game on 8 May, and in the notice expressed its thanks to S. Mangan, Esq, for "giving his kind permission to play on his land, the old favourite cricket grounds, the Woods." One of its first games in 1904 was against the Emmet CC (Skerries), and this resulted in a win for the Skerries team. When the game ended, "there were songs rendered by the members of both teams suitable for the occasion." Among the other teams which Garristown played during this season were Wimbleton, Castleknock and Fairyhouse. The one game listed for The Grallagh for 1904 was played against Corbalton, and it resulted in a win for Corbalton.

For 1905, the only fixtures listed for Garristown were home and away games against Emmet CC, Skerries. Towards the end of this season, there was a movement towards putting league structures in place, and a league confined to Sunday clubs in Meath was established at a meeting in Robinstown on 15 October 1905. This initiative had obvious implications for Garristown, the Grallagh and Ballymadun because many of their games were played against teams from Meath, and there was less inclination or necessity to play friendlies if there was a league structure in place. This had already occurred in Dublin when structures were put in place for junior clubs to play league and cup competitions.

The Meath Cricket League was established in 1906, and nearly twenty teams participated in the competition. In view of developments throughout the country at that stage and in subsequent years, Mr Paddy Daly who was elected Chairman and later became Chairman of the Fingal Cricket League provided his perception of the value of cricket when he stated that "cricket is the most rational as well as the most suitable form of sport for the summer season".

Insofar as Garristown CC was concerned, it is difficult to know if it played less cricket or if the Secretary decided against submitting the results of friendly games. Mullafin CC gave notice of a game against Garristown on 12 July 1908, and requested that its players convene at McGrath's Cross, the starting point. The score in this game was Mullafin, 34 to Garristown's 29 runs. Both teams were commended for the quality of their bowling and fielding, the best batsmen for Garristown were J. Andrews, J. Donnelly, and C. Holly, and the after-game festivities were enjoyed by all:

> After being entertained in a manner worthy of the highest praise, but in keeping with Garristown's traditional hospitality, our boys took the road for the Old Hills via the Lazy Banks well-pleased with their day's outing.

Between 1910 and 1914, only four fixtures are mentioned for either Garristown or Ballymadun. In 1909 and 1910, Garristown played Mullafin, and in 1909 and 1914, Ballymadun played Ratoath and Corbalton.

The Fingal League was fully operational in 1927 and detailed reports of games were furnished to the *Drogheda Independent*. The teams which competed in the Fingal League in 1927 were Skerries, Knockbrack, Macraidh (Knockbrack Seconds), Ballymadun, Knightstown, Black Hills, and Ring Commons. The first fixtures were played on Sunday, 15 May 1927 and the final game was played on 18 September 1927. In 1928, the number of teams had increased to 10, with the three new teams Barnageeragh, Baldwinstown and Balrothery joining the seven teams which had played in 1927. It was now necessary to create two divisions, and there was a play-off between the two teams which finished top of their sections. Ballymadun finished second in Division A. In 1929, the number of teams had increased to fifteen. There were no defections from the previous year and the new teams were Balbriggan, Naul Hill, Skerries B, Balcunnin and Curkeen. Knockbrack beat Skerries in the semi-final and beat Baldwinstown in the final on a score of 24 runs to 16. In addition to Fingal

League games, challenge matches were still being organised. Baldwinstown was due to play Ballymadun on 6 October for £5 a side and to avoid any allegations of bias, neutral umpires were appointed.

## A Period of Growth, 1930-1940

At the Fingal League's AGM in March 1931, the playing regulations were amended, and a decision was taken to play two innings per side in the semi-finals and finals. When the fixtures for the season were announced, seventeen teams had entered for the league. The new teams were Baldwinstown Second XI, and Rush, with the Black Hills, the British Legion and Balcunnin dropping out of the League. The Management Committee decided to organise a "Fingal Cricket Championship" which would be played as a knock-out tournament during the month of September. The final was played at Balbriggan on 27 September between Portrane and Baldwinstown. No information is available on the result of that game, but in the Garristown Notes in the *Drogheda Independent* of the 11 November 1931, it is reported that Baldwinstown won the championship outright so that can be taken as confirmation that Baldwinstown CC was the first winners of the Fingal Championship.

For the 1932 season, Baldwinstown, Ballymadun and Garristown were affiliated again to the Fingal League, and the three clubs were proactive on the cricket field and in organising social activities. On 25 September, Ballymadun hosted a challenge game between Deanhill (the Meath Champions) and Balcunnin (the Fingal Champions). On the same day, Garristown hosted its first Annual Dance at St Mary's Hall, with music by O'Farrell's Band. Dancing was from 9.30 p.m. to 4.00 a.m. and admission for Gents was 3s, Ladies, 2s and Doubles, 5s (including supper). As an added attraction, there was a draw for £1 during the dance. The event was very successful and over one hundred couples attended. The £1 was won by a person from Drogheda, and the only problem was Miss Crosby's coat being taken by mistake. Not to be outdone by the other two clubs in the parish, Baldwinstown organised a Whist Drive on 9 October 1932.

For the 1933 season, the three teams from the area were in separate sections, but there were signs that the playing resources might be stretched too thinly. Ballymadun played a 6-match programme, won one game, and finished last in its section. Baldwinstown played eight games, winning four and losing four, while Garristown had a successful season, finishing joint top of its section with Curkeen, and it won seven of its nine games. Garristown CC organised a Sports Day which featured a wonderful array of events. There was a 10-mile cycle race, a Market Race, a Potato race, a race on cycles, tug-o-war and a greasy pig race which caused a level of consternation for the ladies who sought refuge behind bicycles and other obstacles in case the pigs should come in contact with them.

In the 1934 season, the number of affiliated teams had fallen to thirteen with Curkeen, Knightstown, Skerries and Balcunnin opting out, and a second team from Naul joining up. It was decided to regionalise the League into two sections, East, and West Fingal, with the winner of each section playing a deciding game for the Fingal Challenge Cup.   Oldtown and Portrane contested the final, with Portrane winning by two wickets.

In 1935, Baldwinstown reached the semi-final of the League, but was beaten by Naul in a thrilling game. Naul went on to win the League, and Garristown was the venue for a challenge game between Naul, as Fingal Champions and a Fingal Selection.   In 1936, there were still ten teams affiliated, but there were significant changes in the membership of the Fingal League. Garristown, Man-O'-War, Balrothery and Balbriggan did not affiliate, but Portrane and Naul Hill had re-entered, and the new teams were Blanchardstown and Clonsilla.

In 1938, only six clubs attended the AGM of the Fingal League, but Ballymadun sent a telegram apologising for its absence from the meeting and indicating its intention to play during the coming season.  In 1939, Ballymadun in addition to playing in the Fingal League, also played a friendly game against Tubbertynan which Tubbertynan won by 20 runs. Two players by the name of P. O'Brien featured on the Ballymadun scorecard, and this confusion regarding the names of the O'Briens occurred on a reasonably regular basis. One of the O'Briens was P.A. and the other was P. P, and it would have been helpful if this distinction had been made on the reports which were submitted to the *Drogheda Independent*.

Tubbergregan CC played in 1940, but it may just have been involved in friendly games during the season because the O'Brien brothers were playing cricket for three teams. Pat O'Brien is listed on the Portrane team, which was playing in the Leinster Cricket League, both brothers featured for Ballymadun in the Fingal League fixtures and a P. O'Brien played against Tubbertynan in a friendly game. The game against Tubbertynan was played on the Duke de Stackpoole's pitch at Tubbertynan and resulted in a win for Tubbergregan. It is noticeable that the reports on the Fingal League games tended to be factual and prosaic, but the reports on the friendly games emphasised the social element of the encounters. After the game against Tubbertynan, "the visitors were entertained to tea which was a suitable finish to a sporting game." One of the highlights of the season was the game between Man-O'-War and Ballymadun which ended in a tie with both teams on 36 runs. Ballymadun made a brilliant start and scored 25 runs before the first wicket fell. Of this total, Peter O'Brien made 19 runs, but in the words of the reporter, "the tail failed to wag", and Ballymadun was dismissed for 36 runs. The most successful bowler for the Man-O'-War was T. Morgan who took 6 wickets for 16 runs. Man-O'-War's score stood at 35 for 7, but M. Rogers dismissed the last three men for 1 run. Kerrigan scored 12, Morgan got 10 and Sheridan got 8 runs for the Man-O'-War. The large crowd present gave the players "a great ovation" at the end of this exciting game.

In 1941, Tubbergregan affiliated to the Fingal League, Ballymadun did not, and analysis of the personnel involved in Tubbergregan would suggest that a change of field had occurred. The Hon. Secretary for Tubbergregan was Anthony O'Brien, the Treasurer was Mr James Stone, the Captain was Mr Pat Lynch, and the Vice-Captain was Mr Pat O'Brien. In one of the games for which there is a report, Tubbergregan beat Walshestown on a score of 26 to 14. The main contributors with the bat were P. P. O'Brien (7), T. Tiernan (6) and T. Caffrey (5) while M. Rogers (5 for 8) and B. Hollywood (5 for 4 ) were the successful bowlers. Tubbergregan also played a friendly game against a Bellew team which was captained by Rev. Fr Pearth (an Australian) and included two clerical students (Rev. Mr O'Grady and Rev. Mr Carroll). The game ended in a draw, 47 runs each, and the "team (sic) were entertained to tea in Mr Peter O'Brien's home, where they spent an enjoyable evening."

For the 1942 season, Rev. Fr Shine was elected President of Tubbergregan CC, the Secretary was Mr Anthony O'Brien, the Treasurer was Mr James Stone, the Captain was Mr P. Lynch and Mr P. O'Brien was Vice-Captain, At the AGM, a vote of thanks was passed to Mrs Gormley for the use of the cricket field. Ballymadun, Oldtown, Baldwinstown and Naul Hill joined Tubbergregan in the Fingal League. This was a successful season for Tubbergregan CC, and it beat Walshestown comprehensively in the Fingal League final which was played at Rush. P. P. O'Brien scored a "faultless" 53 out of a score of 69 runs for Tubbergregan and Walshestown ended up on a score of 29 for 7. Unfortunately, two of the publicans in Garristown and some of the cricketers fell foul of the Law due to after-match festivities on one Sunday which necessitated a trip to the District Court:

> The Justice said that as he saw it there would not be much doing in
> Garristown on a Sunday evening. The nightlife would not be very exciting

and whatever café life would be available would be created by these two public houses.... These men were not bona fide travellers though they may have been bona fide cricketers. He imposed a fine of £3 without an endorsement and fined the men 3s each.

Baldwinstown and Ballymadun's return to Fingal League cricket was short-lived, and Tubbergregan was the only club from the area which affiliated for the 1943 season. The highlight of the season was a game between a Phoenix Eleven which contained several international cricketers and a Fingal Eleven which was played at Clonard grounds. Thanks to "admirable fielding" and some superb bowling by Mooney, Russell, Murphy, and Hoare (5 wickets for 0 runs), Phoenix was restricted to 59 runs. In reply, Fingal scored 62, with the main contributions coming from Caprani (19*), P. P. O'Brien (10) and Coleman (10).

Garristown was back in Fingal League cricket in 1944, but only played one season before leaving cricket again.  Tubbergregan  continued in Fingal cricket for a number of seasons. At its AGM in 1945, Mrs Gormley was again thanked for the use of the field, Anthony O'Brien and James Stone continued as Secretary and Treasurer respectively, the Captain was Patrick Lynch, the Vice-Captain was Chris Morgan, and Bob Doyle NT, was elected Vice-President.  In one of the early games in the season, Tubbergregan's victory over Balrothery was the big surprise of that weekend. Balrothery had only lost three times at home since the club was founded eleven years ago, and Tubbergregan was the first team from West Fingal to beat them. On the day, much of the credit for the victory went to the bowlers, Pat O'Brien who took 4 wickets for 8 runs (including a hat-trick) and M. Kiernan, 3 wickets for 8 runs.  Later in the season, P. O'Brien scored 51* while playing for Rush in the Leinster League and he was presented with a bat by an anonymous donor for being the first Rush batsman to make 50 runs after 1 August.

The 1946 Final was not played until 1947 because Tubbergregan indicated that it would not fulfil a fixture that was scheduled for so late in the season (27 October). The game should have been played a month ago, but "harvesting operations had delayed the holding of the game." The 1946 final was eventually played on 29 June 1947 and resulted in a facile win for Balrothery who scored 53 runs against Tubbergregan, who only scored 15 runs having "collapsed before the splendid bowling of Russell and Mooney."

In 1947 and 1948, Tubbergregan did not affiliate to the Fingal League, but opted to play in Meath. It is a matter of conjecture whether this decision related to the impasse which had occurred regarding the arrangements for the previous year's final. Also other sports may have been taking priority. Ballymadun Athletic Club was thriving, and the driving force was P. P. O'Brien, who in addition to acting as an official, took part in a few of the competitions, and dead-heated with P. C. Creagh in the one-mile walk event. The Handball club in Garristown was also doing well, and again P. P. O'Brien was involved. This was also a period when emigration was rife in Ireland, and the Garristown Notes of 29 September 1951 gave details of one person from the area who was emigrating, and going to meet three other people from Garristown who had already emigrated to Australia. One of those emigrants was Peter P. O'Brien who had left Tubbergregan in 1950, and was the recipient of a valuable present from Danestown CC prior to his departure. There are no further references to cricket in Tubbergregan after the 1948 season.

In the early 1950s, cricket was in decline in Fingal, but there was a brief resurgence in 1953, and Garristown affiliated to the Fingal League again. However, Cottrellstown, a new club, was an even more significant addition because among its membership was Peter O'Brien who was home on holidays from Australia. In addition to playing with Cottrellstown during the season, he played in the Leinster League with Bellew and Deanhill. His impact on Cottrellstown was immediate, and the team reached the final of the Fingal League in its first year of membership when it lost to Walshestown in a low scoring game, 18 runs to 11. The following year, the same two teams contested the final, but on this occasion, the result was reversed. Walshestown batted first and scored 22 runs. In replay, Cottrellstown scored the runs for the loss of 6 wickets. The Fingal League Cup was presented to Mr T. Moore, Captain of the winners, "amidst great applause". That season Cottrellstown also competed for the Dunsany Cup, and eliminated Mounthanover, the Headford Cup winners in the semi-final. The team was captained by P. P. O'Brien who returned to Australia on the Wednesday after this great victory. Cottrellstown also reached the Fingal League Final in 1955 but lost to Balrothery on a score of 26 to 22 runs. At the Fingal League's annual dance, when P. P. O'Brien's name was called to receive a runners-up medal, the President of the League, Mr P. J. Daly, paid him the following handsome tribute:

> [I sincerely regret] that Mr O'Brien that night was far, far away from Fingal. Their absent friend was a good Irishman and grand all-round sportsman, and he felt confident that all present that night in the hall would heartily join with him in wishing Peter O'Brien a bumper measure of happiness and prosperity in the land of his adoption.

In 1956, soaring emigration had impacted on all sports and all aspects of life. With specific reference to cricket, the number of teams affiliated to the Fingal League had declined appreciably and a special meeting was convened in late November to review the state of Fingal League cricket. Some members argued that the Fingal League should be dissolved, but the majority viewpoint was in favour of persevering.

The revival campaign was unsuccessful in the short-term, because only five teams affiliated for the 1957 season, and half-way through the season, Cottrellstown withdrew from the League. The report on the *Drogheda Independent* was unsure if the withdrawal was due to a shortage of players or a lack of interest, but it was sad that a team which had won the Fingal League as recently as 1954 was forced to withdraw from cricket. Some of its players had featured with Tubbergregan when it won the Fingal League in 1942, and prior to that the "big guns" in the area had been Ballymadun and Baldwinstown. The loss of Cottrellstown was a body blow for the Fingal League, and it meant that "after some 35 years in West Fingal, cricket gets a rest."

It is pointless to speculate on the reasons for cricket dying out in an area, and invariably, it is never one reason, but a confluence of them which are triggered by a tipping point. In some instances, it is the loss of a field to play on. In other instances, it is the loss of players or the loss of interest by a small group which over the years had managed to keep a club afloat, but then run out of energy or enthusiasm. In the case of Garristown, and in the absence of conclusive evidence for the decline of cricket, rather than apportioning blame, it is more appropriate to commend the patrons, administrators, and players who over a 75-year period provided a sporting, social and cultural outlet for the people of Garristown and surrounding districts.

Garristown in 1860s

Murtagh's, Ballough

Photo courtesy of Joe Curtis

# Drogheda Independent, 29 June 1901

BLANCHARDSTOWN v GARRISTOWN.—Match played at Blanchardstown on Sunday, the 23rd June. The home team winning the toss, sent the visitors to bat, who did fairly well. Notwithstanding the splendid bowling of Lawler, Dominick, and M'Intee, they put 44 runs to their credit. The home team going in to defend made a short stay against the expert bowling of J Brown and A Moore, and only put 27 to their credit, leaving a victory for the visitors of 18 runs. The Garristown men were most hospitably entertained by the home team, who paid every attention to their comfort. The band played from the field out of the town. When parting well wishes were passed, and the visitors returned home well pleased with their day outing.—J MOORE, Sec.

# Garristown, 1920s

The Garristown & Dublin Motor Service.
Taking up passengers at Garristown.

# Drogheda Independent, 25 August 1934

**East Division.**

| | P. | W. | D. | L. | PTS. |
|---|---|---|---|---|---|
| Portrane | 10 | 8 | — | 2 | 16 |
| Knockbrack | 11 | 7 | — | 4 | 14 |
| Black Hills | 12 | 7 | — | 5 | 14 |
| Man o War | 12 | 7 | — | 5 | 14 |
| Ring Commons | 10 | 4 | 1 | 5 | 9 |
| Balbriggan | 12 | 3 | 1 | 8 | 7 |
| Balrothery | 11 | 2 | — | 9 | 4 |

**West Division.**

| | P. | W. | D. | L. | PTS. |
|---|---|---|---|---|---|
| Oldtown | 10 | 8 | — | 2 | 16 |
| Naul | 10 | 6 | — | 4 | 12 |
| Ballymadun | 10 | 6 | — | 4 | 12 |
| Baldwinstown | 9 | 5 | — | 4 | 10 |
| Garristown | 8 | 2 | — | 6 | 4 |
| Naul Hill | 9 | 1 | — | 8 | 2 |

Peter O'Brien, all-round sportsman, killed in an accident on a building site in Australia in 1959.

# Chapter 8: Cricket in Portrane

The psychiatric hospitals in Ireland have had a long and distinguished involvement in sport, and this stemmed from a belief in the value of sport as a form of therapy, as worthwhile exercise or as an escape from mundane reality. The Asylum Committee which had overall responsibility for two hospitals, the Richmond (Grangegorman) and Portrane, had a consistently positive attitude to the role which sport played in the well-being of staff and patients. The annual report on the administration of the Richmond Hospital for 1899 stated that the "beneficial effect on the health of the patients of indulgence in football and cricket, in which games the officers and staff also join, was plainly noticeable". The hospital in Portrane which was located on a 460 acres site in North County Dublin, was opened in 1903, and at a cost of £300,000 it was the most expensive building ever commissioned in Ireland by the British Government. With a fully operational farm and an abundance of labour to work the farm, the hospital was self-sufficient with regard to vegetables and meat. It was deemed equally important for the hospital to be self-sufficient in terms of recreational activities because its relatively remote location deprived the residents and staff of the benefits which the Richmond enjoyed because of its "close proximity to the city and its attractions."

In 1926, the Management Committee of the hospital sought to introduce a games programme to Portrane which was similar to that which already existed in the Richmond. To facilitate this initiative, there was a proposal to the Committee that a grant of £110 be made available to cover some of the players' travel expenses to away games because if there were no incentives, the staff would join outside clubs, and this would defeat the purpose of the recreation programmes which were seen "as an invaluable means of diverting the minds of the patients and ... also useful in enabling the staff to engage in harmless and health giving outdoor recreation." In support of this proposal, it was stressed to the Committee that "most large employers nowadays find it to their advantage to contribute generously to the recreation of their staffs".

This recommendation was accepted, and not only did the Management Committee re-imburse travel expenses, but it also provided the playing equipment. When it is also factored in that the male patients looked after the preparation of the pitches for games, and the male patients served the teas which were provided at the expense of the Health Board, it can be seen how advantaged the cricketers of Portrane CC were. Unlike other clubs in Fingal which affiliated to the Fingal League prior to joining the Leinster League, Portrane affiliated to the Leinster Cricket League before it played in the Fingal League, and this decision was justified on the basis of the proximity of the hospital to Donabate Railway Station.

In its first season (1926) in the Junior League, Portrane fared reasonably well insofar as it is possible to ascertain based on the results which were published. In one of the early games in the season, Portrane lost to Raheny on a score of 123 to 84, and it was also well-beaten in the return game (113 to 57 runs), but Alfie Pownall was successful with the ball (4 for 35). It beat Sandymount, home and away, with good performances with the ball from Pownall (5 for 16) and the bat from Rudkins (35 runs). In a low-scoring game against R. S. P. U., Portrane scored 50 and in reply, R. S. P. U. was restricted to 33 runs, with Pownall again taking wickets (5 for 10 runs). Pownall's good form with the ball continued when he took 7 wickets for 13 runs against Pembroke Wanderers, and on this occasion, Breen "batted merrily for 45 runs".

In 1927, there were ten teams in the A Division of the Junior League, and the other teams in this section were a blend of works' teams such as Players, Jacobs, St James's Gate plus Malahide 1, St John's, and the junior teams of Leinster, Monkstown, and Pembroke Wanderers. Portrane's season commenced with a friendly match against St James's Gate which it lost on a score of 63 to 37 runs. The team had a slow start to the season and when the league tables were published in mid-June, it had only played 1 game which it had lost. By the end of June, it had still only played 2 games, and lost both of them. On 18 June, Portrane was involved in a strange ending to its game against Pembroke Wanderers. Portrane batted first and scored 152 runs for 7 declared. In reply, Pembroke had scored 139 for 4 when Portrane indicated that it was unable to finish the game because the players had to catch a train. Pembroke, "on appeal to the umpires" was awarded the match. In another game, Portrane lost on a score of 91 runs to 64 its game against Bellshire, the eventual winners of the section, but P. Higgins returned the wonderful figures of 7 wickets for 21 runs for Portrane. At the end of a less than memorable season, Portrane had played 12 games, won three and lost nine for a total of 9 points, and finished second last in the league. Pembroke Wanderers who had claimed a win in controversial circumstances were the only team to finish below them.

In 1928, the Grangegorman Cricket Club (Richmond) and the Portrane Gaelic Football team placed a requisition for playing outfits. In a comment which showed how carefully the Management Committee oversaw expenditure, it was noted that this was not an extravagant request because the last time that the football team had been given new jerseys was ten years previously. The recommendation was accepted with the proviso that the suits "should be of Irish manufacture".  On the playing front, this was a far better season for Portrane CC. For example, in its game against St James's Gate, the score was 141 to 98, with Pownall taking 7 wickets for 27 runs.  Revenge was also gained for the previous year's loss against Pembroke Wanderers when Portrane won on a score of 93 runs to 38. On this occasion, the wicket takers were J. Skelton (6 for 17) and Pownall (3 for 21).  Portrane finished top of the Division, but in that era, there was a play-off against the winners of the other section so that the overall winners of the league could be decided. In the play-off, Portrane played against Leinster 3rds, but it was comprehensively beaten on a score of 226 runs to 48.  In its review of the season, the Management Committee was exercised by the expenditure on outdoor sports for the year 1928-29 insofar as Grangegorman had spent its allocation of £90 by November and there would be no further funds available until March 1929. Portrane had been allocated £110 because its travel expenses were greater, and it was suggested that the overall grant of £200 was "hardly adequate in view of the number of pastimes which are now provided for the entertainment of the patients." Whether the grants were being spent appropriately then became a bone of contention, and it was asserted that "outsiders" were being paid expenses to play for Portrane:

> Mr Curran: If I come here to play a game – cricket, hockey, or football, would I be entitled to get my train fare?

> Chairman: If a man is not on the staff of the Institution, he is not entitled to anything.

This reply did not satisfy Mr Curran who asserted that the "outsiders" would not be playing for Portrane unless they were being given the train fare. The matter was referred to the Finance Committee for further investigation.

In 1929, the Junior League was re-organised into three sections, and Portrane was in Division B along with CYMS, National Bank, Malahide, St John's and RSPU 3rds.  Portrane was top of the section with 5 wins and 1 defeat on 11 August.  It played one other game (against CYMS) and won on a score of 50 for 5 wickets to 34. The wickets were taken by Meade (5 for 22) and Pownall (5 for 8).  With three divisions in the league, it was necessary to have a semi-final, and Portrane was drawn against Leinster. The game was played at Civil Service's Ground in the Phoenix Park, and apart from the opening pair of Rudkins (35) and

Neville (13), no other batsman got into double figures. Portrane ended on 72 all out, and Leinster 3rds got the required score for the loss of 1 wicket.

The report on the financing of outdoor sports in Grangegorman and Portrane was submitted to the December meeting of the Management Committee, and the gross total of expenses was £118-19s-7d for Association Football, Gaelic, Hockey, and Cricket. Mr Curran was still unhappy, and he said that one team, which was possibly Portrane CC, had nine "outsiders" on it, and "only they had jam on it, they would not be taking part." On this occasion, the Chairman took a different stance to the position which he had articulated previously, when he argued that "the meaning of the games was to afford recreation to the patients and to them it was immaterial whether the players were officials of not." No decision was taken other than to have another report drafted for the next meeting.

Despite the queries and implied criticism, Portrane Cricket Club was in an expansionary phase, and at its AGM in February 1930, it reviewed a successful season, and elected Dr P. J. Dwyer, who had been responsible for founding the club, as its President. A prize was presented to P. Neville for having the best batting figures (627 runs) and J. Rudkins (597 runs) also received a favourable mention. The club expressed its appreciation of the Management Committee for the generous grant made by them for the upkeep of outdoor games. A decision was made to form a second team which would play in the Fingal League. However, there was a proviso with this decision because it was hoped that the club would be allowed to play most of its games at home because there were specific difficulties regarding playing away games on Sundays. The problem which the club faced was that Hospital Staff were rostered for a seven-day week, and it would have been both a logistical nightmare and inherently inequitable if cricketers were given every Sunday off to play cricket while their colleagues were obliged to provide cover. Home games were more straightforward because with patients involved in playing, preparing the pitch, preparing, and serving teas, it was possible to argue that the staff members who were playing cricket were involved in the supervision of patients. For away games, a level of flexibility and goodwill were involved, and if a staff member brought some patients to a game, it was deemed that they were involved in providing an outing for the patients. However, this flexibility could not be overused, and this was the reason for the application to have as many games at home as possible. The other option was for a player to switch shifts if he could find somebody to change with him, but the Hospital Authorities never became involved in these arrangements, and payment was made to the person who was rostered as distinct from the person who actually worked the shift.

In addition to its appeal to the altruistic instincts of the Fingal League Executive, Portrane CC presented compelling arguments for all clubs to travel to Portrane:

> The Portrane Club have (sic) a first-class Crease, surrounded with beautiful scenery, most admirably situated and very convenient to most clubs in the League. There is also a regular train service to Donabate on Sundays, throughout the season, with bus connection to the M. H. (Mental Hospital) Sports Ground. With these facilities, it is certain the visiting teams would enjoy their game, and afterwards appreciate the cool refreshing breezes from the briney (sic) on the splendid stretch of silvery strand which is nearby.

It has not been possible to deduce from the results whether this request was successful, but the club was welcomed into the Fingal League, and with the increase in the number of teams, the League was organised into three divisions. The auguries for the 1930 season were positive for Portrane CC. At the novices' net practice, it was noted that there were "a few new uns (sic) of exceptional merit, and the prospects for success in the Fingal League were "particularly bright".  The first game of the season was a friendly match against Malahide, and this was the opportunity to try out a few of the new recruits. This was a positive occasion for all concerned, with weather on its "best behaviour and pitch in splendid order, with the result that a very pleasing exhibition of cricket was given by both sides." Malahide won by 36 runs, but the "new 'uns" acquitted themselves well and it was anticipated that they would be seen to "greater advantage" as the season advances.

The links between Portrane and Malahide CC were strong, and over the years, many players from Malahide CC have played hockey with Portrane. P. A. Neville and John, his brother, played cricket with Malahide when it became a senior club, and Billy Goodwin, the O'Neills, Billy Behan, Jimmy Connelly and Podge Hughes among many others played hockey with Portrane. Joe Caprani of Clontarf, Leinster, and Malahide fame played hockey with Portrane, and played and coached cricket at the club as well. These links between Malahide CC and Portrane Hockey are still strong and in the recent past, Ronan McGeehan of Malahide CC has captained a Portrane Hockey team and Cameron Shoebridge has featured on the team sheets of Malahide CC and Portrane Hockey Club.

The club's Leinster League campaign opened with a victory of the "much-fancied" *Irish Times*. It was another of those wonderful days of years gone by with the weather "on its best behaviour and the pitch in first class condition with the result that a fine exhibition was served up to a large attendance." A. Pownall was in "wonderful all-round form", and he took 5 wickets for 30 runs. For good measure, "with the bat he hit up 28 runs". Breen took 3 wickets for 25, and J. Rudkins "hit up a very useful 40 with some beautiful strokes and P. Greary 28". The No. 11 bat for Portrane was listed as Neville (Jnr) who was 1 not out at the close of the innings. It may have been P. A. Neville who would have been 10 years of age in 1930 or John, his brother. Among other games listed for that season are a cup tie versus CYMS which Portrane won thanks to the fine batting of P. Neville and A. Byrne, and the bowling of A. Pownall who took 5 wickets for 21 runs. Pembroke travelled to Portrane with only nine players and lost on a score of 104 runs to 30. Pownall took 3 wickets for 11 runs and Meade took 5 for 11, with M. Brannagan contributing 21* with the bat.

From this point onwards, the main emphasis will be on Portrane CC's involvement in Fingal League cricket, and references to Leinster League cricket will only be made if they are relevant to the Fingal League or important personages in the history of Portrane CC. The Fingal League campaign commenced with a victory over Ballymadun in a "rather one-sided affair". Ballymadun was all-out for 56 because the "bowling and fielding of Portrane on a very fast pitch was deadly accurate, which proved too much for the visiting batsmen". The second game of the season was against Baldwinstown, and again Portrane was at home. Portrane batted first, but then there was heavy rain, and the game was discontinued. The interruption to the game was unfortunate for Baldwinstown because according to the report, it had the game "well won thanks to their bowlers who got all Portrane's wickets rather cheaply". For the third game in a row, Portrane was at home, so it appears that the Fingal League teams had acceded to its request for most of its games to be played at Portrane. In its game against Barnageera, the team resumed its winning ways. Barnageera batted first and compiled a score of 74 runs. Portrane scored 159 for 2 declared, with the partnership of Meade (82) and Rudkins (70*) making a record 2nd wicket stand for the ground. By the end of the season, Portrane had played 10 games in the Fingal League and won 6 of them. Significantly, it had scored 994 runs which was 435 runs more than the team which topped the Division, and this was a positive reflection on the quality of the ground at Portrane. Portrane's first team finished top of its section in the Leinster League, but its play-off game against Leinster was rained off on 13 September, and the ground Phoenix was deemed unplayable on the second attempt to play the game.

In 1931, Portrane tied for second place in Division A of the Fingal League, with 5 wins and 3 defeats in an eight-match programme. It scored 713 runs in 8 games which was 314 runs more than Skerries which topped the table. The Management Committee of the Fingal League then decided to organise a "Fingal Cricket Championship" which would be played as a knock-out tournament during the month of September. In the semi-final, Portrane had a comfortable victory over Balbriggan and qualified to meet Baldwinstown in the final which was eagerly awaited because "both sides are evenly matched."

The final was played at Balbriggan on 27 September 1931 between Portrane and Baldwinstown. Unfortunately, it is not possible to give a definitive answer regarding the name of the winning team because two separate reports in the *Drogheda Independent* gave conflicting accounts. In the first article, it is reported that Mr J. T. Ennis presented Portrane with the championship medals, and Baldwinstown and Knockbrack also received medals as winners of their respective grades. The following week it is reported that at the same function, championship medals were presented to Mr G. Reynolds, Baldwinstown CC. Finally in the Garristown Notes in the *Drogheda Independent*, it is reported that Baldwinstown won the championship outright so it appears that Baldwinstown were the first winners of the Fingal Championship unless some person can produce evidence to contradict this assertion.

In 1932, Portrane qualified for the play-off stages of the Fingal League, and it played Oldtown "under ideal conditions" at Rush. In a two-innings per side game, Portrane's composite total was 131 to Oldtown's 60 runs, but Oldtown's second innings was not completed due to the darkness, and the result was based on the first innings' scores. (Portrane 68 and Oldtown 42). J. Neville featured on the Portrane team sheet, but for some unexplained reason, he did not bat in the second innings. The final of the Fingal Cricket League between Portrane and Balcunnin was played at Balbriggan on 11 September "before a large number of spectators". Balcunnin batted first and scored 80 runs and in reply, Portrane scored 48 runs. Balcunnin declared in its second innings when its score was 80 runs for 6 wickets down. Portrane could only score 47 in its second innings, and this gave Balcunnin its first victory in the Fingal Championship Cup. On this occasion, the Portrane team featured at least 4 players (K. O'Neill, J. O'Hanlon, J. Armstrong, S. Mills) who played regularly for Malahide CC in the Leinster League.

In 1934, Portrane reached the final of the Fingal Cricket League, and its opponents were Oldtown. In an exciting, low-scoring game in which "none of the batsmen seemed at home with the bowling", Portrane won by two wickets to take the Fingal Challenge Cup for the first time. The bowlers for Portrane were A. Griffin and Pownall, and the top-scorer in the game was C. McGarvey of Oldtown with 15 runs.

There is a dearth of information for the 1935 season, and the only reference to Portrane CC in the 1936 season is to its "easy defeat of Knockbrack" on a score of 46 for 3 to 35 for Knockbrack. At the AGM in 1937, the club's prospects appeared to be rather gloomy because it had "lost a number of prominent players for the coming season.". Despite this, the club decided to enter a team in the Leinster Junior League and the Fingal League. The list of officers is noteworthy because many of the people on the list rendered magnificent service to Portrane CC and to Fingal Cricket over many years:

Captain: A. Pownall; Vice-Captain: J. Boyce; Hon. Sec. and Treasurer: G. Skerrett; Ass. Sec.: J. Lea. Selection Committee: A. Pownall, G. Skerrett, S. O'Donnell, J. Ennis, and J. Boyce.

Unfortunately, there is no information available for the 1937 season other than a fixture for Portrane versus Leinster 3rds which was to be played on 26 June 1937.

The 1938 Fingal Cricket League final between Portrane and Balrothery is enshrined in the folk memory because of the series of events which unfolded. The final was played at Balbriggan and "after a very exciting game, the result was a draw of 60 runs each." The principal scorers for Portrane were O'Brien (13), J. Boyce (13) and A. Byrne (11*). The reply was scheduled for the following Sunday, and amazingly, there was another draw, with both sides on 57 runs. The only players in double scores for Portrane were P. W. A. Griffin (12) and S. O'Donnell (10). The third game was played at Skerries because the Balbriggan ground was unavailable. P. Neville won the toss, and Portrane batted first. The principal scorers for Portrane were P. Breen (11*) and P. Neville (10) while V. Farrell (14) and H. Russell (10) were the main contributors to Balrothery's score. On the bowling front, Pownall took 4 wickets for 7 runs, and Griffin took 2 for 7. Portrane's final total was 47 runs and Balrothery ended up on 34 to give Portrane its second Fingal Championship Cup.

In 1939, Portrane played Santry in the semi-final of the Leinster Junior Cup and had an easy victory thanks to the "accurate and spectacular bowling of

Mr A. Pownall who got 6 wickets for 3 runs. It is a record in cricket and being the veteran of the team, showed a good example to the younger members". Portrane batted first and scored 65 runs, with the principal scorers being P. Neville (16), John Neville (14), Joe Boyce (8) and W. Meade (7). Santry was bowled out for 14 runs, and other successful bowler for Portrane was John Neville who took 3 wickets for 7 runs.

On 13 August, Portrane played Balrothery for the second year in a row in the final of the Fingal Cricket Cup. Balrothery batted first and accumulated 58 runs thanks mainly to C. J. Mooney (16 runs) and V. Farrell (11 runs). In reply, Portrane lost early wickets, but the third wicket partnership between W. Meade (20 runs) and P. Neville (15 runs) brought the score up to 32. That was the end of Portrane's resistance, and it was bowled out for 54 runs. The main bowler for Portrane was Pownall who bowled unchanged and took 5 wickets for 25 runs. P. Neville's fielding was also mentioned because his three slip catches were adjudged to have been "excellent efforts".

After the disappointment of the Fingal game, Portrane played Rush in the final of the Leinster Junior Cup. The game was played at Rathmines on 19 August 1939. G. J. Bonass, a leading administrator in Leinster and Irish cricket, reported on the game for the *Sunday Independent*, and his report was of a patronising nature. He praised the wicket at Rathmines as being a "real cast iron" one, but according to Mr Bonass, Portrane did not appreciate its quality, and was dismissed for 75 ones. In his opinion, "one man might have made that score on that wicket." He was not impressed with Rush's approach to chasing the total:

> Stop ball is the order of the day. Many a wild one goes unpunished to leg. Dull cricket. A stray dog relieves the monotony and by his twelfth man fielding lends at least a canine interest to the game... Rush have now lost 4 wickets. There is little variation in the Portrane bowling. Sling 'em in appears to be the slogan. A great mistake even in (sic) a hard wicket.

The only positive element of either side's display was their fielding which he deemed to be a "headline for some of our somewhat bored Senior cricketers". Having completed his analysis of the shortcomings of both teams, it is mentioned in passing that Rush won the game. He finished his report by advising the lawn bowlers that the shorter route to the pavilion was behind the sightscreen rather than in front of it because "their passing usually disturbs the batsman at the far end and may or may not bring tears to his eyes". The report in the *Drogheda Independent* on the game is less jaundiced and more factual. Rush won by 10 runs because "they played the game in a real earnest way, and they have proved themselves by this victory over Portrane to be the best cricket team in Fingal". Rush is commended for its bowling and fielding while "Portrane bowling, and fielding was not up to their usual standard."

Assessment of the 1939 season for Portrane therefore depends to some extent on one's perspective on life and the answer to that deep philosophical question, "Is the glass half-full or half-empty?". The team had played in two finals, and had been beaten in both, but there were many clubs that would love to have been capable of reaching finals so from that viewpoint, the 1939 season was a successful one for Portrane CC. In 1939 also, a Fingal League Selection which was drawn principally from Skerries, Balrothery, Portrane and Knockbrack played Pembroke. Fingal batted first, and scored 90 runs, with P. Neville contributing 20 of this score. Pembroke "never mastered the bowling of A. Quinn and C. Mooney and were all out for 29".

In 1940, Portrane and Rush were in the Intermediate League of the Leinster Cricket Union, and the Leinster Cricket Union Annual for 1941 provided some significant comments on the two Fingal teams. The teams in the league in addition to Rush and Portrane, were the *Irish Times*, Carlisle Seconds, Merrion Seconds, Monkstown Seconds, Civil Service Seconds, and Imperials who withdrew. In terms of personnel on the Portrane team, Dr Blake and Alfie Pownall were employed in the hospital; Paddy Neville and John Neville (both of whom later played Senior cricket with Malahide) were sons of Paddy Neville, Senior, a hospital employee, but there were also some distinguished "outsiders" such as Christy Russell of Balrothery, P. O'Brien of Tubbergregan and Mick Gosson of the Black Hills (and later Balrothery). In the Fingal derbies, honours were even. In the first game, Portrane was dismissed for 51, with Simon Hoare taking 6 wickets for 24 and Kit Mooney taking 4 for 21. Rush scored 152 runs with J. P. Coleman top-scoring with 50 runs. In the return game, Portrane scored 86, and P. Neville was the main batsman with 33 runs. Rush was bowled out for 50, with P. Neville taking 5 wickets for 9 runs. P. Neville's century was scored against Civil Service Seconds, and unusually, Portrane declared when the score was 196 for 3. P. Neville was the outstanding batsman in the Intermediate League, and among his scores were 57, 61, 64*, 54*, and 102*. Not content with starring with Portrane, he scored a number of centuries for Dundrum Asylum and with V. Buggy (Leinster Seconds), he was involved in a number of first-wicket century partnerships. Rush won the Intermediate League with a record of 12 games played, 10 won, 2 lost, and 30 points accumulated. Portrane was right behind Rush, and it had lost 3 games by comparison with Rush's 2 losses.

The people mainly responsible for winning the league were S. M. Hoare (for his bowling), J. A. Martin and J. P. Coleman (for batting) and C. J. (Kit) Mooney for "excellent work in both spheres".

There was little of note in the 1940 season in the Fingal League other than to record that Mr Joe Boyce of Portrane was elected Vice-President of the Fingal League, and Portrane played in the same section as Balrothery, Skerries, Naul Hill and Mulhuddart. In 1941, Portrane was obliged to withdraw from Fingal League cricket due to the foot and mouth epidemic, but the club made a presentation to Dr B. Blake, captain of Portrane hockey and cricket teams, on his appointment to a post in Limerick Hospital. This was the second presentation of the evening because earlier Dr Blake's father, Dr S. Blake, the RMS of Portrane Hospital, had presented a cup and medals to the Portrane Hockey team which had gone through the season unbeaten. From a cricketing viewpoint, there was a significant overlap between the players on the hockey and cricket teams, and the following players received medals: Dr B. Blake (Captain), Messrs James O'Toole, A. Byrne, B. Dockrell, J. T. Kavanagh, John Neville, Jas. H. Lee, A. Griffin, Edward Ennis, P. Neville, and G. Kemp. Portrane was listed on the league table at the end of the season for the Leinster League, and according to the table, it had played 13 matches and lost 11, but it may just have given walkovers when the foot and mouth restrictions were imposed. Some cricket was played in September, and Mulhuddart played Portrane in the first cricket game after the lifting of restrictions. Mulhuddart batted first and scored 24 runs, and Portrane made 26 runs for 7 wickets in reply. The following week, Portrane travelled to Balbriggan to play against Clonard who were making their debut in the Fingal League. Clonard won on a score of 47 runs to 27 because Portrane were "short of some of their favourite cricketers and had to travel with some real amateurs."

The clubs in Fingal were zealous in ensuring that other clubs complied with the rules and regulations of the League. In 1943, Walshestown lodged an objection to Portrane, the grounds for which were not specified in the report other than to state that the objection was over-ruled. The two more usual objections were either biased umpiring decisions or queries regarding the eligibility of players to participate in Fingal League games. With Walshestown's objection being over-ruled, the way was clear for Portrane to play Balrothery in what ended up as a one-sided final of the Fingal League. Balrothery batted first and only scored 15 runs. Portrane made 73 for 6, and of this total, Neville was "over 50, not out". That season there was also a knock-out competition, but Portrane's interest in it was ended in the first round when it lost to Rush.

In 1946, Joe Boyce was re-elected as President of the Fingal League but unfortunately, his health had begun to fail, and he resigned the following year. His resignation was accepted by the League with regret and "tributes were paid to his great sportsmanship and organising ability during his term of office." The loss of a key administrator can have a detrimental effect on a club, and it may have been coincidence but in June 1947, Portrane was unable to field for a cup match against Harding. Portrane dropped out of the Leinster League for a number of seasons but continued to play in the Fingal League. In its first game of the 1950 season, it beat Knockbrack on a score of 64 for 7 to Knockbrack's 63. The top scorers for Portrane were J. Neville (25) and A. Blake (25). On 16 July, Portrane beat Walshestown by 4 wickets. Walshestown batted first and scored 63 all out. Portrane lost 3 wickets cheaply, but J. Neville and E. Fitzgerald got the necessary runs. There is no query regarding the actual details of the report, but it was stated that this victory made Portrane League Champions, and this has not been corroborated by any other sources. In the Fingal League Archives, it is reported that Balrothery won the Championship in 1950. When Balrothery won the Championship in 1955, it was stated that this was the 9th time that it had won it, and this was corroborated by another report in 1971 which indicated that Balrothery had won the Championship on 13 occasions. These figures can only be correct if 1950 is included as one of the years that Balrothery won the competition.

Portrane returned to Leinster Cricket in 1951 and had immediate success when it beat Civil Service Seconds by 5 wickets to win the Minor Cup. Civil Service batted first and scored 117 runs. Both Portrane opening batsmen were out without scoring, but a solid display by the remaining players brought Portrane home with relative ease. The successful batsmen were E. Fitzgerald (22), R. Neville (26, the report says Reville), S. Pownall (33*), J. Byrne (22), and D. Kelly (14*). Fitgerald took 5 wickets for 22 runs, S. Pownall took 2 for 42, A. Pownall took 1 for 29 and Snowe's figures were 1 for 21. Portrane completed the double that season by winning the Leinster Minor League.

The Fingal Cup final was not played in 1951 due to "unforeseen difficulties", but it was agreed that the final between Knockbrack and Portrane would take place on 25 May 1952. The game was played on a "very fast and hard wicket at the Park, Skerries", and Portrane won by 2 runs. Knockbrack batted first in "glorious sunshine", but Jim Young took 2 wickets for 7 runs. By the fall of the fifth wicket, Knockbrack had only managed to score 26 runs, and according to the report, many of these runs were byes. The final 5 wickets fell cheaply, and Knockbrack was all out for 36 runs. Portrane was circumspect in chasing this target and needed only 4 runs with 2 wickets left. Another wicket fell when 3 runs had been scored, and the last man went to the wicket with one run required. The winning run was made, with "one extra for good measure", and Portrane had won the Cup "midst much excitement and applause from the large number of spectators."

In 1952, Portrane struggled in its defence of the Cup. It was well-beaten by Knockbrack on a score of 128 runs to 32, and later in the season, it also lost to Skerries. For the game against Skerries, Portrane batted first on a "perfect wicket" at Portrane, but the team was soon in "dire straits" against the bowling of R. Byrne who ended up with the wonderful figures of 8 wickets for 32 runs. The only resistance came from Liam Tolan who scored 34 runs out of a Portrane total of 62 runs. The necessary runs were obtained with consummate ease, with W. Beggs (25) giving an "exhibition of hitting. One of his shots went over the pavilion, and the last hit over the bowler's head for four gave Skerries the victory.

In 1953, Walshestown and Portrane featured in a quintessential Fingal final. Walshetown batted first, but the "hard wicket" suited the bowlers, and Walshestown was bowled out for 18 runs. Fitzgerald and Pownall were the successful bowlers for Portrane. However, the game was ended when "T. and J. Murphy skittled the Portrane batsmen for 11 runs. T. Murphy took 6 wickets for 8 runs, and Jim, his brother, took 3 wickets for 1 run. There is no reference to Portrane playing Fingal League cricket in 1954, but it was involved in Fingal cricket in 1955 because it was drawn against Knockbrack in the first game of the season.

There is no evidence of Portrane playing Fingal cricket in 1954, but it played a full programme of fixtures in the Leinster League. During this season, it played against Leinster 1V, North Kildare, Clontarf, Old Belvedere. On 27 June, it beat Leinster on a score of 110 for 4 to 109; it lost to CYMS on a score of 145 to 102, and in early May, it had a decisive victory over Clontarf when it scored 96 runs for the loss of 6 wickets, and then dismissed Clontarf for 14 runs.

In 1955, it was one of six teams in the Fingal League when the fixtures for the first games of the season were announced. It was scheduled to play against Knockbrack. The other games were Balrothery v The Hills and Walshestown v Cottrellstown. That is the extent of the information which is available on Portrane's involvement in Fingal cricket during that season, but it featured in two noteworthy games in Leinster competitions. In its game against

Old Belvedere, Portrane was in the news because Lloyd, the Old Belvedere bowler, took 8 wickets for 8 runs – all clean-bowled, and the other two wickets were run-outs. Portrane eventually finished on 32 all out, and Old Belvedere got the required total for the loss of 4 wickets.

In the cup, Portrane was drawn against Longford, and the reports on cricket in the *Longford Leader* were always good value. In the report, it is asserted that Longford "made a present of the match to Portrane who were well and truly beaten but for lax fielding midway through the latter's innings. A lesson that should be long remembered by fielders". Longford batted first and scored 132 runs. The outstanding feature of the match was "Ian Cox's innings of 64 during which he was lauded for the ease and grace in dealing with the bowling. Truly a class batsman lost in junior ranks". There was praise for the bowling of Cox and Shaw, but "most of the fielders lent little or no assistance to their efforts. Without a doubt Portrane should have been out for not more than 50 runs". In addition to being unhappy with the fielding, he was also unimpressed with the field placings, and at the end of this tale of woe, Portrane got 135 runs for seven wickets. The main contributors to Portrane's score were D. Kelly (40) and S. Pownall (41).

1956 was a significant year for Portrane CC. It played Bellew in the final of the Leinster Junior Cup at the Civil Service Grounds. Con Martin, formerly of Rush and Aston Villa, had signed to play for Waterford in the League of Ireland, and thus, he was available to play cricket because he was not returning to England for pre-season training. There was no cricket team in Rush at the time, so he joined up with Portrane. In addition to Con Martin, Stan Pownall of Drumcondra AFC was also on the team, Dick Neville (younger brother of Paddy and John who were playing senior cricket with Malahide), and the Carty brothers from Rush were other significant members of a formidable team.

That was the fifth occasion that Bellew had reached the final of the Leinster Junior Cup in seven years, and it had been beaten in the four previous finals. Bellew batted first, but Stan Pownall in a terrific spell of bowling took 7 wickets for 29 runs. Kevin Farrell (26) was the only Bellew batsman to make a score of any significance, and R. Byrne (12) was the only other batsman to score double figures. Portrane achieved the target of 59 with the loss of three wickets, and D. Kelly (27) was its top scorer.

At international level, a momentum had been building up for P. A. Neville to be capped for Ireland in view of his exploits for Malahide CC in Leinster Senior competitions. In June 1956, he provided more evidence of his right to an international cap when he scored 110 for Leinster when playing against Munster. When Noel Cantwell, another dual player cried off the Irish team, Paddy Neville was called up for the team to play against the British Combined Services in Belfast on 17 and 18 August 1956. A summary of his achievements gives an indication of not just his versatility, but the high level at which Paddy performed. He played hockey for Ireland for three seasons and was on a Triple Crown winning team. He played in goal for Drumcondra and was awarded representative honours when he played for the League of Ireland team. He played Gaelic football for Parnells, and was on a Dublin Championship winning team, but this achievement went under the radar because of the GAA's ban on foreign games. In addition to all this talent, his temperament and sportsmanship were legendary. When his brother, Dick, was asked about Paddy's greatest moment, he said that it was during a cup final when Paddy told an umpire that a goal that had been credited to him, had gone into the goal through a hole at the side of the net.

Paddy Neville was one of three brothers, John. and Richard (Dick) being the others who starred for Portrane in hockey and cricket, but it would be remiss of me not to mention some of the other families whose members have contributed so much to Portrane over the years. Alf Pownall who had a wonderfully long career and his sons, Stan and Alfie, Junior. Andy Byrne was a wonderful full back, and his sons, Tommy, and Ando, were regular members of the cricket and hockey teams. The Breens, John and Ted, played both sports with distinction, and Dr Blake's two sons, Bertram and Adrian captained the hockey and cricket teams. In more recent times, Paschal Henchy ensured that Portrane played Fingal League cricket for many years after Portrane (St Ita's) left Leinster cricket.

In 1957, Portrane reached the final of the Fingal League when it played against Knockbrack at Kenure. Portrane batted first, and only managed to score 43 runs, with the main contributions coming from T. Byrne (14) and R. Neville (9). In keeping with the theory that a winning score is never known until the second team bats, Knockbrack was dismissed for 33 runs due to superb bowling from J. Neville, J. Young, and O. Meenan. The 1958 final was not played until 1959 and the same two teams contested it. On this occasion, Knockbrack won by 11 runs on a score of 59 to 48. Seán Moore took 4 wickets for 4 runs for Knockbrack, while J. Neville took 5 for 29 for Portrane. Knockbrack again beat Portrane in the final which was played at the Ballast Pit in Skerries on 22 June 1960, and the same two teams were scheduled to meet in a final on 28 June 1961, but Portrane withdrew from the League. No reason was given for this decision, but the club continued to play cricket in Leinster, albeit with the different name which had been adopted in 1959. The Health Board had insisted that the hospitals be known by specific names with Mental Hospital being removed from the name, and Portrane CC became known as St Ita's.

St Ita's played in the Intermediate League of Leinster Cricket until 1965, and there were still local derbies because Balrothery CC was also in the Intermediate League. The two teams met in the Intermediate Cup in 1961, and Balrothery batting first was dismissed for 51 runs, the main wicket takers being Bates (4 for 25) and Young (6 for 22). St Ita's lost 3 quick wickets for 17 runs, but McMorrow (24*) and Bates (4) ensured that they were into the semi-final of the Cup. There are no further details available, but the Cup run was ended at the semi-final stage because the final was between Royal College of Surgeons and Leinster 3rds. On the weekend of the victory over Balrothery, St Ita's beat Old Belvedere at Cabra. St Ita's batted first and scored 93 runs, with contributions from Kelly (29), P. Neville (23) and Henchy (20). Belvedere looked to be in the pole position while Delaney (57) was batting but he was caught at square leg by Fenlon off the bowling of Henchy. The other successful bowlers for St Ita's were Young (4 for 16) and Bates (4 for 50). St Ita's was well in contention to win the league in 1961, but a weekend of mixed fortunes damaged its hopes of a league victory. On 15 July, St Ita's lost to St James's Gate by 15 runs. However, on 16 July, St Ita's beat Railway Union 3rds on a score of 124 to 3rds. The main contributors for St Ita's were D. Kelly (27), Byrne (25), Ryan, (12), Young (18).

The 1962 season was a more difficult one for St Ita's, and one of the few games for which it was possible to obtain a result was a game against YMCA on 2 June, and a score of 18 runs all out did not augur well for the season. By 9 August, it had played 13 games, won 2, drawn 2, lost 9, and was second last on the league table with a 21% total. It looked as if the 1963 season was going to be equally difficult because St Ita's was knocked out in the first round of the Intermediate Cup by Harding on a score of 59 to 63 for the loss of 3 wickets. After this setback, there was a resurgence, and the team was involved in some good victories during the rest of the season. On 1 June, St Ita's dismissed Railway for 56 runs with Henchy (5 for 13) and Bates (3 for 9) being responsible for the rout. The required runs were obtained for the loss of 3 wickets by T. Byrne (16) and Henchy (10*). On 8 June, St Ita's batted first against St James's Gate, and accumulated 152 runs, with solid contributions from D. Kelly (47), P. Henchy (41*) and J. Neville (22), but St James's Gate scored the winning run off the second last ball of the game. The following day, St Ita's batted first and scored 113, with T. Byrne (22), P. Henchy (20), P. Neville (20) and J. Neville (17) getting the lion's share of the runs. In reply, Civil Service only got 41 runs, with Henchy taking 4 wickets for 18 runs.

On 7 July 1963, St Ita's played an exciting game with Clontarf. Batting first, St Ita's went from 33 runs for 1 wicket to 78 all out, with only T. Byrne (38) and Noel Bates (20) making any runs. Clontarf were 70 for 8 in the second last over, but Noel Bates took 2 wickets to give St Ita's a thrilling victory which owed a lot to accurate bowling from Bates (3 for 26), P. Neville (3 for 32) and P. Henchy (3 for 9). The top scorers for Clontarf were D. Lee (16), and a future Irish International, Enda McDermott (17). By mid-July, St Ita's was third in the table, but a poor weekend ended any hopes it had of winning the League. On Saturday, 13 July, St Ita's was fortunate to escape with a draw in its game with Phoenix who batted first and declared at 194 for 5. In reply, St Ita's scored 130 for 8 wickets. On Sunday 14 July, St Ita's was set a target of 150 by Railway Union, but there was then a complete batting collapse, and they were all out for 35 runs. All hopes of a League title finally disappeared a fortnight later when St Ita's was well-beaten by St James's Gate on a score of 109 runs to 66, with D. Kelly (23) and Sean Hannon (14), the only batmen to make any impression on the bowling. The wickets were taken by S. Neville (5 for 18), P. Henchy (3 for 27) and Noel Bates (3 for 32).

In June 1964, St Ita's lost to St James's Gate in a low-scoring game. St Ita's batted first and scored 98 runs and St James's Gate reached the target for the loss of 7 wickets. The main batsmen for St Ita's were T. Riordan (22) and A. McCann (16). In the return game at Portrane, St James's Gate won by 5 wickets. St Ita's had scored 40 runs before the fall of the first wicket, but ended all out for 86 runs, and the only significant contributions were from Thomas Byrne (15) and Dermot Kelly (20). By mid-July, the League Table showed that St Ita's had played 8 games, won 3, lost 5, and was on 38%. In late July, St Ita's lost to Clontarf by 1 wicket. Batting first, St Ita's scored 68 runs, with T. Byrne (15) being the top scorer and S. Ryan and J. Coll also in double figures. N. Bates (4 for 31) and P. Henchy (5 for 36) bowled for the entire innings, and Clontarf only scraped home on a score of 70 for 9 wickets. On 25 July, St Ita's welcomed Civil Service to Portrane, and the home team had a nine-wicket victory. Civil Service was restricted to 87 runs due to the excellent bowling of Pat (sic) Henchy who took 6 wickets "at a very low personal cost". In reply, T. Riordan and J. Kelly had no bother in reaching the target against a "Service attack which was devoid of any great thrust".

Information on the last season (1965) that St Ita's played in Leinster Cricket is very sparse, and for the most part, all that is available are details of fixtures rather than results. There were league fixtures against YMCA and Phoenix. The League game against Trinity was not played for some reason, and St Ita's was drawn in the preliminary round of the Intermediate Cup against Clontarf but lost. The one positive element in the entire season is that Portrane was back in Fingal cricket, and it was drawn against Knockbrack Seconds in the Cup. Portrane played Fingal cricket intermittently for the next 35 years and it was represented at a Fingal League meeting which was held in 2001.

Why did cricket die in Portrane when hockey, the complementary sport continued to thrive in the peninsula? In addressing this question, we will leave aside the more general arguments regarding cricket as a sport vis-à-vis other sports and concentrate on issues specific to Portrane. As the salaries of staff improved, there was no longer any necessity for them to live in hospital-owned accommodation, and many of them bought houses in other areas. The tendency then was to gravitate towards recreational facilities close to one's residence rather than the workplace. It was noticeable that when Portrane ceased playing cricket, very few players transferred to other clubs because once the convenience of a ground near home was lost, interest in playing cricket dissipated. Secondly, a hospital team would have players of different abilities and in the later years, Portrane could field only one team which meant that the ambitious cricketers joined some of the bigger clubs in the area, and this was also applicable to novice cricketers. As the number of cricketers declined, the difficulties caused by the inflexibility of work rotas exacerbated the problems involved in fielding teams. Thirdly, there was no youth programme in place and therefore as players retired, there was not a stream of young players ready to take their places. The Hockey club has had a thriving youth programme in place for many years, and this has enabled it to become one of the most successful hockey clubs in the country. There may have been undue dependence on the hospital for institutional support, and as changes began to occur in the treatment of persons with psychiatric illnesses, there were less people available to prepare and maintain pitches whereas the hockey had a greater level of input from the people living in Portrane and Donabate. Fourthly, over the years, Portrane CC was fortunate to have some wonderful administrators such as Joe Boyce, Stephen O'Donnell, and Tim Riordan, and often the work of these administrators is only noticed when they are no longer available.

The comments above are of a conjectural nature but it is more important to reference the contribution which Portrane CC made to the life of the community, and to commend the visionaries who were years ahead of their time in seeing the value which sport served in engendering a sense of well-being in patients and staff. It enabled members of the community of St Ita's Hospital to enjoy a leisure time activity together, and it was invaluable in inculcating a sense of self-worth for people who might have been struggling with low self-esteem. Over the years, some magnificent cricketers such as Paddy and John Neville, the Pownalls, Dermot Kelly and Noel Bates among many others played with Portrane, and they were an adornment to the game, not just because of their sporting prowess, but the spirit with which they played cricket. Portrane CC more than fulfilled the aspirations of the Management Committee of 1926 who saw sports "as an invaluable means of diverting the minds of the patients and... useful in enabling the staff to engage in harmless and health-giving outdoor recreation."

## Notes

I acknowledge with gratitude the assistance and photographs which Paschal (Percy) Henchy has given to me during the preparation of this chapter. However, errors in fact or omissions and the opinions expressed are my responsibility.

Portrane Asylum, F.C.

1st JANUARY, 1904

Irish Hockey Team
P. A. Neville is second from left on front row.

Joe Caprani

Paddy Neville

*Stan Pownall*

Ronan McGeehan and Paschal Henchy

# Chapter 9: Cricket in Balbriggan

## Early Days, 1831-1925

In 1831, the diaries of Mrs Taylor of Ardgillan contain references to cricket and tea on two occasions at Hampton, Balbriggan. Hampton was again the venue when cricket was revived in Balbriggan in 1844. "Several gentlemen amateurs of that manly sport have applied to Mr George A. Hamilton for the use of the old ground in his demesne. Mr Hamilton being desirous to promote an amusement of which he is an ardent admirer, kindly granted their request." The availability of a train service was a crucial factor in forming a cricket team because players came from Drogheda and Dublin to play for Balbriggan, and transport was not a problem for visiting teams. Balbriggan issued a challenge to the Rathmines team, and a game between Balbriggan and Rathmines was played on Monday, 15 July 1844. Balbriggan accumulated 120 runs, with James Ennis scoring 32 runs, Nicholas Ennis got 19 runs and there were 35 extras. Rathmines batted twice but only managed to score 91 runs and was beaten by an innings and 36 runs.

Balbriggan Cricket Club was re-established on 12 May 1863 with George A. Hamilton, Esq as President of the club. At the inaugural meeting, it was reported that "nearly the whole of the gentry of the neighbourhood and surrounding country have become members, and everything looks as if the Balbriggan Club, will ere long, become one of the best in Ireland." Balbriggan played Malahide on Saturday, 25 July 1863 on its "nicely situated ground." Batting first, Balbriggan placed what the newspaper report referred to as a "very respectable number of 75 to their account." The main scorer for Balbriggan was L. Filgate with 34 runs, and his brother, W. Filgate scored 14 runs. The top scorer for Malahide was T. Casey who had the honour of being the first player to score a century for both Dublin University and Malahide. After a game of two innings per side, the result was a win for Malahide, but this was deemed "highly creditable" for a young club to have played with "such success against such good players as the Malahide."

The report of the game between Balbriggan and Westown which was played on 31 August 1863 encapsulated the stratified nature of the society which existed in that era. It commenced with a reference to the "match coming off at the beautiful seat of Malachi S. Hussey, Esq. before "a great concourse of spectators, including the ladies and gentlemen, and all the peasantry of the neighbourhood." Balbriggan batted first, lost early wickets, and the last wicket in the first innings fell for 44 with "Mr Whyte making the largest score, "by good play, all singles." Westown only scored 28 in the first innings but came into their own in the second innings. In his innings, "Mr Hussey played in his usual fine style and his young son and heir, Master Anthony, who is home for vacation, played and bowled beautifully." Balbriggan really had no chance against such talented cricketers, and Westown got the required score in the second innings for the loss of eight wickets. H. G. Carey was praised for his "spirit and energy in getting up the Balbriggan Club, and the report on the *Freeman's Journal* ended with a wonderful account of the after-match hospitality:

> Mr and Mrs Hussey displayed their usual hospitality by entertaining the players and visitors to a sumptuous dejeuner. Mr Hussey presiding, and after drinking the usual loyal and complimentary toasts, the company parted at a late hour pleased, after indulging in the feast of reason and the flow of soul.

The return game between Balbriggan and Westown was played in Balbriggan on 7 September 1863 "in the presence of a large and fashionable attendance of spectators." Balbriggan scored 46 in the first innings, and Westown scored 52 in reply. Young Mr Strong Hussey again got favourable mention and it was reported that "although, (he was) a juvenile in years, promises fair to be a significant player, and he at present forms a very worthy example for many older players." He did not play as well in the second innings because he only got one run, Westown was bowled out for 18 runs, and Balbriggan won by 42 runs. Balbriggan CC was praised for the quality of hospitality, and the report ended with an expression of good wishes for the future development of the club:

> The want of a cricket club at Balbriggan has long been felt and the present club so admirably managed and the subscription so small, we have little doubt of its meeting with the success we wish it.

For the 1864 season, Balbriggan expanded its playing programme considerably. There are reports available on four games, with the first game being against Malahide on 29 June. The top scorer for Balbriggan on this occasion was Mr Creagh, but the reporter was not impressed with his running between the wickets:

> Mr Creagh in the first innings played well, obtaining 23 not out, but had he exerted himself and run out every hit properly, we are inclined to think that he might have doubled his score; for where he got only singles, he might easily have obtained doubles.

In a two innings per side game, both teams scored 49 in the second innings, but Balbriggan was deemed to have won because it was ahead at the end of the first innings. Other games played during this season were against Eagle CC which Balbriggan won, helped to some extent by the fact that the Eagle CC had only eight players, and a return game against Malahide which Malahide won by 9 runs. The final game of the season was played against Fingal on 23 September 1864, and strangely, the Balbriggan team was referred to as an "Eleven of Balbriggan", with none of the usual names appearing on the team sheet. The result was a one-run win for Balbriggan.

By 1866, Balbriggan CC was thriving, and this was recognised by John Lawrence's very influential, *Handbook of Cricket in Ireland*. For the 1866 season, Lawrence reported that Balbriggan CC had forty members who paid an annual subscription of 10s. He praised the club for "greatly" promoting cricket in the district by playing regular matches and for taking part "in a good deal of practice".

The only games on which there are accounts for the 1866 season are a home game against Dundalk which Balbriggan won and a game against Leinster which Leinster won by one innings and seven runs. The overall playing record for the season was played 8, won 4 and lost 4. With everything going so well, it came as a surprise to read that the club folded in the 1867 season. No reason was given by H. G. Carey in his note to Lawrence, and Lawrence expressed his disappointment at this development:

> It must be a source of regret that a club so near the metropolis, possessing all the advantages of easy transit, to contend with first-class clubs, should be allowed to pass away. Possibly, our esteemed correspondent could, if he took this matter in hand, resuscitate this club, and once more give our noble game a habitation in his neighbourhood".

From 1867 onwards, Balbriggan CC had no entry in Lawrence's Handbook. An exhaustive search of national and local papers failed to elicit details of games played, and it seems reasonable to conclude that cricket ceased in Balbriggan for a very considerable period. It was at this juncture that cricket became embroiled what in modern parlance would be referred to as a "perfect storm". A Land War commenced in 1879, and the existence of very prominent landlords in the area meant that members of the gentry had concerns far removed from cricket during this time.

In 1881, a team called Balbriggan Wanderers played Onaskella CC in Navan on Tuesday, 6 September. The best bowlers for Balbriggan were J. McDermott and J. Landy, but the home side won comfortably on a score of 51 runs to 20 runs. There was a comment that the fielding of both sides was "capital", but "particularly so on the part of the home team. They did not let one chance escape them. In fact, they owe their victory to their excellent fielding." The following year, the cricket team was called Balbriggan Rangers, and it played Garristown, home and away. In the away game, Garristown won by an innings and 4 runs. Balbriggan scored 16 in the first innings and 16 in the second innings. In 1887, the team was called Balbriggan Rovers, and in its game with City of Dublin Workingmen's CC, Balbriggan won on a score of 69 to 62. It was still called Balbriggan Rovers in 1888 and played a game against the *Irish Times*.

There was a lull in cricketing activity in Balbriggan between 1888 and the late 1890s, partly because of lack of access to a field. Balbriggan CC held its annual meeting on 23 May 1900, and it was explained that there was no point in meeting any earlier because the club had no ground but Terence O'Neill, businessman and landowner, came to the rescue and "placed one of his fields at their disposal". The captain for the season was G. Hayes, the Hon. Secretary was R. Spencer, and the Treasurer was R. Harford. It appears to have been an eventful season. Briarland CC had been unbeaten until it played Balbriggan, but Balbriggan was declared the winners at 6 o'clock, thanks to its first innings lead. The victory was ascribed to the bowling of Mr J. Reynolds who took 7 wickets, including 3 in one over. The following week, Iveagh CC, "the Dublin crack" visited Balbriggan, but in "erratic weather conditions" and in front of a "large concourse of people", Balbriggan won again on a score of 54 to 24. On 29 June, Balbriggan played the return game against Briarland, although one paper did not use the name, Briarland, it called the visitors, Ring CC. The report in the *Drogheda Independent* is matter of fact. Ring CC won an exciting game by 8 runs, due in "great measure to the excellent bowling of C. Hagan," who took 7 wickets. Others to receive honourable were T. O'Neill of Balbriggan whose batting "was the feature of the match and Jem Browne who trundled the leather to best advantage". The *Drogheda Argus and Leinster Journal* provided more detail on this game. Mr O'Neill scored 18 not out, and Mr Reynolds who was not mentioned in the other report took 6 wickets, while J. Browne took 4. A large concourse had attended the previous game against Iveagh, and the crowd again received mention in this report:

> The rough element of some of the local supporters which made itself apparent during the progress of the match on last Friday, reflects a

serious stain on the reputation of the club. The club means to deal seriously with persons causing a disturbance on their grounds, for if such a state of things were allowed to continue, the club would soon cease to exist.

Gormanstown CC was the next visitors to Balbriggan and won on a score of 48 to 33 runs. The crowd was in the news again and featured in P. J. Curtis's report to the *Drogheda Independent*:

> We would suggest to Mr Terence O'Neill who kindly lent the ground for the occasion, to keep the roughs away from going to the ground who came for no other purpose than to cause a row between the two elevens.

The final game of the 1900 season for which there is a report available was played on the grounds of Iveagh CC. Balbriggan won on a score of 36 to 20, and the season ended on a positive note:

> The hospitality accorded to the Balbriggan men was more than friendly. After the match, an open-air concert was held, and members of both teams contributed largely to the programme.

The AGM for the 1901 season was held in the Town Hall on Wednesday, 12 June; Mr T. O'Neill was elected President, and the other officers were re-elected. Cash in hand was 7s 4d (about 36c) and the club also had a stock of "cricketing utensils". The meeting ended with a vote of thanks to the O'Neill family for the "generous manner in which they befriended the club during the season." Among the games played during this season were away to Oldtown CC which Oldtown won on a score of 33 runs to 35, and home to Naul CC. Naul beat Balbriggan by 4 runs, and the main contributors for Naul were J. McDermott (15), W. Sherwin (5) and J. Whyte (5); for Balbriggan, J. Reynolds scored 11 not out and J. Hamlet scored 6.

Balbriggan CC did not confine its activities to cricket, and on 2 November 1901, it organised a "grand concert and theatrical entertainment" in the Town Hall. According to the report, the concert "was thronged in every part and the club must have realised a substantial sum." The arrangements for the concert were deemed to be "perfect in every detail", and every performer was mentioned by the name in the review. The report ended with "special praise" for the person who painted the "beautiful scenery".

In the 1902 season, games were played against Civil Service, Drogheda, *The Irish Times*, and Co. Meath. The team was four players short for the game against Drogheda and lost on a score of 80 runs to 66. *The Irish Times* provided the opposition on 5 July, and Balbriggan won by 24 runs on the first innings. The main contributors with the bat for Balbriggan were O'Neill (16), P. Cumisky (12) and J. Reynolds (17), while Reynolds and Bannon shared the "bowling honours". Balbriggan's game against Co. Meath was played on a bitterly cold day, and Co. Meath ended a successful season with a comprehensive win. Balbriggan started badly, losing the first four wickets without scoring. Hamlet (18), Mundell (17) and Cumisky (13) "put a better face on things", and Balbriggan's score eventually reached 65. Co. Meath accumulated 136 runs, with one player, C. F. Bomford getting 84 of this total "by grand cricket and carrying his bat." The final game of the season was against Corduff, a team dubbed the Social Invincibles. On the day, the Invincibles met their match with O'Neill (30) and Hamlet (14) being the main contributors to Balbriggan's total of 108. In the words of the reporter, Purfield (19) was the "only one of the Corduff side who could do anything against the good bowling of Reynolds and Bannon."

The season ended with a "grand concert" which was "largely attended by all the elite of Balbriggan and district". The personnel who organised last year's concert were involved again, and the list of artists who contributed to its success were Miss Agnes Treacy (Gold Medallist Feis Cheoil), Miss Corry (Drogheda), Mr J. C. Doyle (Gold Medallist Feis Cheoil), Mr T. J. Graham (Balbriggan), Mr A. C. Watson and Mr L. Farrington.

In 1903, games were played against Civil Service 2, Drumcondra, Ulidia, Holmpatrick, Drogheda, Corduff and the *Irish Times*. Balbriggan won the game against the *Irish Times* on a score of 64 to 51 runs. The main contributors were W. Bannon (13), J. Love (15) and R. Spencer (10). Reynolds and Bannon were in their usual miserly form with the ball, and they both took 4 wickets. Changes were occurring in the junior cricket scene in Dublin as the junior clubs brought pressure to bear for league and cup competitions to be organised. These initiatives meant the clubs no longer had any desire or need to arrange friendly games because there were league structures in place. The exception to this comment was Civil Service 2 which played league cricket and friendlies. In 1904, the Balbriggan correspondent for the *Drogheda Argus* took the cricket club to task for its tardiness in preparing for the new season:

> What is the matter with Balbriggan CC? On all sides one reads and hears of preparations being made for the coming season, but the committee of the BCC seems to be still in that comatose condition attributed to the bear in winter! Surely, it is not possible that the Club will be allowed to lapse in the same way as was the ever to be regretted Balbriggan Sports.

The following week, he again urged the committee of Balbriggan to prepare for the season:

> Today will see the close of the football season in Balbriggan…. We hope that as the season is now over that the committee of the cricket club will now take steps as to promoting cricket here, before the season ends.

Balbriggan's season started eventually with a game against Civil Service on 28 May 1904. Games were also played that season against Castlebellingham, Incogniti, Drogheda and Knockbrack. There is a puzzling reference to the serious loss which the club had suffered "in the person of Mr T. J. O'Neill who defended the wickets so splendidly for the last few years." No further details are given because it is assumed that the reader knew what had happened to Mr O'Neill but based on information from the obituary of his brother, Edward, it appears that Mr O'Neill had emigrated to the USA.

In addition to inter-club games, business houses and factories also played cricket. In a game between Balbriggan and Belfast Banking Co., a player called A. Slogger got runs (18) and took 5 wickets. The club secretary, Mr Spencer, also organised a game against a team from Smyth and Co which ended in a victory for Mr Spencer's team. From 1905 to 1912, there are three hundred and twenty two references to cricket in the local newspapers, but Balbriggan is only mentioned once and that is a game against Corbalton in 1912. Whether or not there was cricket in Balbriggan during this period, it is not possible to come to any definite conclusion. There may have been difficulties in getting teams out because in 1904, a game against Castlebellingham did not take place, because Balbriggan did not turn up, but in the absence of evidence, one way or another, it is futile to engage in conjecture. However, in 1911 in a related story, there was a reference to lands at Coney Hill being bought from Mr T. W. Hamlet so that a golf course could be developed. In 1961, this information was re-produced in an evening paper and Mr G. L. McGowan was asked if he knew anything about the proposed golf club at Coney Hill. He stated that lands were obtained at Bremore, a pavilion was purchased, and the necessary funds were obtained to bring this project to fruition, but a problem arose regarding the lease, and the project was abandoned. The pavilion was sold to Balbriggan Cricket Club which "was very progressive at the time". (1911). Subsequently, this structure was dismantled and relocated to a site on Dublin Street where it was used by children who were learning Irish dancing.

## Balbriggan CC, 1926-1970

In 1926, there were cricket teams in Balbriggan, Ring Commons, Knightstown, Skerries and Knockbrack, but fixtures for the most part were still being arranged as challenges, as there were no official structures in place. Balbriggan entered the Fingal League in 1929, and one of its first games in the league was against Knockbrack, and while Balbriggan lost by 15 runs in a game which was attended by a large crowd, there were complimentary comments regarding the "beautifully laid out grounds".

Shortly after, there was an incident-packed game when Balbriggan visited the Black Hills. The game was terminated unsatisfactorily and there were scenes and "ebulllitions of temper not usually associated with cricket". Two Balbriggan players were adjudged to be LBW by the local umpire, and there were ironical cheers and laughter from all sides of the ground because the decisions were palpably incorrect. One decision was reversed, and the batsman was allowed to continue. Balbriggan was dismissed for 24 runs. The Black Hills lost 6 wickets, and when P. Pollis was clean bowled by Vernon, there was a pitch invasion with the local players saying that the bails had been dislodged by the keeper. The umpire, Mr John Reynolds, "one of the oldest and best-known cricketers in the Co. Dublin, whose knowledge of the game and integrity as an umpire are widely-recognised," was abused and the stumps were pulled by the home side. Such a report was never going to be left unchallenged, and a fortnight later, there was a reply which criticised the intemperate language of the previous article, and alleged bias and prejudice on the part of the *Drogheda Independent's* Correspondent. When the league tables for the season are analysed, Balbriggan and the Black Hills have 1 point each for a draw, so it appears that the officers of the Fingal League deemed both sides to be equally culpable or equally innocent.

The semi-finals and finals of the 1929 Fingal League competition were held in Balbriggan, and Skerries' reign as champions was ended when they lost the semi-final to Knockbrack in Balbriggan. The crease which was laid 24 years ago by the late Terence O'Neill and Patrick Cumiskey was reckoned to be "one of the finest in Ireland and "still in perfect order."

At the end of its first season in Fingal League cricket, Balbriggan finished third in Division B, with a record of 7 wins, 6 losses and 1 draw. While Balbriggan CC may not have won the Fingal League, the club and the town were pivotal elements in its development because it provided visionary administrators, superb venues for finals and the annual dances and meetings which it hosted for many years.

In the 1930s, there was an upsurge of interest in cricket in Fingal, and Balbriggan CC reflected this general trend. The club had twenty two playing members and a large number of honorary members. The accounts were in a healthy state and the custom-built wicket on Market Green had been sponsored by Mr G. L. Mc Gowan. The captain for the season was Mr J. Purfield, Mr C. McCombe was vice-captain and Mr P. Daly was one of the officers on the committee. One of the first games in 1930 was against Knockbrack, and it commenced late because there was a procession at the church. Ayres took 5 wickets for Knockbrack, and the best batsman for Balbriggan was Kearns who scored 20 runs. Daly took 4 wickets for Balbriggan and Crilly took 1 wicket. Knockbrack won on a score of 42 to 41 and fielded very well. Unfortunately, the same could not be same for Balbriggan:

> Their fielding was very bad, particularly the younger members of the team. The older players were the better fielders; they were able to run much faster which is surprising.

As an example of creative thinking at Balbriggan CC, there was a raffle for a pound at the end of the game, and it was won by C. McCombe, the vice-captain of Balbriggan.

During this era, Balbriggan was a hive of cricketing activity, and in addition to Balbriggan CC, the British Legion also fielded a team There were also games on four successive evenings between visitors to the town and Balbriggan, and the honours ended up even, with the visitors winning two and Balbriggan winning two. A friendly was played on the Sunday between Balbriggan and the Pioneers (Dublin), and Balbriggan won easily chiefly due to the "excellent bowling of Duignan, who is a visitor to the town." There was a street league for children which drew big crowds to the games every evening. The reporter saw some "promising left-hand bowlers and for batsmen some of them could make their elders blush". In the semi-final of the street league, Mill Street beat Quay Street, 27 runs to 26. Jackie Dunne took 5 wickets for Quay Street, and Peter McAleer took 5 wickets for Mill Street, with J. Bissett taking 3 wickets and Jack Bissett taking 2 wickets. The final was played between Clonard Street and Mill Stret at the Market Green. There was a large crowd at the game, and "the cheering when a wicket fell could be heard all over the town". The best batsman was J. Bissett who scored 15 runs out of his side's total of 25, and the best bowler was Peter McAleer. The fielding of the Mill Street side was superior as "they swarmed around the wicket like a swarm of bees". Mill Street won the game, and in an aside, the team was praised for winning in adverse circumstances due to two of their members deserting them to play for another team, but the two players who initially were thought to be too small, came in and fielded well. The umpires were Messrs G. A. Cashell, and A. H. White, and Mr Lewis Whyte was the score marker. The winning team was presented with a cricket set.

For the 1931 season, G. L. McGowan was captain, the secretary was Mr J. A. Purfield, and the treasurer was Mr T. Reynolds. The season commenced on 3 May and Balbriggan was in Division B along with Balrothery, Ring Commons, Barnageera, Knightstown and Ballymadun. Balbriggan beat Knightstown very easily in one of the first games of the season. Knightstown only scored 17 runs, "being unable to stand up against the bowling of Daly and Howard and Mc Combe behind the wicket made some beautiful one-handed catches". Dignan and Mc Gowan made 18 runs between them, "thus making victory sure". The rest of the team took things easy, and all were dismissed for 25".

The most noteworthy element of the season was a cricket match on 29 June in aid of Balbriggan Parochial Funds which was played between the Married and Single men, with players selected from Balbriggan, Balrothery, Man-O'-War and Ring Commons. There was also a football match on Inch Lawn between Rush Mars and Balrothery Rangers for which the Parish Priest, Rev. J. Hickey had agreed to throw in the ball. This fund-raising activity illustrated the extent to which cricket clubs were centrally involved in Fingal as distinct from being a minority sport on the periphery of the community. The season ended with the Fingal League's first annual dance which was held in the Town Hall, Balbriggan, and attended by 150 couples.

For the 1932 season, P. J. Daly replaced Mr J. T. Ennis as President of the Fingal League, and Balbriggan CC proposed the formation of an Umpires' Association. There was general approval for this proposal and the issue was to be addressed more fully at a special delegate meeting on 24 April. This meeting was held, and the sixteen teams for the new season were arranged in Divisions A, B and C, but there was no reference to the formation of an Umpires' Association. For this season, Balbriggan played in Division B along with Ring Commons, Rush, Knockbrack Seconds, Balcunnin and Man-O'-War. The results to hand for this season are a win for Balbriggan against Balcunnin on a score of 43 to 27, and a loss by 4 runs in a friendly against Drogheda YMCA. Balbriggan also appeared to have been involved in one of the highlights of the season. The *Drogheda Independent* of 23 July 1932 referred to "one of the most marvellous bowling feats ever accomplished in the history of Fingal Cricket League". Balcunnin batted first and scored a total of 13 runs. There is then a typographical error because the report states that it looked as if Balcunnin would have an easy victory. By a process of elimination and by checking the teams which played in that division, the report should have stated Balbriggan. The Balbriggan reply foundered very quickly because "Murphy and Hoare found form, and it was amazing to see wicket after wicket fall in quick succession and final to see the visitors dismissed with the incredibly low score of three runs."

A street league was again organised, and the final between Balrothery and Mill Street was played over two innings per side. In an exciting game, Balrothery won by one run, and some of the legendary figures of Fingal cricket are mentioned in the report. Mooney and Russell were outstanding for the winners, and J. Cannon who carried his bat; Rex Canning, and J. Bissett starred for the losers. The winners received a cricket set which was presented by Mr Lewis Whyte.

Balbriggan had high hopes for the 1934 season and in the words of the *Drogheda Independent*, it had "got a very useful side together which should go well … in the Fingal League." The season started with a convincing win over Balrothery on a score of 91 runs to 43. Brogan, Grimes, and Howard were the outstanding batsmen and Coyle bowled well for the losers. However, it was not to be. Oldtown and Portrane contested the final, with Portrane winning by two wickets. Balbriggan members continued to play a pivotal role in the affairs of the league and in promoting the Fingal League's corporate identity. On 9 September 1934, the Fingal League played the Meath League at Balbriggan for a "handsome set of medals presented by Mr G. L. McGowan". In a low-scoring game, Fingal won by 5 runs (31 runs to 26); Griffin took 5 wickets for 14 runs and Hoare took 3 wickets for 11.

Over the next number of years, the initial enthusiasm for cricket seems to have diminished to a certain extent, and by 1935, the number of teams had fallen to ten. In 1936, there were still ten teams affiliated, but there were significant changes in the membership of the Fingal League. Garristown, Man-O'-War, Balrothery and Balbriggan did not affiliate, but Portrane and Naul Hill had re-entered, and the new teams were Blanchardstown and Clonsilla.

Mr John Reynolds died in 1938, and his obituary highlighted the fact that in his young days, he was one of the best bowlers in the area and turned out regularly for Balbriggan CC even when advanced in years and continued to be a threat to batsmen. Mr McGowan did not contest the 1938 General Election, citing pressure of business, but he continued to act as Secretary of the Fingal League.  Mr McGowan was in the news again in 1940. He became engaged in August 1940 to Miss Kathleen Barrett, and he was described as "dapper, debonair and endowed with tremendous energy". There was also a brief outline of his sporting achievements – a member of the Dublin GAA minors, and he also played with Pioneers, Balbriggan; played for Balbriggan Rugby team which won Provincial Towns Cup and helped Rush CC to win a Junior Cup. Prior to his wedding, the Fingal Cricket League made "a handsome and valuable presentation" to him at a supper in the Grand Hotel.

Although Balbriggan continued to be the venue for finals and dances, the club was dormant in 1940.  It re-formed in 1941, had a practice game on 11 May, entered the Fingal League and decided to elect a Committee at a later date. On 1 June, Balbriggan beat Ring Commons on a score of 36 to 35, the game was deemed to have been an "interesting struggle with some displays of cricket on both sides."

Normally, references to the dances sponsored by the Fingal League and the various cricket clubs are very positive, but Eddie Dunne of the Black Hills CC had cause to complain to the Town Commissioners about the state of the dance floor in the Town Hall. The substance which had been sprayed on the floor, had caused the dancers to sneeze and had destroyed their clothes. The Shamrock Ceili Band reiterated this criticism of the dance floor, and it appeared that the Badminton club was at fault because it was trying to make the floor less slippery.

The big event of the 1943 season was the game between a Fingal League Selection and a Phoenix Selection which was played at the Clonard Grounds, Balbriggan on 15 August. As part of a great occasion, the Balbriggan LSF Band played the teams on to the field, rendered a delightful programme and concluded with the National Anthem. After the match, the teams were entertained by the Fingal League Committee.

Balbriggan CC was back in cricket in 1945, and there is an account of a friendly game played in Balbriggan when the visitors were Navan CC. The best bowler for Balbriggan on the day was T. Hagan who took 3 wickets for 11 runs. In 1946, the club entered a team in the Leinster League, was placed in Section B of the Minor League and drawn against Monkstown Thirds in the Cup. There are no results available for Balbriggan's season, but the Minor League was won by

Phoenix Thirds and the Minor Cup was won by St James Gate, the conquerors of Malahide in the first round.

The 1950s was a very depressed decade in Ireland, with unemployment and emigration soaring, and there were difficulties in getting teams out in every sport. In 1961, there were only four teams affiliated to the League, but the positive developments were the re-forming of Ring Commons CC and Balbriggan. The newly formed Balbriggan Cricket Club held its first general meeting in the Library, Balbriggan. There was a satisfactory attendance, and "prospects of the game coming back to its former high position in the North County Dublin town are, at present, very encouraging." The officers elected were President: Mr P. J. Daly, Chairman: Mr F. X. McGowan, Secretary: Mr F. Seery and Treasurer: Mr T. O'Connor. In its first year back in Fingal Cricket, Balbriggan lost to Balrothery in the semi-final of the Fingal League.

Mr P. J. Daly died in October 1962 at the age of 88. He had come to Balbriggan in 1916 and had taken an active part in many community activities. In addition to the Fingal Cricket League and Balbriggan Cricket Club, he had a strong interest in local history and was for many years the local correspondent of the *Drogheda Independent*". One of his daughters was Eily Daly who was Town Clerk in Balbriggan from 1953 and had succeeded Mr William Bannon, a cricket man, who had served as Town Clerk for over 40 years.

During its early years back in cricket, the club had a nomadic existence, and played at various fields around Balbriggan including Glebe North FC, Bulls' Lane, and the Pump Lane field. Initially, the team only played in the Fingal League, but in 1966, Balbriggan entered the Leinster League, and the following season won the Leinster Junior Cup. In the semi-final, Balbriggan defeated Phoenix by 4 runs on a score of 112 to 108 and met CYMS in the final. Batting first, Balbriggan scored 90 runs, with opener, J. Quinlan, contributing 31 runs to this total. CYMS was bowled out for 54 runs, with Tom Colgan taking 5 wickets for 21 runs and Ray Kelly 5 for 27.

In 1968, Balbriggan re-located to Mosney, and won the Leinster Junior League having been undefeated for the season. Even more success followed on 15 September when Balbriggan beat Balrothery at the Man-O'-War ground to win the Fingal League for the first time. Balbriggan scored 62 runs, with the main contributions coming from Tom Colgan (13), Jack Harper (11), Martin Russell (11), Brendan Guildea (11) and Terry Quinlan (8), Balrothery was dismissed for 51 runs, with Tom Colgan and Ray Kelly sharing the wickets. The other members of the successful team were Seán Donnelly, Joe Kelly, Gerard Harper, John Quinlan, and Hugh Reilly.

During this season, the Leinster Junior Cricket Committee formed a Ground Inspection group with the avowed aim of ensuring that all junior grounds were up to the required playing standard. The initial emphasis was on the grounds outside Dublin city, and members of the committee visited the grounds of Balbriggan, Balrothery, Knockbrack, and the Man-O'-War. The committee's verdict was positive, and the hope was expressed that the Leinster Cricket Union "might be able to assist these clubs and keep the game alive in the country."

During the period of consolidation, there was an important development which was crucial in ensuring the continuity of cricket in Balbriggan. Balbriggan Juvenile Cricket Club was founded in 1965, and its officers and committee included people such as Richard Hammond, F. X. McGowan, Patrick Gavin, Eddie Guildea and Martin Russell. This club was a separate entity from Balbriggan Cricket Club but received assistance from Jack Harper, Pat McMahon, and Joe Kelly leading members of Balbriggan Cricket Club. The juvenile club's membership included players whose families had ties with other clubs in Fingal, so this may provide a partial explanation for the existence of two separate clubs. During 1966, Balbriggan Juvenile Cricket Club had twenty members, it entered the Leinster League at U15 level, and it also made itself available for friendly games with teams from Dublin, Meath, and Kildare. There were some difficulties experienced in getting teams from Dublin City to travel to Balbriggan, and in a prescient comment, the Evening Herald's Correspondent anticipated the establishment of a Fingal League Juvenile section which occurred in the early 1970s.

The Juvenile Cricket Club went from strength to strength, and in 1968, it began a series of coaching sessions in the Boxing Club Hall. Martin Russell had attended a course in Dublin which was facilitated by two top English coaches, Messrs Canning, and Holt, and along with Mr R. Hammond, put his knowledge at the disposal of the juveniles. There was another boost for juvenile cricket in Balbriggan when Mr J. N. Brophy, the Manager of the Munster and Leinster Bank and a former Irish International, agreed to assist with coaching.

With coaching progressing well, the next item on the agenda for the club was to obtain security of tenure so that a ground could be developed and in 1970, Fr O'Beirne gave the club access to its present ground. Unfortunately, some of the people who had been involved in the club from its early days did not get the opportunity to see it develop. Mr F. X. Mc Gowan died in 1969 and his brother, Mr G. L. Mc Gowan died in 1971.

## Balbriggan CC, 1971-2021

Balbriggan CC left Leinster League cricket in 1971 and did not return to the Leinster League until 1979. The treatment of the period from 1979 to 2021 will concentrate on Balbriggan in the Leinster League because Balbriggan's involvement in Fingal League cricket has already been discussed in a previous section.

Any review of the history of Balbriggan CC would be seriously deficient if it did not emphasise the role which the Harper family has played in the development of the club. Jack Harper was a founder member of the club when it was re-established in 1961; he captained the winning teams in the 1960s and he served as Chairman of the club for many years. He was also President of the Fingal League for a lengthy period. In addition to his administrative roles, he looked after the grounds, the wickets, and the ancillary facilities. Lila, his wife, provided the teas for visiting teams, and when Balbriggan had no clubhouse, the teas were served from Jack and Lila's house. They had a family of ten children, and the seven boys all played cricket. Gerald played for Balbriggan, Man-O'-War and The Hills. Noel travelled a slightly different route to The Hills; he played for Balbriggan and Balrothery before transferring to The Hills so that he could play senior cricket. The other five boys, Albert, Ivan, David, Clifford, and Brian, all featured on Balbriggan CC teams over many years, and the debt which the cricketing community of Balbriggan owes to the Harper family is incalculable.

Balbriggan began to have an impact on Leinster League cricket in the mid-1980s, and Albert Harper played a starring role. In July 1985, Balbriggan played Malahide IV in an Intermediate League game, and Albert scored 103*. In the semi-final of the Intermediate Cup, Balbriggan beat Addinstown in a low-scoring game; Addinstown batted first and scored 83 runs; Balbriggan reached the target for the loss of 7 wickets.

Balbriggan's opponents in the final were Railway Union, and the *Irish Times* devoted a considerable amount of space to a preview of the game. Alan Guildea, the captain, was mentioned for his match-winning innings of 29 in the game against Addinstown; Albert Harper was referred to "as one of the best bowlers in junior cricket", and there were also mentions for Clifford and David Harper, Brendan Guildea, Terry Quinlan, and Patrick Hickey ("strong middle-order batsmen"), and Hickey who had taken over 30 wickets already that season. The key men for Railway were Brian Cross, David Varian, Kieran Byrne, Stephen Fitzgibbon, Gavin Ralston. Cross and Butler had taken over 60 wickets between them, and the all-rounders were Peter Tipping and Trevor Dagg. Only 30 overs of play were possible on the Saturday, and Balbriggan ended on 87 for 5. When its innings resumed, it managed to bring its score up to 143 (P. Hickey, 25, B. Guildea, 24). In reply, Railway scored 108 with the wickets being shared between A. Harper (5 for 52) and P. Hickey (4 for 46).

In 1986, Balbriggan went through the season unbeaten, and won the Middle B League, the Fingal Cup, and it retained the Intermediate Cup. In the final of the Intermediate Cup, its opponents were Merrion IV, and the game was played at Phoenix. Balbriggan scored 132 and in reply, Merrion scored 104 runs. The Middle A League was won in 1987, and this meant that Balbriggan played in the Senior 3 League in 1988.

In 1988, the club's number had increased to such an extent that it was able to field three teams, and it was also very busy off the field as it sought to develop its ancillary facilities. In April 1988, it received a grant of £15,000 from the National Lottery as a contribution towards erecting a clubhouse. The club received approval from Fingal Council regarding tenure of the site, and this enabled it to apply for planning permission to build, with the proviso that the site for the proposed building was marked-out and approved by the Parks Department. That requirement proved to be contentious and developed into a saga which was only resolved eventually by two controversial Section 4 motions by local councillors and an on-site meeting which was attended by the councillors. The cricket club's argument was that the site favoured by the officials would encroach on the playing area, and the officials wanted a site which would not compromise the tennis club's facility to expand. On the basis of a revised plan, there was an agreement eventually, and the club was then in position to draw down the Lottery grant which had been held in abeyance until agreement was reached regarding the site.

The First XI had a solid start to its first season in Senior 3, and it commenced with a win over Phoenix by 2 wickets. Clifford Harper (3 for 18), Albert Harper (3 for 38), Pat Hickey (2 for 28) and Terry Byrne (2 for 18) took the bowling honours and there were runs for Colm Reilly (24), Brian Harper (10), Albert Harper (12), Paddy Byrne (15) and Pat Hickey (12). Old Belvedere played Balbriggan at Balbriggan Park, and was dismissed for 56 runs, with Albert Harper (4 for 21), Terry Byrne (3 for 11), Pat Hickey (2 for 12) and Clifford

Harper (1 for 6) taking the wickets. Balbriggan got the necessary runs without the loss of a wicket (Colm Reilly 29* and Brian Harper 23*).

In the return game against Old Belvedere, Albert Harper was again in form, taking 6 wickets for 34, and scoring 24 runs to give Balbriggan an easy win. By August, Balbriggan and Pembroke were the main teams in contention to win the Senior 3 League, and it appeared that the game on 20 August between the two leading teams would decide the league. It was important however not to lose focus because other games had to be played before that crucial game. Balbriggan had a comprehensive win over Railway Union despite not batting particularly well. Balbriggan struggled to 134 with Tony Clarke's 34, the only score of any consequence. Railway was dismissed for 59 with Albert Harper (4 for 30) and Pat Hickey being the main wicket-takers.

The top of the table clash between Pembroke and Balbriggan ended in a draw. Pembroke batted first and scored 167 runs for 5, with Pat Hickey taking 5 wickets for 79 runs. In reply, Balbriggan scored 131 for 7, with Albert Harper (53), Colin Reilly (38) and Ivan Harper (16*) being the main batsmen. For Balbriggan, it was vital not to lose the game, and the points garnered from the draw kept up its challenge for league honours. There was a 3 wickets win over YMCA and a walk-over from Phoenix, and Balbriggan's First XI had won the Senior 3 League at its first attempt. Balbriggan's Third XI reached the Minor Cup Final and it was due to play The Hills IV at Civil Service, but overnight vandalism at the ground meant that the game had to be switched to Rush. The Hills batted first and scored 171 for 9. Balbriggan was bowled out for 69, and the star of this game was the 70-years old Dick Byrne who took 5 wickets for 30 which included a hat-trick.

With the planning issues resolved and the finance in place, work on the new clubhouse started in November 1988, and was almost finished by April 1989. The project was spearheaded by Frank (Franco) Guildea, the club chairman, and Jack Harper, the vice-chairman, and most of the work was done by voluntary labour. The accommodation consisted of dressing rooms, toilets, showers, kitchen, and a dining area. Balbriggan's first game in Senior 2 cricket was to have been against the high-flying Man-O'-War team, but this game was rained off which meant that the match with Phoenix was the club's first game at that level. Any fears that Balbriggan might struggle in Senior 2 were allayed by the team's performance in the Phoenix Park. Clifford Harper took 5 wickets for 21 runs, Patrick Hickey took 5 for 18, and Phoenix was dismissed for 59 runs.

The required runs were scored for the loss of 2 wickets with Terry Byrne (24*) and Brian Harper (18) being the main contributors to the score.

In the Senior 2 Cup competition, Balbriggan was drawn against Leinster who scored 115 runs, and Balbriggan did the needful for the loss of 5 wickets. In the next round, Railway was bowled out for 69, and Balbriggan reached the target for the loss of 3 wickets. In the semi-final, Balbriggan played North Kildare who batted first and scored 187 runs. Albert Harper (3 for 22), Clifford Harper (3 for 43) and Patrick Hickey (2 for 42) were the wicket-takers. Balbriggan lost 2 wickets for 13 runs, but Patrick Hickey (46), Albert Harper (16), David Harper (37), Terry Byrne (50*), and Clifford Harper (14*) all contributed to a 4 wickets win. With North County winning the other semi-final, the scene was set for the first all-Fingal Senior 2 final since 1982 when The Hills had played Balrothery.

The final at Park Avenue was disrupted by rain, but Balbriggan having won the toss, elected to field first. The report in the *Irish Times* referred to Balbriggan's gamble as having paid off because North County's main two batsmen had been dismissed, and North County had only scored 27 runs in 18 overs. Afficionados of cricket in Fingal would have been well-aware that Fingal League teams managed to thrive on low scores because of the combination of clever bowling and very committed fielders. When the teams returned to Park Avenue on Monday, North County managed to bring its score up to 99 runs, with Anthony Rooney (28), Liam Rooney (15) and Alan Rooney (15) making some runs, and Albert Harper taking 3 wickets for 10. Balbriggan was dismissed for 75, with David Harper's score of 15, the only batting contribution of any consequence and James ("Bisto") Mooney was voted Man-of-the-Match for taking 3 wickets for 16 runs. It was not all doom and gloom at Balbriggan because Balbriggan Second XI beat Malahide IV in a close game in the final of the Junior Cup. Malahide scored 148 for 7, and Balbriggan reached the target for the loss of 9 wickets, with P. Donnelly (57) getting the top-score for Balbriggan.

In 1991, Balbriggan's First XI was playing in the Senior 2 League, but on a cursory appraisal of its results that season, there seemed to have been a major problem in scoring runs. For example, on 6 July, Balbriggan scored 102, and Pembroke reached the target for the loss of 3 wickets; on 17 August, Phoenix scored 230 for 3, and in reply, Balbriggan scored 121; on 31 August, Balbriggan scored 102 runs, and Rush got the necessary runs for the loss of 3 wickets. It was therefore no surprise, that Balbriggan was relegated to Senior 3 for the

1992 season, and it remained in that league until the end of the 1996 season, when it won promotion. Balbriggan played in the Senior 2 League from 1997 to 2000 when it was relegated again, and it was in the Senior 3 League until the end of the 2009 season.

The most noteworthy events on the cricket field in the 1992 season concerned Balbriggan's junior teams. The "evergreen" Franco Guildea made a triumphant return to cricket when he scored 25 runs for Balbriggan's Third XI in its victory over Pembroke. Guildea's knock ended when he was run out, and Balbriggan ended on 150 for 9 after 41 overs. In August, Balbriggan's Second XI won the Whelan Cup when it beat North Wicklow by 4 runs in the final. Brian Harper (34) and M. Carr (26) were the top scorers for Balbriggan, and Patrick Hickey took 4 wickets for 24. Despite the First XI's travails in Leinster League cricket, it won the Fingal Cup in a thrilling final against Balrothery. Full details of that game have already been described in the Fingal League section.

Arguably the most important event for Balbriggan CC in the 1992 season was the official opening of its clubhouse in September by Mr Ray Burke, T.D. and in his speech, Mr Burke made specific reference to the work which Mr Jack Harper had done for the club in his dual role of Chairman and groundsman. Among the other guests present were David Pigot, President of the Leinster Cricket Union, Thomas McGrane and Gerry Byrne of the Fingal League, and local politicians, Seán Ryan, Cllr Seán Gilbride, and Brian Purcell of the Balbriggan Town Commission. Albert Harper, the club secretary, provided some background details on the project; the total cost of the building was £20,000, and the club managed to raise £5,000 to supplement the Lottery grant of £15,000. He thanked the many people who had given their labour voluntarily, and he name-checked Franco Guildea, Jack Harper, Joe Donnelly, Jack Dunne, Franny Hogan, Willie Rooney, Dermot Murray, Paul Kenny, and Liam Rooney Snr, the overseer.

After the Whelan Cup win in 1992, it was five seasons before Balbriggan won another trophy, and again, it was one of the junior teams. Balbriggan's Third XI won the Minor Cup when it beat Leinster in the final in 1997, in a game that went on for three days due to weather interruptions. At the end of Day 1, Balbriggan had scored 52 runs for the loss of 2 wickets; on Day 2, Balbriggan completed its innings and ended on 89 runs, with Terry Morgan, the top scorer on 43 runs. In reply, Leinster had scored 21 for 5 in 16 overs when the rain came again. On Day 3, Leinster was all out for 40 runs, and it had been 35 years since Balbriggan had won the Minor Cup previously. Before the start of the new season, Franco Guildea died, and he had been one of the stalwart members of the club since it was re-established. The Minor Cup win in 1997 meant an awful lot to Franco because Alan, his son, had come out of retirement to play for the team. The First X1 had a lengthy sojourn in the Senior 3 League, but the Second X1 won Junior League C in 2004 and Junior League B in 2007.

In 2007, the Harper family suffered two devastating blows. Mrs Lila Harper died on 9 May, and Jack, her husband, died on 12 September. Mr and Mrs Harper had given a lifetime of service to Balbriggan CC and to the Fingal League. Jack Harper played his last game of cricket at the age of 61 and Lila had provided the teas for the players in her own home before there was a clubhouse and after that in the clubhouse. Their legacy would live on through their seven sons, all of whom had played for Balbriggan, and also served the club in the upkeep of the grounds and in administrative roles.

On the cricket field, Balbriggan managed to retain its Senior 3 League status after a struggle. The crucial game was played against North Kildare, and it started after a minute's silence as a mark of respect for the late Jack Harper. North Kildare was bowled out for 80, with Albert Harper taking 8 wickets for 12 runs, and Clifford Harper taking 2 wickets for 15. In reply, Glen Russell (30), David Harper (15), Albert Harper (15*) and Kevin O'Herlihy (15*) ensured that Balbriggan would be playing Senior 3 cricket in 2008.

In 2007, Fingal County Council agreed to undertake a development programme on the playing facilities, and over the next two seasons, Balbriggan CC's ground was improved out of all recognition. The orientation of the wickets was changed to North-South, the ground was extended, an artificial practice area was established, and the outfield was improved. With these improvements to the playing facilities, a number of top-class cricketers joined the club for the 2009 season, among them Gavin Morgan (brother of Eoin), Barry Archer, an Irish international, Duane Harper, a 5-times winner of Irish Senior Cup medals with North County and Ben Heathcote, an Australian. Roger Kear who had been unavailable for much of the 2008 season was available once again, and with this strong squad assembled, the immediate aim was to win promotion to the Senior 2 League.

The first games of the 2009 were season were an augury of things to come. Clontarf was bowled out for 64 runs, and there were  wickets for Duane Harper (2 for 18), Albert Harper (3 for 18), Roger Kear (2 for 14) and Paddy Martin (2 for 9). The necessary runs were scored by Barry Archer and Gavin Morgan. The next game was against North County, and an opening partnership of 132 (Heathcote 109*, Archer 68) set the game up, and Gavin Morgan (25), Asif

Iqbal (26) and Roger Kear (38) also made significant contributions to Balbriggan's total of 290 for 6. North County scored 128, with most of the runs coming from Derek Rooney (77), the former Balbriggan player. The wickets were shared among Duane Harper (3 for24), Albert Harper (3 for 25), Gavin Morgan (1 for 32), Roger Kear (2 for 28) and Paddy Martin (1 for 16). This pattern of facile wins continued into August, at which stage, Balbriggan had won 8 games out of 8. The ninth game was against Malahide, and Malahide was bowled out for 100. The wickets were taken by Roger Kear (5 for 32) and Paddy Martin (3 for 15). Heathcote (38*), Kear (24*) and Archer (20) ensured that another victory was achieved with consummate ease. Balbriggan was unbeaten for the entire season, and with the batting and bowling talent available to the team, it was ready to challenge for Senior 2 honours as distinct from hoping to maintain its place in the Senior 2 League.

By July 2010, Balbriggan was in third place in the Senior 2 League and had reached the final of the Senior 2 Cup for the first time since 1990. The only survivor from that team was the 50-years old Albert Harper who despite threatening to retire every year for the previous ten years was still taking wickets, and on the Saturday prior to the final, he had taken 5 wickets for 6 runs. In the final, Balbriggan was opposed by Phoenix, and Balbriggan was deemed to be favourites to win, although this was a mantle that never rested easily on a Fingal League team which much preferred to be underdogs. The Balbriggan squad was Paddy Martin, Glen Russell, Barry Archer, Adrian Harper, Duane Harper, Roger Kear, Albert Harper, Sarfraz Anwar, Seán Malone, Kevin O'Herlihy, and Hugh Cashell.

On the day after Eoin, his brother, had scored a Test century, Gavin Morgan had an absolutely brilliant, chanceless knock of 119* runs. With Barry Archer and Glen Russell both scoring 36, and Roger Kear weighing in with 52*, it was reasonable to speculate that a score of 278 for 3 was going to be well beyond Phoenix's reach. Duane Harper (4 for 21) and Sarfraz Anwar (2 for 16) ensured that Phoenix never got into the game. With Roger Kear taking 3 for 17, and Paddy Martin tying up the other end, Phoenix was all out for 79 runs. That win was the most significant result in Balbriggan's history, and the party that followed did not end until 7.00 a.m., although Albert was allowed to leave at 1.00 a.m. out of respect for his age. The honours kept coming for Albert, and in August, he was named Sports Star of the Month by the Fingal Independent. Despite this accolade, he confirmed that he intended to retire at the end of the season, but that was possibly open for negotiation. By January of the following year, Albert had decided against retirement because of requests from his teammates to carry on.

There was not a lot of information available for Balbriggan CC in the 2011 season. There was a reference to a defeat by Dublin University which was followed by a 4-wickets win over Malahide for whom Brian Gilmore scored 58 runs, and S. Kiran scored 38. Clifford Costello, a grandson of Jack and Lila Harper, took 3 wickets for Balbriggan, with Roger Kear and Paddy Martin also taking wickets. Barry Archer scored 95 from 66 balls, and he was aided by Gavin Morgan (22), but a middle order collapse meant that the bowlers, Duane Harper and Sarfraz Anwar had to come to Balbriggan's rescue to give Balbriggan the win.

In the Tillain Cup, Balbriggan played Malahide again, and in the words of the report, Malahide "crawled" to 106 for 8 in 20 overs. The man responsible for keeping the brakes on Malahide was Duane Harper who bowled 3 overs for 13 runs. Barry Archer continued his run of good form with a "quickfire" 48, but two-run outs meant that Duane Harper was on duty again to steer Balbriggan home. The Tillain Cup final brought together the new pairing of Balbriggan and Oakhill. Balbriggan scored 174 for 4 in 20 overs with big scores from Gavin Morgan (70) and Roger Kear (48*). In reply, Oakhill scored 117 for 8, with Duane Harper being the main wicket-taker with 3 wickets for 23 runs.

The Harper family suffered another bereavement in December 2011 with the death of David ("Bellies) Harper. David had played with Balbriggan CC for many years, and a match is played in July of each year for the David Harper Memorial Trophy.

2012 may possibly have been the best year in the history of Balbriggan CC. The First XI was entered in the inaugural National Cup, and it played against Cliftonville from the NCU in the first round. Cliftonville scored 170, and in reply, Barry Archer scored 100* and Glen Russell scored 49, to give Balbriggan a win by 9-wickets. The wickets were taken by Paddy Martin (3 for 32), Albert Harper (2 for 20), Duane Harper (2 for 35), and Ali Qasim (2 for 20).

In the next round, Balbriggan beat Galway by 108 runs. Glen Russell led the way with 39 runs, and Paddy Martin took 4 wickets for 20, Ali Qasim took 2 for 10 and Roger Kear took 3 wickets. The semi-final of the National Cup was an all-Fingal League clash between Balbriggan and Rush. Balbriggan batted first and scored a total of 172 all out; the main run-scorers were Sarfraz (61), Derek

Rooney (31) and Roger Kear (76). In reply, Rush was bowled out for 125, with Ali Qasim taking 3 for 34 and Albert Harper 2 for 27.

The final of the National Cup which was played at The Vineyard was a wonderful occasion. Balbriggan batted first but lost 2 wickets in the first over. Barry Archer and Adrian Harper (60) brought the score up to 97; at 118 for 6, Balbriggan was in serious trouble, but a 59-run stand between Nathan Rooney and Duane Harper gave Balbriggan renewed hope. Three quick wickets fell at that stage, and Balbriggan ended on 183 for 9. Muckamore was 28 for 3, and 60 for 4, but a fine innings by Kamtekar, the overseas player, was the difference between the two sides. He scored 68 which left Muckamore needing 50 runs off 8 overs. Richard Keates hit 34 runs off 18 balls, and that was it as far as Balbriggan was concerned. Muckamore won by 3 wickets, and its name would be the first on the National Cup.

In the final of the Senior 2 Cup, Balbriggan played The Hills CC at Malahide. The Hills scored 171 for 7, with Joseph Clinton top-scoring on 57. In reply, Barry Archer, the former Hills' player, scored 56, Glen Russell scored 43, and Balbriggan won by 3 wickets.

When the Senior 2 League table was published on 21 August, Balbriggan lay in 4th place with 3 wins, 2 losses and 3 no results. By early September, after a combination of wins, a defeat by Civil Service and results of the other teams going in favour of Balbriggan, it was in contention to win the Senior 2 League. By a strange irony, its last game of the season was against The Hills who needed a win to avoid relegation. The Hills scored 243 with Jonathan Andrews scoring 54 runs, but Barry Archer with 5 catches was the hero of the first innings as far as Balbriggan was concerned. In the reply, Balbriggan lost wickets early on, but Archer and Qasim put on 85 runs for the ninth wicket partnership to give Balbriggan a win by 2-wickets. With favourable results elsewhere  Balbriggan had completed the Senior 2 League and Cup double and would be playing in Division 2 (Senior 2 League in old money) the following season.

For a number of seasons, it was off-field initiatives which were the most noteworthy. In February 2013, there was a proposal at Balbriggan Town Council that the cricket ground be re-named "Jack Harper Memorial Park". The Fingal County Council had no objection in principle to the proposal but indicated that any commemorative plaque or stone would have to be provided by the club. The ground was re-named in April 2013, and a memorial plaque was unveiled which paid tribute to a great cricket man and a wonderful servant of Balbriggan CC.

In 2014, the club embarked on a 5-year development programme, with the most expensive item being an investment in new practice facilities which it was reckoned would cost somewhere in the region of £30,000. The membership of the Junior section had trebled in two years, and the extra practice facilities coupled with professional coaching structures were essential if the club was to reach the pinnacle of Leinster League Cricket – the Premier Division.

In 2016, Balbriggan's First XI was well in contention for promotion to the Premier Division, but a defeat by Terenure in mid-August rendered their prospects of promotion very slim. In the next round of games, Balbriggan had a comfortable win over North Kildare, but a narrow loss to Cork County committed Balbriggan to another year in Division 2. Balbriggan's Second XI ensured that some silverware came to the club during the season, and in the final of the Middle Cup, the Seconds played Castleknock who batted first and scored 181 runs. The wickets were taken by Raja Akber (3 for 22), Roger Kear (3 for 20), Waleed Iqbal (2 for 28), Agha Shariq (1 for 41), and Tariq Faheem (1 for 24). Faheem led the reply with a knock of 86*, and with Syed Mehidi (42) and Kear (38*) also contributing, Balbriggan reached the target in 28 overs. .

The following day, the Seconds beat North County IV in a top of the table clash, and this strengthened the Seconds' hold on the top place. North County had scored 183, but an opening stand of 100 of which Justin Kavanagh scored 50 gave the necessary impetus to the chase, and Balbriggan ended up with a victory by 7 wickets. The Third XI won OCD14 that season, and the following season, the Thirds won the YMCA Salver and OCD12.

Over the years, there has been a strong awareness in Fingal of the place of cricket in the social history of the area, and in August 2016, the Fingal County Council Heritage Officer organised a game of cricket at Ardgillan Castle to commemorate one of the first games of cricket played in Fingal between Ardgillan (Taylors) and Kenure (Palmers). On this occasion, The Hills and Balbriggan were the rival teams, and in addition to two International cricketers (Max Sorensen and Ciara Metcalfe), there was a blend of young and old on both teams. The first ball was bowled by Darragh Butler, Mayor of Fingal, and the Balbriggan team was captained by Albert Harper.

Between 2016 and 2019, Balbriggan's First XI just fell short each year in its quest for promotion to the Premier League, but during the close season of 2020, plans were put in place for a concerted drive for promotion in 2021. The first step was the recruitment of André Botha, the former Irish international as club coach. Greg Ford joined Balbriggan from Malahide, and Shahid Iqbal transferred to the club from Rush. There was already the nucleus of a very strong team in place, and there were also other new faces at Jack Harper Memorial Park which put Balbriggan as favourites for promotion to the Premier League.

Due to the Covid pandemic, the league was reduced to 7 games, and the top two teams would play off for a place in the Premier League. Balbriggan won 5 games, lost 1 and had 1 no result, and finished the season on 22 points. North Kildare finished second, and the play-off occurred at Sydney Parade on 12 September 2021. In terms of omens, that date was the 14th anniversary of Jack Harper's death, and Albert Harper expressed the view before the game that his father would be looking down on the Balbriggan team. Balbriggan batted first and got off to a flying start with Connor Fletcher scoring 81 runs. Further acceleration was provided by Greg Ford (61), Chris de Freitas (53*), Nathan Rooney (21) and Dylan Lues (30*) which meant that Balbriggan had achieved a total of 276 for 7. North Kildare wickets fell early to Lues (4 for 30) and Darroch (2 for 19), and the tail was finished off by Chris de Freitas (3 for 11). The margin of victory was 167 runs, and Balbriggan had achieved Premier League status for the first time in its long and distinguished history.

In 2020, Balbriggan CC celebrated 50 years at this present ground, and in 2021, the club had been in existence for 60 years. This is by far the longest continuous period of cricket being played in Balbriggan, and the members, past and present, deserve the highest commendation for the manner which they have developed their facilities, their teams, and provided a wonderful leisure-time activity. Cricket is part of the cultural and sporting heritage of Fingal, and people in Balbriggan have been pivotal in ensuring that cricket has been preserved and developed for this generation and for future generations.

Postcard no date.   circa 1912

Balbriggan from Wavin Silo (Joe Curtis)

Bob Spencer, Hosier, lived next door to Northern Bank (south side)

Community Centre

Garda

Balbriggan's Cricket Ground c 1965

Figure 3, Back: Michael Gavin, John Murphy, Jimmy Tolan, Alan Guildea; Front: Tom Murphy, Fr Comer, Patrick Gavin, Fr Murphy, Jim Brophy

Balbriggan Youth Cricket Club

G. L McGowan

## Jack Harper

## David Harper

## Clifford Harper

## Noel Harper

## Gerald Harper

## Ivan Harper

## Albert Harper

## Brian Harper

Balbriggan CC, 1988

John Mooney, Tom Fanning and Francis Morgan

Franco Guildea

Benton / Curtis 1999

© Benton / Curtis 19

Michael McInerney and Jimmy Richardson

© Joe Curtis 2005

2013

2019

## Albert Harper, Paul Smyth

## Gavin Morgan

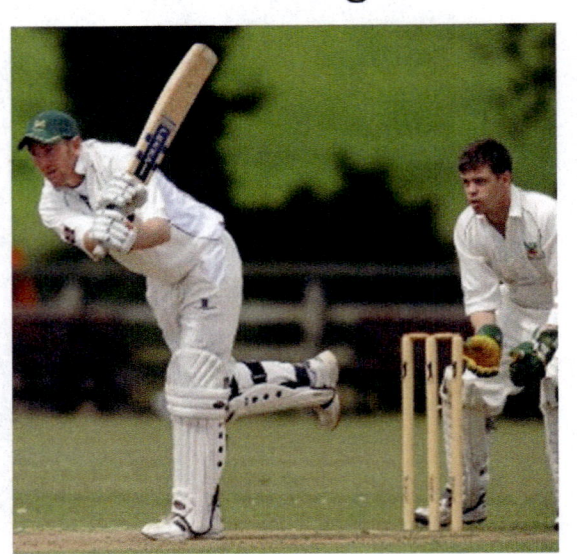

## Adrian Harper

## Roger Kear

Nathan Rooney

Tommy Geraghty and Kathy McCann

Barry Archer

Paddy Martin

Winners Balbriggan (©Tommy Geraghty)

# Chapter 10: Cricket in Malahide

## Early days, 1861-1914

Malahide CC was very firmly embedded in the "Big House" tradition because the club was established by the Hon. Richard Talbot in 1861 and played its home games on the grounds of Malahide Castle demesne. Although we are referring to Malahide as a club, it would be more correct to classify Malahide as a team, because concepts of club membership and organisational structures were very loosely defined. Matches were arranged by advertising availability in the national press or by issuing challenges. They were essentially social events, and there was no league structure as such so people played for whichever team invited them to play. For example, Arthur Samuels, who wrote the paper, "Early Cricket in Ireland", played for nine teams during his cricketing career. Anthony Strong Hussey of Westown House played for Westown, Naul CC, Balbriggan, Malahide, Phoenix, and Co. Meath. A. C. Blackburne played for Malahide and was Secretary of Balbriggan CC.

The club played its first game against Mr Crawley's XI on 15 June 1861 on Mr Crawley's ground. Paradoxically, Mr Crawley's XI had only seven players, and Malahide won with an innings and 13 runs to spare. Mr Gartlan of Malahide was singled out for the excellence of his batting and bowling, and Mr Byrne's underhand bowling was also deemed worthy of favourable mention. A return game was played at the "Nine Acres" in the Phoenix Park on the following Saturday. Mr Crawley was involved again, and his team was now called "The Amalgamated Amateurs". Messrs Gartlan and Byrne were again to the fore, and the "Amateurs" were bowled out for 38 runs. In reply, Malahide scored 98. "The Amateurs" fared slightly better in the second innings, and were bowled out for 48 runs, leaving Malahide the winners by an innings and nine runs. On this occasion according to the *Irish Times*, "the batting of Mr Crawley and bowling of Mr Glover deserve notice; and Messrs Gartlan, Byrne and Keegan batted well for the Malahide Club." Other games played during the 1861 season were against Charlemont (home and away) and Mr Casey's XI. Malahide lost to Charlemont in the away game because "the batting was not quite as good as usual with the exception of Gartlan whose defence was masterly. However, the fielding and bowling nearly compensated for this defect". In the return game against Charlemont, the weather conspired against Malahide because according to the *Irish Times*, "the day being wet between the innings proved most detrimental to the game". The final game of this season for which there was a report available was against a team organised by a person who played for Malahide in earlier games (Mr T. Casey) and resulted in a loss for Malahide on a score of 76 runs to 74. Mr Gartlan continued to star for Malahide, and he ended with the highest score (26 runs) of the game.

As a grand finale to this season, a sports day was organised in a field adjoining the cricket ground. The stratified nature of Irish society at this time is illustrated by an extract from the *Freeman's Journal* report of the event:

> There was a large assemblage present, including the gentry residing either permanently or for the season in this agreeable district and also a considerable body of the country people, to whom the sports, races and music were a great treat.

Members of the cricket club appeared to have dominated the different events. Mr H. A. Dillon threw a cricket ball 76 yards; Mr J. H. Byrne won the 100 yards race in a time of 15 seconds, and he also threw the 56 lb shot the farthest. He won the 440 yards race and Mr Dillon came second. Nobody had the temerity to compete against Mr Byrne in the 880 yards hurdle race, so he won this event on a walk-over. The sack race provided "great merriment" and the evening ended with a "grand display of fireworks."

From 1862 onwards, membership expanded to such an extent that the club was able to field two teams. The second XI played games against the Academic Institute on 24 May and Winton CC on 2 July. The logistical advantage for teams comprising of members of the gentry was the availability of the players for games on weekdays as well as Saturdays. For the game against Eblana, the wickets were pitched at 11.00 a.m. on Wednesday, 13 August 1862, the game against the officers of the 58th Regiment was also played on a Wednesday. Malahide played Ephemera on Tuesday, 5 July 1864, and the game against Civil Service was played on Friday, 24 June 1864. The match programmes for the next few seasons were broadly similar to the 1861 season with games being played against schools such as Rathmines, Santry and the Academic Institute, selected sides such as Eblana, Ephemera, Mr Otway's XI, club teams such as Winton, Civil Service and Kingstown and Army teams such as the 58th Regiment. From a logistical perspective, the availability of a train service was a tremendous asset in arranging games, and as a result, teams were very willing to travel to Malahide, or Malahide played most of its away games in the Phoenix Park and in what is now referred to as Dublin 4 because of the convenience of travel. The last train left Dublin for Malahide at 9.30 p.m., and there were trains from Malahide to Dublin from 5.50 a.m. onwards.

In 1863, Malahide had another Fingal rival with Balbriggan CC being re-established after a lapse of almost twenty years. Balbriggan played Malahide in its first game on Saturday, 25 July, with Messrs Blackburne and Hussey now lining out for Balbriggan. The main contributors to Balbriggan's first innings score of 73 were the Filgate Brothers (L Filgate, 34, T. Filgate, 14) and in reply, Malahide scored 54 in its first innings (T. Casey, 14). Balbriggan scored 28 runs in the second innings and Malahide needed 53 to win, but only scored 30 thus conceding bragging rights to the newly formed club.

In the 1864 season, the playing programme was expanded considerably, and Malahide CC played sixteen matches. The club received very favourable mention in *John Lillywhite's Cricketers' Companion for the Present Year*:

> The Malahide Club possesses an excellent ground, close to the village of that name, 9 miles north of Dublin and about 20 minutes by rail. It has been newly laid down and is situated in the delightfully picturesque demesne of Lord Talbot de Malahide... Malahide is a favourite marine village, the attractions of the game,... generally command a large attendance of the visitors and residents of the neighbourhood.

In 1865, the rivalry between Malahide and Balbriggan was renewed when the two teams played at Malahide. Malahide scored 115 runs (Messrs Downing, Gartlan, J. Kelly contributing respectively 20, 39 and 20); there were 29 extras of which 21 were wides. In reply, Balbriggan scored 88 runs with fine contributions from Mr Madden, 39 and Mr Blackburne, 21. The anonymous reporter in an untypically critical comment mentioned that "the fielding on both sides was good. The bowling of Malahide was excellent, whereas that of the opponents was not up to the mark".

In his report for the 1866 season, John Lawrence was unimpressed by the fact that Malahide had only played three games in the season:

> This club has not, we regret to say, shown so much life during the past as in previous seasons, although only hailing from a district within a few miles of the city: they seldom take a lesson from the metropolitan clubs. We hope during the season of 1867 they will show more vigour and venture away from home.

There was only a slight improvement in the 1867 season, with four games being played. Lawrence paid tribute to the indefatigable efforts of the Hon. Sec, Henry A. Dillon "who does all in his power to keep it together and play his team whenever he can get a suitable match". Ironically, Balbriggan CC which had been the recipient of high praise for its progress during the previous year, ceased to exist during the 1867 season.

In 1868, the slide was arrested, and Malahide CC was again on the crest of the wave. Twenty-four games were played, a new square was laid, and it was hoped to have a new pavilion in place for the start of the 1869 season. Pen Pictures of the squad were appended to the report for the 1868 season, and each player is the subject of fulsome praise. Pressure on space prevents the list being quoted in full but a few examples will provide an illustration of the style adopted by the anonymous author. For example, J. G. Felix, captain, is described as a "hard-hitter and good man all round; the 3 Caseys, T. J., E. H. and P. F., are "members of a family well known in the cricketing world and so good at everything it would be difficult to particularize (sic);"; the Hon R. G. M. Talbot is " a very steady bat and good point"; his brother, the Hon M. G. Talbot is "a very promising cricketer and remarkably fine bowler; " J. O. Jamieson is "a very showy bat, good bowler and perfect field" and A. S. Hussey is the complete all-rounder because he is a "very useful man, can bat and bowl well, and take any place in the field".

In 1869, the club played a 16-match programme, and a "handsome pavilion was erected." The number of members had increased vastly, and according to Lawrence, "among the Eleven may be found names well known to cricketers in England as well as Ireland". The teams which Malahide played were the eclectic mixture as before. There were selected teams such as the Cynics, the Ephemerals, Mr R. Barry's XI, Mr Blackburne's XI; military teams such as the Grenadier Guards, the 65th Regiment, the 56th Regiment and Dunbar's Royal Military Academy; school teams such as Kingstown School and teams from established clubs such as Dalkey, Pembroke, Navan, and Phoenix CC. In 1869, a second club (Waverly CC) was formed in Malahide, but it only played three games in the season.

In his report on the 1870 season, Lawrence expressed his concern regarding the balance in Malahide CC between social cricket and the pursuit of excellence. He referred to the distinguished initials (MCC) of the club and he speculated that the day might come if Malahide CC aimed "at being admitted into the ranks of the leading clubs in Ireland". He praised the "well-laid down ground and the handsome pavilion", but he suggested that Malahide should concentrate on playing recognised clubs possessing their own grounds. He saw minimal value in beating teams such as "Bummers, Chimney Pots, and Stragglers etc".

In the 1871 report, Lawrence was more complimentary regarding the 16-match programme which the club completed: "Malahide played several very good matches, amongst them the Garrison of Dublin and several of the regiments quartered in the town…. From being a small local club, it may now be looked upon as one of the leading Irish Clubs." However, it was also obvious that the club was not neglecting the social aspects of cricket, and when the military teams came to Malahide, "the ground of the club was enlivened by an unusually large attendance of the fair sex and the performance of a military band." Indeed, on one occasion, in a report on the game versus the 84th Regiment, equal prominence was given to players' scores and to the programme of music which the band played.

In 1872, the Waverly Club was absorbed into Malahide CC, with the result that the club had over forty members, and of this number, at least two-thirds were playing members. Lord Talbot continued as President, Major R. H. French was Vice-President, H. A. Dillon who was also Lord Talbot's Agent, combined the roles of Treasurer and Secretary, T. J. S. Casey was Club Captain and Hon. R. G. M. Talbot was the Deputy Captain. The principal players during this season were the Hon. R. G. M. Talbot, G. D. Casey, R. Manders, R. D. Jameson, J. Kirwan, Hon, M. G. Talbot, H. A. Dillon, A. S. Hussey (102nd Regiment), E. H. Woods, A. C. Courtney, T. J. S. Casey, A. S. Deane, H. Hussey, W. St. L Woods, S. D. Smith.

The 1873 season was a difficult one for the club because in August, Lady Talbot and one of her grandchildren died due to typhoid fever. As a direct consequence of these deaths, Malahide CC's match programme was curtailed, and only twelve games were played during the season. After the travails of 1873, the 1874 season was much more positive. The pavilion was repaired and re-roofed. The ground was in "much better condition and has played on the whole very well". The club fielded two teams, with the First XI playing twenty-three games, and the second XI played eight games.

Malahide CC continued to thrive in 1875. It played a 20-match programme, and was according to Lawrence, "fast gaining a position second to none among the clubs of Ireland." Malahide defeated Phoenix, the self-styled Premier club of Ireland, chiefly due to a magnificent innings of 111* by T. J. S. Casey. [Incidentally, Mr Casey had the unique distinction of being the first player to score a century for Dublin University and for Malahide. His 103 for Trinity was scored against Leinster on 11 June 1867. Earlier, the club had been criticised for not venturing too far from Malahide, but during this season,

Malahide played and defeated the Ulster Club, Belfast at the Civil Service Ground.

The 1876 season was not as successful, because there were difficulties in fielding strong teams due to the unavailability of some of the leading players. The club played a 17-game programme, but the top player, T. J. S. Casey, only had 4 innings during the season, and it must be borne in mind that each side had 2 innings in a game. In terms of appearances, J. J. Byrne had 25 innings, and the next highest were F. B. Collier with 15 innings and J. Robertson with 13 innings. Lawrence's match reports contain frequent references to "weak" teams being well-beaten by Leinster, Phoenix and a "weak and short" team being beaten by Navan.

The problems which had been flagged in 1876 became more pronounced in 1877. Lawrence described the season "as a very poor one indeed" for Malahide CC. There were difficulties in getting the ground into playing order; several prominent members declared themselves unavailable at different times and this was illustrated by a game against Phoenix being called off "in consequence of Malahide not being able to get up a team". A limited match programme (8) was completed and the results in the games played were indifferent; Malahide won three and lost 5 games.

For the 1879, 1880 and 1881 seasons, Malahide CC had no entry in Lawrence's Handbook. An exhaustive search of national and local papers failed to elicit details of games played, and it seems reasonable to conclude that cricket ceased in Malahide for a very considerable period. A Land War commenced in 1879, and the existence of a very prominent landlord in the area such as Lord Talbot meant that members of the gentry had concerns far removed from cricket during this time. On 6 December 1880, a meeting was convened in Malahide for the purpose of establishing a branch of the Irish Land League. In attendance were John Dillon, MP and Michael Davitt, and the meeting was chaired by Mr Andrew Kettle, whose opening remarks gave a foretaste of things to come:

> Malahide might be looked upon as the centre of that district of Fingal, and … they could not find a district better rented and better taxed, and notwithstanding this, better farmed. The enterprise of the people there had led to competition which had placed the rents at an unmakeable and unplayable standard. The great bulk of the occupiers of land there were completely in the power of landlordism.

During the different addresses by the speakers, there were calls for landlords to be boycotted and catcalls when the names of individual landlords were mentioned. The jeering grew to a crescendo during Michael Davitt's speech, and his message for the landlords of the area was as follows:

> I can tell the Howths, the Ion Trant Hamiltons, the Talbots, the Palmers and Moncks and the rest of them,.... there is no rampart of injustice in Ireland now which Irish democracy cannot scale and no garrison of landlord oppression which the weapons of the Land League ------- justice, reason and combination, cannot bring to the ground... Stand together... and landlordism will soon be compelled to give up the ghost before the national demand of the land for the people and quit Dublin County and Ireland for ever.

Many of the landlords were patrons of cricket clubs so it was obvious that they were not going to be involved in sporting activities when there were acts of violence being perpetrated on people, property, and livestock. The passing of the Land Acts brought a period of comparative calm, but the Gaelic Revival of the mid-1880s onwards caused general support for cricket to be eroded further.

What of Malahide CC in this cultural milieu? The club was re-formed in 1891 and was the subject of a letter to the *Irish Times*. A gentleman, E. J. Sedgewick journeyed to Malahide by train to listen to the band of the Royal Irish Constabulary, which was due to play at St James's Square, Malahide. Unfortunately, when he arrived in Malahide, there was no sign of the band, because it had been re-located "to some little cricket ground in some remote corner of the district." During 1891, there are records of at least six fixtures. Games were played against Jervis Street Hospital (home and away), Balbriggan Wanderers, "Old Stagers", Mr Godley's XI and Naul. A fixture was made with Belvedere College, but there was some confusion regarding dates, and there is no evidence to show that this game was played. The team which played against Balbriggan on 8 August was J. Daly, J. McBlaine, S. J. Guest, J. C. Collins, T. H. Robertson, R. T. Robertson, J. G. Musters, H. Wallace, G. Burton, J. Wallace, P. J. Kieran. In terms of continuity between the two eras, J. J. Byrne, the outstanding athlete, played against Naul, and A. S. Hussey was now playing for Naul. The other members of the team which played against Naul were J. Robertson, S. J. Guest, F. O. Stoker, W. Deverill, H. Wallis, (sic), Capt Musters, J. McBlaine, A. Wallis, T. Cannon, J. H. Robertson, and Dr Elliott. It is noticeable that the papers have dispensed with using the title, Esquire, and only two players are given titles, Capt Musters and Dr Elliott. It is a matter of conjecture whether this reflected cricket in Malahide becoming more egalitarian or if the members of the gentry were no longer members of the club.

For the 1892 season, a meeting of Malahide CC was held in the Reliance Assurance Office, O'Connell Street. The news item referred to the club as being "resuscitated" and it was reported to be in a "most flourishing financial condition", with the sum of £50 in credit. It was decided to employ a Notts colt as professional coach and to commence playing in early April. The playing programme for the 1892, 1893 and 1894 seasons followed broadly the same pattern as has existed during the 1870s. There were games against club sides (Leinster Seconds, Pembroke, Workingmen's CC, Cursis Stream, Wanderers, Phoenix, Clontarf), army and police teams (the Duke of Cornwall's Regiment, the Army Service Corps, the RIC, Scots Guards), rural teams (Athboy, Reynoldstown, Stedalt, Dundalk), hospital teams (Adelaide), business house teams (Dublin Metropolitan Journalists and selected teams (Mr Donnelly's XI and Mr Alleyne's XI). Stedalt was in the "Big House" tradition and played its home games on the demesne of Mr Tunstall-Moore who was a notable patron of cricket. When he died at the early age of 42, his obituary mentioned that "as a cricketer he had few equals in local combinations and on his invitation leading clubs tried conclusions on his perfectly equipped green at Stedalt." Malahide had a very busy season in 1894. Most of its games were now against club sides (Pembroke, Sandymount, Phoenix, Chapelizod, North Strand, Co. Wicklow, Civil Service, Co. Meath, Wilton, and Leinster. The only business house team which it played in 1894 was the Great Southern and Western Railway, and there was a game against the Army Service Corps. A significant proportion of Malahide's games were played at home which showed the value of convenient access to the rail service. The other factor which explained the unequal proportion of home and away games is that many of the junior teams did not have their own grounds but depended on the generosity of other clubs for access to facilities when the resident club did not have a game on the ground.

While the senior clubs continued to be opposed very strongly to the concept of competitions and league structures, the junior clubs started to make tentative steps during the early 1890s towards putting structures in place. Malahide CC was represented at a meeting of junior clubs in 1894 which sought to put the "Leinster Branch of the Irish Cricket Union on a proper basis". At its AGM in January 1895, the Leinster Branch decided to organise a cup competition for junior clubs and schools. Seven clubs (Sandymount, Melrose, Westmeath, the Land Commission, Clontarf, Athy and the High School) entered the inaugural competition. The final between the Land Commission and Athy was played at the Phoenix Park on 14 September, and Athy emerged victorious in a two-innings per side game.

Although Malahide CC fulfilled a 19-game programme during the 1894 season, there are no reports of cricket being played in Malahide between 1895 and 1900, although a team photograph has been located which may relate to 1897. Games may have been played and reports not provided to the local and national papers, but this is a matter for further research.

At the same time as Malahide CC appeared not to be playing cricket, the cricketing scene in Leinster was changing. Junior clubs were lobbying for a Junior League to be organised so that structures could be put in place and fixture-making could be co-ordinated. The columnists in the *Evening Herald* and the *Irish Daily Independent* were supportive of the junior clubs' demands, with the *Irish Daily Independent* publishing unofficial league tables at various intervals during the 1900 season. In the Junior Cricket Gossip Column of 5 June 1900, the correspondent gave vent to the perceived grievances of the Junior Clubs. He argued that cricket in Ireland was in decline because of "class distinction", and he suggested that there were cricketers playing on Sundays who were as good if not better than many of the "first-class" cricketers. He recommended that the Junior Cup should be open to all clubs who wished to enter it, and not confined to those clubs whose members were wealthy enough to rent and maintain grounds. He took to task the clubs who were unwilling to arrange matches with their less fortunate brethren, and in a telling play on words, he suggested that the possession of private grounds did not necessarily imply that the "owners are gentlemen". The demand for a junior league built up momentum, and on Friday, 29 March 1901, the Leinster Junior League was formed. The Junior League was divided into two divisions, with seven teams in each section. From a Malahide perspective, the teams in the league were particularly significant, because many of these clubs had played against Malahide over the years. In Division A were Sandymount, Leinster Seconds, Old St Mary's, Clontarf, Pembroke Seconds, Civil Service Seconds, and GS and W. R; and in Division B were Richmond Asylum, Beaumont, Ordnance Survey, Iveagh, Old King's Hospital, Greenmount, and Acme.

Thanks to the brilliant work of some members of Malahide CC, there is photographic evidence to show that the club was definitely back playing cricket in 1901. Included in the photograph are Tom Kettle, academic and poet, Charles Adams, an Irish rugby international, and his brother, Archibald. With senior cricket and junior league cricket now occupying space on the national press, there are less accounts of the friendly games played during the season. Malahide CC played Skerries on 29 June 1901 and won by 4 wickets, having successfully chased the Skerries' total of 20 runs. The club was listed as having a home game against Greystones on 30 August, but it was not possible to ascertain the result.

For the 1902 season, a new Secretary, Archibald Adams was elected, the AGM was held at Mr Cook's, Main Street, Malahide and five new members were enrolled. The club was now able to field two teams, and a comprehensive match programme was completed. Among the teams which played against Malahide during this season were Clontarf, Molyneaux, Balbriggan, Greenmount, Beaumont, Drumcondra, Myra, Calaroga, Ordnance Survey, Acme, and Irish Railway Clearing House CC.

During the 1903 season, Malahide again fielded two teams and played at least 23 games, with its final game of the season being played against Clontarf on 1 October. The club entered the Leinster Junior League in 1903, but it did not have the most auspicious of starts. By 11 July, it had only played two games in the league, and it had no points. It had drawn the game against Iveagh, but unfortunately was deducted the point for fielding an ineligible player. The club played Beaumont on 3 August, and there were four points at stake because Beaumont had no home ground. Beaumont scored 71 runs in the first innings, and Malahide scored 20 in reply, with extras (7) being the chief contributor to the total. Malahide lost 5 wickets for 36 runs in the second innings, and Beaumont were declared the winners by an innings. The best bowlers for Malahide were Adams, C. and Tyler, and the main batsman was Smyth who scored 18* in the second innings.

The match programmes for the 1904 and 1905 seasons were broadly similar to the previous year. In 1905, Archibald Adams was elected to the Committee of the Leinster Cricket Union, and the club held "a most successful" concert in the Tea Rooms, Malahide on Wednesday, 1 March 1905. The club was in the news in late July 1905 for a less salubrious reason. The Medical Officer had drawn attention to the fact that there was "nuisance inside the walls at the entrance to the cricket field, both dangerous and injurious to public health." This matter was investigated by Mr P. Cannon, and he named the persons responsible for depositing the contents of privies at the entrance to the cricket ground. Notice was served on the parties not to offend again.

The 1906 season was a successful season for the club. It fulfilled a 20-match programme which included a game against a Trinity team which was entitled the Long Vacation team. Among the other teams which it played were Clontarf, Sandymount, Drogheda, Pembroke, Leinster, Civil Service, Croydon, Workingmen's CC, RSPU, Richmond Asylum and GSWR. Malahide Seconds contested the Junior League Final against Clontarf Seconds on 15 September 1905. At close of play on Saturday, Clontarf needed 46 runs to win with 6 wickets in hand. The reporter on the *Irish Daily Independent* was not too impressed with Clontarf's attempt to chase the score when play resumed on Monday evening. In his words, Clontarf "failed miserably. Down they went like nine-pins before the Malahide bowling." The 6 wickets were lost for 36 runs, and the reported deemed the result "a big surprise". The *Drogheda Independent's* report was more positive, and it commented on the "admirable bowling of Adams, backed up by splendid fielding". Harper (sic, it should have been Hooper) took "2 magnificent catches", and the game which was fought with "great keenness" was witnessed by a "good crowd". The Malahide team on this historic occasion was E. Crowley, P. Powell, D. Murray, A. Adams, T. Courtney, Taylor, H. Holton, W. Hooper, J. Reardon, W. Perrin, and C. O'Shea.

After the excitement of the 1906 season, it was difficult to ascertain if Malahide played any cricket between 1907 and the outbreak of the first World War. There are no fixtures given for Malahide during this period, and by checking the fixtures of clubs such as Phoenix, Civil Service, Croydon and Leinster, there are no games fixed against Malahide. Civil Service listed home and away games against Malahide for the 1908 season, but Malahide's name does not appear on the league table for that season, so it appears that the games were not played. There were twelve clubs entered in the Junior League for the 1909 season, and among new entrants to the league were Croydon Park, Palmerstown, Dublin Jewish Association, Pembroke Wanderers, GSWR, but there is no sign of Malahide CC.

It appears therefore until other information comes to hand that Malahide CC played cricket from 1861 to 1877, 1891 to 1894 and 1901 to 1906. The absence of cricket from 1914 until 1925 is readily explained by a combination of the Great War, the 1916 Rising, the War of Independence and the Civil War, but the other blank periods are more difficult to explain and require further research.

## Malahide returns to League Cricket

When Malahide returned to league cricket in 1925, the cricketing environment in Leinster had undergone a fundamental change. The cataclysmic events of the previous eleven years and their consequences forced the senior clubs to abandon their distaste for competitive league structures, and the Leinster Cricket Union was founded in 1919. The other major change for Malahide CC was that it relocated to its present ground on the Dublin Road.

The teams which entered the junior cup for the 1925 season were Carlisle, Raheny, St Pauls, Pembroke Wanderers, CYMS Seconds, Leinster Thirds, *Irish Times*, Blackrock Hospital, Merrion, St James's Gate, Jacobs, Monkstown, St John's, Wills, YMCA Seconds, Sandymount Seconds, RSPU Thirds and Malahide. Among the players who lined out for Malahide during 1925 and 1926 seasons were C. and A. Adams, G. and K. O'Neill, E. Crowley, J. Finch, J. Keddie, F. Fitzsimmons, S. Mills, K. Healy, W. Taylor, D. O'Brien, V. Stack, N. Tiernan, W. Polley, T. Burke, A. Weldon, T. McMahon, J., and C. McCreadie, G. Harrison, A. Spadaccini. Some of the names on the above list (C. and A. Adams) had played for Malahide before World War 1, and with other names such as the O'Neills were to render wonderful service to the club over many years. The club fielded a second team in 1926 and in a departure from existing practice, it indicated its willingness to play Sunday fixtures away.

For the next four seasons, 1927, 1928, 1929 and 1930, the level of commitment to the players to their club was self-evident, and team-sheets showed minimal changes on a weekly basis. The 1930 season was a successful one as both Malahide teams reached finals. At that stage, the leagues were divided into sections, and there were play-offs to decide the eventual league winners. The Seconds played Leinster IV at the Imperial Tobacco grounds at Crumlin but lost by 34 runs. Leinster scored 75 runs, and restricted Malahide to 41 runs. The Malahide team on the day was C. McCreadie, J. O'Hanlon, J. Armstrong, H. Payton, L. F. Hughes, J. Scott, J. Moran, A. Spadaccini, J. McCreadie, K. Talbot, and J. Richardson. The top scorer for Malahide was J. McCreadie, with 13*, while J. Armstrong took 4 wickets for 26 and H. Payton took 3 for 26.

The First XI played the National Bank in the Junior Cup final at the Civil Service Ground and won on a score of 105 runs to 43. The Malahide team on that glorious day was K. O'Neill, H. Peyton, E. Crowley, S. Mills (13), C. Hughes, L. Hughes, S. Whieldon (18), T. O'Hanlon, J. Keddie (11), J. Armstrong (10*), and R. Harris. The successful bowlers were K. O'Neill (2 for 16), J. Armstrong (3 for 11), C. Hughes (2 for 6) and S. Mills (1 for 7).

During the next decade (1931 to 1940) the commitment of the players to their club continued to be self-evident, not just in terms of playing regularly, but also in becoming involved in the administration of the club. This is illustrated by a list of officers elected at the AGM in 1931. The patrons were Lord Talbot de Malahide and Mr M. G. Jameson; President: Mr George Bolton; Hon. Sec: Mr Arthur Spadaccini; Hon. Treasurer: Mr E. Crowley; Captain: Mr Kevin O'Neill; Vice-Captain: Mr S. Mills; Committee: Messrs J. Hughes, C. Hughes, J. Mc Creadie, J. Keddie, and J. Scarff.

In 1932, Malahide CC was playing in the Intermediate League, and when teams are promoted, it invariably takes time for the team to be accustomed to the higher standard in the new league. No trophies were won during the season, but the club awarded its "Cricket Club Cup" for all-round efficiency, batting, bowling, and fielding to Jackie O'Hanlon, who during the season "gave a brilliant and masterful display". During this transitional period, the club introduced younger players such as A. B. Robertson, and he was to have a major influence on Malahide CC over the next thirty years. The members also showed that they valued the social aspects of the club, and in 1936, about 200 guests attended the annual dance at the Grand Hotel. The *Irish Independent* report gave the names of practically every attendee, but brevity demands that in this instance, only the names of the Committee members are named: Messrs E. J. Crowley, K. O'Neill, J. H. McCreadie, L. F. Hughes, C. J. Hughes, A. B. Robertson, L. P. Boyle, and G. McSwiggan.

In 1938, the Leinster Cricket Union reduced the number of teams in the Senior League to 6, and it formed a Qualifying League. This initiative was intended to increase the interest of players and the general public, but strangely there was no automatic promotion and relegation. Qualifying teams would only be promoted when they had proved "their mettle". This change had two consequences insofar as Trinity would now be able to complete its league programme and Malahide was promoted to the Qualifying League. The other teams in the Qualifying League were YMCA and Civil Service who had been relegated from the Senior League, Monkstown, Carlisle, and Imperial Tobacco. It was hoped that by freeing up some weekends, clubs could undertake tours and play friendly games with teams outside Dublin.

Malahide topped the Qualifying League in 1938, and as a result was invited to play in the Senior Cup in 1939. The team reached the semi-final where its opponents were Phoenix. According to the report in the *Irish Press*, "Malahide put up a good performance, considering the exceptionally strong side fielded by Phoenix and knocked up a total of 138." However, Malahide's fielding was not up to the standard of the batting, and Phoenix reached the target in $1\frac{1}{2}$ hours with the loss of only two wickets. The main contributors for Phoenix were F. M. Quinn (52*) and J. C. Boucher (41*). For Malahide, the successful bowlers were Hughes (1 for 30) and Armstrong (1 for 50). Later in this season, the First XI produced a wonderful performance against Monkstown at Serpentine Avenue. Monkstown had scored 180 for 5 wickets, but the last 5 wickets fell for the addition of only 7 runs. The successful bowlers for Malahide were Quinn (4 for 42) and Robertson (3 for 52). In reply, Malahide had a second wicket stand of 170 between Armstrong and Robertson, and the Monkstown total was passed for the loss of three wickets. Armstrong made 90 in what was described as a "grand freely-hit innings", and Robertson scored 102 by "right good hard-hitting cricket". 415 runs were scored in this game, and in the words of the reporter, it was "an example for the seniors". However, this level of performance was not maintained for the season, and the Qualifying League was won comfortably by YMCA. Malahide's record was played 9 games, won 4 and lost 5.

By virtue of very settled squads and strong leadership through the club, Malahide CC was the dominant force in Leinster Junior cricket during the 1940s and early 1950s. The run of successes commenced in 1941 when in the words of the *Drogheda Independent*, Malahide won the "much-coveted" Intermediate Cup for which twenty-two teams had competed when it overcame Clontarf Seconds at the Postal Services Ground. The main contributors on the day were A. B. Robertson (58) and J. Armstrong (26), and Clontarf was beaten on a score of 154 to 128 runs. The Intermediate Cup was retained in 1943 when Malahide beat Pembroke Seconds in a very low-scoring game. Pembroke was all-out for 26 and Malahide reached the target for the loss of 2 wickets. In 1944, the Intermediate League was won after a play-off against Clontarf Seconds.

The Senior 2 Cup competition was inaugurated in 1942, and Malahide won it in 1945 by beating Cremore in the final. The Malahide team was I. Cashell, N. Mc Connell, H. Darlington (30), C. Hughes, J. Armstrong, J. J. Hughes, Jackie O'Hanlon (38), A. B. Robertson, R. Gilmore (13), H. D. Cashell and H. Booker. A. B. Robertson took the main bowling honours with 5 for 47, and he was ably assisted by Joe Armstrong, 3 for 37, and Cyril Hughes, 1 for 26. To make the season complete, Malahide Seconds won the Minor League Cup by beating 3rd OBU on a score of 94 to 93.

The Senior 2 Divisional League Final was won in 1946 by beating Carlisle at Clontarf. Malahide batted first on a pitch "admirably suited to [the] spins and breaks" of Samuels who took 7 wickets for 16 runs, and bowled Malahide out for 48. According to the *Drogheda Independent*, Malahide was "undaunted", and the steady bowling of Robertson (4 for 12) and Armstrong (6 for 29), backed up by the "brilliant keeping by Des Cahill (sic, should have been Cashell) and the keenest fielding", left Carlisle all out for 43 runs. During this season also, a junior interprovincial game was played between Leinster and Ulster, and Malahide provided two players, A. B. Robertson (Capt) and N. McConnell.

Malahide went one better in 1947 by winning the Senior 2 League and Cup. In the cup final against Cremore, John Neville, formerly of Portrane, was the match-winner for Malahide. The First XI was undefeated for the entire season, and the Second XI also won a League and Cup double. In the final of the Junior Cup, Malahide Seconds defeated 3rd OBU on a score of 97 to 6, while Butler and O'Hanlon shared the wickets. The top scorer for Malahide was J. O'Neill (31). The *Evening Herald* summed up the double, double season with the pithy comment – "some going". At representative level, A. B. Robertson again captained the Leinster Junior team in its game against Ulster at Lisburn, and he was joined by two Malahide colleagues, I. Cashell and J. Neville. This season also, there was a trip to the Mardyke when Malahide Firsts beat Cork County.

In 1948, the Senior 2 League and Cup double was repeated. Malahide again played Cremore in the cup final at Sydney Parade and was in some trouble early on until an eighth wicket partnership of 88 between A. B. Robertson (73) and R. Gilmore (30) turned the tide. In reply, Cremore only scored 59 with J. Armstrong taking 7 wickets for 33 runs. In 1949, the League was retained for the 4th season in a row, by beating CYMS in the Divisional Play-Off. The five in a row was achieved in 1950 when Malahide beat Clontarf in the Divisional Play-off at Rathmines on 14 September. Malahide scored 158 runs, and Clontarf's reply was 123 runs. The "deadly duo" of Robertson and Armstrong took the wickets, with Robertson taking 7 wickets for 61 runs and Armstrong, 3 for 50. Malahide Seconds won its section in the Intermediate League but was beaten by Old Belvedere in the Divisional Play-Off. By comparison with previous years, 1951 was somewhat less successful, but the Second XI won the Intermediate League, and A. B. Robertson, J. Neville, and I. Cashell were selected for the Senior 2 League side to play against the Senior 1 League side.

For the 1952 season, the Malahide First XI was strengthened by the arrival of that wonderful all-round sportsman, Paddy Neville. In the play-off for the Senior 2 League, Malahide played Old Belvedere at Rathmines. At the close of play at the end of the first day, Malahide had scored 188 runs, with contributions from H. Darlington (71) and an eighth wicket partnership of 76 runs between R. Gilmore (35) and G. O'Neill (47). Malahide had also taken 5 wickets for 60 runs, and the other 5 wickets fell on Monday for 27 runs leaving Malahide very easy winners. Robertson took 4 wickets for 35 and Armstrong took 5 for 25.

By virtue of winning the Intermediate Cup in 1951, Malahide's Second XI was invited to play in the Irish Junior Cup. In the semi-final of the Leinster Zone, Malahide played Longford, and the first game ended in a tie. Longford won the replay by 3 runs after a titanic struggle, and the *Longford Leader*'s report was a classic of its type. Longford, a team "which is struggling for its existence" defeated a Malahide team composed of senior and intermediate players. With Malahide needing 4 for a win and with one wicket in hand, Pickett of Malahide was given out LBW with a ball from Smith, and without a hint of bias, the reporter was able to assert that this ball would have hit the middle stump. The best player for Malahide on the day was Billy Deane who scored 51 runs.

Unusually, Malahide also entered a team in the Fingal Cup, but did not fare too well in the game against Skerries on a wicket which the reporter described as being "desperate". Skerries scored 85 runs and then for Malahide, J. O'Hanlon, and D. Kerr "hit out lustily for a merry 39 runs before being separated. The rest of the visiting batsmen failed to impress, and the innings closed with the total at 48". Jimmy Walsh took 5 wickets, including a hat-trick for Skerries, while for Malahide, H. D. Cashell, normally a wicketkeeper, took 6 wickets for 25 runs. Malahide's Second XI was more successful than the Fingal League Cup team, and it rounded off a very fruitful season by winning the Intermediate Cup.

### Malahide joins Leinster Senior League

At its AGM in 1952, Malahide voted to apply for Senior status. The fact that Malahide's record in Junior Cricket over the previous twelve years had been unsurpassed, should have made it impossible to refuse the application, but each of the existing senior clubs had a representative on the Senior Executive, and there was always the fear that allowing a team to join the league would result in the introduction of relegation. Once the Executive decided that this would not occur, Malahide was assured of promotion to the Senior League. Malahide thus became the first club outside the greater Dublin Area to achieve Senior League status, and for its first season in senior cricket, the captain was A. B. Robertson.

For the 1953 season, there were some new faces at the Village. Tommy Dawson from Cremore and D. Rimmer, on holidays from India were valuable additions to an already strong squad. Managers of teams which are promoted often hide behind the cliched concept of consolidation being the main objective, but Malahide's season got off to a tremendous start by beating Leinster at Rathmines. This superb result was followed up by beating Clontarf by 4 runs in the first round of the Senior Cup. Star of the semi-final was Paddy Neville who scored 142 runs to help Malahide beat Phoenix. Previews of the final between Malahide and Leinster were effusive in their praise of the contribution which the club had made to senior cricket during its first season at that level, with special mention being reserved for the quality of its fielding. Things did not go well for Malahide on the Friday evening, and Leinster scored 235 runs, of which, J. D. Caprani who was to join Malahide at a later stage of his career, contributed 55 runs. By close of play, Malahide had lost 7 wickets for 96 runs, and the headline on the *Irish Independent* on the following morning read "Malahide in Dire Straits in Final". However, a team which prided itself on its fighting spirit did not surrender easily. A. B. Robertson (53) and J. Neville (40) put on 40 runs for the seventh wicket, and then J. O' Neill and Neville added 47 runs for the ninth wicket, but when Neville was bowled by Matchette, the game was over three balls later. The final margin of victory was 62 runs, but the game was adjudged to have been the "most interesting and well-attended final for years".

Malahide and Leinster met on two further occasions during this season, and each game produced what modern media refer to as "champagne moments". In the first game, Malahide batted first, and got off to a wonderful start. The first wicket, that of Darlington (49) fell when the score was 105. According to the *Sunday Independent*, Leinster never looked like getting Paddy Neville out and nothing disturbed him on his way to a "majestic" 105*. There was not much hope for Leinster at the other end either with D. Rimmer ending up on 37*. Malahide declared when the score was 203 for 1. In reply, Leinster lost its first wicket when one of its openers was out first ball, but Burke and Joe Caprani steadied things, and as long as Caprani remained, Leinster looked like winning, but then that man, Neville, intervened again. Caprani hit what looked like being a six, but Neville raced along the boundary and took a wonderful one-handed catch. This effort was described as "the catch of the season", and even Caprani "waved his bat in appreciation of a magnificent catch". In this tremendous game, there were moments when either side looked like winning, but in the end, the last Leinster pair "put up the shutters" because they were content with the draw.

The teams met again in the final of the Mid-Week League, a competition which was the brainchild of A. G. Murray of Pembroke. The games were played over 25 overs per side initially, but later this was reduced to 20 overs per side. When the LCU took over the administration of the tournament, the competition became known as the Alan Murray Cup in honour of its originator. The attendance at the game was 400 and the receipts were £20. Malahide batted first and scored 118 runs, of which D. Rimmer contributed 58 runs. The total did not appear to be enough, but D. O' Shea, "the find of the season", had other ideas. He bowled straight to hit the stumps, and he took 7 wickets for 24 runs in 7.4 overs. It seemed that no game in which Malahide was involved during this season was complete without a magnificent catch by Paddy Neville when he caught Spenser off a "skier", and Malahide ended up getting a modicum of revenge for the Senior Cup defeat with its winning margin of 63 runs.

Malahide reached the Senior Cup Final again in 1955 by beating Clontarf and Pembroke while Leinster defeated Railway Union and Merrion. Leinster dropped S. S. Heighway, their opening bowler, and replaced him with J. A. Chillingworth. As usual when Malahide was involved in a final, the team was very well supported, and there were over 500 in attendance when the game started at Park Avenue on Friday evening. Leinster batted first and at the end of the first evening's play, J. D. Caprani was 38 not out, G. A. Duffy was 25 not out, and the Leinster score was 111 for 3 wickets. The next day's play was of the attritional variety as Leinster brought their score to 272 runs, with Caprani scoring 67 runs before being caught by Gilmore off the bowling of O'Neill, while Duffy was out caught by J. J. Neville off the bowling of O'Shea. In terms of stamina, O'Shea bowled 61 overs, of which 32 were maidens, and took 6 wickets for 70 runs. On Day three, Malahide scored 85 runs, but had lost 4 wickets, including the vital wicket of P. A. Neville. On Day 4, nothing went right for Malahide as J. J. Neville was out without adding to the score. A. B. Robertson scored 21 and S. O'Brien scored 30, and Malahide's reply was well-short on a score of 165 runs.

After the cup finals of 1953 and 1955, a period of comparative calm followed for Malahide CC, but there were some outstanding individual achievements. P. A. Neville won the Marchant Cup for best batsman in senior cricket in 1956, and D. O'Shea and A. B. Robertson won the O'Grady Cup for best bowler in 1954 and 1958 respectively. When Malahide reached the Senior

Cup Final in 1959, the team contained five former or future Irish Internationals. These were P. A. Neville, J. D. Caprani, D. E. Goodwin, S. W. Ferris, and G. P. O'Brien. It was therefore a very strong team which faced Leinster at Park Avenue in the final. Leinster won the toss and opted to bat first and scored 40 runs without loss. The pundits were predicting a score for Leinster in the hundreds, but D. Goodwin came on to bowl and within three balls, Duffy was out, caught brilliantly by who else? Paddy Neville. After this reverse for Leinster, things got progressively worse, and on a drying pitch, Leinster was bowled out for 83 runs, with Goodwin taking 5 wickets for 28 runs and A. B. Robertson getting 4 wickets for 26 runs. J. D. Caprani and W. Behan opened for Malahide, and Caprani scored 36 before he was out, caught by the wicketkeeper, Fitzsimons, off the bowling of Harkness. Sean O'Brien was out for 4 runs, but Paddy Neville (18*) and Behan (22*) brought Malahide home without any further alarms.

During the next few seasons, Malahide players won further individual awards. P. A. Neville won the Marchant Cup on two more occasions, in 1960 and 1963, and L. P. Hughes won the O'Grady Cup in 1963. In 1964, Malahide was in contention for all three trophies and met Old Belvedere in the Leinster Senior Cup final at Cabra. The game was decided on the first evening when a last wicket partnership of 53 enabled Old Belvedere to finish on 158 runs, and then Malahide lost 4 wickets before the close of play. Alec O'Riordan took the wickets of G. P. O'Brien, P. A. Neville, and C. D. Smith, while the other opening bowler, Leslie Lloyd, took the wicket of J. D. Caprani. The following day, the wicket of Sean O'Brien was lost nearly immediately, and a rear- guard action by R. J. Gilmore (18) and L. P. Hughes (29) brought Malahide's score up to 123, but it was too little, too late.

Malahide was back in cup action on 11 August 1964 when it met Leinster in the final of the Alan Murray Memorial Trophy. The star batsman on this occasion was the veteran J. D. Caprani who scored 58* and this was the foundation for Malahide's final total of 99 runs. In the Leinster reply, Murrough McDevitt scored 30 runs, and when the last over was called, Leinster needed 13 runs with three wickets standing. Dougie Goodwin dismissed H. Buttimer, thanks to a "superb catch" by his brother, Billy, and with the next two deliveries took the wickets of Doyle and Geraghty, the final wicket falling to a catch in the outfield by L. P. Hughes. Goodwin ended with a hat-trick, and his figures for the evening were 7 for 45.

Winning a league is a reward for consistency throughout a season, and when Malahide played Pembroke on 22 August, the team only needed a draw to win the league. Pembroke scored 157 for 2 wickets and declared, thanks to 100* by Stanley Bergin. The target of 158 was achieved with 20 minutes to spare, and the manner in which Malahide approached its cricket was exemplified by Paddy Neville hitting three consecutive sixes for the winning runs. His partner in this run chase was L. P. Hughes who scored 86* and this rounded off a season, in which Hughes had starred with bat and ball. At a personal level, he had at that stage of his career won Cup medals with Dublin University and league honours with Malahide and Clontarf. The icing on the cake for Malahide was that A. B. Robertson was the President of the Leinster Cricket Union in in 1964.

In 1965, Malahide's defence of the senior league started and ended badly, but in between the team reached the final for the second successive year and lost again to Old Belvedere in the Senior Cup final. The following year, Malahide again met Old Belvedere in the Senior Cup Final. With the game being played at the Phoenix Park for the first time, it was not permitted to charge an admission fee, but there was a souvenir programme. The game was sponsored by *Mineral Waters Distributors* Ltd; a public address system was installed and there was a refreshments marquee. Old Belvedere captained by R. D. Daly was firm favourites to record the treble, and that was how the game turned out. Old Belvedere scored 210 runs, and Malahide ended up with a score of 65. The consolation for Malahide was its involvement in the Alan Murray Memorial Tournament, and in an exciting game, Malahide defeated Clontarf, the holders, by a single run. The scores at the finish were Malahide 90 and Clontarf 89. The main contributors with the bat for Malahide were T. Taylor (23) and P. Hughes (21); Dougie Goodwin took 3 wickets for 47 runs.

**1971 to 1979**

In this section, the emphasis will be the highlights for Malahide's First XI during a 50-year period because a full-scale review of Malahide CC would more correctly be a task for a club historian. Up to 1971, the 1964 season had been dubbed as the best season for Malahide, but the achievements of 1971 surpassed all the achievements of previous years. R. D. Daly, who had captained Old Belvedere in 1966, was now captain of Malahide. The Senior Cup final between Clontarf and Malahide was played at Castle Avenue, and in a less health-conscious era, was sponsored by Players, No. 6, a cigarette company. Malahide did not have a good day with the bat, and only scored 102 runs. The following evening, the Malahide opening bowler, Ray Kelly took 2 wickets, and on the last ball of the evening, the night watchman, Michael Delaney, was run out. Thus, at 33 for 3, it was very much game on. In a preview, Sean Pender of the *Irish Times*, commented that Clontarf only needed 68, and with "Carroll batting soundly, and Noel Grier, Dickie Spence, John Nolan, Fergus Carroll and Podge Hughes – all of whom are quite  capable of big scores – still to come, such a total should really be within their reach." That was not the way it worked out. Dougie Goodwin bowled 26 overs in total and took 4 wickets for 26. Ray Kelly took another two, and his figures for the game were 5 wickets for 16 runs. Clontarf's final score was 73, and the margin of victory was 29 runs. Both sides fielded brilliantly, and R. D. Daly was commended for his "courageous field placings with so few runs to play around with".

With the first leg of the double achieved, Malahide could now focus all its energy on winning the League. By the end of August, the league had also been won, but there was no let-up for Malahide, and it finished the season undefeated. The batting honours for the season went to R. D. Daly (487), J. D. Caprani (299), D. Connerton (284), G. P. O'Brien (252) and S. O'Brien (247). Dougie Goodwin took 55 wickets and won the O'Grady Cup, while the other successful bowlers were R. Shaw (38), Ray Kelly (31) and G. J. Ward (30). In taking 20 catches in the field, S. O'Brien broke a 50-year-old league record, and the "stern and inspiring captaincy" of R. D. Daly was praised for adopting a bright and attacking strategy if there was even a remote chance of victory.  It was not just the First team which brought glory to Malahide during 1971, as the Third X1 also won the Intermediate League and Cup Double.

It was 1974 before Malahide's First XI encountered another success, and it came in the Alan Murray 20 overs league. In the final, Malahide played Pembroke, and apart from Pat Smith who scored 25, Pembroke never managed a quick run rate. The wickets were taken by A. J. Hughes (3 for 20) and D. Goodwin (2 for 21), and Pembroke ended on a moderate score of 83 runs. Seán O'Brien (16), Barry O'Brien (12) stabilised matters for Malahide after it lost two early wickets, and Clifford Caprani's 18* gave Malahide a win in the 18th over.

Malahide had an unfortunate start to the 1976 Wiggins Teape League when it was well-beaten by Carlisle for whom Stephen Molins (77*) and Rodney Molins (4 for 41) played starring roles. There was a change of fortune in the next game when in the first instance a solid batting performance gave Malahide a score of 171 for 9 overs with runs being scored by Goodwin (40), B. J. Gilmore (20) and R. Shaw (2). A very good bowling performance then reduced Pembroke to 99 all out with wickets being taken by A. J. Hughes (4 for 20), Goodwin (3 for 14), B. O'Brien (2 for 20) and Shaw (1 for 16). After 5 games, Malahide had won 3 games, lost 2, and was 20 points behind Phoenix who were unbeaten after 5 games. In a crucial game, Phoenix scored 232 runs, and Malahide lost 2 wickets for 23 runs, but Gerry O'Brien (80) and David Martin (52) combined for a third-wicket stand of 134 runs. Bobby Shaw's 30 runs maintained the momentum, and Malahide chased the score down in 48.4 overs. The decisive game of the competition was played between Old Belvedere and Malahide at Malahide. Old Belvedere batted first, and Doug Goodwin in a superb spell of bowling took 5 wickets for 49 in 25 overs. Gerry O'Brien batted beautifully for 50* and Malahide won by 7 wickets. That was Malahide's first time to win the Wiggins Teape competition, and it collected the first prize of £300.

At the start of the 1977 season, R. D. Daly, the double-winning captain, who had not played cricket for two seasons due to an injury suffered during a rugby game, decided to return to Old Belvedere. By 6 May 1977, Malahide had played 4 games, won 3, drawn 1, and lay in second place in the league. Leinster led the league, but Malahide opened up the league race when it beat Leinster by 56 runs. Malahide scored 200 for 8, with David Martin top scoring on 68. Doug Goodwin took 5 wickets for 56 in 24 overs, Alan Hughes took 4 for 58 in 20 overs, and Leinster was bowled out for 144. With two games to play, Malahide needed 13 points to win the league. Malahide's second last game in the league was against YMCA, and it won by 9 wickets. YMCA was bowled out for 95, and the wickets were taken by Hughes (4 for 40) and Goodwin (4 for 43). Gerry O'Brien (35*) and Barry O'Brien (43*) ensured that Malahide only needed one point from its last game to win the league. The game against Pembroke was referred to as a "dull draw", but that was all that was required to win the league. Pembroke scored 113 in 65 overs, with Alan Hughes taking 6 wickets for 23 and Dougie Goodwin taking 3 wickets for 34. David Connerton (39), Brian Gilmore (21) and J. Pryor (19) ensured that the necessary points were obtained, and Malahide had won the league for the first time since 1971. In the league, Malahide had played 10 games, won 6, lost 0, drawn 4, and finished on 88 points, 8 points ahead of Leinster. The bowling honours were taken by Alan Hughes (65) and Dougie Goodwin (41) and the best batsmen were G. P. O'Brien (428), B. O'Brien (364), D. Connerton (339) and D. Martin (277).

That was not the end of the successes for Malahide in the 1977 season, and it played YMCA in the final of the Alan Murray Cup. Malahide batted first, and thanks mainly to Bobby Shaw (35), scored 87 runs. Les O'Shea took 3 wickets for 25, and Dougie Goodwin took 1 wicket for 11 in 6 overs. YMCA scored 81 runs for 7, and Malahide added the Alan Murray Cup to the League Championship. That win was an ideal send-off for the team as it set off for a 5-game tour of Wales.

In 1978, Malahide needed at least 4 runs to stay in the Alan Murray Cup. Old Belvedere had scored 99 runs, and Malahide was on 96 with one ball left. Don Henderson (39*) hit 6 off the last ball, and Malahide was in the final where it met up with YMCA yet again. YMCA scored 78 for 7, with the wickets being taken by Brian Gilmore (3 for 13), A. Hughes (3 for 20), and G. Ward (3 for 23). Malahide was on 53 for 3 in 15 overs, and the game appeared to be well under control, but when Richard Murphy (30) was dismissed, a crisis developed. At the start of the last over, Malahide was 73 for 7, but John Morgan and Alan Hughes brought Malahide home, with the winning run coming off the last ball.

## 1980-1999

In 1980, Malahide beat Dublin University by 102 runs, but the most noteworthy aspect of that game was Tom O'Neill's feat of taking 9 wickets for 17 runs on his 24th birthday. This was a new club record which had previously been held by Paddy Murphy (9 for 18) and Dougie Goodwin had taken 9 wickets in an innings on two separate occasions. By the end of June, Malahide had won 5 games, drawn 3, lost none, and had accumulated 97 points; Phoenix lay in second place but had played one game less. In the second last league Malahide beat Merrion by 4 wickets. The wickets were taken by Shaw (3 for 7), O'Neill (3 for 23), Brian Gilmore (2 for 14), Hughes (2 for 22), and Merrion was dismissed for 77. Malahide struggled to get this score and lost 6 wickets in the process. There were runs for C. Smith (23) and Brian Gilmore (20).

With one game left, Malahide was 17 points ahead of Phoenix who had two games left to play. In its last game, Malahide played Clontarf and did not look anything like prospective league champions. Clontarf scored 143 runs, and Malahide was dismissed for 51 runs, with Podge Hughes, the former Malahide player, taking 7 wickets for 21 runs. Phoenix needed 22 points from its last two games; it won one of them, and went into the last game needing 5 points to win the league. Gerry Delany of Leinster who was in inspired form, scored 69*, Gerry Duffy scored 21* and John Byrne scored 30. Phoenix had batted first and scored 155; Leinster scored 159 and Phoenix only managed to get 3 points from the game thus leaving Malahide League winners by 1 point. The main run scorers were Brian Gilmore (538), Gerry O'Brien (434), David Martin (293), Barry O'Brien (238), and the main wicket takers were Tom O'Neill (45), Dougie Goodwin (36), Alan Hughes (33), Brian Gilmore (31), and John Murphy (28).

In 1981, Malahide was in third place in the Wiggins Teape League with 8 games played. In the ninth game, Clontarf was bowled out for 74, with the wickets being shared among A. Hughes (4 for 33), T. O'Neill (3 for 33), and Brian Gilmore (3 for 7). Brian Gilmore then scored 30*, John Morgan got 26 runs, and Malahide achieved its target for the loss of 4 wickets. The last game of the season between Pembroke and Malahide was reduced from 50 overs to 25 overs, and Pembroke struggled to get 82 for 7 in 25 overs. There were three run outs among the catalogue of disasters, and Pembroke had only managed to score 44 runs in 20 overs. In reply, Barry O'Brien scored 33, Brian Gilmore scored 19, and Malahide got the required runs for the loss of 5 wickets which enabled the club to collect the £400 prize for winning the Wiggins Teape League.

In 1982, Malahide reached the final of the Leinster Senior Cup where it was opposed by Phoenix. On Saturday, Phoenix scored 235 runs with substantial scores from Alf Masood (87) and Stan Mitchell (48). When play was disrupted on Saturday evening by poor light, Malahide had scored 99 runs for the loss of 3 wickets. On the following day, Malahide had four run outs, and apart from the 19-year-old Colin Wolfe (32*), none of the other batsmen could look back on the evening's performance with any degree of satisfaction. The margin of Phoenix's victory was 66 runs, and the Man-of-the-Match was Alf Masood.

In the Wiggins Teape League in early September 1982, Malahide's quest to retain the title gathered momentum, and in a re-arranged game against Pembroke, scored 225 for 7 with John Morgan contributing 87 runs. Dougie Goodwin bowled 9 overs, 3 maidens, 3 for 26, and Pembroke was dismissed for 141. With 8 games played, Malahide topped the table with 70 points, and it was tied with Old Belvedere who had played one game more. The following week, Malahide won a closely contested game against Clontarf by 6 runs. Malahide batted first and scored 167, with Peter Moynan (32) the top-scorer and Dougie Goodwin getting a valuable 18 runs when batting at No. 9. Clontarf was dismissed for 161, with Dougie Goodwin taking 5 wickets for 34 and Alan Hughes, 3 for 54. The destination of the league depended on the last game of the season between Malahide and Old Belvedere. It has not been possible to access details of this game other than to report that Old Belvedere won, and there was a tie for the Wiggins Teape League.

Even though the share of the Wiggins Teape League was the only honour which Malahide won during the 1982 season, its overall record for the season was very good. It had only lost five games in total during the season; it had finished runners-up in the Senior League, and it was beaten in the final of the Senior Cup. Brian Gilmore had a tremendous season with bat and ball; he scored 777 runs and took 37 wickets; other significant performers with the bat were John Morgan (587), Barry Gilmore (467), Gerry O'Brien (403), and Frank Furey (304); the other wicket takers were Tom O'Neill (54), Alan Hughes (33) and Dougie Goodwin (24).

In 1985, Malahide reached the final of the Alan Murray Cup where it was opposed by Phoenix. Batting first, Malahide was restricted to 75 runs, with only Brian Gilmore (17) and Alan Martin (12) getting into double figures; extras added a useful 13 runs, but it was highly unlikely that 75 runs would be even remotely competitive. Stan Mitchell scored 26, Alf Masood 26, and the target was achieved in 18.5 overs.

In late August 1985, Malahide was still unbeaten in the Wiggins Teape League, but it had two rain-affected games. On 24 August, Pembroke was bowled out for 41 runs, with Alan Hughes bowling 18 overs, of which 13 were maiden overs, and finishing with figures of 5 wickets for 8 runs. Tom O'Neill took 2 wickets for 26 in 16 overs, and in a late burst, Brian Gilmore took 2 wickets for 2 runs in 2.2 overs. Malahide scored the required runs for the loss of 3 wickets. CYM gave Malahide a fright in the next game by restricting Malahide to 134 runs; the main run-scorers were Brian Gilmore (45), F. Furey (21) and J. Morgan (21). CYM was beaten by 12 runs with Tom O'Neill taking 7 wickets for 64 runs, thus ensuring that Malahide would be contesting the final against Clontarf.

In the final, Clontarf won the toss, and opted to bat first, but lost Deryck Vincent and Enda McDermott with only 4 runs on the board. Brian Bergin led the resurgence, but was clean bowled by Brian Gilmore, just as he was approaching his 50. Clontarf had 3 run outs in the last 10 overs and finished up on 144. Tom O'Neill took 3 wickets for 56 runs; Alan Hughes took 2 for 28, and Brian Gilmore took 2 for 33. Gerry O'Brien's captaincy was a significant element in Malahide's success, and his astute field placings during the first 25 overs restricted Clontarf to 34 runs, with the first boundary not being scored until the 17th over. The total of 144 gave Clontarf something to defend against a team whose batting had been inconsistent during the season. The Gilmore brothers put on 47 for the first wicket, and this was followed by three quick dismissals. The pivotal partnership of 82 between Barry Gilmore (60*) and Michael Murphy (35) put the game beyond Clontarf's reach, but the winning runs did not come until two overs before the end courtesy of 4 byes. Michael

Murphy, the former youth international had been suffering with a virus, but O'Brien decided to risk playing him for his batting only, and the gamble paid off with Murphy scoring 35 vital runs.

Malahide earned a place in the final of the Wiggins Teape League in 1988 when (according to the critics), it confounded everyone "by reducing the YMCA batting to shreds at Claremont Road." YMCA was bowled out for 47 by the combination of Alan Hughes (6 for 14) and Tom O'Neill (4 for 27). At one stage, Alan Hughes's mastery of the YMCA batting was such that he had 5 wickets for 6 runs, and his 19 overs included 12 maidens. There was honourable mention too for the stand-in wicket keeper, Barry O'Brien who took 5 catches.

In the final, Malahide played Clontarf, won the toss, and asked Clontarf to bat. Clontarf was restricted to 58 for 8, with Hughes taking 4 wickets for 29 and O'Neill taking 4 for 26. Deryck Vincent (24) and Alan McClean (10) were the only Clontarf batsmen to reach double figures. Unfortunately, the rain came, it never relented, and the game was re-fixed for the following Saturday. Dave Martin, the Malahide Captain, was definitely unavailable for the next game due to holiday arrangements, and some other Malahide players were also doubtful starters. Not only had Clontarf all eleven who played in the first game available, but Brian McNeice and Fergal O'Mahony who had been on holidays were also available for selection.

In the replayed game, Clontarf was struggling again, and at 37 for 4, everything was going in Malahide's favour, but Tony Karam and Brendan Bergin had a fifth wicket stand of 73 which brought Clontarf up to 110 before Karam was bowled by Brian Gilmore. The last five wickets only added 25 runs, and Clontarf's total was 135. Malahide had its own early order difficulties, but after being 40 for 4, John Morgan (30) and Damian Ryan (14) were enabling Malahide to claw its way back into the game. Karam was in the game again when he took a catch off the bowling of Gerry Kirwan to dismiss John Morgan. Alan Hughes and Alan Brophy, the last wicket pair, had scored 27 runs when Kirwan took an outfield catch off the bowling of Karam to dismiss Alan Hughes. On a difficult day for Malahide, the only consolation for Alan Hughes was that he had won the O'Grady Cup for being the best bowler in Leinster cricket for the season.

At one stage in the 1994 season, Malahide was in the running to win lots of silverware; it had beaten Brigade from Derry in the quarter final of the Irish Senior Cup, it was in the running for the Belvedere Bond trophy, and it had reached the final of the Conqueror Cup by beating Clontarf. At the final, Kevin Price, the Malahide Captain, won the toss against YMCA and decided that

Malahide would bat first on a pitch that deteriorated during the course of the day. Despite the wickets of Masood and Rubbathan being taken early, Brian Gilmore batted positively and had scored 53 when he misjudged the flight of a ball from Taylor and was caught at extra cover. Malahide then struggled to reach 117 at the break, but it had still 4 wickets in hand. The last four wickets were taken in 5.2 overs, and Malahide had not managed to bat its full allocation of overs. Malahide ended on 156 runs, and then proceeded to dominate much of the second innings. Whan, the young Australian, took 3 wickets for 20 and Masood took 4 for 17. John Ridgeway and Neil Bailey, the 9th wicket pair for YMCA, faced the task of scoring 34 runs to get past the Malahide total. Ridgeway hit the winning run in the 50th over and this was the preface for a pitch invasion by the YMCA players. Alan Lewis for his 28 runs and 5 for 17 was given the Man-of-the Match award, but according to many observers and Peter O'Reilly of the *Irish Times*, it should have gone to Ridgeway in recognition of his resolute innings.

Having lost the Conqueror Cup final by one wicket, Malahide played Limavady in the semi-final of the Irish Senior Cup and lost that game by one wicket as well. Malahide scored 218 for 6, with Rubbathan scoring 52, Masood scoring 51* and Ryan, 48*. In reply, Decker Curry scored 107, Masood took 3 wickets for 22, but Limavady scored 221 for 9, and Malahide's season of great promise had ended without a trophy.

In 1995, Malahide reached the final of the Wiggins Teape League, and it was opposed by Carlisle. Jason Molins was unavailable, and his uncle, Stephen promoted himself to open the innings. Stephen scored 78, and Trent Johnston, the Carlisle overseas player, scored 79. Carlisle's final score was 250 for 7, and there was a lot of pressure on Justin Benson because he had been unable to field for most of the first innings due to a back strain. Brian Gilmore and Stephen Rubbathan were out cheaply, and Benson, who started badly, managed to score 65 out of 79 runs, but then misjudged a sweep shot. David Fleming scored 61, and there were cameos from Robert Weir (20) and Alan Brophy (19), but Malahide ended up well-short on 199 all out.

In 1998, Malahide was a team in transition. Brian Gilmore was captain, Damian Ryan, Alan Brophy, and Robert Weir were survivors from the 1995 season, but it had Adrian Barnard as overseas player and Michael Morson, an Australian, who was over in Ireland on an extended holiday. Dara and Conor Armstrong had joined the club from Rush; David McGeehan was the club's Development Officer, and Stephen Smith and Anto Weir had come through the club's youth system. In the final of the Lewis Traub League, Merrion batted first and scored 211 runs; the main wicket-takers were Smith (3 for 34) and Gilmore (4 for 46). Brian Gilmore (42) and David McGeehan (54) gave Malahide a solid start, but Bernard (10) and Morson (17) were dismissed cheaply, and it looked as if this was going to be another one of those difficult days for Malahide. Rain stopped play, and Malahide had 136 runs for 4 wickets after 34.4 overs. On the following evening, three more wickets fell cheaply, but an outstanding eighth wicket partnership between Conor Armstrong (34*) and Anto Weir (29*) ensured that Malahide reached its target in 49.3 overs.

Malahide also reached the final of the Conqueror Cup where it was opposed by Leinster, but it was not a game which the club would look on with any satisfaction. In a poor game, Malahide scored 194 in 58.5 overs, with Dara Armstrong (50) being the main run scorer. Leinster approached the task of getting 195 runs in a very circumspect manner. Joe Byrne scored 75* runs, Johnny, his brother, scored 72 and Leinster reached its target for the loss of 3 wickets in 57.5 overs.

## 2000 – 2021

In 2002, the very talented Eoin Morgan joined the club that John, his uncle had represented with distinction over many years. Jim Govan, the former Scottish international, was now resident in the area and was a tremendous addition to Malahide CC. The team was a blend of experience and the products of a very fine youth development programme. A realistic aspiration for the season was a good run in the Irish Senior Cup.

The first game in the Irish Senior Cup campaign was against Bready from the North-Western Cricket Union. Jim Govan took 4 wickets for 24, Damian Ryan took 3 for 28 and Bready was dismissed for 124 runs. In reply, Malahide got the necessary runs for the loss of 5 wickets, with David McGeehan top-scoring with 42*. Robert Weir scored 26 and Eoin Morgan scored 20. In the second round, Malahide played CYM, and batting first scored 129 for 8 wickets in 35 overs. David McGeehan (52) and Damian Ryan (20) were the main contributors to the score. In reply, CYM had the game under control with Michael Lax (34) going well, but he was out to a brilliant catch by John Pryor off the bowling of Peter Saville, and Saville bowled Conor Kelly (20) with the next ball. CYM lost 7 wickets for 14 runs and ended on 119 all out. The quarter-final game was against Brigade, and Brian Gilmore was recalled to the team to take the place of Richard Gale who was unavailable. That was an inspired piece of selection because Gilmore scored 51 runs and was voted Man-of-the Match. The other main contributors to the Malahide score were Damian Ryan (35), Jim Govan (23) and David McGeehan (29). In reply to Malahide's score of 187, Brigade scored 176, with Ryan taking 4 wickets for 44, Govan taking 3 wickets for 38 and Pete Saville taking 3 for 38. In the semi-final, Malahide played Donemana, and won by 4 wickets. Jim Govan starred with bat and ball. He took 6 wickets for 46 runs and scored 41 runs, with the other scores coming from Brian Gilmore (29), John Pryor (25), and David McGeehan (18).

The final was played at Clontarf, and that was a great Fingal occasion between Rush, a Fingal League team and Malahide, a Fingal team which had only played Fingal League cricket in one season. Rush batted first and made a solid start with runs for Gavin Morgan (26) and Collie Doyle (40), but the crucial incident in the game was the LBW decision on Naseer Shaukat when he had only scored 2 runs. Rush never recovered from this setback, and although Alan Butterly scored 21 runs, Rush was on the back foot and ended on 148 runs in 47.3 overs. Malahide approached the low target in a circumspect fashion, and with Shaukat taking 3 of the first 4 wickets, it was game on at 92 for 4. The individual battle in the Morgan household was won by Gavin because Eoin was out, caught Worrell, bowled G. Morgan for 9 runs. Brian Gilmore had opened the batting and he batted very carefully for his 43 runs; John Pryor scored 22, Damian Ryan scored 20, and Malahide reached the target of 149 in the 49th over to give Malahide its first ever Irish Senior Cup trophy.

In 2003, Malahide reached the final of the Alan Murray Cup where it was opposed by Phoenix. In an attritional struggle, Phoenix scored 109 runs for 7 wickets, and E. Goodward was the top scorer with 27 runs; Peter Saville took 3 wickets for 32 runs. Malahide scored 110 for the loss of 7 wickets in 18.4 overs, and the main contributors with the bat were M. Smith (20), R. Weir (19), and D. Ryan (18).

Malahide's First XI reached the final of the DGM (45 overs) League in 2006 where it was opposed by Railway Union who batted first and scored 271 runs. Kevin O'Brien scored 100, John Anderson scored 80 and Kenny Carroll scored 54. A target of 272 was a serious proposition for Malahide, but at 100 runs in 20 overs without the loss of a wicket, and Wotherspoon (60) and Simi Singh (43) going well, Malahide was very much in the game. With 3 wickets for 15 runs in 9 overs, John Anderson gave renewed hope to Railway, and when Mike O'Brien (33) was out, Pete Markey (26) was the only other batsman to score runs of any consequence for Malahide.

Between 2006 and 2018, Malahide's First XI had an inconsistent existence; it was relegated from Senior League A in 2006, promoted in 2007, relegated in 2008 and promoted in 2009. When the competitions were re-branded as OCD 1 down to OCD 13, Malahide finished last in OCD 1. It remained in OCD 2 until 2014 when it won that section. In 2015, it was relegated from OCD 1, and it did not gain promotion back to OCD 1 until the end of the 2018 season.

As a result of playing in OCD 2, Malahide was eligible to play in the National Cup in 2013, and it embraced the opportunity with great enthusiasm. On 8 June, it played Muckamore, batted first and scored 201 for the loss of 8 wickets, with Fintan McAllister top scoring with 59 runs. Muckamore was bowled out for 116 with A. Kamal taking 3 wickets for 10 runs. In the next round, Malahide beat Co. Galway by 162 runs, with McAllister (67), A. Reynolds (66), Y. Kashyap (50) being the main batsmen. Callum Riches took 4 wickets for 27 and Glen Kirwan took 3 for 23. The semi-final against Rush was the Ryan Gallagher show. He took 3 wickets for 41 runs, scored an unbeaten 101, and Malahide beat Rush by 8 wickets.

The final of the National Cup between Malahide and Derriaghy was played at Downpatrick on 25 August. Derriaghy had a dream start when the wicket of Andrew Pyne was taken before there was a run on the board, but that was as good as it got for Derriaghy. Fintan McAllister scored an unbeaten 163, Ryan Gallagher scored 68, Jim Govan scored 27, and Malahide's total was 284 for 3 in 50 overs. Yokesh Takawle, Derriaghy's overseas player, scored 109, but with none of the rest of his team managing more than 20 runs, Derriaghy ended on 238 runs with Callum Riches (2 for 27), Peter Savile (2 for 42) and Peter Chase (2 for 45) taking the wickets. Malahide had then added the National Cup to the All-Ireland Senior Cup which it had won in 2002.

Malahide played again in the National Cup in 2017, and its first game was against Glendermott at The Rectory. Glendermott batted first and scored 179 runs; the wickets for Malahide were taken by J. Newland (3 for 9) and D. O'Shea (3 for 49). In a rain-affected game, the par score was 55 runs in 15 overs, and Malahide scored 70 runs for 1 in 15 overs, with McAllister top scoring on 26*. In the next game, Malahide played Downpatrick, and the Northern team was bowled out for 80 runs, with the wickets being shared among D. O'Shea (3 for 11), S. Davey (2 for 6), K. Reynolds (2 for 9) and C. Riches (2 for 15). The required runs were achieved in 12.3 overs with S. Davey finishing on 31*. In the quarter final, Malahide played Midleton who batted first and scored 93 runs; O'Shea (5 for 14), Chase (2 for 19), Boyne (1 for 22) and Riches (1 for 19) were the wicket-takers. Malahide achieved the target in 12.4 overs with A. Reynolds top-scoring on 43. The pattern of facile wins continued in the semi-final when Derriaghy was bowled out for 78 runs in 28.3 overs; Newland (4 for 8), O'Shea (3 for 10), Chase (1 for 17) and Boyne (1 for 5) were the wicket-takers. Malahide scored 81 runs in 7 overs without losing a wicket (O'Shea, 43*, A. Reynolds, 36*).

Malahide's opponents in the final were Terenure, and there was an ebb and flow to that game which kept supporters of both sides on tenterhooks for the entire game. In a game which was punctuated by stoppages for rain, Seán Davey (108*) was Malahide's main batsman, with McAllister (17), Callum Riches (18) and Alan Riches (15) getting into double figures. With a target of 214, it was essential that Terenure would have a good start, and it was provided by Jeremy Bray who scored 92 runs; with Cheema scoring 33 and Dónal Lynch scoring 15, Terenure needed 19 runs off 18 balls. Cameron Shoebridge took the last two wickets, with Lynch being caught and bowled, and Cheema adjudged LBW to give Malahide a win by 17 runs.

In 2019, the four teams in the semi-finals of the Alan Murray Cup were Malahide, Clontarf, Merrion and Leinster. Malahide played Leinster in the semi-final, and it appeared that it would be chasing a huge score as Gareth Delany scored 46 from 24 balls. However, with Newland taking 3 wickets for 27 and Chase taking 2 for 31, Leinster was restricted to 135 runs. Alan Reynolds (59) and Mehta (31) had an opening stand of 89 in 98 overs, and Danny Mortimer's 20 overs enabled Malahide to get over the line despite a mid-innings wobble.

In the final, Malahide played Clontarf, for whom it was its third year in a row to reach that stage of the competition. Matthew Ford (79) and McAllister (22) enabled Malahide to score 160 for 8. Clontarf was given a solid platform by Mac Wright (37) and Andrew Poynter (31), but then Keith Reynolds took 3 wickets, and Clontarf went from 81 for 2 in the 10th over to 128 all out. There were two wickets each for Newland, Chase, and Donnelly, and Malahide had won the Alan Murray Cup for the first time since 2003.

### Other Developments

Over the years, members of the Malahide club have performed administrative and honorary roles in Cricket Leinster and Cricket Ireland because of a desire not just to develop Malahide CC, but also to develop cricket in Ireland. The next phase in their vision was the aspiration to have Malahide designated as suitable for the hosting of international games, and in this regard, Malahide CC published very ambitious development plans in February 2007 when it applied to Fingal County Council for grant aid to enable the club to build an international standard cricket ground. In April 2007, Malahide CC received a grant of £40,000 to relocate the boundary wall so that the playing field would be up to international standards and specifications. In 2010, the club was granted £450,000 by the Department of Tourism, Culture and Sport for the development of the ground. It was hoped that the capacity of the ground would be somewhere in the region of 12000, and it had been nominated as the preferred venue for international games. After weeks of preparatory work, the official sod turning ceremony took place on 28 April 2011, and it was attended by representatives from Cricket Ireland, Fingal County Council and Malahide CC.

All the developments came together on a wonderful day for Irish cricket and for Malahide CC when practically 10,000 people attended the game between England and Ireland at the newly developed ground. England was captained by Eoin Morgan, a former Malahide player, and Ireland was captained by William Porterfield, a former Rush player. On the day, both captains scored centuries, and Boyd Rankin, a former Irish international, took 4 wickets for England, but the abiding memory was of the wonderful achievement by Malahide CC and Cricket Ireland to host a game which was watched by a record crowd. The second great occasion in the history of Irish cricket from the club's perspective was the hosting of Ireland's First Test match when Ireland played Pakistan between 11th and 15th May 2018. Again, Malahide CC and Cricket Ireland pulled all the stops on an historic occasion for Irish cricket which was graced by many former Irish international players, and it was enhanced by a wonderful century by Kevin O'Brien.

Malahide CC has provided Presidents of Cricket Ireland, Presidents of Cricket Leinster, and the Secretary of the Irish Cricket Union. It achieved senior status, won the Senior League, the Leinster Senior Cup, the Alan Murray Cup, the "Short Overs", the Irish Senior Cup, and the National Cup, and also won numerous trophies at junior level. Its players have been capped for Ireland, won individual awards for excellence, and provided coaches for youth international teams. The officers and members of the club have rendered magnificent service to Irish cricket by hosting international games and a test match efficiently, which is even more laudable when it is noted that the vast majority of those involved are volunteers. It was established in 1861 as a social and sporting outlet for the gentry, and over the next 160 years, it has evolved into an inclusive organisation which has provided sporting and social activities for men and women, boys, and girls. Its origins were elitist, but over the years, the club has ensured that members and visitors are always welcome at the Village.

*Note: Thanks to Alan J. Hughes for providing access to Malahide Cricket Club: Souvenir Brochure, 1981 which was edited by his father, Ivan. I am grateful to Brian Gilmore for his comments on earlier drafts and for providing some photographs, many of which are on www.malahidecc.com. I also consulted with Alan J. Hughes, John M. Pryor, Ray Daly, Ian Talbot, and Gerard Siggins, but I am responsible for any factual errors or omissions.*

Malahide Cricket Eleven. 1901.

T. Kettle, A. Lawler, F. Lawler, D. O'Brien, C. O'Connor, E. Crowley, C. Adams.

A. Adams. (Vice-Captain)    J. Stubbings. (Umpire)    D. Campion. (Captain)

**Malahide 1st XI 1925**
J. Keddie, J. Finch, J. O'Connor, F. Fitzsimmons, K. O'Neill (Capt.) S. Mills,
G. O'Neill, J. Leonard, K. Healy, R. Healy, C. A. Nc McEadie

# MALAHIDE C.C. Iˢᵗ XI.
WINNERS OF SENIOR CUP & LEAGUE, DIVISION II. 1947.

J.F. O'Neill, Esq.(Pres.) Mr. Cooney, H. Darlington, R. Gilmore, C.J. Hughes, J. Neville, Mr. T. Flynn, Mr. Hudson.
J. Armstrong, H.D. Cashell (Vice-Capt) A.B. Robertson (Capt) I. Cashell, I.J. Hughes.
H.G. Booker, P. Butler, Inset:- N. McConnell.

250

MALAHIDE C.C. 1st XI 1953

D. Rimmer   R. F. Gilmore   T. Dawson   E. R. Foster   D. A. Neville   E. Martineau   R. Golden   L. F. Hughes

H. Darlington   J. J. Neville   A. R. Robertson   H. D. Cashell   L. O'Brien   D. C. Shea

*Figure 4, 1959*

## Cricketer's Golden Wedding.

I notice that Mr. Thomas Julian Smith Casey, B.L., eldest son of the late Edmund H. Casey, D.L., The Donahies, Raheny, celebrates his golden wedding on the 1st December, 1930. Few cricketers in Ireland had a more varied or brilliant career in connection with the game than "Tom Casey," as he was best known by his numerous friends and admirers. He captained a team of Trinity Past and Present against the first Australian team that visited Ireland, composed of the best cricketers in Australia, including such brilliant men as Murdock (capt.), Spofforth, and Bannerman. The match was played in the College Park—and Trinity was not defeated. During a period of ten years he captained teams of the Gentlemen of Ireland in most of their important matches, including those against M.C.C. For many years he captained the Phœnix Cricket Club. I believe he was the first cricketer in Ireland to make a century in first-class matches against Leinster C.C. In a match Phœnix v. the Curragh Brigade, going in last man he made 102 runs not out, which, I believe, constituted a record. Mr. Casey was a brilliant wicket-keeper and fielder. An all-round athlete, he won the 120 yards hurdle race in T.C.D., held the Irish croquet championship, the Trinity tennis and billiards championships and several veteran golf cups. He was succeeded in the captaincy of the Trinity C.C. team by his brother, P. F. Casey (a very fine left-hand bat) and George (a very successful fast bowler). The three were well known in Dublin as the popular brothers. "Tom" Casey, although 85, is still playing golf. Success to him.

MR. T. J. S. CASEY.

## ·Cup Final.

**Malahide, 105; National Bank, 43.**

At the Civil Service Ground, Phoenix Park, in glorious weather Malahide won the Junior Cup, defeating National Bank by 62 runs. Details :—

**Malahide**—K. O'Neill lbw b Heaney, 4; H. Peyton b Nesbitt, 0; E. Crowley b Heaney, 10; S. Mills b Heaney, 13; C. Hughes b Heaney, 0; L. Hughes b Nesbitt, 12; S. Whieldan b Heaney, 18; T. O'Hanlon c Beamish b Robertson, 1; J. Keddie b Heaney, 11; J. Armstrong not out, 10; R. Harris b Robertson, 6; extras, 11. Total—105.

**Bowling**—D. Robertson, 2 for 33; L. C. Heaney, 6 for 36; J. Nesbitt, 2 for 25.

**National Bank**—F. Connor b O'Neill, 0; J. H. Nesbett run out b Hughes, 7; H. Beamish b Armstrong, 2; F. Lane c Keddie b Armstrong, 1; L. J. Heaney b Hughes, 11; D. Robertson lbw b Mills, 2; A. P. Swaine b O'Neill, 4; J. Cooney not out, 12; J. O'Neill b Armstrong, 1; L. Thornton lbw b Hughes, 0; E. J. Rowan run out b Armstrong, 0; extras, 3. Total—43.

**Bowling**—K. O'Neill, 2 for 16; J. Armstrong, 3 for 11; C. Hughes, 2 for 6; S. Mills, 1 for 7.

Figure 5, 1947 Scorecard v Cremore

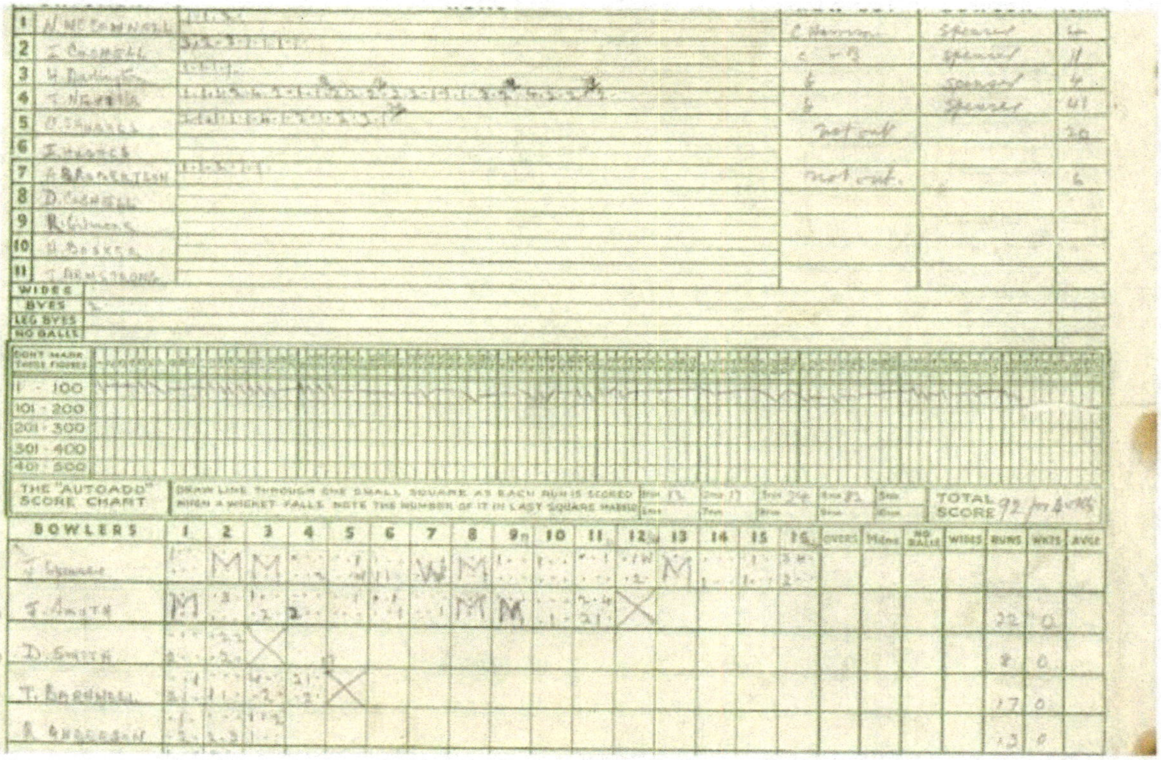

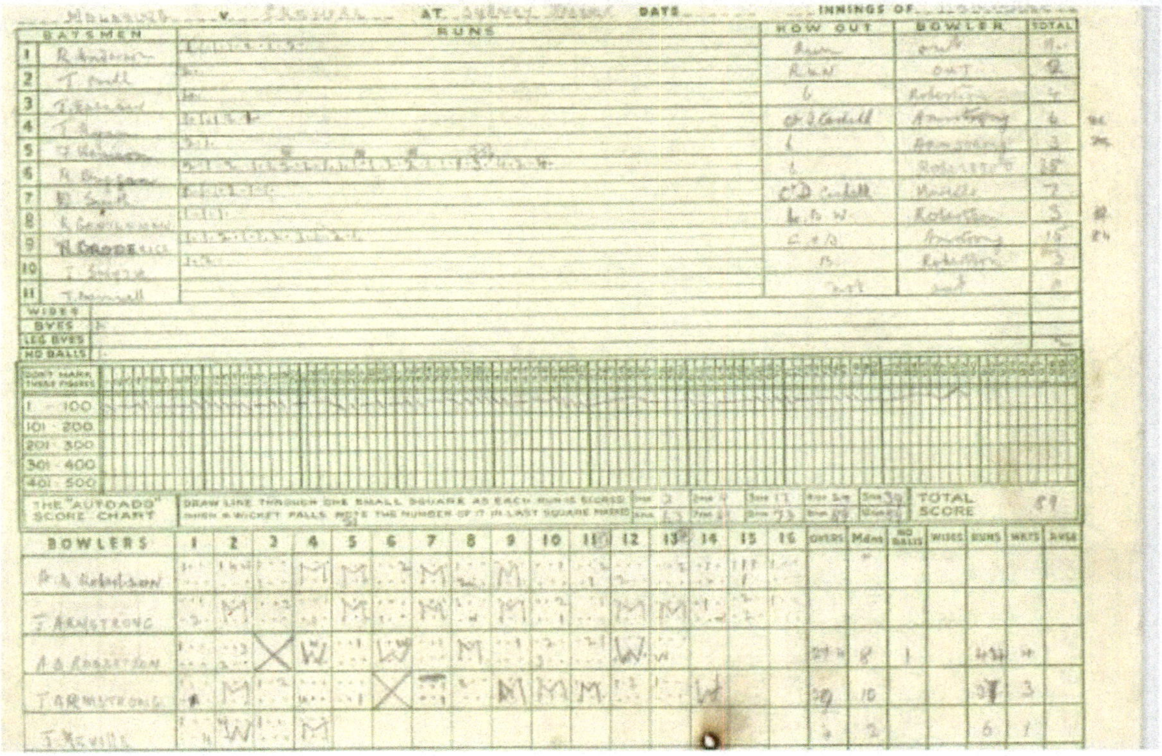

*Figure 6, A. B. Robertson leading team out for first Senior Game, 1953*

J. F O'Neill    L. A. Hughes A. B. Robertson    Hon Rose Talbot    Lord Talbot

Figure 7, R. Gilmore and H. Darlington

1963

MALAHIDE C.C. IV.<sup>th</sup> XI. WINNERS OF MINOR CUP, 1963.

J.O'BRIEN (PRES.), R.T.MAYS, J.GILBERT, K.MAYS, J.B.Mc.CLEERY, R.YOUNG, S.REILLY, R.HAMMOND, B.O'BRIEN, I.R.WRIGHT (CAPT.), J.W.PRYOR, M.ROCHE-KELLY.

Youth Cup Winners, 1969

WINNERS — LEINSTER SENIOR CUP & LEAGUE

(Top) J.B. McCleery. (Hon.Sec), D.Goodwin, R.Shaw, D.Connerton, R.Kelly, G.Ward, C.Caprani (12th Man)
(Bottom) J.Caprani, S.O'Brien, G.Ireland, R.Daly (Capt) B.O'Brien, G.O'Brien

# MALAHIDE C.C. 3rd XI 1971

L.T. Hughes, Past Pres. W.D. Smith    J.N. O'Neill    P. Needle    A. Smith    A. Ingram    B. Gilligan    R. Young
B.W. Gilmore    H.D. Cashell    D. Keegan Captain    R. Smith    S. O'Shea
R. McClancy

EXHIBITION MATCH BETWEEN MALAHIDE CC AND PRESIDENT'S XI CELEBRATING THE OPENING OF THE CLUBHOUSE IN 1975

(L/R) Joe Caprani (umpire), BA ("Ginger") O'Brien, DE Goodwin, D Connerton, R Waters, S O'Brien

BACK ROW.:
M.Howard, D.Keegan, J.Pryor, B.Saville, I.Talbot, D.E.Goodwin, A.Hughes, W.Grimson, W.Goodwin, J.Morgan, C.D.Smith, G.V.Wright.

Front Row.:
N.Adams, P.O'Connor, C.Geelan, E.Harmon, H.D.Cashel, J.Rodgers, D.Geraghty, R.D.Daly, G.P.O'Brien

**MCC President Lunch 2012_names.jpg** - President's Tribute Lunch to H.D Cashell in Royal Dublin Golf Club on thursday 22/11/2012

© Liam Donnelly 2012

G. P. O'Brien and Joe Doherty

Don Geraghty, John Pryor, John Andrews

Anna and John Morgan

## Brian Gilmore

## Brian Saville

## Alan Hughes

## Robert McClancy

Malahide CC. Winers of 2017 National Cup

© 2017 Joe Curtis

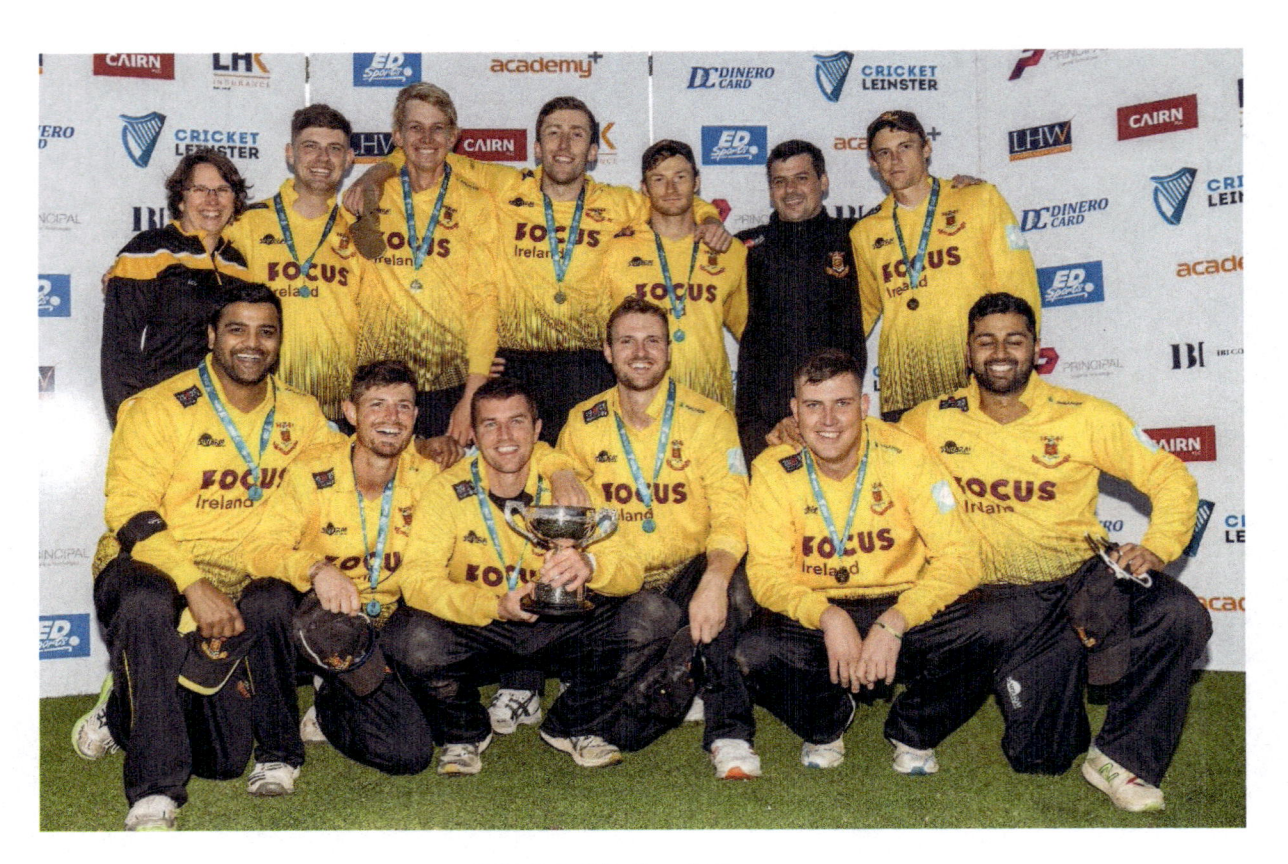

2019 T20 Cup Winners

# Chapter 11: Cricket in Rush

## Early Days, 1825-1920

The earliest references to cricket in Rush are contained in the diaries of Mrs Taylor of Ardgillan when she mentioned cricket in Rush on 19 August 1825. The Taylors also played five games of cricket in 1827, but the opposition is not named, although it is reasonable to assume that some of the games were played against the Palmers of Kenure House, Rush. In 1831, there were two references to cricket matches between Ardgillan and Rush; one game was played on 22 July and the return game was played on 18 August.

The *Freeman's Journal* of 26 August 1891 contained a specific reference to a cricket team in Rush. It mentioned "that the Workmen of York Street turned up smiling against Rush and lost their match". In the first innings, Rush made 35 runs, and of this total, P. Murphy scored 10 runs. In reply, The Workmen scored 26 runs, with T. Kelly (12) being the main contributor. In the second innings, Rush got 30 runs, "without a single double", and in reply, the Workmen scored 21, with M. Bulger getting 11 runs. For the 1898 season, Gormanstown CC's fixtures' list contained home and away games against Rush CC, and these fixtures were repeated in 1899 and 1900. In 1899, the Workmen of Skerries CC (not to be confused with the Workmen of York Street) played Rush and Lusk CC on the "splendid grounds" at Rush, and the game resulted in an easy win for Rush on a score of 66 runs to 16. The evidence of local sensitivities is reflected in an item which appeared the following week in the *Drogheda Independent* regarding Rush and Lusk being referred to as a combined team:

> In our report of the match Rush and Lusk CC versus Skerries (Workmen's CC), we should not have included the name Lusk, as the members of that club took no part in the proceedings.

Although there were no league structures in Fingal at this time, it should not be assumed that games were not fiercely contested. It is also necessary to make allowances for context when commenting on abandoned games because there are invariably two sides to every story, and this is reflected in the Rush correspondent's account of a game between Rush and Skerries Emmet CC which was played in Skerries on 29 July 1900. In suitably ironic tones, he referred to the game as a "friendly", "but it turned out a rather unpleasant one at the finish". Rush scored 64 runs, and J. Bell played "grand cricket "for his score of 34 runs. Skerries had lost 7 wickets for 30 runs when one of its batsmen was adjudged run out by the umpire. He was ordered by his colleagues to stay put because in their opinion, he was not out so he refused to leave the field, and the game was abandoned. The Rush reporter, in reflecting on the rationale for this stance came to the following conclusion:

> For what reason, we do not know, unless they do not want to be beaten. If this is their motto of winning matches, it shows the sportsmen they are.

There are no further references in the local newspapers to Rush CC until 1904 when a report on the Navan CYMS excursion to Skerries referred to a "great cricket match" between Skerries and Rush which was played in a field "just immediately beside the town". There was also a team at Ballykea, and many of the names which appeared on the Rush team sheet in 1900 were now playing for Ballykea. This was common because with no league structures, with concepts of clubs being loosely defined, and the fields changing regularly, cricketers could play for several teams during a season. Arondales, Ballykea played cricket during the 1904 and 1905 seasons. In 1904, Ballykea played Man-O'-War at Ballykea and won handsomely.

Between 1910 and 1913, there are very few reports of cricket being played in Fingal. From 1913 until 1925, the only report in the local press is a reference to a schoolboys' game which was played in Rush in 1920 between Leinster and Rush. Leinster won easily, and the main contributors to the Rush score were C. Stringer and Blake.

**Rush CC, 1930-1960**

At the AGM of the Fingal League in March 1931, there were 25 clubs represented, and the existing officers were re-elected. When the fixtures for the season were announced, seventeen teams had entered for the league, and the new teams were Baldwinstown Seconds and Rush CC.

The Rush CC flag and website record the club as having been formed in 1931, but that is not quite correct. The club was founded in November 1930, but it began to play league cricket in 1931. Rush CC constitutes an interesting case-study because it was a composite of "Big House" and Fingal League cricket. In the earlier era, Irish society was highly stratified, but by the 1930s, it was obvious that cricket was an area of activity in which all members of Irish society met on an equal footing. This is reflected in the list of officers of Rush CC who were elected at the inaugural meeting: Patron, Col Fenwick-Palmer; President, Rev. Fr Perkins, CC; Vice-President, Dr Cooney, Rev. P. Quigley, R. M. Carey, J. Follenus, J. Martin, H. H. Pembrey; Chairman, Dr Cooney; Vice-

Chairman, M. Kelly; Captain, M. Kelly; Vice-Captain, G. T. C. May; Hon. Sec, C. O'Dowd, St Enda's, Channel Road, Rush; Hon. Treasurer, H. S. Pembrey, Hill House, Rush.

In the first year of its existence, the *Drogheda Independent* reported that the Rush team was "going on wonderfully". They had played games against Naul, Oldtown, Hely's, CYMS and Loughshinny, and won them all. It played its early games at the Drummonds, and for a brief period at the end of the 1931 season and in 1932, cricket was also played at a field on the Skerries Road belonging to the late R. M. Carey. The first game on the new pitch was played against Knockbrack Seconds, and Knockbrack won on a score of 52 runs to 16 runs. Writing in the *Drogheda Independent*, "Reflex" was not impressed with the team's efforts:

> This sudden reversal of form is unaccountable as their scores on the previous Sundays left them miles ahead of their opponents. Perhaps they were a little over-confident.

In 1933 season, Lieutenant-Colonel Palmer made a field available to the club and, he also assisted in preparing the pitch. In the words of Ciarán Clear, this was the beginning of an idyllic era:

> The setting was lovely - the picture-book cricket ground, it was called, with the "Big House", the gate lodge, extensive park – the trees, the wooden styles, and fences, even the lowing of cattle and horses. Add to this, after some very hard work, a beautiful wicket.

By affiliating to the Leinster League, Rush was in a position to recruit players from the other Fingal clubs who wished to play in this league:

> The club is anxious that it should be known that it does not confine its membership to persons residing in Rush. Last year it was a source of satisfaction to the Committee that members living as far away as Balbriggan joined and played regularly throughout the season. This year the Committee hopes that the membership of the Club will be further increased by additional members from Skerries, Balbriggan and other adjacent districts.

Over the years, some of Fingal's finest cricketers such as Simon Hoare, Tom and Jem Murphy, Kit Mooney, Christy Russell, Fran Grimes, J. K. Mooney, Dick Byrne, P. O'Brien, Mick Gosson and Seán Moore played Leinster League Cricket with Rush, and Fingal League cricket with their own clubs.

Rush won the Junior Cup Final in August 1933, with the main contributors to the score being Simon Hoare (42) and J. Coleman (36). Hoare took 6 wickets for 43 runs and P. Carty had 4 for 21. During the period, 1936 to 1939, Rush CC was very successful. The Second XI won the Minor Cup in 1936, 1937 and the League and Cup in 1939. One of the reasons for the club's success was the emphasis on high standards, and not resting on its laurels. For example, in 1936 when Rush won the Minor Cup against Bellshire on a score of 50 to 21 runs, the correspondent was very critical of some lapses in the field, and in referring to Bellshire's innings which only lasted 40 minutes, he commented that the score would not have reached 12 if the Rush fieldsmen had accepted "two dolly catches that were offered them."

The First XI won the Junior Cup in 1937, 1938 and 1939, and completed the league and cup double in 1938 and 1939. In 1938, the Leinster Women's Cricket Union was formed, and Rush was one of its founder members. The other teams which played in the Women's Cricket League were Leinster, Civil Service, Bellshire and Carlisle. The league was won by Leinster and Rush finished in third place, winning 3 games, and losing 5. The actress, Marie Keane, and Mildred Carrick were members of this team, but it only played for two years because of transport difficulties during the Emergency.

At the presentation dance in October 1939, P. J. Keane, Chairman of the club, congratulated the club on "establishing a most unique record in the history of Junior Cricket in Leinster". He reckoned that the achievements of the club were "even more remarkable when one considers the numerous disadvantages a country club must overcome, and in a sign of things to come, he expressed the view that:

> Surely the Executive of the Cricket Union must at last recognise the playing strength and great possibilities of our Club and so bestow on us that long overdue honour of promotion to Intermediate status.

Promotion to Intermediate status was granted in 1940, and after six attempts, Rush eventually won the Intermediate Cup in 1945 when Bellshire was beaten in the final at Sandymount. The Rush correspondent to the *Drogheda Independent* gave a lyrical account of the "most thrilling game ever seen in Dublin." With the last batsmen in, Rush needed 6 to win, and in the words of the reporter, "hopes for success looked blue, but once again the club (sic) fighting spirit prevailed and both Dickie Byrne and Joe Kane were carried shoulder high to the pavilion when the winning hit for 2 was scored." Rush CC did not confine its playing exploits to Leinster, and in 1945, it went on tour to Cork and played three games. A notable inclusion on the team sheet was Rev. W. O'Grady who in addition to "fielding excellently and scoring 15 runs, celebrated a special Mass on Sunday in the Church of the Holy Trinity, Cork."

Rush contested the Intermediate Cup Final again in 1950, with Phoenix Thirds as its opposition. The main contributors to the Rush score were T. Murphy (17), P. Carty (21), and J. O'Connor (26), and the *Drogheda Independent* referred to O'Connor as "at last revealing his true form with a brilliant 24." S. Carty's figures were 4 for 10, James Murphy took 3 wickets, and Tom Murphy took 2 wickets to leave Phoenix well-beaten on a score of 78 all out. This victory qualified Rush for an invitation to play in the newly inaugurated Irish Junior Cup, and in the semi-final, Rush defeated Galway County on a score of 65 to 55. The final was staged at Sydney Parade, but Rush was well-beaten on the day by a youthful Cork Bohemians team for whom Jim Kiernan, brother of Tom Kiernan, the Irish rugby international scored 46* and Fitzgerald took 5 wickets for 12 runs. The only Rush batsmen to reach double figures were Murray (21), Connolly (13) and O'Connor (11), and Rush's final score was 80 runs.

Balrothery joined the Leinster Cricket Union in 1949, and two Fingal teams, Balrothery and Rush, met in the Intermediate Cup Final in 1951. The game was played at Civil Service's ground in the Phoenix Park. Balrothery batted first, and scored 141 runs, of which the main contributors were C. Russell (36), V. Farrell (32), J. Mooney (23) and M. Gosson (20). The report mentioned that P. Carty and T. Murphy "trundled in good style" for Rush. The game was continued on Monday evening, and the Rush batsmen were in trouble against the bowling of Russell and Mooney. Rush was all out for 71, with Con Martin (26), T. Murphy (15) and J. Heraty (10*) being the principal run scorers.

From a Rush perspective, there was little of note to report for several years. The team played in the Intermediate League in 1954 and 1955, and it competed in the Junior Cup in 1957. For the 1959 season, the omens were propitious, and the *Drogheda Independent* reported that because of a recent meeting, "big things may be expected in the coming year" from Rush CC. Stalwarts such as Paddy Carty, Paddy Martyn, Andrew Monks, Gay Jones, and Richard Foley were going to play "a whole-hearted part in the pursuit of success". There is no mention of the Fingal League, but it was decided to enter two teams in Dublin competitions. However in May 1959, Rush was forced to withdraw from League cricket mainly due to changed family circumstances for several players, and cricket was not played in Rush in 1960 either.

## The Reawakening, 1961

The lack of recreational facilities for young people in Rush was not a new phenomenon. Cricket clubs in general provide worthwhile sporting activity during the summer months, and they also organise social and cultural events during the close season. The various events such as dances and whist drives may have been primarily for fund-raising purposes, but it is arguable that their social function was of equal value in the contribution which they made to life within the community. The cricket club had been established in 1930, and towards the end of the summer of the following year, an article in the *Drogheda Independent* painted a profoundly depressing picture of social life in Rush and showed the necessity for sports clubs and other recreational facilities in the town:

> Now that the visitors have taken their departure and gone back to their various occupations, the atmosphere of the town has returned to normal, and the people have gone back to the usual routine of hard work and little pleasure for another nine months…. The natives seem to enter into the holiday spirit too, and it is nothing unusual to see the young people knocking off work as early as nine o'clock in the Summer evenings and parading the strands and roads, taking part in the pastimes that attract them most and evidently enjoying to the fullest extent the only few hours leisure that they get in the year, for well they know that with the coming of winter there is no more play for them.

It can be seen therefore that organisations such as the Cricket Club were of vital importance in the town, and in this regard, the club played its part in contributing to community spirit. This can be readily illustrated by the activities which it organised during the 1950s and 1960s. On 30 April 1955, music for the Cricket Club dance was provided by Hugh Lennon and his Orchestra, admission was 4s. The following year, Kevin Keogh and his Music Makers were the main attraction at the opening dance of the season, and the cover charge was still 4s. In 1957, the cover charge was increased to 6s for the visit of Hughie Trainor and his Orchestra. In 1961, the cricket club dance was held in the Palladium, the music was provided by the Pirates Showband, and admission was 2/6. One of the social highlights of the year was the very enjoyable annual dinner at the Holmpatrick Hotel, Skerries.

In 1960, the lack of recreational facilities was still an issue, and Pat Doolan, brother of P. J, convened a meeting of some of his friends to discuss the possibility of organising some social and sporting activities for the young people of the town. About the same time, P. B. Martyn distributed flyers inviting people to discuss the possibility of re-forming the cricket club. This confluence of initiatives resulted in a delegation comprising of Michael McGuinness and Anthony Sourke visiting Colonel Fenwick-Palmer to request permission to play soccer on one of the fields in the Kenure Estate. Permission was not forthcoming, but a second delegation of Ciarán Clear, Anthony Sourke and Pat Doolan called to see the Colonel to see if he would give permission for the cricket field on his estate to be used, and permission was readily granted. Rush CC was re-established in 1961 and a number of friendly games against Fingal rivals such as Knockbrack and Ring Commons were arranged. At the end of the cricket season, a soccer league was organised, but once Rush re-affiliated to the Leinster Cricket Union, soccer was no longer played on the field because there would not have been sufficient time to get the outfield and pitch back in a fit state for the start of the cricket season.

In its first season back in Leinster Cricket (1962), Rush won the Minor League, but lost the Cup Final to a Leinster CC team for whom one player, A. Kati, scored 197 runs. The following season, Rush CC was beaten in the final of the Junior Cup, but shared the league title with Leinster CC. At the AGM in 1963, Anthony Sourke, Club Secretary, was optimistic about the future of the club. There was a growing interest locally in activities of the club, and the younger members were showing "remarkable enthusiasm and ability." There were plans for a tour of Lancashire in 1964, and it was intended to enlarge and renovate the pavilion, while work was proceeding on improving the wickets.

For the 1964 season, cricket proceeded as normal at Rush. The teams played in the Leinster League and the Fingal League, and a team from Carmarthen in Wales played at Kenure in early June. A report in the *Evening Herald* was very complimentary regarding this very enterprising initiative by the club and he praised the ground "at Kenure Park [which] is very picturesque when seen at its best on a sunny afternoon." The Welsh players enjoyed their visit to Rush, and it was planned to turn this trip into an annual event. On the day, proceedings were ended by the Welsh players singing the Welsh National Anthem to which the Rush players responded by singing Amhrán na bhFiann.

With everything going so well for Rush CC in 1964 what could go wrong? The years of maintaining the residence proved to be too much of a struggle for Colonel Fenwick-Palmer, and the Kenure Park Estate was put up for sale in May 1964. The auction notice indicated that the estate was "held entirely in freehold with vacant possession." The reference to vacant possession had serious implications for Rush CC who were tenants, and a period of great uncertainty followed for the club. The 260-acre estate was bought by the Land Commission for £75,000, and it was intended to sell this land to farmers with small-holdings so that their standard of living would be improved.

In 1965, Rush CC was in the words of the *Drogheda Independent*, "seriously inconvenienced by the loss of their beautiful ground at Kenure Park", and it was forced to play its Leinster and Fingal League matches "away". As a result of having no ground, the points system that applied to Rush that season was the same as the dispensation given to Trinity College - there were double points for a single game. In a review of the season, the Honorary Secretary, Eddie Scanlan, described 1965 as the most "difficult year in the history of the club", but despite all the difficulties, the second team managed to finish second in the Minor League".

Just after Christmas 1965, P. B. Martyn convened an Extraordinary General Meeting in the Library in Rush and the only item on the Agenda was the action that could be taken to ensure that cricket would continue in Rush. Eddie Scanlan resigned as Secretary prior to the commencement of the meeting and P. J. Doolan was asked to take notes. A letter from the Land Commission was read indicating that the club could not purchase its present ground, but it offered the club 2.5 acres of woodland for the sum of £600 + interest at 6.5%. This was the market price (£240 per acre) whereas the Land Commission was selling arable land to small holders at £100 per acre. The club was offered the choice of two sites, and there was a time-limit to the offer. Despite the club having a somewhat precarious financial position, the twelve people present agreed unanimously to accept the Land Commission's offer. Michael McGuinness and P. J. Doolan were asked to inspect the two sites and to return with a recommendation for the next meeting. In view of the decision that was taken and its far-reaching consequences for cricket in Rush, it is appropriate that the twelve people who were involved in making that momentous decision should be named: P. B. Martyn, Ciarán Clear, Edward Scanlan, Michael McGuinness, Michael Butterly, P. J. Doolan, Andy Monks, Gay Jones, Hugh Sheelan, Harry White, Roy Whelan, and Noel Harford.

With the decision made, fund-raising became imperative as Rush CC sought to finance the purchase of a ground, and a Variety Concert was held in the Tideway Cinema on Wednesday and Thursday, 19th, and 20th January 1966. Among those who appeared were Maurice Kane, Paddy Carty, Seán Smith, Andy Moore, Jim Carty, Joe Murtagh, The Pirates, the Ely Folk Trio and many more. The hall was packed to capacity on both evenings, and no less than forty-six artists contributed items to the show. The Pirates Showband opened proceedings, there were lots of topical sketches, the Ely Folk Trio (Leo Dunne, Eddie Scanlan and Avril Clear) was applauded to "the echo", and the evening was rounded off with some rousing choruses from a local ballad group consisting of M. J. Butterly, P. J. Doolan, Larry Kane, Michael Mc Guinness, Ciarán Clear and Eddie Scanlan.

The next fund-raiser was a dance in the Palladium Ballroom at which the Skerries Showband, Tony and the Graduates was booked to play. The dance was to be held on Saturday, 19 February, and the club was fortunate to have been allocated this night because this was the era when the Catholic Church prohibited dances being held during Lent, which was commencing on the following Wednesday. Admission to the dance was 7s 6d, and buses were also organised to leave Liberty Hall in Dublin at 9.30 p.m. The all-in price for bus fare and dance ticket was 12s. 6d. Because this was a prime night, there was always a fear that there might be a clash of fixtures, and on the same evening, Dickie Rock and the Miami Showband were booked to play at Palm Beach Portmarnock. In this instance good fortune shone on the cricket club, the dance in Portmarnock was sold-out, and the disappointed patrons flocked to Rush with the result that this was the most lucrative event that the club had organised up to this time. As a postscript to this story, Dickie Rock collapsed on the stage in Portmarnock, and it was feared for some time that he might be unable to represent Ireland in the Eurovision Song Contest on 4 March 1966.

With the fund-raising proceeding satisfactorily, Rush CC was in a position to close the sale on the ground, and the contract was signed on 28 March 1966. The deposit had been £50, and there were eleven instalments of £55 plus interest to be paid. The contract was signed by three Trustees, P. B. Martyn, Michael McGuinness, and Joe Connolly, Senior, and the final payment was made on 8 December 1970. Other fund -raiders organised during this time were a "Gigantic Christmas Fair in the CYMS Hall on 15th and 16th December 1967, and according to the publicity blurb, "there were bargains for everyone." Variety concerts were also held in January 1969, and the report explained that the impetus for the concerts came from the necessity to raise funds for the new grounds. It was anticipated that the cost of the new pitch and the development of it would eventually be somewhere in the region of £1,200.

The club decided to enter teams in the Junior and Minor Leinster Leagues and Cup competitions. The situation regarding a ground was resolved by a magnanimous gesture from Balrothery CC who allowed Rush CC to use its ground at the Matt until its new ground was ready. The arrangement with Balrothery continued until 1969, and Rush CC officially recorded its indebtedness to Martin Russell who prepared the pitch for the club at Balrothery.

While the teams were playing their home games at Balrothery, the enormous task of turning a wooded area into a cricket field continued for several years. A contract was drawn up between Patrick Durnan, Contractor, and Rush CC in relation to the removal of trees and scrub. The best quality trees were marked and removed prior to the sale by the Land Commission and the sale of the other trees covered the cost of removal. It would be invidious to name the people who worked so hard to prepare the new ground, but this information will be provided by P. J. Doolan who is working on a more detailed history of Rush CC.

The first game was due to be played at the ground on Sunday, 29 June 1969, but the weather conditions on the day meant that the game was abandoned after six minutes of play. Eventually after years "of toil and sweat", the first full game at the new ground between the Past XI and the Present XI was played on 20 July 1969. The *Drogheda Independent* report of 25 July 1969 paid tribute to the members who had worked so hard "clearing and reclaiming forest land in the effort to save this 30-years-old club." In the game which preceded the official opening of the ground, the Past XI accumulated 142 runs, with Con Martin (37), Jim Coleman (25), Simon Hoare (18), Stephen Carty (12*) and Tom Walsh (10) being the principal contributors to the score. The Present XI was captained by Brian Morgan and scored 138 runs. Alan Caren was in great form, hitting 41 runs, the other batsmen to figure were Ciaran Clear (20*), Brian Morgan (14) and Eddie Scanlan (11).

## Rush CC, 1970-2019

Once the club had obtained possession of its own ground, other initiatives then became possible. For example, on St Stephen's Day, 1971, Rush played a team called the Santa Claus XI which was captained by David Williams who played Fingal League cricket with Rush. No overall score was given for the game except to state that Michael McGuinness scored 26 runs, Joe Connolly took two wickets and Mike Joe Butterly bowled and fielded well and took two catches. On this occasion, it appears that other activities took precedence over the cricket because the players warmed up with mugs of soup on the field, went to the Palladium for a roast chicken meal, and then retired to the Cradle Rock. This concept of early season cricket was maintained, although it appears that the St Stephen's Day experiment was not repeated. Instead, Rush CC opened its season annually with a fixture on St Patrick's Day, and in 1985, this game was played between the home club and a Selected XI, captained by Dick Forrest.

Rush played in the women's Leinster League from 1977 onwards, and this was the prelude to Rush players winning individual and international honours. Angela Murphy won the Division 2 Batting and Anne O'Brien won the Division 2 Bowling Awards in 1979. Colette McGuinness was the first Rush person to be awarded an international cap, to be followed later by Caitriona Beggs, Ciara Metcalfe, Carole McGuire, and Aoife Beggs.

With its new ground opened, Rush played Leinster League and Fingal cricket for a twenty year spell with a modicum of success at junior league level, and without causing any alarms for the Leinster cricketing establishment. It is only proposed to give details of its successes in tabular form before proceeding to an initiative which tantalised the Executive of the Leinster Cricket Union for two years.

| Year | Team | Competition |
|------|------|-------------|
| 1971 | Rush | Intermediate League B |
| 1972 | Rush 2 | Junior League |
| 1976 | Rush 2 | Intermediate League B |
| 1977 | Rush 2 | Junior Cup |
| 1977 | Rush 4 | Junior League |
| 1979 | Rush | Middle League |
| 1980 | Rush 3 | Junior A League |
| 1986 | Rush | Middle League |
| 1987 | Rush 3 | Junior A League |
| 1990 | Rush | Senior 2 League and Cup |
| 1991 | Rush 3 | Whelan Cup |
| 1992 | Rush 2 | Intermediate League A and Junior Cup |
| 1992 | Rush 3 | Junior A League |
| 1992 | Rush 4 | Junior C League |
| 1994 | Rush | Senior 2 League |
| 1994 | Rush 2 | YMCA Salver |
| 1996 | Rush 2 | Middle A League |
| 1999 | Rush 2 | Middle Cup |
| 2003 | Rush 3 | Intermediate Cup |

By 1990, Rush had several very promising male and female cricketers, among them Colette McGuinness who had been picked to represent Ireland in the World Cup, Caitriona Beggs, Claire Scanlan, Katie Polland, Dara Armstrong who was to be selected for the Irish U19 team, Alan Butterly, Michael Donnelly, Brendan Wilde, Cyril McGee, and Alan Beggs. The Executive of Rush CC decided that a top-class player who would also provide expert coaching was required to bring the club to the next level, because it had seen The Hills and North County, its Fingal League rivals, being granted senior status by the LCU. In 1990, an application was made to the Leinster Cricket Union to register Alf Masood as a professional player for the season. The Union rejected the application on the grounds that Masood did not have the required coaching certificate. Despite this rejection, Rush submitted Masood's name on its list of registered players, and it was hopeful that permission to play him would be forthcoming once the League "became acquainted with the full facts of the case". The appeal was successful, and Masood was given permission to play Senior 2 cricket for the 1990 season.

It became apparent very quickly that the doubts regarding giving permission for Masood to play Senor 2 cricket were well-founded because he was in a class above any other player in the division. He played against Balbriggan in one of the games for which a report has been accessed, and he scored 71 runs and took 7 wickets for 50 runs. In most games, he contributed with bat and with ball, and there was no game in which he did not make a significant contribution with either bat or ball. Later in May, he scored 89 runs out of a total of score of 224 for 4 to Leinster's 99 for 8. In the first round of the Senior 2 Cup, Rush scored 118 for 2 to beat North Kildare, and Masood got 45 of those runs. It was noticeable that each week, Rush rarely had to bat past Number 4 because Masood was so dominant.

In July 1990, Seán Pender, in criticising the performance of the Irish team offered as an aside that Masood "was wasting his talent in junior cricket.". This comment provoked an immediate response from Ciarán Clear, a leading member of Rush CC, who asserted that far from wasting his talent, "Masood is doing quite the reverse." In addition to his coaching and advice, Masood was exerting a "significant psychological influence on his junior team-mates who at first hand have examples of his talents to emulate". Pender accepted that Masood might be doing "good work with Rush", but he was "still far too good a player to be operating in non-senior cricket."

Further justification for Pender's opinion was provided when Rush played Balbriggan in the semi-final of the Senior 2 Cup. Rush scored 341 runs, of which Masood contributed 168, Brendan Wilde scored 55, and in reply, Balbriggan scored 110. In a game against North Kildare, Masood scored 100* out of a total of 182 for 3, and in reply, North Kildare scored 123. The Senior 2 Cup Final was an all-Fingal League affair with Rush opposed by The Hills Second XI, and untypically Masood did not contribute with the bat; the main contributors to the Rush score of 167 were Brendan Wilde (77), Michael Donnelly (56) and Matt Sheridan (23). The Hills' reply was 92 runs, and Masood took 3 wickets for 23 runs to give Rush its first Senior 2 Cup triumph by a margin of 75 runs. By the end of the season, Rush had also won the Senior 2 League, and Masood headed both the batting and bowling averages for Senior 2. Emboldened by the double success, Rush applied for senior status, but not only was its application rejected, but there were murmurings that Masood would not be allowed to register for Rush for the 1991 season.

In an effort to head off a rebellion among the other Senior 2 clubs, the Union appointed a sub-committee to deal with registrations, and there was a specific reference to players being registered for a division where they were deemed "to be too good". It had been argued by the other clubs that Senior 2 cricket had been ruined last season by "Masood's continuing brilliance", and it was assumed that objections to his registration would come flooding in. Some clubs had intimated that they would give a walk-over rather than play Rush if Masood continued to play for Rush, while other clubs were thinking of withdrawing completely from the Senior 2 League. As an indication of the angst which this issue was causing, the Union had taken legal advice, and it was informed that it was within its rights to refuse a registration.

Rush made two applications to have Masood's registration accepted, but the Registration Committee ruled that the player was "too good to be playing in any grade of cricket below senior level." Rush decided to appeal this decision to the Executive of the Union, but it was rejected by a substantial majority of the delegates on the Executive Committee. Masood was allowed to play in the Leinster Senior Cup, although a "move had been gathering momentum" to have him barred from this competition as well. This was blatantly illogical because the recommendation was that he could only play at senior level, but this move may have had something to do with the perception that Masood was being paid to play cricket whereas Rush had argued consistently that he was only being paid to coach.

Rush was drawn against CYM in the first round of the Senior Cup, and Masood starred with bat and ball. Rush scored 222 for 8 with runs for Masood (67), Donnelly (56), McGee (33*) and Carthy (22). In reply, CYM scored 184 runs with Masood taking 3 wickets, Donnelly taking 3 wickets and Michael Marsh also taking 3 wickets. In the second round, Rush played North County, and restricted the senior team to 180 runs with solid bowling performances from P. Carthy, Alf Masood, and Michael Marsh whose 12 overs cost only 18 runs. At 95 for 5, Rush was well within sight of victory with Masood going well, but when he was out, having scored 40 runs, Rush ended on 107 runs, giving North County a margin of 73 runs. Rush made a valiant effort, without Masood to retain the Senior 2 League title, but two defeats in its last two games put paid to that dream. However, Rush did not end the season empty-handed because it won the Fingal Challenge Cup and the Fingal Championship Cup, and these victories have already been mentioned in an earlier section.

When it seemed that the Masood saga had run its course, Rush was summoned to attend a Leinster Cricket Union meeting to answer charges that the club had misled the Union regarding Masood's status at the club. There are no details available regarding the outcome of this meeting other than to report that Masood was going to be back playing senior cricket in the 1992 season, and The Hills was among the clubs being mentioned as a potential destination for him. By April 1992, Masood was still the subject of controversy because it was argued by some clubs that his paid coaching commitments at Rush and Balbriggan could mean that he would be unavailable for some games thus disadvantaging those clubs against whom he would be available to play. In the end, the major issue was whether he was being paid by Phoenix to play cricket because for the "true-blue amateurs", it was anathema for people to be paid to play cricket in Ireland. Phoenix insisted that no remuneration was involved and, on that basis, Masood's registration to play for Phoenix was sanctioned by the Executive. Alf Masood was allowed to play Fingal League cricket with Rush, and he played in the 1991, 1992 and 1993 seasons.

Any reference to Alf Masood's time at Rush would be incomplete if comments on his influence as a coach were excluded. In the three years that he was involved with Rush, the men's teams won the Whelan Cup, the Intermediate A League, Junior Cup, Junior A and Junior C League; the Women's team won the Division 2 League and Cup, and the U15 team won the All-Ireland when it beat Downpatrick by 98 runs. The batsmen who contributed most to that victory were S. Archer (42), P. Mooney (42), A. Butterly (26*), D. Moore (24), and R.

Wilde (20); Wilde took 2 wickets for 8; Archer took 2 for 13 and Donnelly took 2 for 21.

With a strong youth structure in place and some very promising cricketers on the Rush First XI, everything was in place for a concerted effort to win the Senior 2 League again and to hope that this would pave the way for Rush to be granted the coveted senior status. The Senior 2 League was won "by a street" in 1994, and it seemed that there was a general acceptance that Rush merited senior status. Untypically for a Fingal League team, its batting was stronger than its bowling, and according to Philip Boylan, Rush's batsmen would more than "hold their own with some of the Section B clubs". He name-checked John Scanlan, "the veteran Mike Harrison", "the more dynamic Michael Donnelly and Dara Armstrong", "youthful Alan Butterly", and the "swashbuckling Cyril McGee" as making a "useful half-dozen". He had some concerns about the "more modest attack", but the team was led by an "astute skipper," Michael Marsh.

Rush was elected to the senior division at the Executive Meeting on 6 October, with a few provisos regarding ground improvements. The Executive requested that higher sight screens be put in place, a scorebox built, and "netting at either end of the ground to protect the neighbours from bombardment". According to the existing regulations, Rush's accession to senior status should have resulted in Merrion's relegation, but there was no provision for relegation in the older regulations. Merrion applied for re-election, and in the "interest of the continuing good health of the sport", there was an overwhelming vote in favour of Merrion's re-election to the senior league. There were then other logistical issues to be addressed such as which league would have eight teams and which section would have seven. It was also decided to facilitate Trinity by playing the Wiggins Teape League at the start of the season. The other major decision was permitting clubs to recruit one overseas player, with the caveat that the player must not be of Test standard. By the start of the new season, eleven clubs had recruited overseas players, and four clubs (North County, The Hills, Rush, and Trinity) did not have an overseas player, but in Rush's case, results and circumstances forced a change of policy.

The eleven players who represented Rush in the first game in senior cricket were A. Banks, J. Scanlan, D. Armstrong, M. Donnelly, C. McGee, T. Carroll, C. Armstrong, A. Butterly, B. Wilde, J. Carthy, M. Sheridan. Rush had a very difficult start in senior cricket and lost five games in a row. In the sixth game however, there were signs that the players were coming to grips with the higher standard of play, and when Malahide scored 245 runs, Rush managed to get within 16 of the target with runs for Wilde (62) and Carroll (49).

Rush's first win in senior cricket was against Old Belvedere, and with Peter O'Reilly playing for Old Belvedere and reporting for the *Irish Times*, a detailed report on this game appeared in the *Irish Times*. Old Belvedere scored 217 runs, and with the benefit of hindsight, it was obvious that the total was well-short in Kenure Park. Michael Donnelly scored 163 runs, of which 126 runs came in boundaries. O'Reilly suggested that very few bowlers would be anxious to bowl from the clubhouse end where the boundary was only a few steps from the 30 yards circle. In fairness to O'Reilly, he was full of praise for Donnelly's innings which he referred to as a "remarkable innings of ferocious pulls and straight drives that will remain in the memory of the fielders unfortunate enough to be standing in their path". Donnelly batted for 36 of the 37 overs required, and Dara Armstrong scored 20* to give Rush the 218 runs that were required for victory.

With the realisation that one swallow doesn't make a summer, the Executive of Rush CC recruited Naseer Shaukat from Pakistan in June 1995 as Rush's overseas player, and he was to make an incredible contribution to the club between 1995 and 2009 inclusive. In his first game for Rush which was played against YMCA, he took 2 wickets and scored 85 runs. By early July, he was fully acclimatised, and he helped Rush to beat The Hills in a game in which he excelled with bat and ball. He scored 51* and took 6 wickets for 46 runs. This gave Rush its first victory in the Belvedere Bond League, and in every game that Rush won that season in the League, he was usually the main contributor. By August 1st, that was the only game that Rush had won, and it was on the bottom of the Section B table with 5 games played, and 4 defeats. Rush's second victory came at Cabra against Old Belvedere, with Naseer taking 6 wickets for 34 runs and Jemmy Carthy taking 3 wickets for 15 runs. On that occasion, the main run-scorer was M. Donnelly with 60 runs. On 19 August, Naseer scored 46 runs, and took 5 wickets for 38 runs in a drawn game against The Hills CC. The following week, Rush was in action against another Fingal League side, and it had a comprehensive victory over North County. Naseer took 5 wickets for 32 runs, and Tommy Carroll took 5 wickets for 29 runs. North County was bowled out for 64 runs, and Rush achieved its target for the loss of 2 wickets. The following day, Rush played Merrion, and bowled Merrion out for 144 in 52.4 overs. The main wicket takers were Naseer (3 for 42) and Tommy Carroll (3 for 44). Cyril McGee scored 52* and Naseer scored 42* to give Rush a 7-wicket victory. At the end of its first season in senior cricket, Rush finished 4th in Section B, with 4 wins. The Section was won by Leinster, with Merrion in 2nd place and Phoenix in 3rd place. The teams behind Rush were The Hills, North County, and Old Belvedere. In a season where Rush had looked totally out of its depth in the early stages, resourceful recruitment by the Executive ensured that there would not be a clamour for Rush to be sent back to the junior ranks.

It is intended to deal with the 1996 season at reasonable length, but from 1997 onwards, it will only be possible to deal with the various seasons in a more synoptic manner. In its second season in senior cricket, Rush was even more successful. It started the season with a win by 55 runs over Clontarf. J. Scanlan scored 42 runs, Naseer Shaukat scored 33 runs, and the wickets were taken by C. Armstrong (3 for 39), J. Carthy, (5 for 26) and D. McCann (2 for 28). In the game against Malahide, Michael Donnelly scored 78 runs, and Naseer scored 50. Malahide with Justin Benson on the team was dismissed in 43 overs for 157 runs, and this gave Rush a victory margin of 67 runs. Naseer took 3 wickets for 21 runs, Tommy Carroll's figures were 2 wickets for 34, Jemmy Carthy took 2 for 45 and Conor Armstrong took 3 for 54. At the end of the "Short League", Rush had played 7 games, won 3 and lost 4.

In the Conqueror Cup, Rush beat Old Belvedere by 7 wickets, with runs being scored by Shaukat (59*), Donnelly (57) and Scanlan (31). Shaukat (4 for 2) and Donnelly (3 for 49) also took wickets to give Rush a comfortable win. Rush played The Hills in the semi-final but lost a close game. This game is dealt with in more detail in The Hills' section.

Rush's first game in the River House League was against Merrion, and it bowled Merrion out for 136 runs, with Naseer taking 7 wickets for 50 runs. In reply, D. McCann (40), D. Armstrong (22) and C. McGee (22) got the required runs. Rush then played a drawn game against CYM who scored 235 for 7 in 60 overs. Rush scored 222 in 50 overs, with Donnelly's good form with the bat continuing as he scored 57 runs. There was another draw against Phoenix for whom Ludick, the overseas player, scored an unbeaten century (107*). Naseer took wickets (3 for 69) and scored runs (61). There was then an unanticipated result when Rush was beaten comprehensively at Cabra by Old Belvedere, despite Michael Donnelly scoring 79 and Naseer taking 3 wickets for 48. Rush was bowled out for 120 runs, and Old Belvedere reached its target for the loss of 4 wickets.

At the end of July, Rush was third from the bottom of the league, with only The Hills and North County below them. In August, Rush had a number of positive results, and it started to climb up the league table. The good run commenced with a 4-wickets win over North County. Naseer took 3 wickets for 39 and Jemmy Carthy took 6 wickets for 29. Naseer scored 36* and Raymond Wilde scored 21. In the game against CYM, Naseer took 7 wickets for 70 and Cian Armstrong took 3 for 50, and CYM was dismissed for 154 runs. McCann (50*), D. Armstrong (23), M. Donnelly (33) and Naseer Shaukat (37*) scored the necessary runs in 33.5 overs to give Rush an 8 wickets victory. Rush beat Phoenix by 7 wickets, and in terms of coincidences, Luddick got the same score (107) as he had done in the previous game against Rush, although on this occasion, he was out on 107. Naseer took 5 wickets for 62 and Jemmy Carthy took 5 for 58. In reply, Naseer scored 75, D. McCann scored 40 and M. Donnelly scored 36. This was followed by a 7 wickets win over Merrion with Naseer taking 6 wickets for 54 runs and scoring 81*. Rush beat North County by 7 wickets, and Shaukat got wickets (3 for 51) and runs (55*). Jemmy Carthy got 2 wickets for 20 runs, and Michael Donnelly scored 53*.

With everything going so well, Rush suffered a surprise defeat by Old Belvedere, when a devastating burst of fast bowling by Owen Butler (7 for 33 in 20 overs) caused Rush to be bowled out for 86 when the target was 185. Naseer took 4 wickets for 48, but he was clean bowled by Butler for a duck as were Dara Armstrong and Collie Doyle. Michael Donnelly scored 4 runs, and John Scanlan (29) and Cian Armstrong (25) were the only Rush players to get into double figures. This defeat meant that the last game of the season between Rush and The Hills was effectively a promotion play-off. The Hills lost the toss and was asked to bat first. Naseer took 4 wickets for 34 runs, Jemmy Carthy took 3 wickets for 34 and Cian Armstrong took wickets for 21 runs. Mark Clinton was the top scorer for The Hills with 37 runs, and the Milverton men were dismissed for 111 runs. In reply, Michael Donnelly batted superbly to score 86*, and his knock included 14 boundaries and 2 sixes. Naseer was there at the end with 19* to complete a magnificent season for Rush CC and for himself.

Naseer Shaukat's figures for the season were 71 wickets and 826 runs. He topped the batting averages for the season with an average of 68.83. He came second in the bowling to Matt Dwyer who took 73 wickets. In *100 Not Out*, it is stated that Naseer won the all-rounder award, but that may not be correct because as an overseas player, Naseer was not eligible to win the award. According to the *LCU Handbook* for 1997, the winner of the Samuels Cup for the 1996 season was Matt Dwyer who also won the O'Grady Cup. Other players for Rush to shine in that season were Michael Donnelly (658 runs), Dara Armstrong (384 runs and winner of the Hopkins Cup for the best wicketkeeper in Leinster), and Jemmy Carthy (36 wickets). At the end of its second season as a senior club, Rush was promoted to Section A for the 1997 season.

Rush's Record in Senior Cricket, 1995 to 2004 was as follows:

| Year | P | W | D | L | NR | Points | Place in League |
|------|---|---|---|---|-----|--------|-----------------|
| 1995 | 12 | 4 | 1 | 7 | | 162 | 4th |
| 1996 | 12 | 7 | 3 | 2 | | 328 | 1st (Promoted) |
| 1997 | 12 | 6 | 1 | 5 | | 218 | 2nd (Section A) |
| 1998 | 12 | 2 | 1 | 9 | | 45 | 7th (Relegated) |
| 1999 | 12 | 4 | 0 | 8 | | 109 | 6th (Section B) |
| 2000 | 12 | 4 | 1 | 7 | | 105 | 7th |
| 2001 | 12 | 3 | 0 | 9 | | 86 | 7th |
| 2002 | 12 | 5 | 2 | 5 | | 142 | 4th |
| 2003 | 12 | 5 | 0 (T) | 5 | 2 (NR) | 151 | 3rd |
| 2004 | 12 | 9 | | 3 | 0 (NR) | 223 | 1st (Promoted) |

**Rush CC and the All-Ireland Cup Competition, 2002 and 2006**

Prior to 2002, Rush's record in the All-Ireland Cup had been abysmal, and on seven previous occasions, the team had been beaten in the First Round, and thus it was more in hope than expectation that Rush welcomed Cliftonville to Kenure Park for the First- Round game in 2002. Kyle McCallan was the most famous name on the Cliftonville team, but Terrett, Turkington, and Menaul had been solid performers in the NCU, and McKee and Cowden had played for Ireland at youth international level. Naseer Shaukat was by then residing permanently in Ireland, and Rush's team was a mixture of experience and youth. Jemmy Carthy was a survivor from Rush's first year in senior cricket, and there was the father and son pairing of Jody and Gavin Morgan. The prospects for any play looked bleak but eventually the day cleared sufficiently for a 10-overs per side to be played. Rush batted first, and there were solid contributions from Gavin Morgan (39) and Alan Butterly (18), and Cliftonville needed 84 runs to win. Terrett (13) was run out, McCallan only scored 9, and most of the runs came from the late order batsmen (Speer 11, Anderson 18). Gavin Morgan's figures were 3 overs, 3 wickets for 11, Jody, his father, took a catch, and Cliftonville ended up 11 runs short on 73 runs for 7.

Rush was drawn against Lisburn in the next round of the Irish Senior Cup, and some of the Northern commentators had described Rush's win over Cliftonville as a 10-overs fluke. That game was reduced to 30 overs per side because of rain, and Rush batted first. Collie Doyle scored 50, extras were 31, and Rush's total was 131 in 29.2 overs. Naseer Shaukat took 4 wickets for 23 runs, Khalil took 3 wickets for 10, and Lisburn was bowled out in 24.3 overs for 67 runs.

In the next round, Rush was drawn against Merrion who at this stage had a very strong team. Naseer Shaukat scored 122 runs out of a Rush total of 245 for 7. In reply, Brad Spanner (36) was the only batsman to get a score of any significance for Merrion; Naseer took 4 wickets for 26, Lee Metcalfe took 3 for 15, and Rush won by 103 runs. In the semi-final, Rush played Downpatrick at Kenure on 10 August. Downpatrick batted first and scored 140 runs for 8 in 48.2 overs. There were wickets for Gavin Morgan (4 for 53), Jemmy Carthy (3 for 33) and Naseer Shaukat (2 for 31). In reply, Gavin Morgan (51) and Naseer Shaukat (59*) were the main contributors for Rush, and the target was reached in 37.3 overs.

The final was played at Clontarf, and that was a great Fingal occasion between Rush, a Fingal League team and Malahide, a Fingal team which had only played Fingal League cricket in one season. There was scope for divided loyalties in the Morgan household because Gavin was playing for Rush and Eoin, his younger brother, was playing for Malahide. Rush batted first and made a solid start with runs for Gavin Morgan (26) and Collie Doyle (40), but the crucial incident in the game was the LBW decision on Naseer Shaukat when he had only scored 2 runs. Rush never recovered from this setback, and although Alan Butterly scored 21 runs, Rush was on the back foot and ended on 148 runs in 47.3 overs. Malahide approached the target in a circumspect fashion, and with Shaukat taking 3 of the first 4 wickets, it was game on at 92 for 4. Brian Gilmore had opened the batting and he batted very carefully for his 43 runs; John Pryor Jnr scored 22, Damian Ryan scored 20, and Malahide reached the target of 149 in the 49th over to give Malahide its first ever Irish Senior Cup trophy.

In 2003, Rush had a reasonably satisfactory season, and finished third in Section B with 5 wins, 2 no results and 5 defeats with Clontarf and The Hills being the promoted teams. It was evident that Rush was assembling a strong team which would challenge for honours in the next season. Naseer Shaukat had been joined in the club at that stage by Saadat (Tipu) Gull and Shahid Iqbal, both of whom had been professionals with other Irish clubs. The club had always had a tradition of developing young players, and among the players who featured on the First XI in 2004 were Fintan McAllister, Lee Metcalfe, and

Niall Mullen. Michael Donnelly, Alan Butterly and Collie Doyle were still playing, and the combination of experience and youth made Rush a very formidable team in 2004. In Section B, it played 12 games, won 9, lost 3 and accumulated 223 points to win the section by 48 points from CYM.

Rush had never won the Leinster Senior Cup, but it made a valiant effort to win this competition in 2004. On 29 May, Rush played Railway Union, and won by 3 wickets. Gull, Iqbal, and Shaukat all took 2 wickets, and Lee Metcalfe took 3. In the Rush innings, Naseer scored 90* and the next highest score was 24 extras. Rush met Phoenix in the next round, and Phoenix had been strengthened by the recruitment of Chris Torrisi and Thinnus Fourie to complement a team which already had Jeremy Bray and David Langford-Smith on it. Rush batted first and Collie Doyle scored 123 runs, and there were contributions from Shahid Iqbal (34) and Alan Butterly (18) to give them a total of 229 runs. In the Phoenix reply, Bray only got 2, and other batsmen got starts, but there was nobody to bring Phoenix home and Rush won by 12 runs. The bowling honours were taken by Iqbal (3 for 38), Shaukat (2 for 40), Akhtar (2 for 34). In the semi-final, Rush played YMCA, and YMCA was dismissed for 136 with Niall Mullen taking 5 wickets for 44 runs. Saadat Gull (55*) and Shahid Iqbal (29) were the main run-scorers for Rush, and the target score was achieved with the loss of 8 wickets.

In the final, Rush played Clontarf, and Saadat Gull's decision to ask Clontarf to bat first was probably not the wisest one that he ever made as a captain. Clontarf racked up the huge score of 290 for the loss of only 3 wickets, with Trent Johnston scoring 102, Dom Rigby scoring 90. Shahid Iqbal scored 90*, but that was the only sizeable contribution from a Rush batsman, and Rush was beaten by 97 runs.

### League Placings for Rush, 2005-2013

| Year | P | W | T | L | NR | Pts | Place in League |
|------|----|---|---|---|----|-------|-----------------|
| 2005 | 12 | 5 | | 4 | 3 | 149 | 4th (Section A) |
| 2006 | 12 | 7 | | 5 | 0 | 165 | 2nd (Section A) |
| 2007 | 12 | 6 | | 0 | 6 | 190 | 2nd (Section A) |
| 2008 | 12 | 3 | | 6 | 3 | 195 | 7th (Section A) |
| 2009 | 10 | 6 | | 3 | 1 | 150 | 3rd (Section B) |
| 2010 | 12 | 7 | | 5 | 0 | 56.6% | 3rd (Section B) |
| 2011 | 12 | 7 | | 5 | 0 | 168 | 4th (Section B) |
| 2012 | 13 | 5 | | 7 | 1 | 128 | 4th (Section B) |
| 2013 | 13 | 7 | | 6 | 0 | 201 | 3rd (Section B) |

## 2006 - The Irish Cup Campaign

That season, it is arguable that the Rush First XI was stronger than the 2004 team. Brían O'Rourke, Cricket Leinster's Development Officer, was residing in Rush and had joined the club in 2005. William Porterfield was studying in England, and he commuted to Rush on a number of weekends during the season. In the Section A League, Rush had its best ever finish when it came second to North County.

With the all-round strength of that team, it was not unrealistic to hope for a victory in one of the cup competitions. Rush played Lisburn in the first round of the Irish Senior Cup, bowled Lisburn out for 143 runs, and achieved the target for the loss of 4 wickets. Ronan McGuire (3 for 44), Shahid Iqbal (3 for 19), Naseer (2 for 20) and B. O'Rourke (2 for 34) were the stars with the ball, and there were runs for O'Rourke (40) and Collie Doyle (63). Rush played North Down in a tempestuous game in the next round. North Down scored 300 for 9 runs, and Rush achieved the target for the loss of 5 wickets in the 49.1 over. Lee Metcalf took 4 wickets for 40, Brían O'Rourke scored 105 runs, and Shahid Iqbal scored 97. Clontarf had been a bogey team for Rush over the years, but with O'Rourke scoring 73 and Porterfield 56, Rush put 249 runs on the board. Despite Trent Johnston scoring 73 runs, Clontarf was beaten by 51 runs, and the star with the ball was again Lee Metcalf (4 for 45).

The semi-final of the Irish Senior Cup brought together two Fingal League teams, Rush, and North County, and it was unarguable that North County had been the best team in Ireland for a number of years. However, in that season, it had shown itself as being fallible in cup games because it had already been beaten by The Hills in the final of the Leinster Senior Cup. As an indication of its intent, North County had flown Eoin Morgan home from London for the game. Rush struggled early on, and Porterfield was back in the pavilion without scoring many runs. Brían O'Rourke (98) and Michael Donnelly (80) batted superbly, and Rush's total was 272 for 6. North County never looked like getting the score, and at one stage, the score was 18 for 4, with two wickets for Shahid, one for Naseer, and Botha had been run out. Strydom and Morgan had a 100 partnership, but Morgan holed out to Niall Mullen at deep mid-wicket for 39, and that was the end of the North County chase, with the winning margin being 59 runs.

Rush's opponents in the final were Railway Union, and it turned out to be a wonderful game. Rush batted first and there were scores for McAllister (36), Van Zyl (36), Iqbal (58), but Naseer, Rush's talisman was out for a duck, caught and bowled by Singh. Railway Union's reply was broadly similar, with batsmen getting starts, but no one went on to get a big score, and wickets were being taken at regular intervals. Kenny Carroll (36), Niall O'Brien (44), A. Murphy (50) brought the target within reach, but with 9 wickets down, it was up to the last pair, Roger Whelan, and James Rogan to get the winning runs, and the concession of 36 extras by Rush was of considerable benefit in Railway Union's run chase. Yet again, Rush had come up short in a final, and that time by one wicket, the narrowest of margins.

| Year | P | W | T | NR | L | Points | Place in League |
|------|----|---|---|----|---|--------|------------------|
| 2014 | 15 | 6 | | | 9 | 174 | 6th (Section B) |
| 2015 | 13 | 5 | | 1 | 7 | 172 | 5th (Section B) |
| 2016 | 13 | 5 | | 1 | 7 | 135 | 7th (Section B) |
| 2017 | 13 | 5 | | | 8 | 131 | 6th (Section B) |
| 2018 | 11 | 7 | | 1 | 3 | 179 | 2nd (Section B) |

The disappointment of losing cup finals, combined with some of the older players wishing to step back or move on, caused a certain amount of reflection at the club and the Executive appear to have decided that the way forward was to focus on youth. Lynal Jansen was appointed as coach and overseas player in 2007, but his main function at the club was as a coach, with his playing role of secondary importance. He stayed with the club until 2017, when a family issue in South Africa forced him to return home, but he left a phenomenal legacy at Rush in terms of the many young players who flourished under his coaching, and that legacy will be main focus of the rest of this section.

Cricket Ireland established a National Cup competition in 2012, and it was intended for teams in each of the unions which were outside the top leagues. Rush had been playing in the Second Division of Leinster Cricket or as it was then called OCD 2, and it was therefore eligible to play in the National Cup. At a general level, Fingal League clubs were very supportive of the concept of National competitions because of the opportunity to play different clubs and to visit different venues. In the first round of the National Cup in 2015, Rush was drawn against Templepatrick from the NCU, and won after a very closely contested game. Rush batted first and did not bat particularly well. Lynal Jansen who scored 26 runs, and Stephen Doheny (10) and Allan Eastwood (17) were the only other batsmen to get into double figures and extras were a handsome 21. With a score of 118, it appeared that Rush's involvement in the National Cup would end in the first round, but defending low scores was not a novelty for a Fingal League team. Saadat Gull took 7 wickets for 15 runs, Lynal

Jansen took 3 wickets for 23 runs, and Templepatrick was bowled out for 109 runs.

In the second round, Rush played Academy at Kenure Park on 6 June, and Academy accumulated a competitive total of 242 runs. The wickets for Rush were taken by Allan Eastwood (3 for 68), Lynal Jansen (2 for 23) and Saadat Gull (2 for 37). Rush achieved the target score for the loss of 4 wickets with runs for Jansen (80), Eoghan Conway (58) and Gull (43*). In the third round, Rush was opposed by Derriaghy, another NCU team. Derriaghy scored 294 runs in 50 overs, but Rush achieved the target for the loss of only 4 wickets. Jansen's run of good form continued with a knock of 94 runs, and there were decent contributions from Butterly (27), Brogan (39), Iqbal (38), Gull (26*) and Patrick Sheridan (47*). In the semi-final, Rush beat Greystones by 8 wickets, and on that day, there were two centurions, Stephen Doheny, one of the many talented young cricketers at the club scored 112* and L. Jansen scored 101 runs.

The final was played at Strabane, and Rush was opposed by Drummond from the North-West Cricket Union. Drummond won the toss, batted first, and scored 171 runs in 46.2 overs. The wickets were taken by Dean Brogan (4 for 26), Lynal Jansen (3 for 14), Saadat Gul (2 for 32) and Allan Eastwood (1 for 34). Rush found runs very hard to come by, and it was only when Eoghan Conway came into bat, that the Rush chase took on any momentum. Conway scored 43 and Eastwood scored 32, but just as the finishing line was in sight, both of their wickets were taken. It was left to Niall Mullen (18*) and Daniel Coffey (4*) to steer Rush home and give it a victory by two wickets. This was a great triumph for a Rush team which was a combination of some long-established players and burgeoning young talent within the club, and it enabled Rush to shake off the mantle of always being "good losers".

Rush's defence of the National Cup in 2016 commenced with a game against Downpatrick. Downpatrick scored 200 runs, and there were wickets for Brogan (3 for 37), Gull (2 for 31), Eastwood (1 for 28) and Jansen (1 for 50). Rush achieved the target for the loss of 3 wickets, and there were runs for Doheny (49), Jansen (34), Seán Monks (28) and Iqbal (61*). In sporting contests, there are sometimes mismatches, and the game between Rush and Dundrum definitely came into that category. Rush batted first and scored 569 runs. Doheny scored 259 runs, Jansen also scored a century (108), Iqbal scored 37 and Gull scored 61 runs. In reply, Dundrum was bowled for 74, and the margin of victory was 495 runs. Jansen took 6 wickets for 15 runs, Eastwood took 3 for

37, and other wicket was taken by Gull (1 for 17). In the game against Balbriggan, Gull (131) and Jansen (107) led the scoring, and Rush ended with a score of 351. In reply, Balbriggan scored 80, and there were wickets for Eastwood (4 for 16), Jansen (2 for 13) and Iqbal (2 for 180). The margin of victory over Woodvale in the semi-final was 86 runs; Doheny (89) and Iqbal (67) were the main run-scorers.

The final of the National Cup was between Rush and Laois, and the pattern of easy wins for the competition was maintained when Rush won by 9 wickets. Laois batted first, and was bowled out for 149 runs, with Brogan (4 for 34) being the main wicket-taker. In reply, Jansen (64) and Doheny (71*) shared an opening partnership of 123 runs, and Rush had retained the National Cup with consummate ease.

In 2017, Rush was knocked out of the National Cup by Terenure, but the title was won by Malahide, another Fingal club. In 2018, Rush's first game in the National Cup was against Lisburn, and at that stage, Conor Armstrong had returned to Rush, and he celebrated by scoring a century. Rush scored 223 for the loss of 7 wickets, and Lisburn was dismissed for 138 runs, with Jonathan Waite (51), the only player to make a significant score. The wickets were taken by Coffey (3 for 42), Eastwood (2 for 28), McGuire (2 for 25), Doheny (2 for 17) and Iqbal (1 for 2). In the next game, Rush played Drummond, and won a rain-affected game by 6 wickets. Conor Mullen scored 49* and Neil Rock, another of the Rush young stars, scored an unbeaten 51. There was a trip to the North-West for the semi-final, and Ballyspallen provided the opposition. Rush batted first and scored 212; the main run-scorers were Doheny (54), Mullen (45), Gull (50*) and McGuire (36*). In reply, Ballyspallen was bowled out for 142, and Doheny was the main wicket-taker with 4 wickets for 13 runs.

The final between Limerick and Rush was played at Kenure Park, and it was a tremendous occasion for a huge, enthusiastic crowd. Conor Armstrong (90) and Stephen Doheny (62) gave Rush a tremendous start, but Limerick stuck to its task, and took wickets at regular intervals. Gull (32*), Ramnathpur (27), Iqbal (28) brought the Rush score up to 269 for 6 wickets. Limerick had a poor start, and lost both opening batsmen fairly cheaply, but Sultan (56) and M. Siddqi (53) brought Limerick back into the game, and solid contributions from Yousafzal (23) and a quick-fire knock of 24 by Burra kept the Rush faithful in tenterhooks until Burra was bowled by Daniel Coffey with the score on 243.

That game was a wonderful advertisement for the National Cup, and it provided vindication for the visionaries who established it in 2012.

In 2019, Rush celebrated the 50th anniversary of the opening of the new ground at Kenure. On that occasion, there were lots of reminiscences of past games and great achievements by individual players and by the club. The club has developed its ground and its ancillary facilities and established an enviable youth coaching programme. Rush CC has been a competitive club in Leinster Senior Cricket since it attained Senior status. It has played in two All-Ireland Senior Cup finals and has won the National Cup on three occasions during a 5-year period. It has produced international cricketers for the Ireland men's and women's teams, and its wonderfully successful youth programme has been demonstrated by the numerous All-Ireland titles which have been won at the various age levels during the past few years. When Ireland played England in that historic game in Malahide on 3 September 2013, both captains, William Porterfield, and Eoin Morgan, had played with Rush. When England won the World Cup in 2019, its captain was Eoin Morgan who has spoken eloquently and frequently of his indebtedness to Rush CC for the start which it gave him in cricket. Rush CC has made a wonderful contribution to the preservation, nurturing, and development of the game of cricket and to the life of the community since it was founded.

**Note 1**: I am greatly indebted to P. J. Doolan for the detailed information which he has given to me in relation to the period from 1961 to 1970, and I take this opportunity to wish him well in his work on the History of Rush Cricket Club.

Rush CC, early 1930s

38 Cup Winners

**LEINSTER INTERMEDIATE CUP FINAL 1951**

RUSH TEAM BEATEN BY BALROTHERY IN THE PHOENIX PARK
IN 1950 RUSH DEFEATED PHOENIX IN THE SAME CUP FINAL

| JOHN HORITY | TOM WALSH | JIM COLEMAN | TOM MURPHY | JEM MURPHY | CON MARTIN | STEPHEN CARTHY | PADDY CARTHY | JAMES O'CONNOR | JOE CONNOLLY | MATT MURRAY |

1950 Intermediate Cup Final                    Rush CC

Back Row:  Umpire Connaughton; Matt Murray, Joe Connolly, Tom Walsh, Stephen Carty, Jim O'Connor, Jem Murphy.
Front Row:  Earl Ward, Jim Coleman, Paddy Carty, Tom Murphy, Sean Hegarty

293

## Dance Committee

Dance Committee

## 1962

*1962/63*
*Back L to R: Michael McGuinness, Ed Scanlan, Tony Sourke,*
*Mike Joe Butterly, Albert Caprani, Stephen Carty*
*Front L to R: Paddy Carty, Ciaran Clear, Paddy Martyn, PJ*
*Dolan, Andy Monks, Iral Ward*

## 1985

RUSH C.C. 1985
BACK: Alan Caren, Michael Connolly, Alan Beggs,
Matt Sheridan, Tom Armstrong, Cyril McGee.
FRONT: Gerry Monks, Robert Murray,
Mike Marsh, John Scanlon.

## Early photo of Simon Hoare

John Gill and Michael Marsh

Brendan Wilde and Alf Masood

Alan Caren and Mike Joe Butterly

David Williams

Thomas Morgan and Matt Sheridan

Pat Mc Bennett and Tommy Mooney

## Barney Metcalfe

## Eddie Scanlan and Friends

## Rush Fans Celebrate

## Grace Sheridan

Rush U15, All-Ireland Winners, 1991

Matthew Tighe, Donal O'Sullivan, and Eoin Morgan

Anne Harford and Friends

Alan Butterly

Caitriona Beggs

Ciara Metcalfe

Colette McGuinness

Naseer Shaukat

Lynal Jansen

Rush U11, 2014

2015

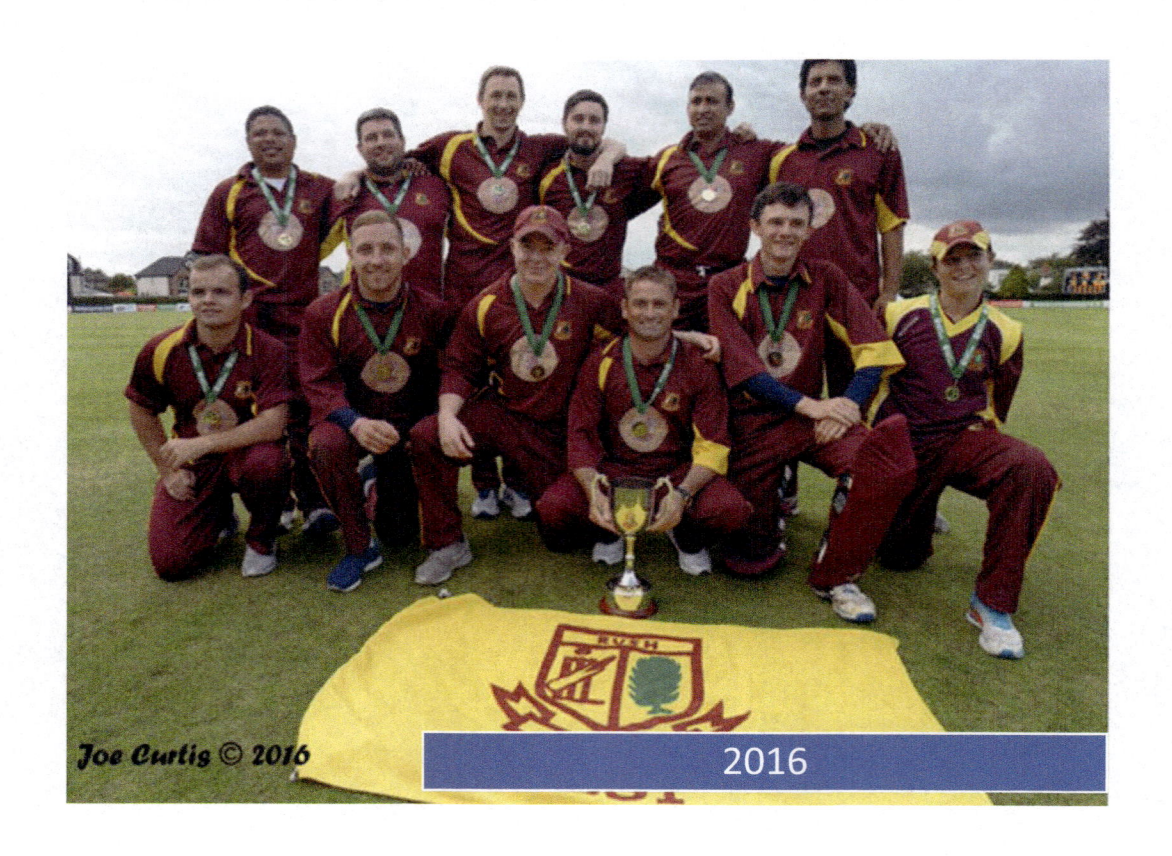

Joe Curtis © 2016

2016

2018

# Chapter 12: Cricket in the Black Hills

## Early Days: 1898-1927

The earliest references to cricket in the Black Hills are contained in the diaries of Mrs Taylor of Ardgillan when she mentions cricket being played in Hampton (Balbriggan) on 5 August 1825 and again in Rush on 19 August 1825. The next reference to cricket in that general area is an account of a game between White Hart and Balcunnin which was played on 31 August 1863 and resulted in a win for White Hart by 31 runs. Every player appeared to have been a member of the gentry because in a very deferential report, it is mentioned that "all is excellent, (and) we do not wish to particularise, but cannot refrain from noticing the wicket-keeping of Mr Gibson which was worthy of the highest commendation."

The Shamrocks CC was based at the Black Hills, and the choice of name is significant because it wished to make clear its identification with the nationalist cause. This espousal of a political ideology flew in the face of the sentiments expressed by Kithogue in the *Drogheda Independent* of 14 October 1899 when he recommended that clubs not be allowed to adopt party or political names or identify themselves in any way with non-sporting matters because in his words, "some Irishmen would drag politics into pitch and toss". Not only was this recommendation ignored completely by the team which became known as the Hills Shamrocks in 1899, but in 1900, it changed its name to the Cronje CC, Black Hills, and its aspiration for the season was "to make as good a stand against their opponents in cricket as the gallant General did against the British forces in South Africa."

In the only game in 1899 for which there is a report, the Hills Shamrocks played Workmen's CC, Skerries, and the result was a comfortable win for the Workmen's CC. In a two innings per side game, the Black Hills scored 11 in the first innings and 28 in the second innings, and the Workmen's reply was 34 in the first innings and 14 in the second innings for 4 wickets.

Results were more positive during the 1900 season. At Black Hills on 19 July, Garristown was beaten on a score of 32 runs to 19, and the bowling honours were taken by Patrick Grimes who "bowled in splendid style for the home team taking seven wickets. Edward Connor batted exceedingly well scoring 15." On 5 August, Corduff was beaten on a score of 49 to 30 in a game played in sunshine and rain on a "very slow wicket". The Cronje's run of success continued on 19 August in "splendid cricket weather" when Oldtown was beaten on a score of 23 runs to 13. The return game against Oldtown in Oldtown ended rather suddenly. The "kind hospitality combined with beautiful weather made the day's outing a pleasant one", but a "singular incident" caused the Cronje team to leave the field. P. Leonard was hit on the head by a full ball, and he was given out LBW:

> We were completely astounded at the fact and immediately left the field and hurried home to spend the remaining few hours of the evening studying the laws of cricket.

In August 1901, Cronje's Black Hills CC played Donabate De Wet's CC and the game ended in a draw on a score of 81 runs each, and this seems to have been a very pleasant social occasion:

> Great respect and thanks to Mr J Smith, Bridge House for his kindness for giving his splendid field and one of his spacious rooms at our disposal which in both we passed a splendid and enjoyable evening's fun.

This club had sufficient numbers in this season to field a second team which played against Balcunning (sic) Major Mc Bride's CC on 18 August 1901 at the Black Hills. The home side scored 79 runs, and the visitors were dismissed for 46 runs due to the bowling of T. C. Clinton and L. Casey. In the return game against Corduff at Corduff, Cronje CC was beaten on a score of 35 runs to 13. The Cronje 1st XI played Donabate De Wet's at the Black Hills on 1 September 1901, and both teams received an interesting invitation from J. Bissett, for the evening prior to the game:

> All bona-fide members of both clubs are requested to attend the annual soiree given by the Cronje CC on Saturday night at 9 o'clock sharp, 31st August without fail.

At its AGM on 4 May 1902, the Cronje CC reverted to being called The Shamrocks CC, The Hills, the "usual officers" were elected, and teams were invited to communicate with Patrick Daly to arrange fixtures for the coming season. That is the extent of the information available on the 1902 season. The only other report on a team in the locality was a reference to a game between Balcunnin and Ballykay which was played on 9 July 1905 and resulted in a win for Balcunnin on a score of 79 runs to 40. Nothing further is known of the cricketing endeavours of the Black Hills CC or Balcunnin until the establishment of the Fingal League in 1926.

## 1927-1969

The establishment of the Fingal League was a catalyst for a revival of cricketing activity in the area. The Black Hills Cricket Club held its AGM on 15 March 1927 and entered a team in the league for the 1927 season. It was not too successful in 1927, but it entered a team again for the 1928 season, and there was also a team from Barnageera in the League. By 8 August 1927, Barnageera had won 6 out of 8 games played, and the Black Hills had won 2 games. The other teams in the section were Balrothery, Baldwinstown, Macraidh (Knockbrack Seconds). There were three teams, Barnageera, Black Hills and Balcunnin, from the area in the Fingal League in 1929. Black Hills continued to struggle and only won 3 games out of 14; Balcunnin won 5 out of 14 games, and Barnageera won 5 out of 10 games.

Black Hills was involved in a very controversial game against Balbriggan which was played at Black Hills on Sunday, 9 June 1929. Details of the incident have already been recounted in the Balbriggan chapter, so the bare outline was that there were a number of LBW decisions which were contested, and this was followed by a contested stumping.

A spectator at the game suggested that the original report contained "intemperate criticism of the game" and was not "calculated to further the interests of cricket in the district." He was very critical of "vituperative comment", and he deemed the correspondent's attitude to the umpire as being prejudiced. He expressed the opinion that a sportsman would never denigrate the actions of an umpire, and he was confident that the Management Committee was well-capable of dealing with the matter because it would take the "sane and proper view of such incidents". The parting shot from the person who signed himself, Fair Play, was that the previous report was not exactly "cricket". There is no account of the decision of the Management Committee and both teams played their full quota of games (14), but they had one draw each, so it is possible that the game was declared a draw.

There is no evidence that the Black Hills played in the 1930 season, but Balcunnin was involved in an exciting final against Knockbrack Seconds on 24 August. The official result of the game was a draw with each team scoring 40 runs, but the correspondent in the *Drogheda Independent* and "a vast number of spectators" were in no doubt that the official marker had got the score wrong and Knockbrack had scored 41 runs. In addition to being unhappy with the marking, the reporter was not impressed by the standard of the cricket which was played. There was "no brilliant batting (and) "most of the score was made through the medium of byes."

The reply was held on the Sunday, 31 August, and one legendary feat was talked about for years after the event. Knockbrack scored 23 runs, with Murphy taking 6 wickets and Hoare taking 4 wickets. The best batsman for Knockbrack was P. Moore who scored 7 runs. Hoare and Gosson opened the batting for Balcunnin, and 9 wickets fell for 14 runs. Hoare (there were 3 Hoares playing) and Power brought the score to 22 when "Murphy send up a fast ball and racing forward made a beautiful one-handed catch to gain victory for his side." Knockbrack Seconds became the first winners of the Fingal Cricket League Perpetual Challenge Cup.

Barnageera played Fingal League cricket in 1931 and won 5 out of 5 games, but Ballymadun, the team which topped the section, won 8 games. Balcunnin returned to the league in 1932, and resumed its role as a force in Fingal cricket. A report of a game on 17 July 1932 encapsulates the main ingredients of Fingal cricket – a low score and brilliant bowling. Balcunnin batted first and scored 13 runs, but in a wonderful response, the opposition was bowled out for 3 runs due to the bowling of Hoare and Murphy. Balcunnin played Portrane in the Fingal League Final of 1932, and in a two innings per side game, won the Fingal Cricket Cup for the first time. Balcunnin defended the trophy successfully in 1933 by defeating Ring Commons in a very one-sided game.

From 1934 onwards, there is no mention of either Barnageera or Balcunnin as playing in the Fingal League, and the Black Hills became the only team in the area. Some of the Barnageera and Balcunnin players such as Hoare, Murphy and Thornton were now playing for the Black Hills, and this may have been because the cricket field was in the Black Hills. The Fingal League Final of 1935 between Naul and the Black Hills resulted in a win for Naul. Naul batted first and scored 33 runs. In reply, the Black Hills were all out for 27. In the second innings, Naul scored 47, and the Black Hills lost 6 wickets for 8 runs in the last 15 minutes of the game. The best batsmen for the Black Hills were Hoare, Murphy, and Thornton, with Murphy and Hoare being the best bowlers. The "outstanding batsmen" for the winners were Hughes, O'Brien, and Rock, with Hughes and Mangan being the best bowlers.

The Black Hills reached the final again in 1936, with Balrothery being the opponents on this occasion. The Black Hills scored 38 runs, with the main contributors being J. Murphy (17), J. Shanley (7) and J. Russell (5). In reply, Balrothery only managed 16 runs, with S. Hoare taking 6 wickets for 9 runs, and

J. Murphy, 4 for 3. C. Mooney made the top score for Balrothery, and he took 6 wickets for 16 runs. These two great rivals met again in the final in 1940, and Balrothery won by 10 runs on a score of 76 to 66 runs.  In 1941, the same teams met when Balrothery CC was attempting to win the trophy for the third year in succession. This game was described as "the most interesting Fingal Cricket League for some years". The Black Hills won by 10 runs, and the victory was attributed to "excellent fielding and bowling. No opportunity was lost by the fielders in making a catch even at times when it seemed impossible". The Black Hills Captain was M. P. Gosson who "inspired confidence", and the other member of the Black Hills team "who distinguished himself was Dick Byrne both with ball and bat". This was the last occasion that the Black Hills won a trophy in the Fingal League until it was re-named The Hills and obtained permission from the Wentges family to use the *Vineyard* as its home ground.

The Black Hills played in the Fingal League during the 1942, 1943 and 1944 seasons, but in the absence of complete records, it is not possible to state with certainty that the club was involved in the Fingal League every year from 1945 to 1947 inclusive. During this period, some prominent Black Hills players such as Mick Gosson, Eddie Dunne, Richard Byrne, Gerry Byrne, and Simon Hoare played Leinster and Fingal League cricket with Skerries at different times. The Black Hills CC was back in the Fingal League in 1948 and 1949.  Eddie Dunne succeeded Tom Murphy as Secretary of the Fingal League, and he was to serve in this position for a very lengthy period.  It appears that the Black Hills did not play in the Fingal League in 1950, 1951 and 1952 and former Black Hills players such as Dick Byrne and Eddie Dunne went back to play with Skerries in 1952 when it resumed playing cricket. 1951 had been a very difficult year for the Fingal League, but Fingal League teams such as Rush and Balrothery had been very successful in interprovincial and national competitions during that season, and it was hoped that their success would act as a catalyst for clubs to re-join the Fingal League. The Black Hills returned to the Fingal League in 1953, and remained in the League under that name until the end of the 1969 season. From a playing perspective, the club was not too successful during this period, and it only made one appearance in a Fingal league final when it was defeated by Knockbrack in 1964.

At an administrative level, the Black Hills members were pro-active in ensuring the continuation of the Fingal League and were always very generous with their time. In addition to Eddie Dunne who served as secretary, Gerry Byrne served as Vice-Chairman in 1955, and Chairman of the League from 1961 until his death in 1993, Seamus Clinton was Ass. Secretary and Treasurer for a period and his brother, Joe also served as Treasurer.  With the Fingal League providing a structure in terms of fixture-making, and landowners such as the Clintons and the Murtaghs providing fields in which to play, cricket was kept alive in the townlands of the Black Hills, Baltrasna, Strifeland, Margaretstown, Milverton, Balcunnin, Barnageera and the Grange until the 1969 generation was ready to take the next step with the establishment of The Hills CC at the Holmpatrick House Hotel in Skerries.

Balcunnin 1930

BALCUNNIN          RUNNERS UP.   19.30

1 S. HORE
2 J. HORE                    SCORE 22 RUNS
3 G. HORE
4 G. THORNTON
5 ? THORNTON
6 G. MURPHY.
7 M. GASON
8 B. MONKS
9 ? POWER
10 ? LAMB
11 ? EVERET

Team Sheet

| | | | | | | |
|---|---|---|---|---|---|---|
| 4 | J. Casey. | l.l.l.l.l.l.l.l.2.l.l. | bowled | " | 14 |
| 5 | J. M. Gowan | l.l.l.3.l.l.l. | bowled | C. Bissett | 8 |
| 6 | G. Delgnam. | l.l.l.l.l.l. | caught + b | m. murphy | 7 |
| 7 | J. Folan. | 0 | bowled | J. Clinton | 0 |
| 8 | m. Cullen. | l.l.l.l. | bowled | C. Bissett | 4 |
| 9 | P. Daly | l. | bowled | J. Clinton | 1 |
| 10 | . Cummings. | | bowled | C. Bissett | 0 |
| 11 | J. Fanning. | 2. | | | 2 |
| | WIDES | | | | |
| | BYES | l. | | | 1 |
| | LEG BYES | | | | |
| | NO BALLS | | | | |
| | | | | TOTAL | 41 |

| RUNS EACH WICKET | 1 FOR 0 | 2 FOR 4 | 3 FOR 4 | 4 FOR 18 | 5 FOR 31 | 6 FOR 32 | 7 FOR 35 | 8 FOR 38 | 9 FOR 38 | 10 FOR 40 |
|---|---|---|---|---|---|---|---|---|---|---|

Black Hills, 1936

# Chapter 13: Cricket in The Hills

The inaugural meeting of The Hills CC was held in the Holmpatrick Hotel, Skerries in late September/early October 1969 and it was chaired by Gerry Byrne. Joe Clinton and Paddy Byrne had inspected *The Vineyard* regarding its possible suitability as a cricket ground, and Gerry Byrne and Joe Clinton were delegated to meet with Mrs Wentges who readily agreed to the request for the use of The Vineyard as a cricket ground. With the permission forthcoming, it was decided to enter a team in the Leinster Cricket Union League for the 1970 season.

A square of wickets was developed in the middle of the field, but the owners cut silage off the field, which meant that it was not possible to play home games until early June. At the end of the season, the square was fenced off to allow for cattle to graze in the outfield. The first clubhouse was a wooden crate acquired at a cost of £19 from Buckleys, the car distributors on Shanowen Road, Santry.

The Hills' first ever game in Leinster League cricket in 1970 did not have the most auspicious of starts. The players drove to the wrong ground, but they were quickly informed by a very superior member of another cricket club, "this is Phoenix CC, Civil Service ground is over there." After this false start, things improved. The Hills amassed 188 runs, with St John Bosco's tally being 12 runs. Johnny Archer scored 80 runs, and Joe Clinton got 28 runs. The wickets were taken by Joe Hoare, Martin Byrne, and Joe Clinton. The first game at The Vineyard was played between The Hills and Knockbrack Second XI on 6 June 1970. Thomas McGrane, long-time Secretary/Treasurer of the Fingal League was captain of the visitors, and the result was a win for The Hills.

In 1971, the all-conquering Hills team under the inspirational captaincy of Johnny Archer had started to make its presence felt in in Leinster Cricket. The Junior A League was won with the team going through the season unbeaten, and it won the Junior Cup by beating Pembroke V in the final which was played at Carlisle on 21 August 1971. This game was played over two days because of rain-interruptions, and with the game finishing on a Sunday morning, it was not possible to have a proper celebration. Michael Sharp, Captain of Pembroke, and Gerry Byrne agreed that the Hills' first cup win had to be celebrated so later in the month a bus load of The Hills team and supporters went to Sydney Parade for a memorable evening. In 1971 also, the Fingal B League was won, and Gerry

Byrne showed his lifelong commitment to youth cricket by donating a trophy for which youth teams in the Fingal League would compete.

In 1972, the Hills First XI went through another season undefeated, and in the process won the Intermediate B League and the Intermediate Cup. There was a perception in junior cricketing circles that junior cricketers did not get as much value for their subscriptions as senior players, and W. J. Whelan of Railway Union agreed to sponsor a trophy for a limited overs competition. In the first year of the competition, the nine teams who participated were Pembroke, Merrion, Leinster, Old Belvedere, CYM, The Hills, Man-O'-War, Clontarf, and Railway Union. The final was played on 8 August 1972 between The Hills and Railway Union, and among the players on the Railway team were Ray Satchwell, Des Stirratt, Archie Noone, Declan Tanham, and Maurice Whelan.

In the final, The Hills batted first, and scored 106 runs for 9, with the main contributors being Anto Byrne (22), Nick Farrell (22*), Paddy Byrne (13*), and Johnny Archer (13). In reply, Railway Union scored 54 runs with Tanham being the top scorer with 16 runs. The wickets were taken by Joe Clinton (4 for 14), Jimmy Byrne (2 for 3), Martin Byrne (2 for 5), and the margin of victory was 52 runs. In addition to winning competitions in Leinster, The Hills also won the B League in Fingal, and formed a Second team.

The 1973 season was equally successful for The Hills CC; the Intermediate A League was won, and on the basis of the latest table which it was possible to access, 10 games were played, 8 were won, 2 were drawn, with an 88% record. The Whelan Cup was retained, with the league and cup double being completed when Rush was beaten in the final of the Intermediate Cup. In this game, Rush batted first, and scored 169 for 7 runs, with the principal contribution to the score coming from Paddy Carthy (76); in reply, the Hills reached the target for the loss of 4 wickets, with major contributions from Liam Archer (62) and Anto Byrne (48). To round off another successful season, the Hills Second XI won the Junior League with a record of 12 games played, 11 wins and 1 draw.

There was a dearth of information regarding the 1974 season, other than to report that The Hills First XI continued on its unbeaten run in Leinster Cricket by winning the Middle A League and Cup. In terms of development in the club, a third team was formed, with the result that extra time would be required on the ground. The Wentges family was approached again, and the club was given permission to use the full outfield for the entire cricket season. The club was also given a five-year lease on the grounds, and this provided very welcome security of tenure.

As winners of the Middle Cup in 1974, The Hills qualified to play in the Irish Junior Cup 1975. In the semi-final, The Hills beat Greysteel from Derry on a score of 137 runs to 59 runs. The final was played in the Phoenix Park against Zingari, the adopted title of Cliftonville 3rds. The Hills batted first with Johnny Archer and Martin Russell opening the batting. One of the opening bowlers for Zingari, W. Irvine, who later played for Bready, took two early wickets. (Liam and John Archer), and The Hills looked to be in very serious trouble. However, Nick Farrell joined Martin Russell at the crease, and for some time, it became a question of survival. Zingari then had the misfortune to lose Irvine because he went over on his ankle and was unable to continue bowling. Nick Farrell (37) and Martin Russell (63) accumulated runs steadily, and there were no further alarms. When Nick Farrell was out, Seán Hoare (24) joined the fray, and he gave further impetus to the scoring rate. Thus, despite of the early setbacks, The Hills batted the full 50 overs and ended on 200 for 9.

In late season, a score of 200 was almost certainly a winning score, but nothing was taken for granted by this incredibly competitive team. Liam Archer took 3 wickets for 20 runs and Martin Byrne took 3 for 22. Zingari was never in the hunt. It only batted 40 of the 50 allocated overs and it ended on 68 runs. This completed a 4-year period during which The Hills won 12 titles at either league or cup level and won several Championship trophies in the very competitive Fingal League.

The 1975 and 1976 seasons were fallow in terms of success at Leinster League level, as the Hills First XI came to terms with the higher standard in the Senior 2 League, but this changed in 1977 when The Hills won the Senior Two League with Man-O'-War coming second. This was not the end of the successes in Leinster because The Hills Second XI won the Intermediate B League and the Whelan Cup.

In terms of development, the opening of the clubhouse on 18 September 1977 was arguably the most important event of the season because for many years, there had been criticism of the "primitive" facilities at some of the Fingal grounds, and this initiative showed that The Hills was willing to complement success on the cricket field with the development of the facilities off the pitch. The official opening was performed by Des Cashell, the President of the Leinster Cricket Union, and an exhibition game featuring current and past international cricketers was played. The most noteworthy element of this game was Joe Archer hitting three successive sixes off Stan Oakes, the last of which cleared the scorebox at the end of the ground.

With the First XI now being very successful in the Senior Two League, it was inevitable that the players would start to win some of the individual awards, and in the period between 1977 and 1982, the Oulton Cup was won by four players from The Hills CC. Liam Archer won it in 1977; Paddy Byrne won the cup in 1978; his brother, Martin, won it in 1980, and Matt Dwyer was the winner in 1982.

The 1978 season was another wonderful season for The Hills CC, with all three teams winning their leagues. The First XI won the Senior 2 League; the Second XI won the Intermediate B League and the Third XI won the Junior A League. The First XI was deprived of the double by Clontarf Second XI who beat The Hills by 4 wickets in the Senior 2 final which was played at Malahide. Liam Archer scored 44 runs; Ernie Bodell took 4 wickets for 44, and Derek Wheeler scored 57 runs for Clontarf.

The 1979 season was a very poor one for The Hills on the field, and at one stage, the First XI was in danger of relegation. Things stabilised to a certain extent, and by winning four games, the team finished third last in the Senior 2 League. In view of the successes at Junior League Level in Leinster and in Fingal competitions, the Executive Committee of The Hills decided that the time was opportune for an application for Senior League status, but the lack of a clearly defined pathway meant that there were lots of obstacles to be surmounted. At the end of the 1979 season, The Hills CC applied for senior status, and the application was rejected on the following grounds: the playing strength and back-up were not up to senior standard, the square was not big enough for senior cricket, and the ancillary facilities at The Vineyard were deemed to be inadequate. Senior status was zealously guarded by the established clubs, and this reluctance to admit other clubs to the inner sanctum combined with the lack of a clearly defined pathway constituted very serious difficulties for clubs that wished to progress from junior to senior status.

Having been beaten in the Senior 2 final in 1978, The Hills had another opportunity to win the Senior 2 Cup in 1980 when its opponents were Old Belvedere Second XI. This game was described as "the most remarkable match that [the participants] had ever played." Old Belvedere was bowled out for 50 runs on a wicket which by any stretch could not be called "a minefield". Martin Byrne (3 for 27) and Paddy (6 for 21) Byrne bowled unchanged, and Johnny Archer took 4 catches at silly mid-on. In reply, The Hills scored 18 runs in the first four overs, and there was no evidence of the carnage which was to follow. The Hills then lost 10 wickets for 14 runs in 30 minutes, with Peter O'Reilly taking 4 wickets for 7 runs, and Bernard O'Donnell's figures were 5 wickets for 9 runs in 4.1 overs.

As a compromise and on a trial basis for one year, it was decided to invite The Hills to play in the John Player Cup in 1981 (The Leinster Senior Cup), but this was a qualified invitation, The Hills would be obliged to play at their opponents' grounds.  The Hills was drawn against Leinster in the Cup, and this provided an opportunity to compare the top team in Senior League with a Senior 2 team. Leinster won the toss, and The Hills missed two big chances before lunch. Short (94) was missed on a run-out when he had only scored 34, and Buttimer (153) was dropped on a caught and bowled. At 245 for 1, it looked as if The Hills would be chasing something in excess of 300, but a combination of tight bowling and good fielding restricted Leinster to 284 for 7. The Hills struggled to reply to this big score, and only Martin Byrne (62) and Gerry Harper (26) got any runs.

This was a learning experience for The Hills, and The Hills Captain, Matt Dwyer's analysis of the game provided an insight into the information which he had gleaned. He mentioned the conversations with the opposition after the game as being invaluable, and he was very specific regarding the differences between Senior 1 and Senior 2 cricketers. The greater level of skill enabled batsmen to place the ball into gaps in the field, and with the grass being much more tightly cut, it was necessary to field on the boundary rather than run after the ball as applied in Fingal where the grass tended to be appreciably longer. Also, the wicket in Rathmines favoured the batsmen, and there was no assistance in it for the bowlers. Having said all that, Matt felt that the team had given a good account of itself, and he did not have any concern regarding The Hills being able to acquit itself well in Senior 1 cricket.

The junior clubs hoped that the participation of The Hills and CYM in Senior Cricket would be the prelude to the launching of a system of promotion and relegation, because there was a perception that it would not be possible to accommodate twelve Senior Clubs in Leinster Cricket, but for some of the existing senior clubs, this would have resembled turkeys voting for Christmas. In October 1981, another application for senior status from The Hills was rejected, but in his annual report for the 1981 season, John Dawson's advice to The Hills was to "keep trying".

The Hills reached the Senior 2 final again in 1982, and its opponents were its near neighbours, Balrothery. The game was played on a sweltering hot day at Rathmines, and on this occasion, The Hills managed to win the Senior 2 Cup at last. Gerry Harper scored 111 runs out of Hills' total of 244, with Patrick Hoare (58) also making a valuable contribution. Balrothery was captained by Noel Harper, Gerry's brother, and he was the top scorer (52) for Balrothery with John Mooney (The Ranger) scoring 34 runs in a total of 124 runs. Matt Dwyer took 5 wickets for 10, and Paddy Byrne's figures were 5 wickets for 10 runs.

In that era, Nottingham Turf wickets (artificial) were seen as a panacea for improving batting techniques, and for combatting the vicissitudes of Irish weather. During the 1981 season, work was started on an artificial wicket, and the wicket was ready for play at the start of the new season, with The Hills being the second club in Ireland to lay an artificial wicket. During 1982, an intensive lobbying campaign was mounted for the support of senior clubs, sectional interests, and the Executive Committee of the LCU. Matt Dwyer, Captain of The Hills First XI waited until 10.00 p.m. in the carpark of a senior club so that he could speak to the President of that club. The President of the senior club was so impressed with this enthusiasm and dedication that he promised that his club would vote for The Hills CC to be accepted into senior cricket. Therefore, by the end of the 1982 season, it seemed that all the auguries were in favour of The Hills achieving the Holy Grail of senior status, and thus it came to pass on 17 September 1982, The Hills CC became the first Fingal League club to be admitted to the Leinster Senior League.

In 1983, there were some in the higher echelons of Leinster cricket who had misgivings about The Hills being admitted to the "top table" because of concerns about the playing standards of the team. The visit of the mighty North Down to The Vineyard for a first -round tie in the Schweppes Irish Senior Cup was seen by many at The Vineyard as an ideal opportunity to answer the critics. A 52-run victory for The Hills provided the perfect response to the critics, and Seán Pender's analysis of the game was as follows:

> The Hills fully deserved their convincing success. Ultimately it was a case of spirited bowling and superb catching making up for some patchy batting. On this performance, more teams than North Down will bite the dust at Milverton this season.

Joe Archer (31) was given the Man-of-the Match award, and in addition to his knock which included 3 "massive" sixes and a four, he also took two magnificent catches. Liam Archer scored 19 runs in a patient knock and then dismissed the top two North Down batsmen and finished with three for 13 in 10 overs. There was also favourable mention for Matt Dwyer's captaincy and his "tight, accurate left arm bowling". The Hills scored 153 for 9, and North Down's reply was 101 runs.

The period from 1983 to 1989 was one of consolidation in Senior Cricket for The Hills First XI, but honours were still coming to The Vineyard. In 1984, the Second XI won the Middle League, and the Thirds won the Junior B League. In 1985, Martin Byrne won the award for the best bowler in Senior 1 (the O'Grady Cup), and Michael Dwyer won the wicket-keeping award (Hopkins Cup). In 1987, the Second XI won the Middle League, and the following year, the Fourths won the league and cup double.

The Fourths' achievement merits more detail because Dick Byrne, a septuagenarian, won the Man-of-the Match award. The Hills' opponents were Balbriggan, and the game was played at Rush on 27 August 1988. The Hills batted first, and scored 171 runs, with major contributions from Joe Clinton (36), Richie Byrne (40), Mark Maguire (29*) and N. Nugent (19). Balbriggan was restricted to 65 runs, and the main bowlers were L. Daly (4 for 15) and D. Byrne's 5 for 30 which included a hat-trick. The other major development in 1988 at The Vineyard was the formation of a women's team which won the Minor League in 1989, the Division 3 Cup in 1990; there were two women's teams in 1991, and the Women's Firsts won League 3, the Second XI won League 4 in 1991; the Firsts won the Division 2 Cup in 1994, and won Division 2 in 1995.

By 1989, The Hills' years of consolidation in the Leinster Senior League were finished completely, and there was now a panel of experienced cricketers with a sprinkling of youth. Among the survivors from the first senior game in 1981 were Matt Dwyer, Michael Dwyer, Martin Byrne, Paddy Byrne, John Archer, Gerry Harper, Patrick Hoare; the additions from within The Hills' own ranks were Liam Archer and Seán Hoare; Mark Clinton and Alan Courell were products of the very successful coaching programme which had been initiated in 1978 under the supervision of Joe Caprani and John Andrews and Noel Harper had transferred from Balrothery because of their desire to play Senior Cricket.

In the final of the Senior Cup, The Hills played Carlisle at Kimmage on 22 July 1989. The Hills won the toss, batted first, and lost the first three wickets for 8 runs; there were 8 wickets down when The Hills had only 97 runs on board. Mark Clinton, The Hills Captain, scored 29 runs, and the 17-year-old Alan Courell got 38 runs. There was also a crucial last wicket stand of 25 runs between

Martin Byrne (20*) and Michael Dwyer (10*) which gave The Hills something to defend, and Fingal League sides were well-used to defending low scores.

The Carlisle reply started well, and the opening stand of 37 runs suggested that The Hills' supporter who left the ground at the end of the first innings was correct in his assessment of the situation. Mark Cohen (18) was out to a brilliant slip-catch by John Andrews off the bowling of Matt Dwyer; Martin Byrne took three of the top four batsmen for 31 runs in his twelve overs, but at 83 for 3, it was still only possible to see a win for Carlisle. In an amazing turn-around, Carlisle lost 5 wickets for 14 runs in 7 overs, with Gerry Harper taking 2 key wickets, Noel Harper took 2 wickets and Paddy Byrne took 1 wicket to leave The Hills the winners of the Leinster Senior Cup for the first time in its history. What about the supporter who went home early? He heard Philip Greene reading out the result on Radio Éireann; he turned the car around at the Railway Bridge in Skerries and drove back to Kimmage.

With a crucial Belvedere Bond League game to be played the following day, the players' celebrations were somewhat restricted because this Hills' team was very focused. On Sunday, Leinster batted first and scored 172 runs for the loss of 9 wickets, with Paddy Byrne taking 3 wickets for 40 runs. In reply, The Hills looked to be in trouble, but Saturday's heroes came to the rescue again. Alan Courell scored 47*, Mark Clinton scored 31, and The Hills chased down the score for the loss of 6 wickets. In the final league game of the season, The Hills played Clontarf, its closest rivals, on Wednesday, 23 August 1989. In a 110 overs game, The Hills opted to bat for 60 overs, and scored 197 runs for the loss of 7 wickets. There were significant contributions from Matt Dwyer (29), Seán Hoare (30), John Andrews (43) and Martin Byrne (33*). It looked as if Brian Bergin (83) and Johnny Daly (30) were going to chase down The Hills' total with ease, but Matt Dwyer clean-bowled Bergin, and then took a catch off the bowling of Noel Harper to dismiss Daly. McClean scored 11, no other Clontarf got into double figures, and Clontarf finished on a score of 166 runs for 9 wickets, with Matt Dwyer taking 4 wickets for 43 and Noel Harper, 4 for 58. The points for a draw meant that The Hills had won the League and Cup double. The Hills' record in the 12-game league programme was 7 wins, 4 draws, 1 loss, 103 bonus points, and a total of 212 points. With one game left to play, Clontarf had accumulated 175 points. The focus then turned to the Wiggins Teape League, with an attempt to win the treble, but it was not to be. In the semi-final at Claremont Road, YMCA scored 107 runs, and The Hills finished on 82 runs.

The double for the Firsts was not the only silverware which came to The Vineyard during the 1989 season. The Women's First XI won the Minor League, and the Fourth XI won the Junior A league. The Third XI played Railway Union in the final of the Whelan Cup and won by 4 wickets. In that game, the father and son combination of Martin and Declan Moore took 6 wickets between them, with Martin taking 3 for 18 and Declan taking 3 for 8. Railway was dismissed for 60 runs, and The Hills scored 62 runs for the loss of 6 wickets. The main contributors to The Hills' score were Nick Farrell (25) and Martin Russell (16).

The cricket scene in Leinster changed completely in the 1990s, with the abolition of the ban on professionals in 1990, but there was a caveat, the professional cricket was obliged to have an acceptable coaching qualification. The ban on professionals was reinstated the following year, and it was not rescinded until 1994 when teams were allowed to have 1 overseas player. The Hills First XI remained competitive, but it did not win any trophy at senior level until 1996. Individual awards continued to come to The Vineyard, Matt Dwyer won the O'Grady Cup for the best bowler on five occasions (1990, 1991, 1993, 1994, 1996), and he won the award for the best all-rounder in Leinster cricket in 1996.

The junior teams continued to bring silverware to the club, with the Third XI winning the Intermediate A League and the Whelan Cup in 1990. In the final of the Whelan Cup, The Hills played North Kildare, and dismissed North Kildare for 96 runs for 7. Stephen Archer (son of Joe) took 2 wickets for 22, and then hit 49* runs with assistance from Mark Maguire (17*) to leave The Hills winners by 5 wickets. The following year, the Second XI won the Tillain Cup, but the only information available on that triumph is that The Hills appeared to have beaten Balbriggan in one of the earlier rounds, although the report is full of contradictions. It is mentioned that The Hills won by 1 run, but according to the scores which are reported, Balbriggan scored 136, and The Hills scored 124.

In 1993, the Second XI won the Senior 3 League, and the Thirds won the YMCA Salver for the first time by beating YMCA, the host club. YMCA batted first, and was restricted to 73 runs for 8, with the wickets being taken by James Carroll (3 for 15), Joseph Clinton, Brendan, and Martin Moore. The first wicket (Barry Archer) fell when the score was 21, James Carroll scored 15* and Nick Farrell got the Man of the Match award for his score of 28*. The other major development that season was that a player from The Hills CC was capped for Ireland at senior level when Marguerite Burke represented Ireland at the 1993 World Cup which was played at the Oval.

In 1995, there was continuing evidence of the impact of the coaching programme which had been initiated by Joe Caprani, as the U18 team won the League, and then won the Seán McGrath Cup by beating Old Belvedere in the final; the Second XI won the Senior 2 League, and Joseph Clinton followed in the line of some very illustrious Fingal cricketers by winning the Oulton Cup.

Off the field, the members continued the drive to develop the infrastructure at The Vineyard, and from the early 1990s, the club was anxious to put a more permanent building in place, but it was necessary to proceed with a certain amount of caution because the club was leasing the ground. The support which the club received from the Wentges family was demonstrated by the fact that Richard Wentges, an architect, designed the pavilion, and Michael Wentges made the weathervane which stands proudly above the clock on the pavilion. Seán Gilbride, a local councillor, helped with the planning application, and eventually, all the legal hurdles were surmounted. For a builder to undertake the work in its entirety, the cost would have been in the region of £110,000, and at that stage, the club had £5,000 in the bank so it was decided that the project would have to be undertaken by voluntary labour. Some grants and loans were sourced, and work began. The members and supporters who were tradesmen and other volunteers gave very willingly of their time, and as a result of a tremendous amount of goodwill and hard work, the magnificent building was ready for the official opening on 6th August 1995, which was performed by Councillor Seán Gilbride and Michael Dwyer, Club Chairman. While the members of The Hills rarely indulged in self-congratulation, the building of the pavilion was an achievement of which all members and supporters of the club could be justifiably proud.

In 1996, The Hills was the first Fingal League club to be invited to host the Leinster Senior Cup final, and this invitation was an affirmation for the work which the club had done on developing its facilities over a number of years. The main objective for the 1996 season was for the Firsts to be playing in the final at the Vineyard. With this in mind, Matt Dwyer was elected captain of the First XI, and Ray Daly, a former Irish international, was appointed club coach.

The first trophy of the season to be decided was the 50 Overs Wiggins Teape League, and The Hills had never won this competition. The final was played at Malahide, and the opposition for The Hills was provided by Leinster CC. The first four batsmen for the Hills, Paul Mooney (39), Patrick Byrne (31), Barry Archer (19), and Declan Moore (36), gave The Hills a solid platform from which to accelerate, but there was a minor slump which was arrested by John

Archer (10), John Andrews (38), and Joseph Clinton (17) to give The Hills a total of 203 runs for 8 wickets. This was deemed by the neutrals to be about 20 or 30 runs short of a good score, but in Fingal, a good score is whatever runs the team scores in the first innings.

In reply, a lot depended on the Byrne brothers, Joe, Johnny, and Peter, but on the day, the players at the other end struggled. Matt Dwyer brought himself on to bowl in the 16th over and the Leinster batsmen had to decide whether to attack the spin or to block it out. Mark Jones decided to attack, and was out, caught sub, bowled Dwyer. Peter Byrne continued to play his shots, but with the run-rate continuing to climb, it became apparent that Leinster would finish well-short of The Hills' total. In the end, the margin of victory was 28 runs, and for his part in arresting the collapse, John Andrews was given the Man of the Match award.

Winning the 50 Overs trophy was a bonus, and then the attention turned to the Senior Cup. The Hills played Rush in the semi-final, and thanks to Noel Harper who took 5 wickets for 2 runs from 17 balls, Rush was bowled out for 154 runs. The required runs were not scored until the last ball of the allotted overs, although The Hills would have won on fewer wickets lost if the scores had remained tied as they had been with 5 balls to be bowled.

3rd August 1996 was one of the great days at The Vineyard. The pitch was adjudged to be one of the best in Ireland, the outfield was in beautiful condition and the magnificent new pavilion was a visually stunning example of what can be achieved by committed voluntary effort. The sun was shining, a marquee was in place so that the great and the good could partake of the legendary hospitality of The Hills CC, and everything was in readiness for the meeting of The Hills and Pembroke. The Hills' team on this occasion was a combination of some of the heroes of the double wins in 1989 (Matt Dwyer, Michael Dwyer, Mark Clinton, Johnny Archer, Noel Harper, John Andrews) and new blood (Joseph Clinton, Patrick Byrne, Barry Archer, Paul Mooney, and Declan Moore). Uniquely, The Hills was the only club in the Senior League at that stage which did not employ the services of an overseas player.

The Hills won the toss but did not have the greatest of starts. There were two wickets down with the score on 23. There was then a stand of 62 runs between Barry Archer (33) and Declan Moore (28) to bring the score to 85, but 3 more wickets fell for 9 runs, leaving The Hills on 94 for 5 wickets. Fortunately, The Hills batted to no. 11, and there were very valuable contributions from John Archer (13), Noel Harper (12), John Andrews (16),

Matt Dwyer (23), Joseph Clinton (23*) and Michael Dwyer (9*). The Hills' final score was 200 for 9, and in the opinion of one former international, 200 was always a winning score in that era.

The Pembroke Professional, Wim Jansen, was out very quickly, caught and bowled by Declan Moore. There was then a stand of 39 runs between Richard Hastie and Trevor Dagg which was ended by Matt Dwyer with the aid of another catch by Declan Moore. Pembroke wickets fell in flurries, 2 for 49 became 7 for 77, 8 for 108, and there was a late revival to bring the score to 140, but it was all too little, too late for Pembroke. The Hills had won the Leinster Senior Cup for the second time. For his achievement with the bat, his superb bowling (12 overs, 8 maidens, 3 for 11) and captaincy, Matt Dwyer was awarded Man of the Match, but every member of the team had contributed to this great day for The Hills CC.

With the First XI doing so well, international recognition came at last to Hills' players when Declan Moore was awarded a full cap and made his debut against Gloucestershire at Clontarf on 7 May 1996. Declan was the first of four Hills' players to receive international caps between 1996 and 1999, with the next international being Matt Dwyer, who very belatedly, received his first cap on 1 May 1998. Paul Mooney was also capped in 1998, and made his debut at Pollock Park, Lurgan, while Barry Archer played against Scotland on 29 June 1999.

Between 1995 and 2001, The Hills had a magnificent Second XI, comprising of some of the heroes of 1989 and emerging talent within the club. During this period, the team won the Senior 2 League in 1995, 1996, and 1997, the Senior 2 Cup in 1997, 1998 and 1999, and the Tillain Cup in 1999. The players from the Second XI who won the Oulton Cup were Luke Clinton (1997), Martin Byrne (1998), and Pat Bennett (1999). Martin Byrne who captained the team during many of those years, has described it as a wonderful time for the players because in addition to continuing to play at a high level with friends, it provided the opportunity to play cricket with their sons.

In 2000, The Hills First XI lost to Phoenix for whom Hendy Wallace scored an unbeaten 127 in the final of the Lewis Traub League. In 2001, The First XI was relegated to the B Division, and spent two seasons in this Division. There was then a promotion to the A League in 2003, and this was followed by another relegation in the 2004 season. The Hills had gone down the overseas player route in 1998 with the signing of Aijaz Farooqui, and he played with the First XI until 2011, but in the early 2000s, the entire cricket scene in Leinster changed because in addition to the designated overseas player, lots of senior clubs had players from overseas who had played to a high level in their own countries and were inspired to come to Ireland by the "Celtic Tiger" phenomenon. The Hills First XI could not compete for honours in this environment, and towards the end of the 2004 season, questions were being asked within the club regarding playing policy. Did the members wish the First XI to play in the B Division on a regular basis with success being defined as promotion to the A League, and then relegation the following year or did the players wish to be competing for honours? There was a consensus that playing in the B Division was setting the bar too low, and that this would have an impact on the more ambitious players who wished to become senior internationals. Two major decisions were taken in 2004 which would have an impact on the club for many years. It was decided to employ as the overseas player a cricketer who had enjoyed previous success in Leinster League cricket because this would reduce any "settling-in period", and Bryn Thomas who had played with CYM was enlisted as the overseas player for the 2004 season. The other major decision was to employ a top-class coach for the First XI, and John Wills, who had coached the Irish senior international team and the Irish Ladies team, joined the club in 2005.

With these building blocks in place, a combination of circumstances resulted in some very good players coming to The Hills for the 2005 season. Michael Lax had played on the same CYM team as Bryn Thomas; Ian O'Herlihy joined the club from Merrion CC; Gavin Morgan transferred from Rush, and Keith Peinke, a South African, came to Ireland on a holiday visa. This infusion of talent allied to the very talented young players who were at the club meant that The Hills was again in a position to challenge for honours. The first target was to escape from Senior League B, and this was achieved with consummate ease. The record for the season was 12 games played, 11 games won, 1 game lost, and 245 points accumulated which was 27 points ahead of YMCA who finished second.

The Hills reached the final of the Short Overs League which at that stage had been reduced to 45 overs per side but played very badly against a very strong Clontarf team and lost by 8 wickets. The opportunity for revenge came very quicky because The Hills and Clontarf reached the Senior Cup final, which was played at Inch, Balrothery on 30 July 2005. Those who arrived early at Inch for the game between The Hills and Clontarf were greeted with plastic sheets covering the pitch and the bowlers' run-ups. The prospects for play seemed remote, thus, it was deemed prudent to repair to the *Merry Cricketer* and to partake of a healthy breakfast. Just as the nicely poached egg and the white pudding were being savoured, word came through from Inch that play would be starting in 10 minutes, so it was necessary to finish eating the breakfast in great haste and return to Inch.

Clontarf who had been having a very successful season, had an extremely strong team with five of the first six batsmen being full internationals. The toss was won by Clontarf, and somewhat surprisingly given the ground and atmospheric conditions, they opted to bat first. The first Clontarf wicket (Bray) fell when the score was 13, the next wicket (Rigby) fell at 29, followed by another wicket (Coghlan) at 32. The international players continued to come to the crease and next in was Trent Johnston who had returned from the USA that morning. His stay at the crease was very short-lived because he was clean bowled by a magnificent delivery from Gavin Morgan. Ronan O'Reilly came and went, and Clontarf were 72 runs for 6 wickets. Greg Molins (99) and Ian Synnott led the Clontarf recovery and put together a stand of 97 runs. There was a huge appeal for a catch against Molins, but the person who mattered, the umpire, deemed that Greg had not hit the ball. The eighth wicket partnership between Molins and Cullen brought the score to 199, but the last three wickets fell for 1 run, and Clontarf's final score was 200 in 58.3 overs. The bowling honours were taken by Joseph Clinton (3 for 31), Luke Clinton (2 for 22), Gavin Morgan (2 for 43), Michael Lax (1 for 26) and Barry Archer (1 for 34).

Bryn Thomas (121*) and Gavin Morgan opened the batting for The Hills, and Gavin was out for a duck when the score was 6 runs, followed by a partnership of 72 runs between Thomas and Barry Archer (12) in which Bryn was very much the dominant partner. There was then a minor collapse, and three wickets fell for 17 runs. Patrick Byrne (31), batting in the unaccustomed position of number 6 assisted Bryn in steadying matters, and when Patrick was out on 187, it was all over bar the shouting. Ian O'Herlihy and Bryn Thomas got the required runs with the minimum of fuss, and The Hills had reached the target in 52.4 overs. Long-time followers of The Hills adjudged Bryn Thomas's innings the finest ever knock by a Hills' player. He seemed to have been untroubled by any of the vicissitudes which had caused the downfall of so many other batsmen, and he made the judging of the Man of the Match award a formality. At the end of this season, there were also individual honours for a Hills' player when Ian O'Herlihy won the Hopkins' Cup, the first player from the club to win that award since Michael Dwyer in 1985.

The following season The Hills reached the Senior Cup final again, and on 29 July 2006 the opponents were North County CC, who by general agreement had been the best team in Ireland over a lengthy period. On that basis, North County was adjudged to be the favourites, but such tags meant very little in Fingal cricket. North County won the toss and opted to bat first. The first partnership of Conor Armstrong (96) and Seán O'Connor (27) put on 38 runs before O' Connor was bowled by Luke Clinton. A partnership of 70 runs between Armstrong and Botha (42) followed before Botha was bowled by Bryn Thomas. There was no other major partnership for North County, and its innings ended on 248 runs. The bowling honours were taken by Barry Archer (4 for 62), Bryn Thomas (3 for 42) and Luke Clinton (2 for 24).

The Hills' innings had a disastrous start when Bryn Thomas, the hero of the previous year's win, was out LBW with the score on 7. Michael Lax (94) and Patrick Byrne (45) retrieved the situation, and in a stand of 157 runs brought The Hills back into the game. Bad light stopped play after 43 overs with The Hills on 179 for 2. On Saturday evening, the critics deemed The Hills to be in the more favourable position, but it is always wise to hedge one's bets when discussing games between Fingal sides. André Botha and Reinhardt Strydom bowled brilliantly on Monday evening, and The Hills lost 3 wickets for 8 runs. The Hills' score was now 188 for 5, and the critics had now decided that North County was in the driving seat. O, ye of little faith! 188 for 5 became 208 for 6, and the game was now in the hands of Michael O'Herlihy (34*) and Joseph Clinton (7*). On the fourth ball of the 58th over, Michael O'Herlihy hit a glorious six over the long on boundary, and The Hills had retained the cup by beating their local rivals.

Over the years, the Alan Murray cup competition had been played in a variety of formats, and in 2007, it consisted of groups at the early stages, followed by semi-finals and finals. That year, Clontarf had already won the Cup, and later in the season, won the League so the Alan Murray cup was the third leg of the treble. The final was staged at *The Vineyard* on the 8 August between The Hills and Clontarf. The Hills won the toss and opted to bat first. Jeremy Bray (64*) batted right through the innings, and he received great support from Max Sorensen (42) and Michael O'Herlihy (24*). The Hills ended on 160 for 3 wickets.

Clontarf got off to a reasonable start, and the first wicket (Coghlan) fell when the score was 35. Jeremy Bray as befitted his status as an all-rounder then had Rigby caught by Michael O'Herlihy. Rod Hokin, the Clontarf Professional had been a thorn in the side of The Hills on every occasion that he had played against them, but not this evening. Max Sorensen had just joined

The Hills and was still adjusting to life in Leinster cricket, but the 4 overs which he bowled were probably the fastest and most frightening ever seen at *The Vineyard*. He bowled Rod Hokin, LBW, and to add insult to injury, possibly broke Hokin's foot, so Rod had to be helped off the field. Jeremy Bray's evening was not finished. He took a stupendous catch on the boundary off the bowling of Luke Clinton to dismiss Andrew Poynter. However, Clontarf was going nicely and chipping away at the target. At 7 wickets for 129, things looked good for Clontarf, but that became 8 wickets for 129. Richie Reid (21*) batting at no. 10 brought Clontarf back into the game, and 3 runs were needed to win off the last ball. Clontarf could only manage 2 with Christopher Cahill being run out, and The Hills winning by virtue of fewer wickets lost. This was a truly memorable game, with some magnificent individual performances. Jeremy Bray was given the Man of the Match award for his batting, bowling, and fielding, and Max Sorensen's bowling spell on that evening is still spoken about at *The Vineyard* and further afield with awed reverence.

The quest for Irish Senior Cup honours had become akin to the Holy Grail for The Hills, but every year the club seemed to be bedevilled with some kind of misfortune in this competition. In 2007, The Hills reached the final which was played at Clontarf, and its opponents were North County, the Irish Senior Cup specialists. North County won the toss and batted first. The main contributor to its score was André Botha (84), but Conor Armstrong (41), P. Mooney (31) and John Mooney (31) also made significant scores to leave North County with the competitive total of 259 runs in 40 overs. Any chance that The Hills had of chasing this score disappeared in the early overs with the dismissal of Jeremy Bray for 9, and then Botha had a hat-trick of dismissals. Barry Archer (52) and Mark Dwyer (36) batted well for The Hills, but the team finished on 154 runs, 105 runs short of North County's score.

In 2008 under the captaincy of Luke Clinton, The Hills won the Leinster Senior League for the first time since 1989. The Hills lost the first game of the season to North County, and there was one other loss to Rush, but with 8 wins and rain draws, The Hills finished the season on 201 points, with Merrion in second place on 166 points   The club's commitment to coaching and development was shown by the appointment of Albert Van der Merwe on a 12- month contract. In addition to working in schools in the locality, Albert continued to work on his cricketing skills in conjunction with John Wills, and his dedication was rewarded in 2009 when he won the Samuels Cup for being the best all-rounder in Leinster cricket and he received a full international cap. At infrastructural level, new practice nets were constructed in 2008 and the club house was refurbished completely in 2009.

In the period 2000 to 2009, the main emphasis has been on the First XI, but other teams from The Hills were also successful during this time. It will be necessary for the review of their successes to be synoptic because of pressure on space. In 2000, the Third XI won the Middle 2 Cup, and the Fifth XI won the Junior C League. The following year, the Second XI won the Senior 3 League, and Martin Byrne won the Seán Pender Fair Play Award. The Thirds win the Intermediate A League in 2003 and the Middle B League in 2004. ICC Trophy games were held in Ireland in 2005, and there were two games at The Vineyard (Bermuda v Scotland, and Denmark v Norway). In 2006, Paddy Byrne organised a Fifths team to play in the cup, and it won the Minor Cup by beating YMCA at Phoenix Cricket Club. Just as he had done in 1977 for the opening of the club house at the Vineyard, Joe Archer starred in this game, and he hit some sixes over the Phoenix clubhouse. The women's First XI won the Minor Cup in 2007.

In 2008, the YMCA Salver was won by the Third XI, with contributions from Jason McGee (24) and Malcolm Byrne (21) to give The Hills a score of 117 runs for 8 wickets. Leinster was all out for 74 with Emmet Brannigan doing most of the damage (4 wickets for 10 runs). In a very successful year for the club, the Fourths won the Junior A League, and the Fifths won the Junior C League. The Second XI won the Senior 2 League in 2009, and there were individual honours for Tracy Fleming (Division 2 Batting) and Miranda Andrews (Division 2 Bowling). The successes for the Women's First XI continued into 2010 when it won the Division 2 League and Cup double. Laura Boylan was capped for Ireland in 2011 and Veronica Fay-Watt won the Division 3 Wicketkeeping award. In 2012, the Women's Second XI won the Division 2 League and the Minor Cup.

For the late Richard Dunne, winning the Irish Senior Cup was an obsession, and at the start of each season, he would ask the same question, "do you think we'll win the Irish Senior Cup this year?" In April 2012 at the Friday morning soiree in Olive Café, Max Sorensen promised Richard that this would be the year when Hills would win the coveted Bob Kerr, Irish Senior Cup. On the way to the final, The Hills beat Bready, won a bowl-out against CIYMS (2-1), beat YMCA in the third round, beat Waringstown at Waringstown in the semi-final, and qualified to meet Merrion in the final which was played at Clontarf on 1 September 2012.

The Irish Senior Cup final is a great occasion, but it is important to bear in mind that it is still a cricket match and to play the game, not the occasion. It is essential not to become distracted by logistical issues such as car-parking permits, tickets for lunch etc, and there was the added complication that year of a film crew looking for live footage to underpin its theme of the importance of cricket in Fingal. Merrion won the toss and opted to bat first. A combination of very accurate bowling and a conservative approach by the openers resulted in a very low scoring rate, and Ben Ackland had only scored 8 runs off 36 balls when he fell to the Mark Dwyer and Nicolaas Pretorius combination. Dom Joyce scored 51 runs off 113 balls, and John Anderson's tally was 47 runs off 74 balls. With the scoring rate as low as this, either Joyce or Anderson needed to be there at the end of the innings, but Joyce was out when the score was 87 and Anderson was out on 133. Merrion scored 152 runs in 48 overs. The Hills' bowling attack maintained the form which it had displayed throughout the season. Naseer Shaukat took 3 wickets for 16 runs, Luke Clinton took 3 wickets for 26 runs, Tomás Rooney-Murphy 1 took for 25, Max Sorensen's figures were 1 for 27 and Mark Dwyer took 1 for 41.

The Hills' reply started steadily. The first wicket partnership of Jonathan Andrews (14) and Darryl Calder (64*) ensured that Merrion would not be let back into the contest. Mike Baumgart (34) and Darryl put on a further 69 runs and Darryl Calder and Cormack McLoughlin-Gavin wrapped up proceedings to give The Hills a comfortable 8 wickets victory.

This was an incredibly emotional day for all involved with the Hills CC, and it was particularly gratifying to have the cup presented by Mrs Hope Kerr who had sponsored the competition in memory of her late husband, Bob. Mrs Kerr and Bob had always been great supporters of the Hills CC and were regular visitors to The Vineyard. This victory was the culmination of a dream which had commenced in 1983 when the Hills played in the Irish Senior Cup for the first time. In subsequent years, there were heartbreaks and near misses, and it seemed as if winning the Cup was always going to be a step too far. The roller-coaster of emotion continued into the evening and while the victory was being savoured, Max Sorensen requested a moment's silence so that he could address the players and supporters. In a very touching speech, he thanked everyone for the support which he had received since he had come to The Hills, and after dedicating the victory to his friend, Richard Dunne, he presented his medal to Richard as a memento of a great occasion. This was a very fitting finale to a voyage which had commenced in Olive Café in early April.

2012 was also a year in which individual Hills' players won awards. Max Sorensen was capped for Ireland; Naseer Shaukat won the John Dawson Fair

Play Award; John Wills won the Coach of the Year Award, and 27 years after he had won the Hopkins Cup, Michael Dwyer was the Division 2 wicketkeeper of the year.

2013 was another momentous year for The Hills CC. The Senior A League was re-branded as Open Competitions Division 1, and The Hills First XI won it with record of 11 wins and 3 losses to finish 11 points ahead of Merrion. For the 2013 season, there was another revamp of the Alan Murray cup with each team playing 6 games, and the top two teams in each group qualified for the semi-finals which were held at Sydney Parade. The Hills met Pembroke in the semi-final, and unfortunately for Pembroke, they met Max Sorensen at his very best. He scored 97* with some of the most fearsome hitting ever seen at the venue. Cricket balls were hit by him over the pavilion, into apartments, into back gardens and down the street. His brilliant knock from 36 balls included 10 sixes and four fours. It didn't matter on the day whether a bowler was a fast bowler or a spinner. Barry McCarthy conceded 68 runs in his four overs, and Paul Lawson conceded 42 runs. Mike Baumgart scored 44 runs and Mark Dwyer added another 34 as The Hills ended on 210 for 6. Pembroke's response foundered very quickly, with their final score being 151 for 8.

In the final, The Hills played Railway Union who had beaten North County in the other semi-final. The Hills batted first, and Mark Dwyer continued his good form from the previous game by scoring 37, and Max Sorensen scored 41 (3 fours and 1 six). The Hills' total was 153 for 7, and in the modern era, a chase of under 8 runs per over is eminently gettable. Railway started very well, and there were solid contributions from Paddy Conliffe (26), Saad Ullah (21) and Mo Tariq (16). Dhruv Kapoor struggled against some very accurate bowling and could only manage 1 run off 8 balls. However, Tim Townend (37) was going very nicely, and with 2 runs required, he was run out by Cormac Mc Loughlin-Gavin going for the second run, thus giving The Hills victory on fewer wickets lost. The wickets were taken by Mark Dwyer, Luke Clinton, and that man again, Max Sorensen. This was a repeat of the Alan Murray Final of 2007 when The Hills beat Clontarf at the Vineyard on fewer wickets lost. There was another raft of individual awards for club members, with John Wills winning the Hall of Fame Award. Other award winners were Luke Clinton (John Dawson Fair Play Award), Mike Baumgart (Solomons Cup for Fielding), Laura Boylan (Wicket-keeping in Division 2) and Caroline Clinton (Fair Play award).

However, the most significant achievement of the season was off the playing field as The Hills CC obtained the freehold of The Vineyard. Milverton

Hall and Demesne had been sold to Treasury Holdings in 2008, and the intention of the purchasers was to develop two golf courses, a hotel, an equestrian centre, and some luxury houses. The Vineyard was included in the sale because it was planned that cricket teams might come from overseas and play games on the ground. The club was assured by both the Wentges family and the purchasers that The Hills need not worry with regard to its tenure of the ground. With the economic collapse, Treasury went into NAMA, and the club was now obliged to deal with NAMA. In 2008, there was a reference to The Hills being given the ground for free, but NAMA was obliged to recover as much money as possible from bad loans, and it became clear that the club would be obliged to purchase the ground. Valuers and estate agents were commissioned to value the Vineyard, and all the legal and financial hurdles were surmounted in October 2013. The club which had been given access to the ground as tenants in 1970 was now one of the few clubs in Leinster which owned its own ground, and it was to the credit of the Executive, the members, and friends that the necessary capital was raised to complete the purchase.

With the freehold of the ground secured, the club could concentrate on cricketing matters, and the Irish Senior Cup was the main target for the 2014 season. In the first round, The Hills beat Glendermott CC at the Rectory in the Waterside district of Derry. In round two, The Hills beat Bready, another team from the North-West. There was a trip to Park Avenue for the third round to play Railway Union who had won both of its previous rounds on bowl-outs. The Hills' bowlers were tremendous, and Railway was bowled out for 148 runs. Manu Kumar bowled 10 overs for 15 runs and took 4 wickets. Although he did not take a wicket, Naseer Shaukat only conceded 7 runs in the 10 overs that he bowled. Cormac McLoughlin-Gavin was brilliant in the field and took 4 catches. Railway's final score was 148 all out. It was obvious from the bowling figures that runs were not going to be got easily on a difficult pitch, and so it proved. A painstaking 54 runs in 95 balls from Patrick Byrne and 23 runs from Manu Kumar helped The Hills to chase down the target score in 49.2 overs for the loss of 8 wickets. The best that could be said about this game, was job done.

The Hills drew North Down in the semi-final, and the trip to the iconic ground at Comber is always eagerly anticipated. In a game which fluctuated wildly, The Hills won the toss and batted first. Nicolaas Pretorius was out in the first over without scoring, Patrick Byrne scored 26 and Mike Baumgart scored 27 runs. As he had done on innumerable occasions for The Hills, Max Sorensen came to the rescue with a brilliant knock of 70 runs which included 6 sixes and 3 fours. He was ably assisted by Jonathan Andrews (22), and Manu Kumar who contributed an invaluable 27* at the end of the innings. The consensus from the home supporters was that 223 runs was well below par.

This indeed seemed to be the situation when North Down openers, Larkin (60) and Terrett (65) racked up 126 runs before Larkin was out in the 30th over, bowled by Manu Kumar and caught by Nicolaas Pretorius. The equation for North Down was 98 runs in 20 overs with 9 wickets standing. At this stage, Terrett went into his shell to a certain extent. He scored 65 runs off 112 balls and was bowled eventually by Manu Kumar, caught by Tomás Rooney-Murphy. At 151 for 2 wickets, the game was still in the control of North Down, they had plenty of batting to come, but the run-rate was climbing, and this tends to induce panic among some batsmen. The very dangerous Taimur Khan was clean bowled by Naseer Shaukat for 3 runs, Ryan Haire scored 22 runs and his brother, Andrew, scored 15 runs.

There were 31 runs needed off four overs with four wickets in hand. In the 48th over, Max Sorensen was hit for 12, and North Down came to the 49th over needing 11 to win. Luke Clinton bowled this over, conceded only 3 runs, and took the wicket of Andrew Haire. North Down needed 8 runs off 6 balls, but 7 would be enough to win on fewer wickets lost. In a situation such as this, Naseer Shaukat's experience was invaluable. In the final over, only 4 runs were conceded, and The Hills had won a great game by 3 runs.

And so, to the final on 23 August at Clontarf against the home side. Over the years, league encounters had tended to favour Clontarf, but on a previous occasion when Hills and Clontarf met in a Cup Final, The Hills had won. In terms of relative strengths of the two sides, Clontarf seemed to be the stronger batting side, while The Hills' strength in characteristic Fingal style was in the bowling and fielding departments.

Clontarf won the toss and opted to field first. The opening partnership of Patrick Byrne (14) and Nicolaas Pretorius (34) yielded 30 runs, and the second wicket partnership of Cormac McLoughlin-Gavin (75) and Nicolaas brought the score to 59 runs. There was then a crucial third wicket stand of 106 runs between Cormac and Mike Baumgart (62), and everything seemed to be set fair for an onslaught by Max Sorensen and co. This did not occur, and only 74 runs were scored for the loss of the last seven wickets. A score of 239 gives a team something to defend, but the impetus was now with the team batting second.

Max Sorensen took a wicket with the third ball of the first over, the second Clontarf wicket fell when the score was 18, but Bill Coghlan and Andrew

Poynter brought Clontarf back into the contest, with a third wicket partnership of 77 runs. Both were out when the score was 95. Coghlan (40) was bowled by Mark Dwyer, caught by William Archer, who was on as substitute fielder, and immediately followed by Poynter (41), caught by Nicolaas Pretorius off the bowling of Naseer Shaukat. The momentum was now with The Hills, but a partnership of 95 runs between Eoghan Delany (41) and Adrian D'Arcy (51) brought Clontarf back into the game with a vengeance. The fifth wicket, (D'Arcy) fell when the score was 190, Delany was out stumped by Pretorius, bowled by Naseer Shaukat, and it was game on. Clontarf needed 45 runs off 40 balls, but the pressure was beginning to tell. Max Sorensen took 2 more wickets, Naseer took one more wicket and there was a run-out, leaving Clontarf 9 runs short.

This was a very competitive game of cricket between two very evenly matched sides. In the final analysis, the batting contributions of Pretorius, McLoughlin-Gavin and Baumgart allied to the superb bowling and fielding performance brought The Hills home. Max Sorensen took 3 wickets for 50 runs, Naseer Shaukat took 3 wickets for 40, Manu Kumar's figures were 1 for 35, Mark Dwyer took 1 wicket for 37, and Tomás Rooney-Murphy took 1 wicket for 23 runs. Luke Clinton did not take a wicket on this occasion but bowled 8 overs for 36 runs. Joy was unconfined as The Hills journeyed back to The Vineyard with the Bob Kerr Irish Senior Cup for the second time in three years.

In 2014, Malahide CC donated a trophy for the best ground in Leinster in memory of Joe McCleery, its patron, and The Hills was the first club to receive this much coveted and much appreciated award. Those with long memories will recall that The Hills was refused admission to senior cricket in the late 1970s because its ground was not up to senior standard, and it was gratifying for the club to be deemed now to have the best ground in Leinster.

By one of those strange anomalies, The Hills had a fixture the day after winning the Irish Senior Cup in 2014, and in losing that game, suffered the ignominy of relegation to Division 2. It must be said that no team is relegated because of one result, but there was a feeling that on any other day, relegation might have been avoided. It was unfortunate to be relegated, but the players were adamant that the sojourn in Division 2 would be brief, and thus it proved. 10 games out of 13 were won, there was one no result, and two losses and the league was won by a 47- point margin. There were individual awards in the 2015 season for Cormac McLoughlin-Gavin (Division 2 Fielding), William Archer (Division 3 Fielding) and Veronica Fay-Watt (Division 3 Wicket keeping).

In 2016, the contribution which Matt Dwyer had made to cricket as a player, groundsman, coach, and administrator was recognised when he was awarded the Hall of Fame by Cricket Leinster. The Third XI won the Division 9 League, but all other silverware was brought to The Vineyard by the women's section whose Second XI won the Division 3 League and Minor Cup; Ciara Metcalfe won the Fair Play award, and Aisling Byrne won the Most Improved Player and Division 3 Batting awards.

A keen interest in youth cricket has been one of the hallmarks of The Hills CC during the past fifty years. In the early 1970s, Gerry Byrne had presented a cup for which youth teams in Fingal competed, and in 2004, the family of the late Billy Tolan sponsored a cup for one of the Leinster Cricket Union's youth competitions. Linked with these initiatives was a very strong belief in the value of coaching, and in this regard, Joe Caprani, the former Irish International, coached at the club from 1978 until 1998 inclusive. The Hills CC was also at the forefront with its organisation of Summer camps and the appointment of Development Officers to oversee the coaching structures within the club. Under Joe's tutelage and with the assistance of senior cricketers and the various Development Officers, many players from the club have represented Ireland and Leinster at youth level over the years, with William Dwyer being the first youth international in 1985.

In view of the disparity in numbers between The Hills and the bigger clubs in Dublin City, it has often been difficult for the club to win trophies at youth level, but over the years, teams have been fielded at all age levels, and they have invariably competed very well. On occasions during the past fifty years due to a happy confluence of circumstances, it is possible to identify some outstanding teams at youth level, but it is intended to concentrate on one game because of its significance for three generations of one of the great Hills' families.

The All-Ireland youth competitions were the brainchild of Rev. Wesley Ferris, and over the years, they developed into very prestigious tournaments with the winning teams from the LCU, NWCU and NCU competitions competing at U11, U13 and U15 age levels. The Hills played in the U15 All-Ireland Final in 1997 but lost to an all-conquering Donemana team which featured many players who were to become senior internationals. In 2016, The Hills Under 11 team which was coached by Joseph Clinton, Mark Clinton and Paul Smyth won the Leinster Cup and progressed to meet CSNI from Belfast in the final which was staged at The Vineyard on 11 September 2016. The word on the street was that this Hills' side was the strongest team to represent the club at youth level for many years. For Adam Clinton, son of Joseph and Barbara, and grandson of Joe and Mary, Seán and Maureen, this was his day of days. In a brilliant knock, he scored 94 runs off 91 balls, and contributed hugely to a Hills' total of 139 for 5 wickets. The other scorers for The Hills were Ben Parker (17), Matthew Weldon (8) and James Ryan (3). For CSNI, big contributions from the top order were essential if they were to chase down this score. Mohammed Aahil (34), Scott Grey (10), Harry Dyer (10) and Yuv Pahuja (16) all got starts, but a combination of superb bowling, (Ben Parker, 3 for 11), Sam Smyth (2 for 11), Ivan Ryan (1 for 13), brilliant fielding (4 run outs) and score-board pressure ensured that the Hills' total was never in serious danger, and The Hills won by 32 runs.

For the players, parents, grandparents, and supporters of The Hills CC, this was an incredibly emotional day. Joe Clinton, Senior, who was very ill at this time, was seated in his car at the boundary, watching his grandson make a major contribution to the Hills' first All-Ireland trophy at youth level. It was especially gratifying for the Clinton family because from the very early days of the club, Joe had been a great supporter of youth cricket and very positive about the contribution which young cricketers made to The Hills CC.

In 2017 Cricket Leinster in its wisdom decided to dispense with the 60 overs per side cup competition and introduced a new cup competition that would be 40 overs per innings. The traditionalists were aghast, but many players thought that the 60 overs per innings competition was an anachronism, and thus, it was that The Hills and Merrion met at The Vineyard in the final of the revised version.

The Hills won the toss and decided to field, and there were 2 early successes for the wily Naseer Shaukat whose final figures were 8 overs, 2 maidens, 2 for 10. Two more wickets fell before the score was 40, and it appeared that Merrion would be dismissed for a very low score. John Anderson kept the innings together, and with a record of not having been bowled since he had scored 100 in the first round of the Leinster Senior Cup 2017, he was Merrion's main hope of putting a reasonable total on the scoreboard. With Patrick Tice (40), he was involved in an 82 partnership, and he had scored 80 before he was bowled by Ryan Cartwright when the score was 177. Tomás Rooney-Murphy got two wickets, and Ryan Cartwright blew away the tail. Merrion's final score was 186 in 39.1 overs. Ryan Cartwright took the main bowling honours (4 for 30), and the other 2 wickets were taken by Luke Clinton. The Hills got off to a reasonable start and the opening pair of Cormac McLoughlin-Gavin and Mike Baumgart scored 32 runs. There was then a minor crisis when Seán Terry was bowled for a duck. The third wicket partnership between Cormac and Hamid Shad brought the score to 82, and The Hills needed

105 runs from 14 overs on the fall of the third wicket. Max Sorensen as he had done so often for The Hills in the past answered the call, and he hit 64* in 37 balls in an innings which included 5 sixes and 4 fours. Sorensen in that type of form is impossible to bowl to, and one over from John Anderson was hit for 22 runs. Max was ably assisted by Albert Van der Merwe (17) and Ryan Cartwright (16*). The Hills won by five wickets, with 14 balls to spare, and this was the first Leinster Senior Cup win for the club since the defeat of North County in the final in 2006.

While attending a funeral in 2018, the comment was made that while people might talk about great men in The Hills CC, the club had been blessed with the number of great women who selflessly had done so much to enhance the club's reputation for hospitality since it was founded in 1969. In terms of catering for players and visitors, the ladies have taken great pride in ensuring that everyone who visits *The Vineyard* is made feel at home, and one of the last tasks before the washing-up commenced was for the ladies to ask a member of the Executive to ascertain if there was anyone who hadn't been invited in for a cup of tea and a sandwich. When there were lunch matches, the roast beef and home-grown potatoes were the talk of Leinster cricket, and now, it is the scones and cream which are the envy of every visiting supporter and player.

Hosting international and representative games is a huge task and it makes great demands on personnel due to the wide disparity in dietary habits, but the varied tastes are always met with great efficiency and courtesy. When it is considered that the people involved are volunteers, the indebtedness of all members and visitors to the many members of the Ladies' Committees during the past fifty years is acknowledged and it is recognised that the club could not have functioned so well without their whole-hearted endeavours.

Being asked to host games is something of a double-edged sword. At one level, it is an acknowledgement that the facilities at a club are of sufficiently high standard to be granted the hosting of a game but hosting always involves an incredible amount of work, and this is especially true when the workers are volunteers. When the Inter-regional tournament was re-branded in 2013, The Hills was asked to host the first game, and this fixture became an annual event on the May Bank Holiday weekend for several seasons. The Hills hosted games in the ICC competition in 2005, and it also hosted the Ireland men's team versus Norway in 2008. Over the years, the Irish women's team has played several games at *The Vineyard* with the most recent being the two games in 2018 against New Zealand. In 2019 Ireland A played Bangladesh in 2019. As part of

The Hills' 50th Anniversary celebrations, the club hosted the Leinster Senior Cup Final and the All-Ireland Final with its customary efficiency and courtesy.

In June 2019, The Hills played Phoenix in the final of the League Cup, and somewhat surprisingly, given that The Hills had beaten Phoenix already this season, the Cricket Leinster preview made Phoenix favourites to win the game. Nothing motivates a team more than to be dubbed second favourites in a two-horse race, and there was a delightful exchange later in the pavilion when the previewer correctly identified one of the photographs in the display to be complimented by a proud Fingallian on getting something right for the first time in a fortnight!

The Hills won the toss and opted to field first. Beecroft and McDonough were batting for Phoenix and at the end of the 5th over, the Phoenix score was 31 without loss. Some of the more pessimistic Hills' supporters were muttering about The Hills chasing at least 300. In the 6th over, in the words of W. B. Yeats, "all changed, changed utterly". The ageless Naseer Shaukat clean bowled Louis McDonagh, and in the next ball, Irish international, Simi Singh, was out LBW, again bowled by Nas. The former Hills player and skipper, Nicolaas Pretorius, negotiated the next two balls from Nas with a certain amount of difficulty, and decided to leave the final ball of the over. From behind, there was the very ominous sound of timber being dismantled, Nas had taken 3 wickets in the over, and 31 for 0 became 31 for 3.

Beecroft was batting very nicely, but he was out to a fine catch by Greg Lamb to became Nasser Shaukat's fourth victim. Adam Chester was out LBW without troubling the scorer, and the Phoenix score was 35 for 5, with all five wickets to the brilliant Naseer Shaukat. Stephen Black was Nas's next victim, and Poonish Mehta was next one out, LBW to Joey Carroll. Amish Sidhu was out when the score was 54, caught by Joey Carroll, bowled by Naseer Shaukat. The score was 65 when Gordon Millar was out, LBW, bowled by Daya Singh. A period of consolidation followed, which was very necessary if Phoenix was to avoid being bowled out for the lowest ever total in the history of the Leinster Senior Cup. Ben White batted very sensibly for 24 runs, but the innings ended when Devender Ranolia induced an edge from Matt Lunson for Mark Donegan to take a very good catch. Naseer Shaukat's figures were 10 overs, 4 maidens, 7 wickets for 20 runs – the best bowling in the 84-year history of the Leinster Senior Cup. This was an incredible performance from an amazing bowler, and given the activities of the winter, it seemed appropriate to misquote Alfred Lord Tennyson, "men may come, and men may go," but Nas goes on forever.

As The Hills prepared to bat, the cry was "remember Old Belvedere!" Phoenix had a very mild glimmer of hope when Cormac Mc Loughlin-Gavin was caught behind off the bowling of Poonish Mehta in the first over. Joey Carroll and Bhavesh batted with great intent, the good balls being blocked, the bad ones being dispatched without ceremony. On the last ball of the 11th over, Bhavesh lost patience and in attempting to hit a ball from Simi Singh out of the ground was caught on the boundary by Poonish Mehta. Joey Carroll had accumulated 35 runs when he was run out, another run-out in a succession of them for the top order batsmen during the previous weeks. Mark Donegan (20*) and Daya Singh (7*) wrapped up proceedings in the 20th over.

Pride of place for the victory must go to Naseer Shaukat, but this was a wonderful team performance – the bowling was excellent, the fielding was very good, the batting was very sensible, and Tomás Rooney-Murphy was a very astute captain. Four Leinster Senior Cup finals have now been hosted by The Hills CC, and the home club has played in three of them, winning in 1996, 2017 and in 2019. On the occasion of the 50th anniversary, this victory, the presentation of the ground, the general facilities, and the hosting are a celebration of the values and vision which drove the men and women to establish the club in 1969 and have been maintained by successive generations of Hills' members and supporters.

Back Row: (L to R) Joe & Seamus Clinton, Johnny Archer, Gerry & Paddy Byrne, Simon Hoare & Anto Byrne
Front Row: (L to R) Joe Hoare, Pat Casey, Richard Dunne & Jimmy Byrne

First Trophy, 1971; 2 umpires are Mr A. Solomons and Mr M. Russell

Leinster Intermediate League and Cup Winners, 1972

Intermediate A League and Leinster Intermediate Cup Winners 1973

Back Row. L to R    Tom Dwyer, Gerry Harper, Paddy Byrne, Anthony & Jimmy Byrne
Front Row L to R  Martin Byrne, John Quinlan (Sham), Liam Archer, Johnny Archer, Joe Hoare & Neil Carpenter.

1974

# Club House, 1975-1995

# Ladies' Committee, 1978

# Executive, 1982

Dick Bourke, Joe Clinton and Michael Chance

Senior 2 Cup Winners, 1982

Richard Dunne

# Senior 3 Cup Winners, 1987

**Second XI. 1987 Winners Leinster Senior III League.** Back Row (L-R): Alan Courell, Brian Higgins, Anthiony Byrne, Tom Dwyer, Noel Harper, Gerry Byrne; Front Row (L-R): Martin Duggan, Paddy Byrne, Joe Keogh, Patrick Hoare, Rory Courell, Martin Russell

Figure 8, Joe Clinton, 1988

Figure 9, Women's Team, 1988

*Figure 10, Marguerite Burke*

Senior Cup Winners, 1989

*League Winners, 1989*

# Division 4 League Winners, 1989, Division 3 League and Cup Winners, 1990

# Marguerite Burke, 1993

Marguerite Burke, representing Ireland World Cup, June 1993.

## Holy Faith Skerries cricket team

**Ladies 1994. Leinster Junior Cup winners and Minor Cup Runners up.**

End of Old Club House, 1995

1995

Richard Wentges, photo taken by Maurice O'Keeffe

# Opening of New Pavilion, 1995

Wiggins Teape Winners, 1996

The Vineyard 1996, Cup Final Day

Senior Cup Winners, 1996

## Paul Mooney

## Barry Archer

## Declan Moore

...an Moore, 1st Cap on 7 May 1996 v. Gloucestershire.

## Matt Dwyer

*Figure 11, The Second XI, 1999*

*Figure 12, First XI, 2005*

*Figure 13, John Wills and Joseph Clinton*

# 2005

Leinster Senior Cup Winnners, 2005

Leinster Senior Cup Winners and Supporters at Merrion, 2006

**Fifth XI. 2006 Winners Leinster Minor Cup.**

**The Hills Cricket Club Ladies, July 2006.**
Front Row (L-R): Tracy Fleming, Kay Rogan, Maureen Byrne, Frances Dwyer, Barbara Clinton; Back Row (L-R): Pearl Costello, Emer Kitteringham, Helen Lynch, Margaret Dunne, Mary Clinton.

*Figure 14, 2008 Whitney Moore Section A Winners*

*Figure 15, 2008*

361

Figure 16, Irish Cup Winners, 2012

*Freehold Ceremony, 2013*

Photo © 2013 Michael Gavin

*Figure 17, Irish Cup Winners, 2014*

*Figure 18, Squad listening intently, 2014 (Michael Gavin)*

© Joe Curtis 2012

Jeremy Bray

Aijaz Farooqi and Michael Dwyer

Bryn Thomas

Nadeem Akhtar

Yaqoob Ali and Seán Terry

Max, Albert and Ryan Cartwright

Hamid Shah

Tomás, Nicolaas Pretorius, Darryl Calder

## Mike Baumgart

## Michael Lax

## Freddie Klokker

## Shaun de Kock

Jane Maguire

Laura Boylan

Katie Boylan

Tracy Clinton

Miranda Andrews

Aisling, Katie, Cara

*Figure 19, Ireland U15 2018*

*Figure 20, All-Ireland Winners, 2016*

# Senior Cup Winners, 2019

The Hills (©Joe Curtis/CricketEurope)

# Chapter 14: Cricket in Ring Commons

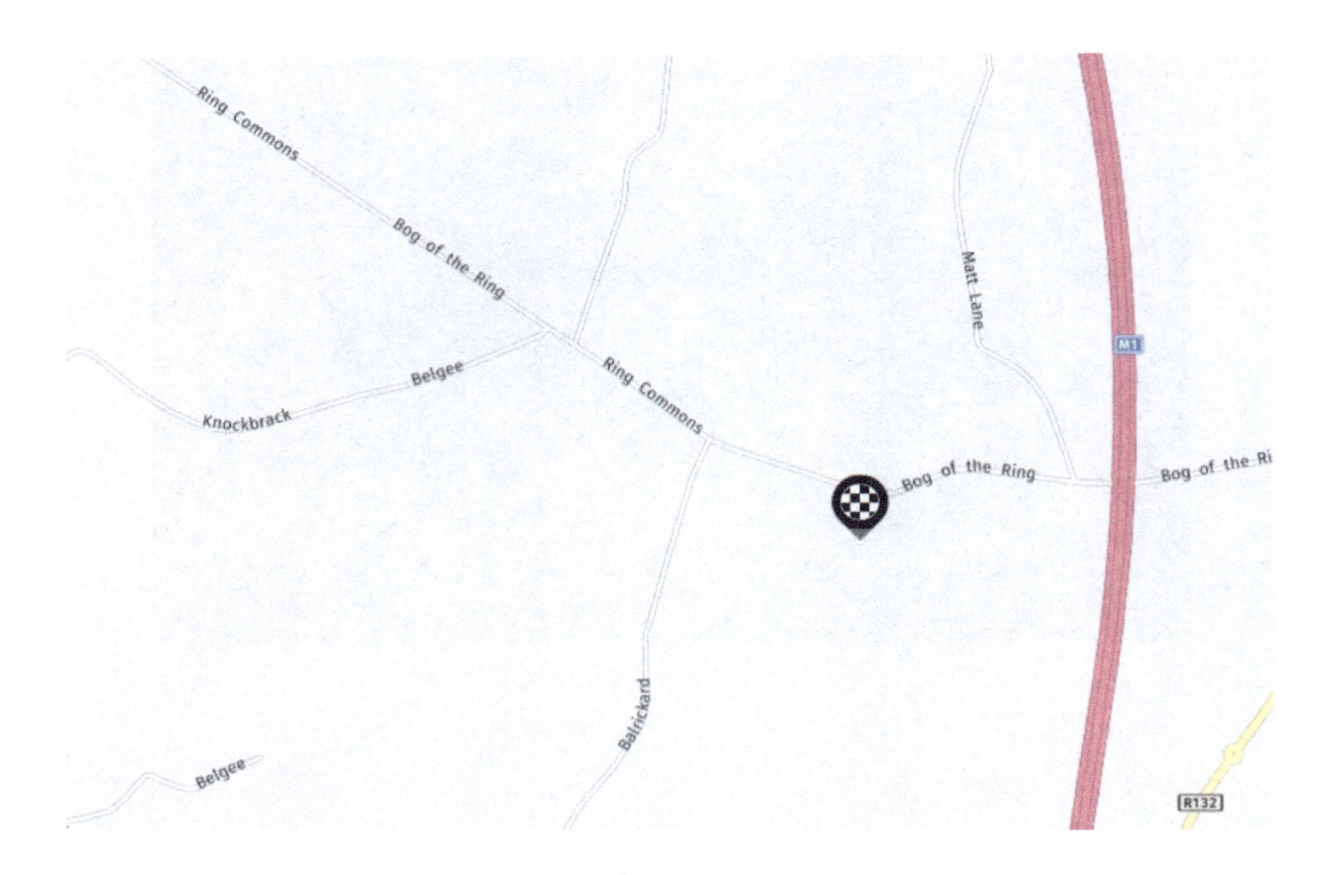

## Introduction

The Ring Commons Sports Centre is testimony to the wonderful community spirit in the area, and its genesis dates to 1977 when a group of young men decided to reclaim some marshy commons land so that they might re-form a cricket team. They showed great foresight in naming the ground, Ring Commons Sports Centre, and not Ring Commons Cricket Club because it was anticipated that in time, other sports would be played on the ground. The Centre now consists of a function room, a members' bar, a club house with changing rooms and showers, two football pitches and a pitch and putt course in addition to a cricket pitch and a cricket pavilion. This development was made possible by a combination of fund-raising, voluntary labour, and a grant from Fingal County Council.  The main focus of this chapter will be the period up to 1977 but it is important to pay tribute to the people who have worked so hard to provide and maintain recreational, social, and cultural activities in the Ring Commons Sports Centre.

**Early Days**

The first reference to cricket in Ring Commons was a note in the *Drogheda Independent*, 19 June 1897 which stated that Ring Commons Cricket Club beat Garristown on Sunday by 20 runs. That is the extent of the report, and in certain respects, it set the tone for most of the accounts of the games played by the club over the years – scores and results, and nothing else.

In its early manifestations, the club played at Briarland, and some of the reports called the club, Briarland while other reports used the title, Ring Commons. This is illustrated by the accounts which are extant for two games which were played in 1900. In the first report, there is a reference to the Briarland Club having some "first class players, as is seen by the fact that they carried their bats to victory on every occasion last season". In addition to being unbeaten in 1899, it was also unbeaten until Sunday, 17 June 1900 when it played Balbriggan Rovers. Briarland batted first, and was dismissed for 20 runs, with J. Reynolds taking 7 wickets in both innings. In reply, Balbriggan scored 37 in the first innings, and of this total, 16 runs were extras. In Balbriggan's second innings, 6 wickets had fallen at 6 o'clock when time was called, and Balbriggan was deemed to have won based on its first innings score. There are two reports available for the return game, and stylistic differences in reporting are very evident. The *Drogheda Independent's* account is prosaic, and it refers to the visitors as Ring CC. The game was played in Balbriggan on 29 June and "after an exciting game", the visitors won by 8 runs. This win was attributed to the bowling of C. Hagan who took 7 wickets. For Balbriggan, the batting of T. O' Neill (the owner of the ground) "was the feature of the match, and Jem Brown trundled the leather to the best advantage". The *Drogheda Argus* reproduced the score card, with the main contributions from Mr O'Neill (18*) batting at no. 9 and J. Magrane (sic) the top scorer for Briarland with 13 runs. The report however did not end with the scorecard, and there was a disquieting reference to crowd trouble which has already been quoted in the Balbriggan chapter.

The above reports are the extent of the information available on Ring Commons CC until April 1913 when William Rooney, the Hon. Sec., indicated that the club was open for challenges for the coming season. Ring Commons CC visited Gormanston Castle on 31 August to play the local team on the "lately well laid out grounds presented to the club by Lord Gormanston". P. J. Curtis, the Gormanstown Secretary, did not lack confidence in his team, and in his report, he mentioned that the home club "proved successful as usual." It is difficult to know if it was much consolation to Ring Commons to be told that they had "hard luck by only getting 22 runs". The home team sent in "their old reliable Johnny Clarke of Stamullen to defend the stumps which he did in fine style, as also did the Purfield Brothers". The bowling on both sides was good, with "Reilly for the home club and Hughes for the visitors doing best". The final score was Gormanstown CC, 58 runs; Ring Commons CC, 22.

For the next twelve years, local, national, and international events dominated the print media, and references to cricket in Fingal are minimal. For Ring Commons CC, the re-awakening occurred in 1925 when it played Kilbride at Ring Commons and won on a score of 74 runs to 51. On three successive weeks in the *Drogheda Independent*, the club advertised the New Year's Dance which was to be held in Ring Commons School. On Week 1, details of admission prices (Gents: 5s; Ladies, 2s 6d, Doubles, 7s 6d) are given, "everyone was welcome", refreshments were included in the price, and this dance would be "the Best One Yet". On Week 2, the advertisement mentioned "Splendid Music and Excellent Catering", and Week 3, it was reported that the Committee had made "elaborate arrangements" for New Year's Night. The fact that the Annual Dance was held in the school showed that the school building in addition to its primary function as an educational establishment, served a vital secondary function for the wider community as a venue for meetings and social events. The close links between the Ring Commons Cricket Club and Ring School have already been mentioned, but the place of the school is enshrined in the history of Fingal cricket because the Fingal League was established in Ring Commons in 1926. The Executive of the League recognised its indebtedness to Rev. J. Hickey by passing a vote of thanks for the use of Ring School for Committee meetings and it made a subscription towards parochial funds. Indeed at an event which was held in 2004 to celebrate the achievements of the school which was closed in the 1970s, a cricket bat was one of the artefacts which was brought to the altar during the Special Mass.

There were only two clubs in the Fingal League in 1926, but it was fully operational in 1927, and Ring Commons CC was one of the seven clubs which entered the league. Ring's first season in Fingal League cricket was not too successful, and it ended up with 12 points by comparison with the winners, Skerries, who obtained 33 points. For the 1928 season, the only game for which there is a report available was Ring Commons versus Knightstown which Knightstown won on a score of 50 runs to 33. Despite not being too successful on the field of play, Ring Commons CC was of crucial importance in the administration of the league because in addition to providing a venue for meetings, Mr Michael White gave a field for the staging of the final between Skerries CC and Barnageeragh.

In 1929, Ring Commons CC was in Section A along with Knockbrack, Skerries, Ballymadun, Barnageera, Knightstown, and Balrothery. It fulfilled its 12 fixtures, but success continued to elude it, and its record for the season was won 1 game, lost 11 and scored 328 runs which was an average of 27 runs per game. In 1930 however there were distinct signs of an improvement, and in its game with Balbriggan, Ring Commons won on a score of 37 runs to 25. It is difficult to know if the reporter was being ironical when he referred to Balbriggan's "stone-wall defence" being a feature of the game, and "the fine hitting of Bergin who made two 2's". The best batsmen for Ring Commons were Dunne (11), McNally (7), R. Lacy (4), and Fanning (4), while Dunne took 6 wickets for Ring Commons.  By the end of the season, Ring had played 10 games, won 6, lost 4 and scored 487 runs which was an average of nearly 49 runs, a considerable improvement on the previous season.

Cricket was not the only sporting activity in Ring Commons during 1930. Some of the young men decided to form a "push bicycle club" and one of its first events was a reliability trial in which twenty competitors took part, but only six finished the course. The trial commenced at Ring National School, went through the playground, via Old Maids' Lane, back to the Commons, and finished with a "tough struggle up Balrickard Hill." The competitors had some difficulties on Old Maids' Lane, and at least half a dozen cyclists came to grief there. The reporter was unable to provide the name of the winner, and in justifying this lacuna, he explained that "he [the winner] appeared at the winning post covered with mud and in such a condition that I believe his own mother would not know him."

Ring Commons CC held its AGM on 15 March 1931. There was an "exceptionally large attendance of members"; it was reported that the Club was in a "very sound position", and that its prospects for the coming season were "very rosy". In a clear statement of priorities, about half-way through the Agenda, "it was decided to have a practice owing to the day being so fine". The meeting was adjourned until 5 April when the remainder of the Agenda would be addressed, and new members registered. The number of teams in the Fingal League had increased to such an extent that it was deemed necessary to have three sections. Ring Commons was in Division B along with Balrothery, Balbriggan, Barnageera, Knightstown and Ballymadun. In one of the early games in the season, Ring Commons beat Ballymadun on a score of 30 runs to 27. By the end of the season, it had played 10 games, won 7, lost 3, scored 329 runs (average of 32.9 per game) and finished second in its section on 14 points. Club members were also involved in the cricket match between married and single men from Balbriggan, Balrothery and Man-O'-War which was arranged to raise funds for Balbriggan Parish, and the club organised a dance on 16 August 1931.

Ring Commons CC had a difficult start to the 1933 season with the death of Christopher Hardford (sic) who was referred to as a "very useful and valuable member, both on the playing pitch and the committee room". On the playing field, Ring had a successful season, and by 19 August, it was joint top of its section with 7 wins and 2 losses. It was involved in a crucial game against Curkeen where a win for Curkeen would give divisional honours to Curkeen while a win for Ring Commons would necessitate a replay. On the day, Ring Commons responded to the challenge and won by 65 runs to 32. The bowling of Dunne and Rooney was reported to have been "excellent", while "the fielding of Ring Commons on the whole was exceptionally good". The two teams met again at Balbriggan and treated the large crowd to a "fine exhibition of cricket". The final score was Ring, 36 runs and Curkeen, 17, and this result was attributed to Ring's fielding and bowling being "well-nigh perfect". Dunne of Ring Commons was given a special mention because of his bowling. This result meant that Ring Commons would play Balcunnin in the final of the Fingal League. Unfortunately for Ring Commons, on a difficult day which was marred by frequent showers, the final was a "one-sided affair", and it "proved unequal to the superior bowling and batting of the Balcunnin team who won comfortably by an innings."

In the 1934 season, Ring Commons was in the same division as Portrane, Knockbrack, Black Hills, Man-O'-War, Balbriggan and Balrothery. The club played 10 games, and won 4, lost 5, drew 1, and finished the season on 9 points. At the AGM of the League, it was indicated that there would be a representative game between a Fingal League Selection and the Meath League for a trophy which was presented by G. L. McGowan. V. McNally was the Ring Commons' representative on the Fingal team.

In 1936, the number of teams in the Fingal League had fallen to ten, and Ring Commons CC was not affiliated to the League for that season. The club did not play in the following two seasons either, but it is possible that some of its players may have opted to play for one of the clubs in Naul because in 1936, Naul and Naul Hill played in the Fingal League. Ring Commons CC was represented at the Fingal League's AGM in 1938 by J. Kearns, and it was obvious that the club had resumed its cricketing and social activities. There are no reports available for games played by Ring Commons in 1938, but the club organised a dance in Naul Hall on Sunday, 30th October, dancing was from 7 to 12 p.m., admission was 1s 3d and there was a guarantee of the "usual good music". There is a similar situation regarding reports on games in 1939 but at the AGM in 1940, it was noted that Ring Commons had tied with Knockbrack for runners-up for the Fingal Challenge Cup. There is more information available on the 1940 season, and on 19 May, Ring Commons beat Ballymadun on a score of 48 runs to 35 in "a well-contested game." The report on the game between the Black Hills and Ring Commons is matter of fact – "Black Hills defeated the home team by two wickets." The return game between Ring Commons and Ballymadun was played at Ring Commons on 30 June 1940, and resulted in a win for Ring Commons. Ballymadun was all out for 35, and Ring Commons' score was 39 for the loss of 6 wickets. The best scorers for Ring Commons were M. Dunne (14*) and J. Maguire (13).

The club joined forces with Knockbrack to host a Ceilidh and Old Time Waltz in the Town Hall, Balbriggan on 26 January 1941, admission was 1s 6d, dancing was from 9 to 1, and the music was provided by Jack Ryan's Band. Ring Commons lost to the Black Hills on a score of 48 runs to 18 in a play-off which would decide who would qualify for the final of the League in 1941. There was a big increase in the club's involvement in social events during this year. It organised a Ceilidh, Old Time and Modern Dance in Naul on 10 August, dancing was from 8 to 12, admission was 1s 6d and music was by Harry Magee's Band. There was a "Grand Novelty Dance" in Naul on 5 October with the same price, same band and same duration. Finally, in conjunction with Knockbrack CC, Ring Commons organised a Ceilidh, Old and Slow Waltz in the Town Hall, Balbriggan on 19 October, and this was advertised as "a dance you are sure to enjoy".

In 1942 the rationing of motor fuel during the Emergency continued to have an impact, and the League was divided into two divisions to minimise these transport difficulties. Ring Commons was in the same division as Balrothery, Clonard, Walshestown, Rush, and the Black Hills. The only other mention of Ring Commons is contained in a report on a game between Rush and the *Irish Times*, in which J. McDermott, formerly a member of Ring Commons CC, scored 30 runs. At the AGM in 1943, the following officers were elected for the season: Captain: John Kearns, Vice- Captain: P. White, Hon. Sec.: E. P. Moore, Hon. Treas.: Jas Kearns; Committee: the above with George and Christy Casey. The meeting recorded its thanks to Mr Patrick Reilly, Saddlestown House, Stamullen, for the use of the field. On 16 May, Ring Commons was due to host Oldtown, but Oldtown did not travel. The continuing importance of the corporate identity of the Fingal League was reflected in the game between a Phoenix Selection and a Fingal League Selection which was played at Balbriggan. E. P. Moore of Ring Commons was named among the substitutes for the Fingal team. Between 1944 and 1947, Ring Commons continued to play Fingal League cricket, but it was evident that the club was struggling on the cricket field. In 1945, it was well-beaten by the Black Hills on a score of 43 runs to 21. In 1946, Ring Commons lost to Bohill, and then it was reported that "Balrothery had a very big win over Ring Commons". At the end of the season, Ring Commons ceased to be involved in Fingal League cricket for a considerable number of years and it did not return to cricket until 1961. The existence of the Fingal League was beneficial to this comeback because a club could play league cricket without going through the rigours of arranging friendlies or issuing challenges.

In the 1950s, the only reference to Ring Commons CC was the report of the bereavement of John Donnelly whose obituary mentioned that he took a "keen interest in sport and was a leading member of the old Ring Commons CC. After the doldrums of the 1950s, Fingal cricket was boosted by the return of several clubs to cricket. In May 1961, upwards of thirty people attended a meeting at which it was decided to re-form a cricket club in the Ring Commons area and to enter a team in the Fingal League. The officers elected for the season were President: Joe Finnegan, Chairman: John Maguire, Captain: John Fanning, Vice-Captain: Paddy White, Treasurer: Matt Magrane, and Secretary: Peter Carey. Ring Commons' ground was chosen to host the Fingal League final between Knockbrack and Portrane. For some unexplained reason, Portrane withdrew from the League, and Ring Commons played a challenge game against Knockbrack. The report on this game mentioned that Ring Commons CC had been revived after a lapse of twenty years, but this is inaccurate because the club's last year in cricket had been 1946. On 4 June, Ring Commons beat the Black Hills on a score of 30 runs to 26, but it lost to Skerries the following week on a score of 75 runs to 51, and a "feature of the game was alert fielding." Later in the same month, Knockbrack beat Ring Commons by 64 runs to 29.

In the 1962 season, the first game for which there was a report available for Ring Commons was a defeat against Man-O'-War on 1 July. Later in the month, Ring Commons played the Black Hills in which the Black Hills batted first and scored 39 runs, with the main scorers being J. Russell (12), J. Clinton (8) and D. Murtagh (6). In reply, Ring Commons scored 22 runs, with P. White (8) being the principal contributor to its score. There was favourable mention for the 15 -years- old, P. Guildea who took 7 wickets for 10 runs. Ring Commons also lost the return game against Man-O'-War on a score of 96 runs to 20.

In 1963, the teams playing Fingal League cricket were Skerries, Rush, Man-O'-War, Portrane, Naul, Balrothery, Black Hills, Knockbrack, Balbriggan, and Ring Commons. The league was again divided into two sections, and in Ring Commons' section were the Black Hills, Skerries, Naul, and Balbriggan. Ring Commons lost to Balbriggan and the Black Hills in the two games for which they are reported. In September 1963, the club suffered a bereavement with the death of Michael Dunne, who with his brothers had been a member of the Ring Commons team for many years. In 1964, Ring Commons' fixture against Naul was not played due to Naul giving a walk-over, and the club joined forces with The Black Hills and Skerries CC to host a "Grand Cricket Dance" at the Holmpatrick House Hotel on Friday, 20 November 1964. Dancing was from 8 to 1, tickets were 6s, music was by the Silver Star Band, and supper was extra.

At its AGM in 1965, the following officers were elected: President: R. Casey; Chairman, P. White; Vice-Chairman, G. Casey; Captain, J. Fanning; Hon. Sec., P. Carey and Treasurer, M. McGrane. The club was reported to be in a "sound financial, position", and there was a vote to thanks to Mr McGrane for the use of his field during the season. In 1966, Ring Commons played the Man-O'-War in the Fingal Cricket League Final (B Section) on 18 September. Thanks to first-hand reports from two members of the Ring Commons team (Joe Curtis and John Coyle) and a photograph of a winners' medal, it has been possible to report that Ring Commons won the final.

**The New Ground, 1977**

Involvement in the final in 1966 was the prelude to Ring Commons' departure from cricket, and it did not return to cricket until 1979 when it had a new ground and immediate success by winning the Fingal Cricket League Cup. This triumph owed a lot to the White family, because Paddy White, President of the Club was the oldest playing member of the team, and he was joined by his sons, Johnny, Joe, Dermot, Peter, and Christopher. This achievement was celebrated at the Cardy Marina, and in addition to League medals being presented, there were also awards for Thomas Bertram (best batter and all-rounder), John Fanning (the best bowler) and Dermot White (special award). The club which now used the title, The North Ring Commons Cricket Club also maintained its commitment to social events, and it organised a Social Evening in the Milestone, Balbriggan on 17 August 1979, with music by the McNallys and admission, £1.50. There was another Social Evening in the Milestone on 16 May 1980, and again the music was by the McNallys. Later in the year, Ring Commons was represented at the function to mark the 50 years of the Fingal Cup, and it received medals for being runners-up in the Fingal B League.

**Postscript**

Ring Commons CC affiliated to the Leinster Cricket Union in 1981, and it won the Junior A League in 1982. It continued to play Leinster League cricket and Fingal League for some time and in 1987 it amalgamated with Knockbrack CC to form KBRC. This experiment only lasted for 2 seasons, but it was successful in the first season when its teams won the Intermediate and Junior B Leagues, and the Middle Cup. For some years, Ring Commons continued to play Fingal cricket until 2001, and the club was re-formed in 2011.

It is a tribute to resilience and the deep-seated affection for the game, that cricket continued to be played in Ring Commons despite challenges and setbacks at different stages during the past 120 years. A desire to re-form a cricket club in 1977 provided the impetus for the establishment of the Ring Commons Sports Centre, and the subsequent initiatives are a wonderful example of what can be achieved when clear vision is combined with concerted community action. The structures which are now in place provide a stability which ensures that cricket will continue to thrive in Ring Commons, and it is appropriate to commend the sense of pride and community spirit which underpin a wonderful Sports Centre.

**Notes**

This chapter is dedicated to Joe Curtis, who played cricket for Ring Commons and who has done such brilliant work in preserving and photographing the social history of Fingal.

Ring Commons School circa 1910

Pupils at Ring Commons School

Left To Right: Charlie Harford, Ned McGrane, Charlie McGrane, Jack White, Kevin Hamilton, John Fitzpatrick, Dick Maguire, Kitsy McNally, Charlie Moore, Jack Brogan, Matt Brogan

Left To Right: Lena McNally, Mary Frances Moore, May Moore, Nellie Vickers, Biddy Fanning, Mary Moore, Bridie Kearns, Julie Vickers, Mary Hagan, Nan Harford

Ring Commons School circa 1930

Ring Commons CC circa 1935

Back Row: George Casey, Johnny Donnoly, James Kearns, Eamonn Moore, Johnny McGowan, Tommy Dunne, Charlie White.

Front Row: Ned Maguire, John Maguire, Mick Dunne, John Kearns, Christy Casey.

Ring Commons School

Back Row L to R: Miss Geraghty, Jem Carroll, Joe Carey, Dick Colgan, James Tolan, Bill Casey, Kenneth Moore, Lou Maguire, Miss Rafferty.
2nd. Row From Back: Mary Brennen, Anna Lindsay, Mag Flynn, Maureen Carey, Bridie Carey, Anna Moore, Josie Moore.
3rd. Row From Back: Tom Carey, Richard Tolan, Maggie Donnelly, Eddie Lindsay, Maura Dunne, Christine Dunne, Paddy Fanning, Connie Moore, Eamonn Kiernan, Tom Fanning, Larry Flynn.
Front Row: Tom McGrane, John McGrane, Andy McGrane, John Fanning, Julia Fanning, Betty Emerson, Nancy Fanning, Kit Ryan, Jim Carey, Peter Carey, Ned Lindsay.

M·Cole, J· McNally, John Coyle, Jem Coyle, Tom Fanning, Joe Curtis
Paddy White, Buster Carey, John Fanning, Tom Lindsay, Bill Casey·

Tom Fanning

John Fanning

389

Joe Curtis

Johnny White

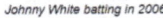

*Johnny White batting in 2006*

1966 Medal

# Chapter 15: Cricket in Man-O'-War

## Man-O'-War, 1930-1940

Man-O'-War is an area of population which is located within the townland of Courtlough in the Barony of Balrothery East, and the origin of its intriguing name has given rise to many theories. The most credible explanations are that the name is a corruption of the Irish phrases, Meann Bharr (Middle Height) or Meann Bhothar (Middle Road). These and the other theories regarding the placename have been discussed in detail by Jim Walsh in the paper which he delivered to Skerries Historical Society in 1999. The first reference to cricket in the area is a game between Wanderers CC, Balbriggan and Man-O'-War CC which was played in Balbriggan on 21 May 1883 and resulted in an "easy win" by 18 runs and 4 wickets for Wanderers on a score of 88 runs to 70. Reynolds and Hammond of Man-O'-War received favourable mention for bowling which was deemed to be "splendid", and for the Wanderers, Purfield, and Kirk "were credible". There are no further references to cricket in this area until 1904 but it cannot be assumed that the game was not being played. The tensions arising from the Land War and the Irish Revival are one explanation , but it is also possible that games were played on a field in a different townland, and accordingly, the name of the team was changed.

The next reference to the Man-O'-War and cricket is a game between Man-O'-War and Ballykea which was played on 16 October 1904. The result was a win for Ballykea by two runs with two wickets to fall. In 1905, there is an account of an annual meeting, and after the meeting, "a most enjoyable evening was passed with bat and ball". Everything was in readiness for the season and players were requested to be "on the grounds, sharp at 2.00 o'clock for practice on Sunday next, 11th June". The first game of the season was played against Knockbrack, and "owing to the day being so fine, the game was witnessed by a large number of spectators." The result of the game was a win for Knockbrack on a score of 57 to 34 runs, and the only other game for which there is a reference was scheduled to take place at Balcunnin on 18th June.

For the next twenty-five years, there are no accounts of cricket being played by the Man-O'-War CC, and it is a matter of conjecture whether to ascribe this dearth of information to pressure on space in the newspapers due to local, national, and international events, games not being played or reports not being submitted. Between 1930 and 1940, Man-O'-War CC played intermittently in the Fingal League, and this did not constitute a problem because if a team opted out for a season or two, it was possible to re-affiliate without the previous difficulty of having lost a place on a fixture list.

There were nineteen teams in the Fingal League in 1930, and Man-O'-War CC was drawn in Division C along with Balcunnin, the British Legion, Skerries Seconds, Oldtown, and Curkeen. The only game for which there is a report in which Man-O'-War was involved was against the Black Hills which the Man-O'-War won on a score of 46 to 22 runs. The additional comments were to the effect that the game was "interesting to the last wicket", and the Man-O'-War "are (sic) improving at every outing." At the end of its first season in Fingal League cricket, Man-O'-War finished a creditable third in the division which was won by Balcunnin.

For the 1931 season, Man-O'-War was again in Division C, and joined by Rush, Naul Hill, Curkeen, Oldtown, and Baldwinstown Second XI. Man-O'-War's record for the season was that it played 10 games, won 8 of them, scored 309 runs, and finished top of the division. The Fingal League was organised on the basis of play-offs, and Man-O'-War played Ballymadun in a two innings per side game. In the semi-final, Man-O'-War was beaten by one innings and ten runs, with the scores being Ballymadun 75 runs, Man-O'-War, first innings, 37 runs and second innings, 28 runs for a total of 65 runs. The best players for Man-O'-War were T. Morgan (9) and C. Dowdall (8).

Information for 1932 is limited, and there is no evidence that Man-O'-War played in the Fingal League during this season, but the club was back in the League in 1933. There were seventeen teams in the League in total, and Man-O'-War was drawn in Division B, with the other teams in the section being Balrothery, Oldtown, Knockbrack, and Baldwinstown Second XI. The team played 8 games, won 3, lost five and finished last in its section. By 1934, the number of teams in the League had fallen to thirteen; Man-O'-War was in the same section as Portrane, Black Hills, Knockbrack, Ring Commons, Balbriggan, and Balrothery. Its record improved from the previous season, and of the 12 games which it played, it won 7 games, lost 5 games and finished joint second in its section.

The decline in the number of teams in the league continued in 1935, and only ten teams were affiliated. It was decided again to divide the League into two sections, East and West Fingal, and Man-O'-War was drawn in the same section as Balrothery, Knockbrack, the Black Hills and Balbriggan. The Perpetual Challenge Cup was won by Naul, but it appears that there were complaints regarding regionalisation and that the strong teams were in the same section.

In 1936, there were still ten teams affiliated, but there were significant changes in the membership of the Fingal League. Garristown, Man-O'-War, and Balbriggan did not affiliate, but Portrane and Naul Hill had re-entered, and the new teams were Blanchardstown and Clonsilla. Man-O'-War was back in Fingal cricket for the 1939 season, and it was drawn in the same section as Portrane, Naul Hill, Skerries, and Mulhuddert (sic). There is no further information available regarding that season, but the Fingal League was the object of glowing praise in a *Sunday Independent* article by G. J. Bonass, one-time President of the Irish Cricket Union which was headed "Flourishing State of Fingal League."

> It is good to see that the Fingal League flourishes.... There are some delightfully named clubs in this most sporting North County Association. Naul Hill, Man-O'-War, Ring Commons, Ballymadun are surely names to conjure with. In North County Dublin, there are few billiard table wickets. Scalps may be had at bargain prices, and it is usually a matter of great difficulty to get runs. Competition is extraordinarily keen.

Man-O'-War was involved in one of those very keen games in 1940 in what turned out to be its last season in cricket for over twenty years. On 16 July, in the game between Man-O'-War and Ballymadun, Ballymadun batted first and at the fall of the first wicket, had accumulated 25 runs. Of this total, Peter O'Brien had scored 19 runs, but in the words of the *Drogheda Independent* reporter, "the tail failed to wag", and Ballymadun was dismissed for 36 runs. The main wicket-taker for the Man-O'-War was T. Morgan who ended up with a tally of 6 wickets for 16 runs. In reply, Man-O'-War's score at 7 wickets down was 35 runs, but with 2 runs needed for a win, M. Rogers dismissed the last three men for 1 run. The best batsmen for the Man-O'-War were T. Kerrigan (12), T. Morgan (10) and T. Sheridan (8). With honours even, "the large crowd present gave the players a great ovation." For the 1941 season, there is no mention of Man-O'-War CC, but it appears to have been succeeded by Walshestown CC because there was some overlap between the personnel in both teams.

## Walshestown CC, 1940-1959

While Man-O'-War's main objective during its somewhat fragmented early existence appears to have been to play a few games of cricket, Walshestown CC which was founded in 1940 in addition to becoming a successful cricket team, also took a full part in the  social life of the community. The first reference to the club in the *Drogheda Independent* is an advertisement for a Ceilidh and Old-Time Waltz which was to be held in the Library in Lusk on Sunday, 15 December.

Dancing was from 8.00 to 12.00, music was by the Gay Gordan's Band, there were numerous novelties and other attractions, and admission was 1/6. The club organised a second ceilidh in Lusk on 16 February, with the same band providing the music. The price of admission was the same but there was no reference to novelties or other attractions on this occasion. Later in the year, the club organised another ceilidh in Lusk, but on this occasion, a rival club, the Ring Commons CC held a ceilidh on the same evening in Naul.

Irrespective of the community involvement, the main business of the club was to play cricket, and it had a difficult introduction to the Fingal League. On 25 May 1941, Walshestown played the all-conquering Balrothery team, and the young players were no match for a much more experienced side. Balrothery scored 57 runs, with C. Russell getting 27 runs and C. Mooney "playing up to his usual form." In reply, Walshestown scored 12 runs, and of this total, K. Murphy contributed 7 runs. The opposition for the second game of the season was Tubbergregan, and again there was a defeat on a score of 26 runs to 14. The Walshestown scorers were J. Moore (5) and M. Ayres (4), and the bowling honours went to K. Murphy who took 6 wickets for 12 runs and A. Ayres whose tally was 4 wickets for 8 runs. As the season unfolded, there were obvious signs of the team improving, and when a cup competition was organised at the end of the league season, the biggest surprise of the early rounds was Walshestown's defeat of the Black Hills, the League Champions, on a score of 32 runs to 15. The report on the game ascribed great credit to Walshestown "for their grasp of the game after such a short time. "A noteworthy element of the display was "the spirit to win amongst the members of the team" which was evident from the start. Walshestown's season ended with a game against Rush in which Jim Murphy scored 22 runs, but Rush won on a score of 69 runs to 48. Despite this defeat, the auguries for the future were positive, and in the words of the *Drogheda Independent*, "their prospects are looking bright for a young team and their sporting spirit will be amply repaid in future seasons."

Despite the difficulties caused by the Emergency during 1941, there was general satisfaction regarding the manner in which the Fingal League had managed games:

> Notwithstanding the amount of difficulties confronting the Fingal [League] cricket this season a very high standard of cricket has been witnessed....

A practical example of the impact of the Emergency on cricket was that on some occasions, games could not be played because the rationing of petrol meant that fields were not cut or only half of a field was cut. This may account for clubs having to make alternative arrangements for their games, and there is a reference to two Fingal League games (Walshestown and Tubbergregan, and Knockbrack versus Balrothery) being played on the same day at Walshestown.

There were thirteen clubs represented at the AGM of the Fingal League in 1942, and the League's divisional structures were amended slightly so that the issues caused by the continuing rationing of petrol could be ameliorated to a certain extent. Walshestown CC was drawn in the East Division along with Balrothery, Clonard, Rush, the Black Hills, and Ring Commons. The improvement from the 1941 season was maintained, and Walshestown reached the final of the League by beating Balrothery. In the final, Walshestown played Tubbergregan, and unfortunately, met up with Peter O'Brien whose innings of 53 was described as "faultless". The final score was Tubbergregan 69 and Walshestown 29 for whom J. Moore (8*) was top scorer.

For the 1943 season, ten teams were represented at the AGM, and Walshestown was paired with Portrane, Balrothery, Rush, and Clonard. Early in the season, Walshestown had two positive results, firstly by beating Clonard and then having a comprehensive victory over the Black Hills on a score of 76 runs to 7. However, this run of victories was halted when it played Portrane, and the final score was 90 runs to 24.

One of the defining characteristics of teams in the Fingal League has been the vigilance with which teams sought to ensure that other teams complied with the letter of the law. It is possibly for this reason that the administration of the League was streamlined to a certain extent in 1943, and a Management Committee consisting of seven members was put in place. The most frequent objection related to the eligibility of players, but at different times, there were complaints about umpires, scorers, and player behaviour. Walshestown lodged an objection against Portrane in 1943, but without access to the Minutes of the League, it is not possible to ascertain the nature of the complaint. In any event, it is irrelevant because the League dismissed the objection and Portrane went on to win the League by beating Balrothery in the final.

In 1944, Walshestown was drawn in the same section as Portrane, Skerries, Naul Hill and Knockbrack, and from a Walshestown perspective, there was nothing of note in terms of the League, but players from the club represented Fingal with distinction during this season. K. Murphy of Walshestown was named on the team which played Phoenix CC on 18 June 1944. The Fingal League team was again in action on 5 August when it played against a

Meath Selection. The result was a win for Fingal League on a score of 106 runs to 73, and one of the main contributors to the Fingal League's score was Tom Murphy (15), a member of the Murphy family who was to have a long and distinguished cricket career. While the club may have had a quiet year at league level, it continued to be active on the social front, and 2 Céilithe were held in Naul Hall on 1st and 8th October. Music was provided by the Whispering Pines, admission was 2s, and there was a cycle park.

Walshestown CC commenced the 1945 season with a Ceilidh in Naul on 29 April; music was provided by the same group, admission remained the same, but there was no reference to a cycle park. The team was in Division 2 along with the Black Hills, Portrane, Skerries, Knockbrack, and Ring Commons. The competitive nature of Fingal cricket meant that it was never possible to predict results. Walshestown lost to Knockbrack and to Skerries, and yet based on other results, qualified to meet Skerries in the semi-final which was played at Clonard. Skerries batted first and scored 49 runs, and in reply, Walshestown had scored 43 runs for the loss of 6 wickets when the excitement became "intense" as three wickets fell in the next over. According to the *Drogheda Independent*, Kevin Murphy, despite injured fingers, "carried the team on his back", … and batting with confidence, they survived to win by 19 runs." The main contributors to the score for Walshestown were Tom Murphy (14) and Kevin Murphy (11). Walshestown played Balrothery, the title holders, in the final, but was beaten by the all-conquering Balrothery team.

Eight teams were represented at the AGM of the Fingal League in 1946, and Tom Murphy of Walshestown was elected Treasurer. The team continued to be inconsistent in the League, and on 26 May 1946, it had a day to forget when in front of its home followers, it only scored 4 runs. Kit Mooney took 5 wickets for 1 run, Christy Russell took 5 wickets for 2 runs, and Balrothery scored 50, with Henry Russell (28) being the main contributor. However, the following month, Walshestown in the words of the newspaper report, "sprang a rare surprise" when it beat Balrothery at Balrothery on a score of 45 to 37 runs. T. Lindsay (17) was described as "the youth who played a big part in Walshestown's success.". In August, Rush needed to defeat Walshestown twice to win the division, but Walshestown beat Rush at Kenure Park on a score of 90 for 8 to 88 runs, and everything now hinged on the result of the second game. Walshestown beat Rush on a score of 35 runs for 3 to 31 runs and qualified to play Balrothery in the semi-final. On this occasion, two of the Murphy family, Jim, and Kevin, ended up with identical bowling figures, 5 wickets for 14 runs.

At the AGM of the Fingal League in 1947, Tom Murphy who had been elected Treasurer the previous year, appeared to have taken on the role of Secretary during the course of the year because he gave his report to the meeting in the roles of Hon. Secretary and Hon. Treasurer. At the AGM, he relinquished the role of Treasurer to R. J. Moore and was elected Secretary for the coming season. Walshestown played Rush in the semi-final of the Fingal Cup and won by 31 runs. Walshestown scored 55 runs, and bowled Rush out for 24. Jim Murphy took 5 wickets for 6 runs, and J. Moore took 4 wickets for 5. Walshestown played Knockbrack in the final, scored 94 runs, bowled Knockbrack out for 34 runs and won its first Fingal Cup after seven years of endeavour. The players who represented Walshestown on this historic occasion were as follows: T. Murphy, K. Murphy, Joe Moore, W. Tolan, P. Murphy, P. Mulligan, John Moore, J. Murphy, N. Lindsay, J. Hughes, C. Lindsay.

For the 1948 season, Tom Murphy continued as Hon. Secretary of the Fingal League, and a decision was made to put two competitions on a more formal basis as distinct from the ad hoc arrangement which had existed heretofore. In defence of its title, Walshestown did not qualify for the final which Balrothery won by beating Knockbrack in a very one-sided game. Balrothery scored 133 runs, and Knockbrack only managed 21 in reply. As Secretary of the Fingal League, Tom Murphy was also responsible for arranging the Annual Dance and Prize-Giving, and it was gratifying to note that there was a record attendance, Ralph Sylvester's Band supplied "a very pleasing selection of music", and "the catering arrangements in the hands of Mrs McKeown, Erin House, Balbriggan could not have failed to satisfy the most fastidious".

It was decided that the 1948 Cup Final between Walshestown and Balrothery which "had been unavoidably delayed" would be played as early as possible. Walshestown batted first, struggled against the "constructive bowling of Mooney and Russell", and was dismissed for 23 runs, with Tolan (7) and C. Lindsay (7), the only batsmen to "give any trouble". In reply, Balrothery scored 80 runs for the loss of 5 wickets when the stumps were drawn. J and T. Murphy are mentioned as bowling best for the losers. When the same teams met in the League, Balrothery beat Walshestown on a score of 69 for 7 wickets to 48. The principal scorers for Walshestown were K. Hughes (11) and T. Murphy 9), while T. Murphy and N. Lindsay were the best bowlers. After these defeats, Walshestown's season improved, and there were comfortable victories over Skerries and Portrane which meant that Walshestown qualified again to meet Balrothery in the final. The Drogheda Argus and Leinster Journal's preview referred to the supporters of Walshestown being "confident that the trophy this year will change hands." There is no report available on the final, but there is no doubt that Walshestown won because it was presented with the Fingal Challenge Cup Perpetual Trophy at the Annual Dance which was held in late 1949. Walshestown retained the trophy in 1950 when it defeated Clonard in the final.

Balrothery's successes in 1950 and 1951 sparked a revival of interest in cricket in Fingal. Eleven teams entered the League, and eight teams, among them, Drogheda YMCA and Malahide entered the cup competition. Walshestown played Drogheda YMCA on 22 June 1952 and won by 43 runs. The innings featured some "glorious batting" by P. O'Neill (45), T. Murphy (31) and J. Tolan (11), and the wickets taken were shared among T. Murphy, M. Brady, J. Murphy, and P. Murray. Walshestown, did not have the most propitious of starts in the game against Balrothery. Balrothery batted first and scored 97 runs. In reply, Walshestown lost the first wickets for only 4 runs, but the day was rescued by the combination of S. Carty and T. Murphy who had a "magnificent stand" of 70 runs, of which, Murphy scored 34. T. Hynes and S. Carty (42*) brought the game to a satisfactory conclusion for Walshestown. In mid-August, confidence was high in Skerries CC because it had accounted for Portrane, and then played Walshestown in Skerries. Walshestown suffered a disastrous day with the bat, with only one player, J. Tolan (11) reaching double figures, the rest of the batsmen unable to cope with the bowling of J. Walsh, W. Beggs, and R. Byrne. Walshestown ended on a "meagre total of 38 runs", and Skerries scored the necessary runs with the loss of 4 wickets. Both of these teams qualified for the final, but Skerries' hopes of winning its first title since 1931 were dashed by a resurgent Walshestown team.

The surge of optimism for cricket continued into the 1953 season, and it was hoped to have thirteen teams playing in the league. It cannot be stated conclusively that thirteen teams played during the season, because only eight teams entered for the cup competition. Walshestown reached the final again and played Portrane in "ideal conditions". Walshestown batted first and was dismissed for 18 runs. Out of this total, Jim Murphy scored 10 runs, and it appeared that a win for Portrane was a foregone conclusion. However, in Fingal cricket, it is never wise to predict whether a score is either a winning or a losing score. Portrane wickets fell like ninepins, and it ended with a score of 11 runs. Tom Murphy took 6 wickets for 8 runs and Jim, his brother, took 3 wickets for 1 run.

In 1954, Walshestown attempted to emulate Balrothery's feat of three league titles in a row and met Cottrellstown in the final. Walshestown batted first, and only scored 22 runs, with Hughes (11), the only batsman to offer any resistance. In reply, Cottrellstown had scored 35 runs for the loss of 4 wickets when stumps were drawn. The main contributors to the Cottrellstown victory were C. Russell and V. Farrell, both of whom had starred for Balrothery in the very recent past. Walshestown continued with its commitment to social activities in the community by organising a social in the Library, Lusk on 18 November, with admission costing 2/6.

In 1955, the social activities continued, and a card night called Three Fifteens, was organised on 21 January in the Library in Lusk. The First prize was £5, second prize was £3, and third prize was £2. Admission for the event was 3s. Walshestown was one of only six teams entered for the Fingal League in 1955, but the only game for which there was a report during this season was its defeat of the Black Hills by seven wickets. The Black Hills scored 13 runs, and Walshestown "had no difficulty in passing the required number with the loss of only three wickets." Cottrellstown played in the 1955 Final but lost to Balrothery on a score of 26 to 22 runs.

There are no references to Walshestown playing cricket in 1958, and the solitary game which is reported on in 1959 was played against Skerries at the Ballast Pit. Walshestown scored 34 runs, and Skerries with two wickets in hand needed 7 runs to win. W. Beggs scored "a wonderful six and Thomas Hand gave Skerries the winning run."

Unless evidence is produced to the contrary, it appears that Walshestown CC ceased to exist at the end of the 1959 season. Over nearly twenty years, the club had played a major role in assisting the development of a sense of identity for its community, and it provided valuable social, cultural, and sporting activities during this period. It was a very successful cricket club as is reflected in the number of Fingal Challenge Perpetual Clubs which it won despite being pitted against Balrothery which during this period was one of the strongest junior cricket clubs in Ireland. The members of Walshestown CC were not finished with cricket however, and when Man-O'-War CC was re-established in 1962, many of the Walshestown players were very influential in its development.

### The Man-O'-War CC, Phase 2, 1962-1969

The Man-O'-War Cricket Club was re-established in 1962, and it is relevant to comment on the contribution which pragmatism and a reluctance to accept authoritarianism made to the existence of two clubs. The Man-O'-War GAA club was founded in Thomas Morgan's house in November 1946. In an area where the population was low, it would not have been possible for a GAA club and a cricket club to survive if the GAA's ban on playing foreign games had been implemented strictly or even implemented at all. Instead, the administrators of the Man-O'-War GAA club ignored this edict, and people from the area played both games very successfully. This very commendable attitude to a restrictive practice was one of the reasons that cricket remained a mainstream sport in Fingal, and it was not achieved at the expense of the GAA clubs, but in conjunction with them. A similar situation existed in Skerries where the Beggs' brothers, one of whom was a double All-Ireland medal winner, played cricket with Skerries, rugby with Skerries and Gaelic football with Skerries Harps.

In addition to pragmatism, it was also necessary to be flexible regarding fixture-making, and there were very few instances prior to the abolition of *The Ban* when players were unavailable to one or other code due to a clash of fixtures. If there was a clash, some very astute strategic planning was brought to bear on the situation. If the Man-O'-War or The Hills won the toss, the Gaelic Footballers batted first, and when they were out, they went off to play the football match. When the football match was over, the players returned to field for the second innings. It was a little bit more complicated if the opposition decided to bat first, now substitute fielders were required, and for this to occur, permission was required from the opposing team's captain, and this permission was not always forthcoming; thus, at times it was necessary to field a number of players short until the Gaelic match was over

The early 1960s saw a resurgence of cricket in Fingal with Ring Commons being re-formed in 1961, Balbriggan returning to the fold in 1962, and Man-O'-War being re-established in the same year. The seven teams in the Fingal League in 1962 were Knockbrack, Balbriggan, Man-O'-War, Ring Commons, Skerries, the Black Hills and Balrothery. With this increase in the number of teams, the officers of the League decided to put the second competition on a more formal footing and to purchase a cup. The Man-O'-War's return to Fingal League cricket was moderately successful. It beat Ring Commons twice and qualified for the semi-final of the League where it played Skerries. No result is available for that game, but it did not win the league because Balrothery CC won the League and was the first winners of the cup competition.

In its first incarnation as a cricket club, the Man-O'-War's objectives were relatively modest and limited to playing Fingal League cricket, but the new version was more ambitious, and in addition to Fingal League cricket, the officers decided to affiliate the club to the Leinster Cricket Union. With three Fingal League teams affiliated to the Leinster Cricket Union, and ten teams playing in the Fingal League, cricket was thriving in Fingal.

The impact of the Man-O'-War on Leinster Cricket was immediate, and in its first season in Leinster, it won the Minor League. In 1964, Man-O'-War had another very successful campaign in Leinster when it retained the Minor League and reached the final of the Minor Cup but lost to Clontarf. In the Fingal League, there was an eagerly-awaited clash with Rush where Ciaran Clear (12) and Tom Walsh (10*) were the only batsmen to play the "accurate bowling of T, J. and K. Murphy". The rest of the Rush batting collapsed, and Rush ended on a score of 48, all out. The Man-O'-War batsmen, T. Murphy (33), T. Sheridan (16*) and K. Gaffney "had no difficulty in knocking off the runs against a variety of bowlers. In the semi-final of the League, Man-O'-War lost to Knockbrack on a score of 36 runs to 15. In the Fingal Cup Final, Man-O'-War faced the mighty Knockbrack who batted first and accumulated 106 runs, thanks to Sean Moore (30) and Eddie Lindsay (20). Man-O'-War was 17 for 6 wickets down when Tom Murphy appealed against the light. At that stage, Murphy was on 10*, and was Man-O'-War's "best batsman by far". The game resumed the following Sunday, but the weight of runs on the scoreboard was too much for the Man-O'-War, and Knockbrack completed a League and Cup double. The AGM for the 1964 season showed the strong links between Walshestown CC and Man-O'-War CC, with Tom Murphy, Treasurer and Captain of the First XI, and Jim Murphy, Captain of the Second XI. The close ties between the GAA Club and the Cricket Club were also evident and Thomas Morgan, a founder member and officer of the GAA club, was vice-captain of the First XI.

During the close season, Man-O'-War CC was active in maintaining the public profile of the club, and in providing social activities for the community. On 5 March 1964, there was a Club Dance in Rolestown Ballroom with music by the Silver Slipper Showband, and admission was 5s. There was another dance in the Holmpatrick House Hotel, Skerries, with the same band, but the admission had increased to 6s. At the end of the season, social activities resumed, and the club hosted another dance at the Holmpatrick House Hotel, with the same band and price of admission, but on this occasion, suppers were available. The ubiquitous Christmas Raffle was a valuable fund-raiser for all the Fingal clubs, and in keeping with the importance of transparency, the names of the winners of the Man-O'-War's Raffle were published in the *Drogheda Independent* on 19 December 1964.

Affiliation to the Leinster Cricket Union brought pressure on the clubs in terms of administration, the quality of pitches and ancillary facilities, but there was no doubt that the Fingal League clubs and the Leinster Cricket Union derived benefit from the presence of the Fingal clubs in Leinster competitions. In 1964, Gerry Byrne, President of the Fingal League, complimented the clubs on their impact on Leinster Junior Cricket, and he mentioned Rush, Man-O'-War and Knockbrack as being responsible for providing brighter cricket in the Fingal area. A potential disadvantage was the possibility of the Fingal competitions being downgraded in importance, but this did not occur for many years because of the very strong commitment of the clubs to the concept of Fingal identity and heritage.

The Man-O'-War CC did not win a League or a Cup in 1965, but it continued to field two teams in Leinster competitions, and to compete very well. It was beaten in the Final of the Junior League by Monkstown and in the Final of the Fingal Cup by Balrothery. The only game for which a report exists was a Fingal Cricket Cup tie against Skerries in which Man-O'-War batted first, scored 57 runs, with F. Morgan (12) and J. Archer (10) being the main contributors to this total. Skerries was dismissed for 20 runs, with K. Murphy taking 5 wickets for 10 runs, and T. Morgan, taking four wickets for nine runs.

In 1966, Man-O'-War reached the Final of the Leinster Junior Cup where it played a Knockbrack team which was in the middle of a golden era for that club. The Man-O'-War batted first, but only two batsmen, V. Farrell (11) and S. Hoare (22) reached double figures and the team was dismissed for 67 runs. In reply, Knockbrack got the necessary score for the loss of 4 wickets. However, the Man-O'-War had better luck in the Fingal competitions, and it completed a League and Cup double. At the AGM on 19 March 1967, the officers of the club were re-elected, Tom Murphy continued as Captain of the First XI and Thomas Morgan became Captain of the Second XI. No competitions were won in Leinster, but the Man-O'-War retained the Fingal Championship Cup.

In 1968, the Man-O'-War teams were involved at the final stages of practically every competition in which they played. Man-O'-War CC played Phoenix in the final of the Leinster Junior Cup, and on the first day, Phoenix struggled to 145 runs, all out. At close of play on Day 1, Man-O'-War had scored 35 runs for the loss of one wicket. Play resumed on Tuesday evening, and Man-O'-War ended up on 89 for 7 wickets down. This saga resumed on Thursday, and unfortunately, no details are available other than the comment in the *Evening Herald* that Man-O'-War had been beaten by Phoenix "in a very exciting finish."

Man-O'-War's tale of Cup woe was made complete when the Second XI was beaten convincingly by local rivals, Balrothery, in the Minor Cup Final. The comment regarding a convincing beating requires clarification because Balrothery had lost 6 wickets for 47 runs when the *Evening Herald* went to print on Saturday evening so it appears that some of the late-order Balrothery batsmen got runs. After these reverses, the strength of the club was shown by winning the Junior A Section of the Leinster League and winning the Fingal Cricket Championship for the third successive year.

In seven years in Leinster Cricket, Man-O'-War CC was making rapid progress through the divisions, and in 1969, it was in the same section as Balrothery, so the number of local derbies increased. Man-O'-War played Balrothery on 3 August and had a poor start, but J. Archer (33) "changed the course of the match with big hits." Balrothery had an opening stand of 29 runs, but then lost wickets cheaply to end on 66 runs, 7 runs short of Man-O'-War's total. The best bowler for Man-O'-War was Matt Gaffney who took 4 wickets for 13 runs. Man-O'-War won Intermediate League B, but it was deprived of the double by Clontarf Thirds which won the Intermediate Cup in a low-scoring game. Only four batsmen, V. Farrell (10), T. Murphy (15). T. Sheridan (13) and J. Archer (10) got into double figures, and its final score was 67 runs. Clontarf reached the required total for the loss of 7 wickets, with T. Murphy returning figures of 4 wickets for 23 runs.

Man-O'-War also had a successful season in Fingal Cricket in 1969. It won the League and Cup double, and had the Indian sign over Balrothery, its old rivals. On 26 July, Man-O'-War played Balrothery and won this game by 6 wickets. Balrothery batted first and ended on 86 for 4 wickets. The best bowler for Man-O'-War was Tom Murphy, and in reply, the opening stand for the Man-O'-War amounted to 50 runs, "helped by a few dropped catches". On the following weekend, Man-O'-War scored 45 for 3 wickets, and in reply, Balrothery got 44 runs, with T. Morgan taking 7 wickets for 10 runs. In the Cup, Man-O'-War played Rush and in the words of the Rush Correspondent in the *Drogheda Independent*, "Rush failed to dismiss the Man-O'-War for less than 64 runs and lost by 4 wickets. When the Man-O'-War met Balrothery again in the Fingal League, the margin of victory for Man-O'-War was 62 runs, and this was an untypical result in a competition where most games tended to be cliff-hangers. Tom Murphy (23) and J. Archer (22) were the main contributors to the Man-O'-War's total, with Joe O'Callaghan of Balrothery taking 8 wickets for 43 runs. In reply, Balrothery had a poor start with only Oliver Murray (25) getting a score of any consequence. The main bowlers for Man-O'-War were Tom

Murphy with 5 wickets for 17 runs, and Seán Moore whose 5 wickets for 24 runs included a hat-trick.

## Man-O'-War CC, 1970 - 1992

The treatment of individual seasons will be more cursory in this section because the aim of this chapter is to place Man-O'-War CC within sporting, cultural and social contexts. It was never intended to provide a history of the Man-O'-War CC because that would require an approach which would involve analysing each season in detail. Cricket Leinster's Centenary Book, *100 Not Out*, referred to the "re-emergence of Fingal in the 1960s", and the impact of the Fingal League clubs on Leinster Junior competitions was even more pronounced in the 1970s. The Man-O'-War, The Hills, Knockbrack, Rush and Balrothery all won cups or trophies during this decade, and of the 45 league championships, outside of senior cricket, Fingal League clubs won 24 of them, a 53% -win percentage.

In 1970, Man-O'-War retained the Fingal Challenge Cup and the Championship Cup. It was less successful in Fingal Cricket in 1971, although it retained the Cup for the 6th time in succession, but it lost the League to Balrothery CC. Winning the Championship Cup for the seventh time in succession proved to be a step too much, and Man-O'-War was beaten by 8 wickets by Balrothery. In the final, Man-O'-War batted first, lost 4 wickets for 7 runs, and was 51 for 9 wickets down. John Murphy (43*) and Dermot Sheridan (10) were the only batsmen to reach double figures. The 56 years old, Kit Mooney, took 7 wickets for 18 runs, off 16 overs, with the first 8 overs being maidens. In reply, John Mooney (43*) and his uncle, Kit (13*) steered Balrothery home, and this gave Balrothery its first cup since 1965, but it was also Balrothery's last success in Fingal competitions until 1982. From 1973 until the early 1980s, the main rivals for Fingal League honours were the Man-O'-War and The Hills CC.

For the 1973 season, John Morgan was elected Captain of the First XI, Tom Murphy was Captain of the Second XI and Liam Rooney was Captain of the Thirds. On the last weekend of the season, Man-O'-War and Clontarf were in the running to win the Senior 2 League, and the two teams met at The Nevitt on Saturday, 13 September. Unfortunately, there was one of those infamous batting collapses which seemed to affect Fingal sides on some of the big days. Man-O'-War was dismissed for 34 runs, with Don Geraghty taking 6 wickets for 22 runs, and W. Dalton-Browne taking the other 4 wickets for 10 runs. Clontarf needed to beat CYM on the following day to ensure a league triumph, but the game was not played due to rain, and the Junior Branch was left with a decision to make because Man-O'-War and Clontarf were now tied for first place. In the end, it was decided to share the League title, and this was a wonderful achievement for a club which had only been in Leinster League cricket since 1963. There was a further triumph for the club when Tom Murphy won the Oulton Cup which is awarded to the best bowler in Senior 2 Cricket. To finish off a successful season for the club, it won the Fingal Championship Cup.

The 1974 season was one of consolidation for the Man-O'-War because it did not win any trophies at Leinster League level, and The Hills CC commenced on a run of Fingal Championship Cup victories which lasted from 1974 to 1978 inclusive. The Challenge Cup was shared between Man-O'-War and Balbriggan, due to a tragic event which occurred on 28 September 1974. Christy Russell, one of the legendary Fingal Cricketers, was playing with Balbriggan in the final against the Man-O'-War, but he suffered a heart attack, and died during the game. As a mark of respect, the game was not re-played but the Fingal League decided that the Challenge Cup should be shared. Additionally, Balbriggan CC presented a cup in memory of Christy, which became the prize for a T20 competition. From 1975 until 1979 inclusive, Man-O'-War won the Perpetual Challenge Cup and won back the Championship Cup from the Hills in 1979.

In 1976, Man-O'-War played Knockbrack in the Intermediate Cup final at Phoenix. There is a photo extant of the Man-O'-War team, and it evoked many memories as some of the players attempted to name the entire team. Details of the actual game are also sketchy. Jody Morgan, father of Eoin, played in the game, and he thought that Man-O'-War scored about 120 runs, Brendan Sheridan got about 40 runs and Liam Rooney took wickets. These details will be clarified when (or if) a scorecard becomes available.

In 1977, Man-O'-War was in the running until late August to win the Senior 2 League, but a poor result against Malahide ruined its chances of winning it. On a rain-affected wicket at The Nevitt, Malahide batted first and declared on a score of 219 runs for 8 wickets. The best bowler for the Man-O'-War was Tom Murphy, who took 5 wickets for 68 runs off 19 overs. The Man-O'-War response started badly but Liam Rooney (43) and Nick Farrell (40) compiled a stand of 80 runs for the 6th wicket to give the score a semblance of respectability. When this partnership was ended, Man-O'-War attempted to bat for a draw, but this effort failed, and Man-O'-War's final score was 125 runs.

The Man-O'-War's Thirds followed up the previous year's cup success by winning the Intermediate C League, and in one of the games in that season for which a report is available, it had a comprehensive victory over Civil Service to maintain its 100% record in the League. Civil Service, for whom the famous umpire, Stuart Daltrey featured, batted first, and was dismissed for 124 runs. Christy Garry took 3 wickets for 20 runs, off his 10 overs. The Man-O'-War reply got off to a brisk start, and Christy Garry completed a successful aal-round game by scoring 32 runs. Other contributors to the Man-O'-War victory were Brian Murphy (21*), Jody Morgan (17), Michael Kiely (16), and Kevin Gaffney (14).

The development of youth cricketers has been one of the defining characteristics of the Fingal League, and this was given formal recognition in 1971 when Gerry Byrne, President of the Fingal League, presented a trophy for youth cricket. In 1977, the Man-O'-War played Balbriggan in a play-off game to decide the winners of this trophy. Man-O'-War batted first, and scored 72 runs, of which Thomas Murphy Jnr, was the main contributor with 29 runs. Balbriggan only scored 43 runs in reply because it struggled against the bowling of the Murphy brothers, with Thomas taking 3 wickets for 12 runs, and Joe taking 3 wickets for 19 runs.

The main success story of the 1978 season again related to a Junior team, and Man-O'-War's Second XI won the Whelan Cup by beating Knockbrack by 7 wickets in the final. Knockbrack scored 61 runs, and the main wicket takers for the Man-O'-War were T. Murphy, 3 wickets for 7 runs, and Albert Harper, 2 wickets for 16 runs. Man-O'-War reached the target for the loss of 3 wickets, with Jody Morgan (17*), T. Murphy (11), S. Halligan (9) and B. Murphy (9*) being the main contributors to the score.

The non-selection of Fingal players for representative teams was a source of grievance for many years, with the most extreme instance being the failure of the Irish selectors to pick Matt Dwyer of The Hills CC until he was 39 years of age, despite the fact that he had won the award for being the best bowler in Leinster on 5 occasions. At underage and junior league levels, the balance was redressed to a certain extent, with John Murphy of Man-O'-War CC being selected to play for the North Leinster U19 team in the Jeyes Cup in 1972. Further representative honours were forthcoming for the Murphy family in 1976 when Tom and John, Father, and Son, were selected for the Senior 2 League team which played against Clontarf in the Centenary Fixture. By this stage, John had become a youth international, and was also playing for the North Leinster Senior side in the Guinness Cup. His brother, Michael at 15 years of age, had already scored a century for the Man-O'-War in a game against Old Belvedere, and was selected for the North Leinster U19 team in 1977.

Over the next 10 years, Michael Murphy won the Bookman Cup for being the best Senior 2 batsman in Leinster in 1982, 1983, 1987 and 1989; his brother, Joe, won the Oulton Cup in 1989, and Liam Rooney won it in 1981, 1983 and 1984. The clamour for Fingal League players to be selected for representative sides was not confined to Fingal, and Seán Pender of the *Irish Times*, an advocate for Fingal cricket, argued that Michael Murphy was in a different class to many other cricketers and that it was "past the time that he should be given the chance to prove this at Guinness Cup (Interprovincial) level". This situation regarding selection issues was not rectified until Mike Hendrick became Coach to the Irish team, and players were judged on results and ability, rather than on their clubs or addresses.

After that digression on selection issues, it is opportune to return to cricketing matters, and in the late 1970s, and early 1980s, the aspirations of the Fingal League clubs changed from being content to play Leinster Junior cricket to a desire to be considered for membership of the Senior League. Unfortunately, entrance to senior cricket was controlled by the senior clubs, and they feared that the inclusion of some other teams would eventually lead to the introduction of relegation, with the consequent loss of senior status for some long-established clubs.

It was argued by some eminent cricket people such as Michael Sharp and Seán Pender that Man-O'-War CC's record in Leinster Cricket in the early 1980s should have ensured its admission to senior cricket. In 1980, it played Clontarf, the holders of the Senior 2 League title, and recorded its highest ever total at that level. It had a poor start, and lost 3 wickets for 39 runs, but a quick 23 runs from Tom Murphy, a "faultless" 102 from Michael Murphy and a patient 33 from Liam Rooney gave Man-O'-War a total of 231 for 8 wickets. The "much-vaunted" batting line-up of Clontarf struggled against the bowling of Michael Murphy (5 wickets for 30 runs) and Liam Rooney (4 wickets for 56 runs) and was dismissed for 110 runs. While Man-O'-War had shared the Senior 2 League title previously, it won the title in its own right in 1980 and again in 1982. Man-O'-War applied for senior status in 1982 but was refused admission to the senior league. The matter was discussed at a Junior Branch meeting, and Michael Sharp, Secretary of the Branch, argued that the system was defective if a club was not provided clear criteria for its application being refused.

In 1983, Man-O'-War had an opportunity to show that it merited admission to the Senior League when it was drawn against CYM, one of the two clubs admitted to the Senior League, for the first round of the Leinster Senior Cup. Seán Pender in his column following this game argued that Man-O'-War was more than ready in terms of playing resources and facilities, and that its promotion to the Senior League should not be delayed any longer. In the game, Man-O'-War scored 149 against CYM's 171, and one of the stars of the game was Tom Murphy, who at 60 years of age only conceded 19 runs off 12 overs. The Man of the Match was Tom's son, Michael, who scored 69 runs, took 3 wickets and 2 slip catches. Man-O'-War reapplied for membership to the Senior League in October 1983, but its application was refused again on this occasion because its ground did not meet the required standard. At Fingal League level, Man-O'-War won the Perpetual Challenge Cup in 1983, won the Fingal League double in 1984 and again in 1985.

Man-O'-War and Balrothery met in the Fingal Championship final, and the first attempt to play the game was abandoned due to continuous rain in Rush on 4 August 1985. The teams met again on 15 September, and Balrothery batted first, but superb bowling from Liam Rooney (7 wickets for 24 runs, off 14 overs) meant that it was dismissed for 61 runs. In reply, Anthony Rooney and Brian Southam scored 49 for the first wicket when Anthony Rooney was caught in the slips by Tommy Mooney, off the bowling off Phil Mooney. Brian Southam and Tom Murphy were out shortly after, and this left Jody Morgan and Liam Rooney at the wicket. Jody Morgan hit a four to tie the scores, and Liam Rooney hit the winning run.

At this juncture, player retention had become an issue for both clubs as some of their better players had begun to transfer to senior clubs. John Morgan had left Man-O'-War in 1977; John Murphy had played for Trinity while in college, and then played for Malahide, and his brother, Michael, had also transferred to Malahide. Gerry Harper had transferred to The Hills, and there was a fear that other players might wish to test their skills in Senior Cricket. Applications for senior status by Balrothery and Man-O'-War had been rejected so it was logical that the new amalgamated club entitled North County would apply for admission to the Senior League for the 1986 season. This application was refused, but it was intimated that if North County won the Senior 2 League in 1986, its application would be looked upon favourably.

For Fingal League purposes both clubs decided to retain their individual identities and to maintain two grounds, the Nevitt and the Matt. Man-O'-War continued to be a successful club at Fingal League level; it won the Challenge Cup in 1987, 1988 and 1990, and it won the Fingal Championship Cup in 1987, 1988 and 1990.

In 1989, Man-O'-War played Balbriggan in the Christy Russell final, and it is appropriate to give a detailed account of this game because it contained all the ingredients of Fingal League cricket – brilliant bowling and fielding in addition to "big hitting" towards the end of the innings. Man-O'-War batted first, and after a somewhat circumspect start, Michael Murphy batted almost the entire innings for 59 runs. His innings accelerated when he hit Albert Harper for 13 runs in an over, but the Harper family had revenge when he was eventually caught off the bowling of Clifford Harper. Liam Rooney (29) and Alan Rooney (12) provided good support, but the momentum in the innings was provided by Joe Murphy who scored an unbeaten 43 runs in 5 overs to bring the Man-O'-War total to 145 for 4 in 20 overs. Albert Harper took 2 wickets for 33 runs, with Clifford Harper and Patrick Hickey taking 1 wicket each.

Balbriggan's reply had a disastrous start. Albert Harper scored 5 runs; Alan Guildea got 6, but Patrick Hickey and Colm Reilly brought Balbriggan back into the game with a stand of 106 runs which left Balbriggan needing 6 runs in the last over to win. Ivan Harper was run out without scoring; Tom Clarke was bowled for a duck; Hickey was left becalmed on 86*, and Balbriggan ended up on 143 for 6, 2 runs short of the Man-O'-War's total. Joe Murphy's figures for 5 overs, were 1 for 12, and Liam Rooney took 2 wickets for 32 runs. Patrick Hickey had the consolation of being awarded the Man-of the Match trophy.

In 1991, Man-O'-War was involved in an interesting test of the Fingal League's residency rules which simply stated that it was necessary for a person to reside in Fingal for one week. There was no prohibition against playing a professional cricketer in the Fingal League, even though professionals were not allowed to play in Leinster League cricket during that season. Man-O'-War recruited Gary Wood, the Malahide Professional, and its argument was that Wood was intended to counteract the influence of Alf Masood who was playing for Rush. In any event, neither player had a starring role in the final, and it fell to Brendan Wilde who scored 42 runs to enable Rush to win the Championship Cup for the first time in 30 years.

Man-O'-War continued to play in the Fingal League, and it won the Perpetual Challenge Cup in 1995 for the last time under its own identity. From that point onwards, the amalgamated team is listed in the Fingal League's Archives as Man-O'-War/Balrothery. In an era where sporting affiliations were divisive at times, Man-O'-War Cricket Club was an outstanding example of a community-centred club whose members played cricket and Gaelic Football. It promoted a sense of identity, and it provided a splendid sporting and social outlet for the people of the wider community. It produced magnificent cricketers who played the game with pride and passion and represented the finest values of the game of cricket by being scrupulously fair. When the question is asked, why did cricket remain a mainstream sport in this part of Fingal, Man-O'-War Cricket Club will feature prominently in the ensuing discussion.

Walshestown, 1945

**Man-O-War Photo, 1966**

Back row: Thomas Morgan, Matt Gaffney, Oliver Murray, Thomas Caffrey, John Archer, Jim Garry, Kevin Murphy, Tom Sheridan, Anthony Rooney, Joe Hoare. (Billy Tolan may be the person beside Thomas Caffrey).

Front Row: Thomas McDonnell, Joe Archer, Tom Murphy, Simon Hoare, Valley Farrell.

*Figure 21, Man O'-War, 1966*

## Man-O-War, 1976 (Winners of Intermediate Cup)

**Back Row**: Kristan Gargia, Jody Morgan, Alo Rooney, Liam Rooney, Brian Murphy, Jim Garry

Front Row: Michael Murphy, Joe Keogh, Niall Hughes, Seán Halligan, Nick Farrell, Brendan Sheridan

*The Nevitt*

## Jody and John Morgan

## Jim Garry

## Thomas Garry

## Liam Rooney

# Chapter 16: Cricket in Balrothery

Cricket was introduced to Fingal in the 1820s by some of the owners of the "Big Houses", and as the game grew in popularity during the 1860s and 1870s, cricket clubs were formed. Some of these clubs such as Malahide, Balbriggan and Rush continued to be heavily dependent on the patronage of the gentry for the use of a ground and playing equipment, but other clubs were formed in townlands where tenant farmers and farm workers were given access to a field by a supportive landowner for a few games of cricket during the season. It was a source of considerable pride for the members of Balrothery CC that over the years they remained close to their rural roots and when the club was involved in the Irish Junior Cup competitions during the 1950s, the reports in the local press drew attention to the fact that the "club and players are mostly composed of farmers and farm workers as well as one schoolboy." This claim was reiterated in 1954 when Balrothery defeated Ballyclare in the semi-final of the Irish Junior Cup:

> It is of interest to note that the personnel of the Balrothery side are all farmers and farm workers, and they all learned their cricket in their leisure hours on the village green.

Prior to the establishment of the Fingal League, it has only been possible to locate one reference to cricket being played in Balrothery when Knock CC defeated Balrothery CC on 23 June 1912 on a score of 115 to 35 runs. However, it cannot be assumed that there was no cricket in the area because teams tended to take the name of the townland in which the field was located, and there were at least twenty teams in the greater Balbriggan/Skerries area during this period.

Balrothery CC entered the Fingal League in 1928, and in its first year in league cricket, did reasonably well by finishing second in its section. In 1929, Balrothery opened its season with two friendly games. It played against Skerries on 14 April and lost on a score of 28 runs to 22. Its second friendly game was against Balbriggan, and Balrothery won an exciting game by 5 runs, but according to a local critic, the auguries for the season were not good. In a typically trenchant assessment of the overall standard, "the father of cricket in Balbriggan said that it would take five years for any of the players to be a perfect cricketer." While the quest for perfection in any aspect of human activity is a laudable if somewhat chimerical enterprise, the sentiments expressed were an accurate assessment of Balrothery's season, because it finished second last in its section with an overall record of 12 games played, won 4 and lost 8. It may be deduced from the league table that batting was a problem because only 310 runs were scored for the season, and this works out at an average of slightly less than 26 runs per game.

On 3 May 1930, Balrothery played the British Legion, and won on a score of 15 runs to 11. This result suggested that the batting woes of the previous season were still an issue, but on this occasion, the *Drogheda Independent's* Correspondent contented himself with the comment that "judging by the display on Sunday last, we are assured of some very interesting games when the League commences." Balrothery finished joint second in its section of the League with a much-improved record. It played 10 games, won 6 and lost 4, but it increased the number of runs scored from 310 to 513, and the average per game was 51.3 which was almost double the average of the previous season.

While the main emphasis of this paper is on cricket, it would be negligent to ignore the Balrothery District Council and Board of Guardians which held its last meeting on 13 October 1930. This august body, which was established by the British Government in 1898 as an experiment in giving Irish people the opportunity to manage some element of its own business, was responsible for many initiatives which improved the lives of the people of Fingal during the thirty odd years of its existence. The District Council oversaw the building of houses, dispensaries, and libraries, and it had responsibility for the development of water supply and drainage schemes in Balbriggan, Skerries, Swords and Malahide. New burial grounds were laid out in Balbriggan, Rush and Malahide, and the Council was also entrusted with the very onerous task of the management of the Public Health and Charities Acts.

While cricket is a summer sport, the cricket clubs in Fingal maintained their profiles on an all-year round basis by organising Whist Drives, Concerts, and Dances. In 1931, the Annual Dance of the Balrothery Cricket Club was held in Naul on Sunday, 8 February and it was deemed to have been "the most successful event of the season". There was a huge crowd present, and the dancing which consisted mostly of old-time waltzes and Irish dances went on from 8.00 p.m. until the "small hours of the morning". There was a raffle for a watch; there were singers, and step dancers, and Tolan Bros Band provided the music. Unlike many other parts of Ireland where cricket and cricketers were on the periphery of their communities, the cricket club was a focal point in the social and cultural life of Balrothery; thus, one of the events on Patron Day on 29 June 1931 at a fund-raiser for parochial funds was a cricket match between the married and single men from Balrothery, Balbriggan, Man-O'-War and Ring Commons. There were also general athletic events, and a football match between Rush and Balrothery for which V. Rev. J. Hickey, PP, threw in the ball. In addition to this sporting activity, the day ended with a dance, and Mrs Pim who had "kindly lent her ground for the occasion", was going to "supervise all". In terms of cricket, Balrothery CC had a poor season. It was drawn in Division B, with Ballymadun, Ring Commons, Knightstown, Balbriggan, and Barnageera. Its record for the season was 10 games played, won 4, lost 6, and only 317 runs were accumulated which worked out at an average of nearly 32 runs per game.

The most significant item of news regarding Balrothery CC during the 1932 season was its involvement in the Balbriggan CC Street League. In the final, Balrothery scored 20 runs in its first innings, and Mill Street scored 23 runs. Balrothery only scored 16 runs in the second innings, and Mill Street required 4 runs to win with 4 wickets in hand. Mooney and Russell, took the last 4 wickets for the loss of 2 runs, leaving Balrothery the winners by 1 run. It is unfortunate that the newspaper report did not give the players' forenames with the result that it is not possible to conclude whether this league was for children or adults. More than likely, it was a competition for children because Balbriggan CC had organised such a league previously and it is difficult to imagine that a team which was competing at adult level in the Fingal League would have been permitted to enter a street league.

Balrothery maintained its membership of the Fingal League during this period unlike many other teams which opted in and out on a season- by- season basis. In 1933, the other teams in its section were Oldtown, Baldwinstown, Knockbrack, Man-O'-War. Of its 8 games, Balrothery won 3 and lost 5. In 1935, there were ten teams affiliated, and Naul won the Fingal Challenge Cup for the first time by beating the Black Hills in the final. A difficulty involved in the regionalisation of a competition is that the strong teams may be in the same section, and this may account for the challenge game which was played on the following Sunday between Naul and Balrothery. The opening sentence of the report on the *Drogheda Independent* asserted that any doubts that existed regarding the superiority of Naul in Fingal cricket were "set at rest" when Naul defeated Balrothery on a score of 81 to 51 runs. The chief contributors to Naul's total were Ennis (39*), Mangan (15) and Corbally (13) while Mooney scored 19 runs for Balrothery.

After some years of moderate results in Fingal cricket, Balrothery CC improved year by year, and in 1936, it reached the Fingal League final for the first time when it played its near neighbours, the Black Hills, in front of a large crowd. The Black Hills batted first and scored 38 runs, with J. Murphy (17), J. Shanley (7) and J. Russell (5) being the main batsmen. Balrothery encountered the magnificent bowling of Simon Hoare who took 6 wickets for 9 runs and Jem Murphy who took the remaining 4 wickets for 3 runs. The same two teams contested the 1937 final, and Balrothery won the Fingal Challenge Cup for the first time. Unfortunately, there is a dearth of information regarding that season, so it is not possible to give any further details regarding the scores in that game.

For the next twenty years, Balrothery CC was the strongest club in Fingal. During this time, individual clubs may have beaten Balrothery in finals, but none of them had Balrothery's consistency over the longer period. For example, in 1938, Balrothery played Portrane CC in the final, and the three matches which ensued are enshrined in the annals of Fingal Cricket history. There were over 200 people present at the first game in Balbriggan which ended with both teams scoring 60 runs. The replay was staged at the same venue, and it also ended in a tie, with both teams scoring 57 runs. The second replay was hosted by Skerries CC because the Balbriggan ground was unavailable. Portrane won the toss and batted first. At the close of its innings, Portrane had scored 47 runs, with P. Breen (11*) and P. Neville (10) being the main contributors to the total, and the Balrothery bowlers who were adjudged to "have made good use of the ball" were C. Mooney, C. Russell, and P. Farrell. In reply, Balrothery could only score 34 runs and on this occasion, fortune did not favour J. Mooney (3), C. Russell (1) and C. Mooney (0), the batsmen who regularly were the top scorers for Balrothery, and only two Balrothery batsmen, V. Farrell (14) and H. Russell (10) managed to reach double figures .

The test of the resilience of a team is the manner in which it addresses a setback, and Balrothery reached the final again in 1939, and again Portrane CC provided the opposition. It is of value to quote at length from the report on this game because it provides an insight into some of the key characteristics of Fingal cricket, and it also features starring roles for two men, C. J. Russell, and C. Mooney who are legendary figures in the history of cricket in Fingal. The highlight of the Balrothery batting was C. J. Mooney's 16 "excellent runs". He received valuable support from Valley Farrell who scored 11 runs, and Balrothery's final total was 58 runs. In reply, Portrane, who ended up on a score of 54 runs, encountered the brilliant "length" bowling of the 19 years old C. J. (Christy) Russell, who took 8 wickets for 19 runs, and his partner, C. (Kit) Mooney, who while not as successful with the ball, took the "all-important" first wicket. The fielding was also of a high standard and some superb catches were taken with Russell also receiving special mention for his performance in the field:

> This boy's fielding was a treat to watch and the manner in which he stopped and gathered fast travelling balls had an inspiring effect on all the members of his side and it was only fitting that he should take the final wicket by bringing off an excellent slip catch.

In 1940 Balrothery reached the final for the fifth consecutive year, played Black Hills, and the Russell brothers, Henry, and Christy, who combined for a stand of 50 for the fourth wicket, enabled Balrothery to compile a score of 76 runs. It appeared that there was going to be an early finish to this game because Black Hills lost 5 wickets for 6 runs, but the later batsmen, more "by good luck than by good resolute batting" brought the score to 66 thus, giving Balrothery a victory margin of 10 runs. Balrothery owed its victory in no small manner to its captain, C. J. Mooney who bowled unchanged, took 7 wickets for 22 runs, and got special mention for taking the last three wickets when the batsmen were on top. As usual, the Balrothery fielding was very good with Dillon's slip catch to dismiss the last batsman being described as "miraculous".

Balrothery's run of successes was ended in 1941 when the same two teams contested the final which was described as the "most interesting Fingal Cricket League final witnessed in Fingal for some years". The Black Hills scored 38 runs, and Balrothery was restricted to 28 runs in its reply, with Mr J. Mooney being "easily the outstanding light on his team". No Fingal event is complete without a "high class tea" and on this occasion it was provided by Balbriggan CC.

Between 1931 and 1961, a knock-out competition was played intermittently until it was put on a formal footing in 1962 and a cup was presented. In 1941, Balrothery played Rush in the final of the knock-out competition, and its tale of woe for the season was made complete when it was comprehensively beaten by a Rush team on a score of 79 to 43 runs. For Rush, T. P. Walsh (37) was outstanding with the bat, and A. G. Quinn took 7 wickets for 19 runs. The only Balrothery batsmen to offer any resistance to the Rush bowling were Henry Russell (30) and J. K. Mooney (9).

For the first time since 1935, Balrothery did not reach the final of the Fingal League Challenge Cup in 1942. However, Balrothery reached the Championship Cup final and was opposed by the Black Hills in a game which was due to be hosted by Clonard CC on 11 October 1942. Unfortunately, an exhaustive search of the local newspapers has failed to elicit the name of the team which won this game, or even if it was played at all.

Balrothery was back in the Fingal Challenge Cup Final again in 1943 but was well-beaten by Portrane. Just as there was an expectation that Balrothery's bowling and fielding would be first class, there was a certain inevitability about the batting woes. Balrothery batted first and was dismissed for 15 runs. In reply, Portrane made 73 for 5, with Neville scoring more than 50*. Portrane appeared to have completed a League and Cup double by beating Tubbergregan on a score of 48 to 11 runs; however, according to the *Drogheda Independent* of 9 October 1943, Balrothery won the Championship by beating Rush on a score of 35 runs to 10. It is definite that Portrane won the Perpetual Challenge Cup (The League), but it is not possible to be definitive regarding the winners of the Cup, given that there were two contradictory reports in the *Drogheda Independent*. In 1944, Balrothery reached the Cup Final again, and played Knockbrack at Clonard, Balbriggan. Balrothery scored 43, with G. McNally taking 7 wickets for 22 runs. Knockbrack was dismissed for 14 runs, with the "deadly duo of C. Mooney (6 for 3) and C. Russell (3 for 10) taking most of the wickets.

Balrothery did not have the best of starts to the 1945 season and it was beaten at home by Tubbergregan on a score of 66 to 53 runs. This result was deemed to have been a major surprise because Balrothery had only been beaten at home three times in eleven years, and Tubbergregan was the first team from West Fingal to lower Balrothery's colours. M. Kiernan took 3 wickets for 8 runs, Pat O'Brien took 4 wickets for 8 runs, and this included a hat-trick. Balrothery recovered from this early season reverse and retained the league title when it overcame Walshestown in the final.

The 1946 Fingal League Final was not played until 1947 because Tubbergregan indicated that it would not fulfil a fixture that was scheduled for so late in the season (27 October). The game should have been played a month ago, but "harvesting operations had delayed the holding of the game." The 1946 final was eventually played on 29 June 1947 and resulted in a facile win for Balrothery who scored 53 runs against Tubbergregan's 15 runs who "collapsed before the splendid bowling of Russell and Mooney." Balrothery CC beat Knockbrack handsomely in 1948 in the final on a score of 133 runs to 21 with Simon Hoare (40) being the main contributor to the Balrothery score. A cup competition was also organised in 1948 but due to a variety of circumstances, the final between Balrothery and Walshestown was not played until May 1949. Walshestown batted first but struggled against the bowling of Mooney and

Russell and was dismissed for 23 runs. The only batsmen to make scores of any consequence were W. Tolan (7) and C. Lindsay (7). In reply, Balrothery accumulated 80 runs for 5 wickets when the stumps were drawn with the most significant contributions coming from V. Farrell (27), S. Hoare (17), H. Russell (16) and C. Russell (14).

At different stages during the preceding years, players from Balrothery such as Simon Hoare, Christy Russell, John, and Kit Mooney had played Leinster League cricket for Rush and/or Skerries, and in 1949, Balrothery decided to affiliate to the Leinster Cricket League in addition to playing Fingal League cricket. This initiative brought variety in terms of games against different teams, and with games being played in Dublin on cricket grounds as distinct from fields which were given over for a few games, the Fingal clubs came under pressure to improve their pitches and ancillary facilities. Balrothery encountered immediate success in Leinster League cricket, and it won the Minor League (Division 5) in 1949. Walshestown won the Fingal Challenge Cup in 1949 and it was won by Balrothery the following year.

With Rush, Portrane, and Balrothery playing in Leinster League cricket in addition to the Fingal League, there was now pressure regarding fixtures with Leinster League fixtures invariably being given precedence over Fingal League games. In his report on the 1951 season, the Secretary of the Fingal League, Eddie Dunne, stated that the season had been a very bad one for the League with only four teams competing for the Fingal Cup, and the final between Portrane and Knockbrack not being played due to unforeseen difficulties. However, 1951 was not a bad year for Fingal teams in Leinster because two Fingal League teams, Rush and Balrothery, contested the Intermediate Cup. Balrothery batted first and scored 141 runs. According to the *Drogheda Independent*, S and P. Carty and T. Murphy "trundled in good style" for Rush. The game was continued on Monday evening, and Rush lost wickets early on and were always "uncomfortable" against the bowling of Mooney and Russell. The top scorer for Rush was Con Martin (25), and Rush's total was 71 runs. By winning the Intermediate Cup, Balrothery qualified to represent the Leinster Cricket Union in the newly established Irish Junior Cup and played Galway County in the semi-final. According to *The Irish Times*, the Galway batting "was all at sea on a wicket at Terenure CYM which was much faster than they are accustomed in the West," and against the bowling of Mooney (5 for 11) and Russell (4 for 11), they were all out for 32. In the final, Balrothery met Bohemians, Cork, the holders of the trophy, and 5 wickets fell for 11 runs, but Simon Hoare (26) and Hugh Russell (13) retrieved the situation with Balrothery's innings closing on 63 runs. Excellent bowling by Kit Mooney (4 for 11) and C. Russell (6 for 8) was mainly responsible for the victory, and according to the *Irish Times*, neither of them "sent down any loose stuff at all, and Bohemians were struggling from the start." Bohemians were bowled out for 20, with six batsmen not scoring a run.

Balrothery celebrated this wonderful year in style by hosting a "Grand Presentation Dance" in the Town Hall, Balbriggan on 9 November 1951. Music was provided by the Savoy Orpheans, Dancing was from 9.00 to 3.00, Admission was 5s, catering was by Mrs McKeown and Supper was extra. That was not the end of the dancing for 1951 because a "Grand Festival Dance" was hosted by the club on 21 December 1951. On this occasion, dancing was from 9.00 to 4.00, music was provided by Stephen Garvey's Orchestra, Admission was 5s, Catering was again by Mrs McKeown and the Supper was extra.

The level of enthusiasm for cricket in Balrothery during this period was such that the club was able to field two teams in the Leinster Cricket League. The First XI won the Intermediate League for the first time in 1952 by beating Leinster in the final game of the season, and the Second XI under the astute leadership of G. L. McGowan won the Minor Cup. The victory for the Second XI was particularly meritorious because the team was mostly composed of young players. In the final, Balrothery played Merrion and bowled them out for 42 runs. The wickets were shared between Frank Casey (7 for 18) and George McNally (3 for 16), and inevitably, there was a reference to "excellent fielding". Balrothery's opening pair of McNally and Hickey put on 23 runs before the first wicket fell. G. O'Mahony and his brother, Dermot, a future bishop of Dublin, saw Balrothery home without any further alarms. At its AGM, Mr Moore, Secretary of Balrothery CC, ascribed the progress of the club since its foundation 17 years ago to the "loyalty of the members and good sportsmanship in defeat as well as victory." The reference to a foundation date is open to question because a team from Balrothery was playing in the Fingal League from 1928 onwards so this comment may relate to the club being put on a more formal footing or to a change of ground.

Balrothery retained the Intermediate Shield in 1953 by beating CYMS in the final on a "rain-soaked wicket". CYMS batted first and scored 59 runs, with C. Mooney (6 wickets for 29 runs) and C. Russell (4 for 27) sharing the wickets. The main contributors to the Balrothery score of 61 for 5 wickets were J. Mooney (17), R. Byrne (16) and S. Hoare (16*). Having had some of its players play for Fingal League teams which had beaten Senior League teams, it was an obvious progression for Balrothery to play a Senior League side and it received a gracious invitation from the recently promoted Malahide to play a friendly game. The Malahide Selection batted first and scored 86 runs, but Balrothery managed to surpass this score for the loss of 9 wickets.

Fund-raising is an essential element in the activities of most clubs, and in addition to the revenue raised and its social function, it is valuable in maintaining a public profile for the club. Before the start of the 1954 season, the club organised a Three Fifteens and Final Card Night at the Town Hall, Balbriggan, with the price of admission set at 6s. The first prize was £20, second prize was £10, third prize was £5, and the other finalists received £1.

Fingal League clubs had a reputation for insisting on strict adherence to the letter of the law by their opponents, and this was evident from the first year of the League when the Executive was kept busy in dealing with objections and queries. This legalistic characteristic manifested itself again in 1954 when Rush and Balrothery became embroiled in a dispute regarding the use of substitutes during the semi-final of the Leinster Senior Intermediate Cup. Rush claimed victory by 2 runs in the first game when a Balrothery player was not allowed to bat because he was deemed to be a substitute. Balrothery lodged an objection, and the LCU ordered that the game be replayed on the basis that the player should have been allowed to bat. Balrothery batted first in the replay and amassed a score of 160 all out. The leading scorers for Balrothery were M. Gasson (36*), S. Hoare (17), J. Bissett (17) and P. Dillon (10). With the exception of Tom Murphy, who scored 24, the other Rush batsmen provided very little opposition for Russell (5 wickets), Hoare (3 wickets) and Bissett (2 wickets) and were dismissed for 75 runs. Balrothery played Cremore in the final of the Intermediate Cup and won by 4 wickets. Cremore batted first and was dismissed for 86 runs. Russell took 6 wickets for 50 runs and Bissett took 3 wickets for 8 runs. C. Mooney (11) and J. Bissett (21) were together when Bissett hit the winning runs.

By winning the Intermediate Cup, Balrothery CC qualified again to represent Leinster in the Irish Junior Cup. It defeated Ballyclare, Co. Antrim in the semi-final, and in the final was opposed by Cahir Park, Tipperary. Unfortunately, the old batting malaise struck and Balrothery scored 48 runs with only Simon Hoare (11) and R. Moore (12) getting into double figures. Cahir Park scored the runs for the loss of 6 wickets, with Mooney (3 for 31) and Russell (3 for 25) being the successful bowlers.

1955 was another successful year for Balrothery. The Third XI won the Leinster Minor Cup by beating Jacobs by 7 wickets. J. Murphy took 6 wickets for 23 runs, R. Byrne took 4 wickets for 16 runs, and the Dublin side was dismissed for 45 runs in 102 minutes. Balrothery reached the required total in 35 minutes for the loss of only 3 wickets. The best batsman for Balrothery on this occasion was J. Sheridan who scored 29 not out. Meanwhile the First XI retained the Intermediate Cup by beating Cremore by 27 runs. Balrothery batted first and scored 133 runs, with the main contributions coming from S. Hoare (33) and T. Murphy (27). This was Balrothery's 5th year in the Intermediate Grade, and it had won the Cup on three occasions and the league once.

Balrothery had qualified again to play in the Irish Junior Cup. In the preliminary round, Balrothery beat Arklow on a score of 162 to 73 runs. In the semi-final, it played Shortt and Harlands, and won by 8 wickets. The top scorers for Balrothery were Val Farrell (28*), C. Russell (15*) and G. Bissett (15). Christy Russell took 5 wickets for 32 runs and Kit Mooney took 4 wickets for 22 runs. In the final, Balrothery met Cahir Park for the second season in succession, and the result was the same. Cahir Park batted first and scored 79 runs. The successful bowlers were Russell (3 for 32), Mooney (3 for 13) and Hoare (4 for 33). Unfortunately, there was another batting collapse with only C. Mooney (13) getting into double figures, and Balrothery lost by 23 runs. Cahir Park created a record because it was the first club to retain the Irish Junior Cup.

Balrothery had not won a Fingal championship since 1950, but this deficiency was rectified in 1955 when it defeated Cottrellstown by 8 wickets. Cottrellstown batted first and was dismissed for 22 runs with Christy Russell taking 8 wickets for 7 runs. Balrothery reached the required target for the loss of 2 wickets. Since winning the cup for the first time in 1937, Balrothery had at that stage won the Fingal League Perpetual Challenge Cup on 9 occasions. At the AGM in January 1956, Mr Pat Hickey, the Secretary, described 1955 as the most successful year in the history of the club.

In 1956, the flag bearers for Balrothery CC were the Second and Third teams. The Second XI won the Junior League, and the Thirds retained the Minor Cup by beating North Kildare at Anglesea Road. At the top of the order, J. Mooney scored 23, and there was a strong showing from the middle and lower order batsmen, with R. Byrne (31), S. Moore (23*), G. Byrne (20), and B. Tolan (15) all contributing to a very respectable total of 136 runs. In reply, North Kildare scored 89, with 4 bowlers, (S. Moore, 2 for 13, J. Mooney 2 for 19, K. Murphy, 3 for 28, R. Byrne, 2 for 25) sharing the wickets.

While the period from 1957 to 1961 was a fallow period for Balrothery in terms of winning trophies, nevertheless, the club was involved in the final stages of the cups or in contention for league honours during most of those years. In 1959, Balrothery Seconds played Leinster IV in the Junior Cup final, and Leinster scored 119 runs when batting first. The main contributor to the Leinster total was W. L. W Goulding (52) who later played for Phoenix and was Headmaster of Headfort School in Meath. In reply, Balrothery scored 81 runs, with only three batsmen, T. Murphy (37), S. Moore 17) and C. Hickey (13) getting into double figures. Balrothery reached the final of the Intermediate Cup in 1961, and again, a Leinster team was its nemesis. Leinster 3rds scored 131 and Balrothery was dismissed for 44 runs, with no batsman getting into double figures, and Sheridan (9) and Fanning (9) being its top scorers. In 1962, the Fingal League decided to put the second competition on a more formal footing and to purchase a cup. Balrothery CC was the first winners of this cup, and earlier in the season, had also won the Fingal Championship.

The minutes and annual reports for the 1962 to 1964 seasons were made available in 2019 by the Byrne Family, and they make fascinating reading because they provide an in-depth perspective on the work of the Fingal League Committee. Meetings were held monthly during this period, and some of the clubs kept the officers at full stretch in dealing with objections and counter-objections. At the meeting on 20 May 1963, Balrothery objected to Knockbrack because two Knockbrack members had "deliberately marked down wrong scores". The Knockbrack response was that the scores were right, and Balrothery should have brought their own scorer. It was only through "goodness" that the Knockbrack member marked the book at all. The score books were checked and did not tally so the Committee declared the game a tie. Knockbrack was very unhappy with this outcome, and one of its members contended "that everyone was against them, especially the Chairman who wanted Knockbrack out of cricket altogether. The meeting became so heated that it had to be adjourned. The Committee re-convened on the following week and decided to reprimand the Knockbrack members for their conduct at the previous meeting. The Knockbrack delegate objected on the basis that his club had not been given a fair hearing. Some committee members wanted Knockbrack suspended, others wanted them reprimanded, but the very minimum requirement was that Knockbrack should apologise to the League for the conduct of its two delegates.

The officers of the Fingal League were back in action on 12 August 1963. A game between Knockbrack and Balrothery was not played, and Knockbrack claimed a walk-over. Games were due to start at 3.00 p.m. but definitely not later than 3.30 p.m. Knockbrack's openers were instructed by their captain to leave the field at 3.35 p.m. because the game had not started. One of the (neutral) umpires was very annoyed that no game was played because there was a big crowd present, and this kind of behaviour was giving Fingal cricket a bad name. The Committee decided not to award a walk-over to Knockbrack but insisted that the game be played. Eventually, cricket was played, and Knockbrack won the Perpetual Challenge Cup by beating Balrothery on a score of 38 to 36 runs.

Another problem arose in late September when Knockbrack was due to play Balrothery and the winners to play the Black Hills in the final, but the games were not played due to two funerals (Mr P. Murphy and Mrs Farrell). Eventually, the final was fixed for 20 October, but the Black Hills could not field a team due to illness and the time of the year. It was decided to allow each club to hold the cup for four months each, and to play the game in June 1964.

Balrothery was back to its winning ways in Fingal League competitions in 1965. It went unbeaten for the season and won both the Perpetual Challenge Cup (League) and the Championship Cup. The members of that successful team were N. Carpenter, C. Russell, L. Mooney, H. Russell, C. Hickey, J. Callaghan, A. Pollis, O. Nolan, P. Mooney, J. Mooney, P. Hickey, P. Hand, and M. Connell. It is always important to celebrate victories and the club held a "Reunion Dance" on 24 November 1965 in the Grand Hotel, Balbriggan with dancing from 9 to 2, and tickets were 25s.

Man-O'-War and Knockbrack joined the Leinster League in 1963 and 1964 respectively, and Fingal League sides were very successful in Leinster cricket during this decade but irrespective of successes in Leinster, it was vitally important for Fingal League clubs to win their own competitions. Balrothery won the League in 1967, and it also received great praise for its generous gesture in allowing Rush to play its home games at The Matt for several seasons due to Rush losing its ground at Kenure. Balrothery, captained by John Mooney Senior, won the Minor Cup in 1968 by beating local rivals, Man-O'-War in a low scoring game. In 1969, Balrothery organised its 5th Annual Dinner Dance, and the occasion was enhanced by the Balrothery Inn's presentation of a trophy to Charlie Hickey as captain of a veterans' team which had "smashed their way to victory" in a challenge match against the present team. With wounded pride being involved, it was anticipated that there would be a return game at the earliest possible opportunity.

Balrothery's next victory in the Fingal Challenge Cup was in 1971 when it defeated the Hills at the Man-O'-War's ground. This game was Fingal cricket at its best. Balrothery bowled 78 overs while The Hills made its way cautiously to 114. The top scorers for The Hills were Hugh Cowling (26), Jimmy Byrne (19) and John Archer (17) while the best bowlers for Balrothery were Bunny Casey (4 for 36), Kit Mooney (3 for 11) and Tommy Mooney (3 for 33). Balrothery conceded 26 extras in the field. There was a successful appeal against the light after one ball, and play resumed on the Sunday. The opening partnership of Neil Carpenter (43) and John Mooney (60*) put on 100 exactly, and John Mooney was joined at the crease by his uncle, Kit who had also been a member of the Balrothery team which beat the Black Hills in the final of 1944. The winning shot was a 6 by John Mooney. There was a very sad postscript to this game when Frank Hand, a founder member of the club, was killed while crossing the road in Swords to come back out to the celebrations at the Balrothery Inn.

Before the start of the 1972 season, Balrothery CC lost another one of its leading members, Charlie Hickey who had provided a cricket ground at The Matt for many years and died after a long illness. In memory of these two former members, a game was played at Balrothery between a Balrothery Selection and a Fingal Selection for the Hickey-Hand Memorial Shield. Balrothery scored 86 runs, of which John Mooney scored 25 and looked like scoring a lot more, until he was run out. The Fingal Selection which ended up on 31 runs never got going, and three run outs did not help its cause. As usual in a Fingal game, there was a brilliant display of bowling and fielding. John Neville of Rush took 4 wickets for 38 runs off his 17 overs and he was supported by a superb display from the Hills' wicketkeeper, John Archer. For the home side, Sean Moore took 5 wickets for 19 runs and Tommy Mooney took 2 wickets for 8 runs.

In 1972, Balrothery won the Middle League by beating Malahide in the final match of the league season. Balrothery also ended Man-O'-War's run of successes in the Fingal Championship in 1972 when it won the cup by a margin of 8 wickets. Man-O'-War lost its first four wickets for 7 runs, and John Murphy (43*) and Dermot Sheridan (10) were the only batsmen to reach double figures. Kit Mooney took 7 wickets for 18 runs off 16 overs, with the first 8 overs being maidens. In reply, John Mooney (43*) and Joe Russell (21) brought the score to 60, and then Kit Mooney (13*) with his nephew, John, achieved the target score. Balrothery's season was made complete with its victory in the Leinster Junior Cup when it beat Knockbrack in the final. "Kit" Russell bowled brilliantly, taking 5 for 34 in 22 overs, while Tom Fanning took 5 for 50 in 18 overs. The top scorers for Balrothery were "Kit" Russell (22), Dick Byrne (27), Martin Moore (18) and Tom Fanning (18). "Kit" Russell received the "Man of the Match" award, and Thomas Bertram at 12 years of age was one of the youngest players ever to receive a Leinster Cup Medal.  In 1973, The Man-O'-War won the Fingal Championship Cup for the 7th time, shared the Senior 2 League with Clontarf, and Balrothery won the Senior 3 League.

By the 1980s, the pressure to grant senior status to one of the Fingal League clubs was gathering momentum, and the Senior 2 Cup Final which was played on 7 August 1982 between The Hills and Balrothery was in the nature of a qualifier for admission to the Senior League. On the day, the Hills won comfortably, thanks to a superb knock by Gerry Harper (111) and brilliant bowling by Paddy Byrne (4 for 45) and Matt Dwyer (5 for 10).  The Hills was granted senior status in October 1982, and this had implications for the other Fingal League clubs in terms of player retention. The two clubs bowed to the inevitable and in October 1985, Balrothery and Man-O'-War amalgamated to form North County CC, but both clubs indicated that it was their intention to maintain their separate identities for Fingal League competitions.

Although the clubs are listed separately in the Fingal Cricket League Archives until 1995, and then the names are combined as Balrothery/Man-O'-War until 2005, it seems appropriate to end this chapter with an account of the Fingal League Final in 1985 before the two clubs amalgamated. Balrothery batted first and lost the first three wickets for only 10 runs. Tommy Mooney who was fifth batsman in brought the score up to 30, and his brother, James, added a few more, but with extras at 14 being the second highest score, it was never going to be enough to trouble the Man-O'-War unless there was an early collapse. The main bowler for the Man-O'-War was Liam Rooney who ended up with the figures of 7 wickets for 24 runs off fourteen overs. Brian Southam and Anthony Rooney, the Man-O'-War's opening pair, put on 49 runs before a wicket fell. It appeared that the game might be over before tea, and given the importance ascribed to the quality of teas in Fingal, "the final that ended before tea" would have been a source of conversation for years. The *Evening Press* Reporter, Karl Johnston, provided a report on this game, and he adjudged the tea as being excellent. He also commended Rush Cricket Club for the work done on the "superbly renovated old schoolhouse." Man-O'-War lost two wickets immediately after tea, but with 5 needed for a win, Jody Morgan  hit a four, and moments later, Liam Rooney hit the winning run.

In October 1970, Tom Corr, a journalist with the Drogheda Independent, described Balrothery as a "nondescript little village on the outskirts of Balbriggan, [which]... until relatively recently the place could boast only one organisation, a cricket club. While a native of Balrothery would quibble with the adjective, "nondescript", there is a modicum of truth in the sentiments expressed. The importance of the cricket club in Balrothery cannot be over-emphasised because it provided a sporting and social outlet for the community over a lengthy period, and it was instrumental in giving Balrothery a unique identity. On its website, the Balrothery Inn describes itself as the "unofficial home of Irish Cricket", and players and officials of the club have represented their community and their country with pride. In 1884, the Catholic Archbishop of Cashel, Dr T. W. Croke, wrote the following to the *Freeman's Journal* on 24 December 1884:

> We have got such foreign and fantastic field sports as lawn-tennis, polo, croquet, cricket, and the like—very excellent, I believe, and health-giving exercises in their way, still not racy of the soil, but rather alien, on the contrary, to it, as are, indeed, for the most part the men and women who first imported and still continue to patronise them.

When John Mooney, a proud son of Balrothery, took the crucial catch in the World Cup in 2007, he soloed the ball in recognition of his friends back home at the local GAA club, and his pride and passion for his country were self-evident. It can be argued that in Balrothery, the game of cricket "has always been racy of the soil", and the administrators, players and supporters who have nurtured, developed, and played the game are worthy of the highest commendation.

The Matt, home of Balrothery CC

Balrothery Cricket Club Circa 1955

Back Row: James Farrell, Seán Farrell, Richard Moore, Simon Hoare, Peter Hand, Vally Farrell, James Bissett, Richard Moore Jr, Pat Dillon, Peter Pollis, John Mooney, Richard Bissett.
Middle Row: Francis Casey, Kathleen Casey, Nick Hickey, Kit Russell, Kit Mooney, Simon Gossan, Henry Russell.
Front Row:          Connor                                        Phil Mooney

Back Row: Jay Mooney, Patsie Farrell, J McGowan, Val Farrell, P Dillon, Christy Cannon,
Frint Row: Henry Russell, Kit Russell, Kit Mooney, W Morgan, John Mooney

Back; D. Bissette, C.Mooney, P.Gilsenan, H. Russell, V. Farrel, R. Moore
Front; P.Farrell, S.Goosan , C.Russell, C. Cannon, J.Mooney.

V Farrell (Balrothery) just avoids being run out as Rush wicket-keeper. J. Heraty, gathers in the Intermediate Cup final in the Phoenix Park. Balrothery won by 70 runs.

26ᵗʰ July 1951

THE BALROTHERY CRICKET CLUB FIRST ELEVEN who retained the Intermediate Cup of the Leinster Branch of the Irish Cricket Union for the second year when they defeated Cremore in the final. Front Row (from left to right)—H. Russell, C. Russell, S. Hoare (Capt.), C. Mooney and J. Mooney. Back Row—J. Bissett, M. Gosson, E. Kieran, V. Farrell, N. Hickey and T. Murphy.

12-8-1955

John Mooney, Senior

Phil Mooney

John Mooney

James Mooney

Back Row: Tom Poynton, James Hagan, John O'Connor, Patsy Farrell, Charlie Hickey, Niall Carpenter.
Front Row: Fr. Walsh, G.L.McGowan, Tony Devine, Kit Mooney.
Balrothery Cricket Club, Dinner Dance Organising Committee circa 1962

## Seamus Russell and Noel Harper

Russell, son of Christy Russell, presenting The Christopher Russell Memorial Cup to Noel Harper, capt of North County

## Kit Mooney and Tommy Mooney

# Chapter 17: North County Cricket Club

Balrothery and Man-O'-War decided to amalgamate after the Fingal League final in September 1985, and to play in the Leinster League competitions under the name, North County CC. It was intended to retain the individual identities of the clubs for Fingal League purposes, and to maintain two grounds, one at The Nevitt and the other at The Matt, Balrothery. The new club applied to the Leinster Cricket Union for senior status for the 1986 season, and while the application was rejected, it was intimated that if North County won the Senior 2 League in 1986, a further application would receive more favourable consideration. The main reason for the amalgamation was the quest for senior status, but player retention had become an issue for both clubs as some of their better players had begun to transfer to senior clubs.

In 1986, North County did not have a particularly successful season, but it won the Senior 2 League and Cup in 1987. In the cup, North County scored 209 runs, with Michael Murphy top-scoring with 76 runs, and in reply, Clontarf was dismissed for 109 runs, with wickets for Joe Murphy (2 for 24), Joey Mooney (4 for 27) and L. Rooney (2 for 24). With the Senior 2 double completed, another application was made for senior status. However, allowing North County into the Senior League would have facilitated the introduction of promotion and relegation, and this was a concept which did not find favour with some of the established senior clubs. Strangely enough, it was suggested that the playing strength might not be good enough for senior cricket which was somewhat ironic since the club had achieved the objective which was given to it when its previous application had been refused. The application for senior status was rejected overwhelmingly (16 votes to 5), but as a concession, North County would be allowed to play in the Senior Cup in 1988.

The dress-rehearsal for Senior cricket did not go well because the North County batsmen struggled against the Old Belvedere pace attack of Con McGrath and John McDevitt. Old Belvedere batted first, and it looked as if the North County bowlers would restrict Belvedere to 125 runs or so, but a last wicket partnership of 35 runs left North County with a target of 161 runs to win. There was a general acceptance that the North County bowling attack was as "good as most, if not better than some senior clubs", and in this regard there was favourable mention for Tommy Mooney (4 for 29), and Joey Mooney, "their best performer in this area", who took 2 wickets for 15 in 12 overs. Unfortunately, the familiar frailty of Fingal batting manifested itself on another big day. Michael Murphy was out LBW to McDevitt in the first over, and he took 3 more wickets plus the valuable runs in the last wicket partnership to make the Man-of-the-Match judging a formality. McGrath took 5 wickets, and the other wicket to fall  was a run-out (John "the Ranger" Mooney). John Andrews (24 runs) was the only batsman to get any runs, and North County was dismissed for a "paltry" 46 runs.

It was not all doom and gloom at The Nevitt and The Matt during the 1988 season because North County's Second XI won the Intermediate League and the Middle Cup. In the final of the Middle Cup, North County played Civil Service at Rathmines, and struggled to a certain extent against excellent fielding, and having scored only 90 runs with overs nearly completed, it looked that they would not post a competitive target. Until the last wicket partnership between James Mooney (20*) and Noel Hickey (11), only Thomas Garry (28) and Thomas Murphy (20) had managed to score any runs, but the last pair put on 31 runs to leave North County on a score of 121 for 9 in 55 overs. James ("Bisto") Mooney also starred with the ball, and he took 6 wickets for 40 runs in 25 overs. He was complemented by Paul Martin (3 for 10) and Kevin Murphy (1 for 31), and Civil Service was all out for 90.  North County also reached the final of the Whelan Cup but lost to YMCA on a score of 125 for 6 to 82.

One of the very positive consequences of the amalgamation was that there were enough players available to field a women's team because at an earlier stage some of the players such as Angela and Deirdre Murphy had played for Rush because neither  Man-O'-War nor Balrothery had enough players to form a team. The women's team in its first season in competitive cricket in 1988 won the Minor Cup and the Division 3 League. Among the most noteworthy performances during this season were Angela Murphy's 99* against Clontarf in a cup game, and then in a league game against Clontarf Angela scored 46*, Deirdre, her sister, scored 36* and Marion Holland scored 28 runs. To round off a successful week, in the game against Mullingar, Angela (57*), Deirdre (39*) and Kathleen Richardson (13) brought the North County score up to 132 for 2. Mullingar was dismissed for 100 with wickets for P. Hickey (2 for 30), D. Murphy (2 for 13), M. Holland (3 for 21), and A. Murphy (2 for 13).  That same season, Paula Hickey was selected  for North Leinster against the South- East in a representative game in which Ann Harford and Geraldine Carty also played. There were also individual awards for the women with Angela Murphy winning the Division 3 batting award and Paula Hickey won the fielding award.  The following season, North County women played in Division 2, and with Deirdre and Angela Murphy starring again, won this league at the first attempt.

For the third successive year, North County applied for senior status, but unlike the previous occasions, the performances on the field had not reached the standard of 1987, and the application was refused again. In reflecting on the decision, Brian Southam, the Chairman, accepted that the First XI had fallen short during the season, but he argued that it was only a matter of time before North County became a senior club. The growth in membership was illustrated by the club being able to field five teams from Senior 2 to Junior B for the 1989 season, and the captains were as follows: Michael Murphy (Firsts), Brian Southam (Second XI), Phil Mooney (Thirds), Dave Powell (Fourths) and William Tolan (Fifths).

With the hierarchy in the club being so upbeat, it was hoped that this positivity would transmit itself to the players, and North County's First XI fulfilled all the club's objectives in the 1989 season. In the semi-final of the Senior 2 Cup, North County played Old Belvedere, and batting first scored 155 runs with contributions from Michael Murphy (37), Paul Martin (27), Alan Rooney (15), and Joey Mooney (15). In reply, Old Belvedere could only manage a score of 107, and there were wickets for James Mooney (4 for 28), Joey Mooney (3 for 27), Liam Rooney (1 for 26), and Joe Murphy (2 for 16). In the other semi-final, Balbriggan beat North Kildare to set up the first all-Fingal Senior 2 final since 1982 when The Hills had played Balrothery.

That Senior 2 final was the first occasion that Balbriggan had reached a final at that level, and it was hoped that Albert Harper could maintain his form with bat and ball. During the early part of the season, he had scored two centuries, and he had taken 11 wickets for 70 runs during the cup campaign. For North County, its main batsmen were Michael Murphy who had scored over 600 runs, which included a double century in the first round, Thomas Garry had scored a century in the same game, and Liam Rooney had scored 50 runs the previous week in the Fingal Final. North County's wicket-takers up to that point had been James and Joey Mooney, and Joe Murphy.

A final between two Fingal teams where the strength of both teams lay in the bowling was never going to produce a lot of runs, and when rain stopped play at the end of the first day, North County had scored 27 runs for the loss of 2 wickets. When play resumed on 7 August, North County managed to bring its score up to 99 runs, and there were significant contributions from Anthony Rooney (29), Liam Rooney (15) Alan Rooney (15). Albert Harper took 3 wickets for 15 runs. In reply, Balbriggan finished well-short on 75 runs, and the only batsman to contribute runs of any consequence was David Harper (15). For his 3 wickets for 15 runs, James Mooney was the Man-of-the Match. North County completed the second leg of the double with a mid-week victory over Railway Union. Michael Murphy (42) and John Rooney (41) helped North County to a score of 163 runs for 5. Railway Union was bowled out for 96, with 7 wickets for Joey Mooney and 2 wickets for Joe Murphy. Balbriggan had a modicum of revenge when it beat North County in the league, but the match was a "dead rubber" because North County had already secured the Senior 2 League title.

North County's application for Senior status was to be heard at a meeting on 28 September 1989, but it appears that the application was deferred for some undisclosed reason. The application was down for a decision at the November meeting of the Leinster Cricket Union, but when the draw for the Wiggins Teape League was made in early November, North County's name was not included. At some point between early November and mid-November, North County was awarded Senior status, but the only reference to this change of status was a throwaway comment that North County had been "belatedly" included in the Wiggins Teape draw, and in another part of the same article it was mentioned that North County had recently "been upgraded." The draw for the Wiggins Teape competition, with North County's name included, was published but not accompanied by any explanatory comment.

North County's elevation to the Senior League caused ripples immediately, because the legislators had been arguing that there were too many clubs at senior level. With that in mind, YMCA proposed that the Leinster Senior League be divided into two sections with eight teams in each section for the 1991 season with automatic promotion and relegation. In this proposal, the teams in the two sections would be based on league placings during the period 1988 to 1990. The matter was to be discussed at the December meeting of the Leinster Cricket Union, and if accepted, it would have meant that Balbriggan and North Kildare would become senior clubs.

This debate was complicated by permission being given again to sign overseas players, and there was a perception that the wealthier clubs would be able to buy success while the clubs that had a conscientious objection regarding hiring overseas  players would be disadvantaged. As a result, they would lose their valued senior status, and this would result in the loss of their better players. Seán Pender placed himself firmly on the side of those who wanted a two-tier system because of his belief that the status quo was causing standards to plummet due to the lack of players of sufficient quality to play senior cricket. Gradually, the tide began to turn regarding acceptance of the two-tier senior league concept, but it was then linked in with a proposal to renew the ban on overseas players.

In a sense, North County's promotion was seen to have exacerbated the situation regarding too many senior teams, and there were frequent references to their new status as being "controversial". Prior to its first senior game, there was evidence of the ambivalent attitude to North County, with the players being anxious to prove that over the "past two decades they were as good as most clubs in the senior echelon", while some critics argued that they would "be found badly wanting." North County did not have an easy start to its senior programme because it was drawn against YMCA, the favourites to win all three domestic competitions. At an individual level, the pressure was on Michael Murphy, the captain, because he had played senior cricket with Malahide, and in the words of Seán Pender, "North County's overall performance this season will hinge very much on how Murphy performs with the bat."

North County lost to YMCA by 41 runs having restricted YMCA to 32 for 1 after 17 overs, but decent contributions from Keith Bailey (46), David Starkey (40) and Clive Davis (26) enabled it to post a total of 163 for 6 in 55 overs. North County's openers, Michael Murphy, and John Mooney, set about this target, and scored 31 for the loss of no wicket in 5 overs. After that brilliant start, things went awry for North County, with John Mooney being caught in the covers, Michael Mooney over-reaching and spooning a low full toss back to the bowler and John Neville being run out. In a final defiant gesture, James Mooney scored 10 off two successive deliveries, but with the light deteriorating, North County ended 41 short of the target. In a review of the game, Seán Pender suggested that there was no necessity for North County to be despondent, and that wins would come if the team continued to bowl and field as well as it had done against YMCA, but he had concerns about the batting. In its first home game at The Nevitt, North County lost to Carlisle by 3 wickets on a day that Joey Mooney took 5 wickets for 51 runs. There was then a draw with Leinster at Rathmines when John Mooney top scored with 39 runs, and there were runs also for Michael Murphy (34) and Anthony Rooney (18*). Joey Mooney had another 5-wicket haul, this time for 25 runs.

North County's first win in senior cricket came at College Park when it beat Trinity by 102 runs. John Mooney scored 62 and Thomas Garry scored 51 while there were wickets for Christy Garry (5 for 13) and Joey Mooney (3 for 17). On the following day, there was a draw with Phoenix when Joey Mooney took 5 wickets for 44, Joe Murphy, 3 for 67, and the runs were scored by John

Mooney (61), Michael Murphy (52) and Joe Murphy (22). With 5 games played, North County lay in 7th place in the league, with a record of 1 win, 2 draws and 2 defeats. YMCA led the league with 4 wins out of 4, while CYM had only played 2 games, and lost both.

With the first league win achieved, North County's attention then turned to the Leinster Senior Cup, and it was drawn against Railway Union, the beaten finalists two years previously. North County batted first, and the redoubtable John ("Ranger") Mooney top-scored with 64 runs; Michael Murphy scored 27 and Joe Murphy scored 24 runs to give North County a total of 181 runs. In reply, Railway who never got to grips with North County's all-seam attack finished 66 runs adrift, with wickets being taken by James Mooney (3 for 16), Joe Murphy (2 for 7) and Liam Rooney (2 for 38). North County's odyssey in the Senior Cup was ended by Clontarf on a day when the batting failed. Michael Murphy (39) and Liam Rooney (21) were the only significant contributors to a score of 138 runs which Clontarf reached for the loss of 5 wickets.

At the half-way stage of the season, North County's performances were making some critics eat their words, and the unfortunate element of North County's promotion was that it had come too late for stalwarts such as John and Tommy Mooney who had been denied representative honours because they were playing with a junior club. There was a perception also that Michael Murphy's loyalty to his club had cost him international caps, but with North County playing senior, there were opportunities for the players to stake their claims for representative recognition, and in that regard, Joey Mooney had been selected for the North Leinster team which played the North-West at Comber on 27 May. Joey Mooney did not take any wickets in his spell of 11 overs for 35 runs, but batting "sensibly", he scored 38*. In June 1990, there were further honours for Joey Mooney when he won the JMA award for the Player of the Month of May as result of taking 19 wickets for 172 runs, and taking 5 wickets on three occasions. It was anticipated that he would add to his haul of wickets the following day when North County visited Cabra to play Old Belvedere, but it was Joe Murphy, his fellow-seamer, who wreaked havoc on the home team by taking 9 wickets for 28 runs.

A review of North County's first season in senior cricket showed that the team finished in a very creditable 7th place, winning 5 games, drawing 4, losing 4, and accumulating 170 points. The prophesied issues with the batting did not manifest themselves to the extent expected, but of the six batsmen who scored more than 200 runs, only two had an average of more than 20. Michael

Murphy topped the list with 565 runs, (average 26.9), and John Mooney scored 421 runs with an average of 24.76. The other significant batsmen were Joe Murphy (274), Christy Garry (230), Joey Mooney (216), and Thomas Garry (207). The bowling honours were taken by Joey Mooney (45 wickets), Joe Murphy (40 wickets), Liam Rooney (21 wickets), and James Mooney (13 wickets).

With the imminent introduction of promotion and relegation, the Leinster Cricket Union continued with its ban on professionals for the 1991 season and added another tier by establishing a registration committee which would provide clearance to play cricket for people who came to Ireland during the summer for holidays or work purposes. A procedure was also put in place to examine complaints if a player was deemed too good to be playing at a level lower than the higher echelon. The teams in the two divisions were to be based on their results for the 1991 and 1992 seasons.

The North County squad for the 1991 season was essentially the same personnel who had achieved a reasonable mid-table slot in the 1990 season. The bowling of Joe Murphy and Joe Mooney was adjudged to be the strongest part of North County's game, but there were continuing concerns regarding the batting. The season started badly for North County because in the first game of the season, North County was well-beaten by Trinity College who scored 201 for 4; Joe Murphy took 3 wickets for 47 runs. In reply, North County only scored 71 runs, and Joe Murphy was the top-scorer with 18 runs. This was followed by a loss to YMCA when North County scored 106, and YMCA reached the target in 40 overs. The team was very handicapped by an injury to Joey Mooney, who was able to bat, but could not bowl. The siege was lifted to a certain extent with a win over Malahide when Michael Murphy had the top score of 28, and there were also runs for Liam Rooney (23) and Christy Garry (20). Malahide was dismissed for 72 when Joe Murphy took 6 wickets for 33 runs, and a fit-again Joey Mooney took 3 wickets.

In the Leinster Senior Cup, North County played Rush at Rush, and was restricted to 50 runs for 2 wickets after 30 overs, but Joe Murphy and Joey Mooney added 51 runs in "double-quick time", and this complemented Michael Murphy's brilliant knock of 76 runs to leave North County with a score of 180 runs. The best bowler for Rush was its captain, Michael Marsh, who bowled 12 overs for 18 runs. Rush's reply got off to a disastrous start, with three wickets falling before tea. Alf Masood batting with a borrowed bat and without his spectacles because his equipment bag had been mislaid, brought Rush back into the game but when he was caught in the covers by John Mooney off the bowling of James Mooney, that was the end of Rush's challenge. In the  semi-final, North County was drawn against Leinster, and was very unlucky to finish 3 runs short of the Leinster total in a great game. Leinster batted first and scored 176 runs, and there were wickets for Tommy Mooney (2 for 13), James Mooney (2 for 23), Joey Mooney (2 for 42) and Joe Murphy (2 for 43). Michael Murphy was out for a duck, but Christy Garry (26), Thomas Bertram (22), John Mooney (22), Anthony Rooney (21) and Liam Rooney (21) kept North County in the game. Joey Mooney (20*) and James Mooney (11*) batted in the last over with 13 required but finished agonisingly short on 174 for 9.

In mid-July, the Merrion versus North County game was a clash between two teams that were struggling. Merrion had not won a game, and North County had only won one. Merrion batted first, and while Rob Stanton (48) was at the wicket, it appeared that it would accumulate a big score, but he was bowled by Tommy Mooney, and Merrion ended on 169 for 9. In reply, Michael Murphy scored an unbeaten 110, and John Mooney, his opening partner was unbeaten on 60 to give North County its best win of the season.  Unfortunately, it was not possible to  maintain this form, and the following day North County was bowled out by Clontarf for 107 runs, with only Michael Murphy (41) making any runs. Clontarf got the required runs for the loss of no wickets (M. Rea, 57, D. Vincent, 43) in 25 overs.  North County's only other win for the season was against Pembroke who it bowled out for 87 runs at The Nevitt, with wickets for J. Murphy (5 for 38), T. Mooney (3 for 21), and L. Rooney (2 for 14). The target score was achieved for the loss of 1 wicket, with Michael Murphy scoring 49* and John Mooney, 32 runs.

Michael Murphy gave a very insightful interview to the *Drogheda Independent* on 22 August 1991 in which he assessed the season's performances. A lack of pre-season practice was one of the factors that he identified, and injuries to Joey Mooney and Liam Rooney left the team without two of its main bowlers at various stages of the season. He was satisfied that the team was able to compete with the best teams in the league, but a lack of concentration at vital times in games deprived them of victories. The ability to play spin bowling was a real weakness, and this was a general problem for all Fingal teams not just for North County. In Michael Murphy's own words, "Nobody really in North County can play the spinners and usually try to hit them out of the ground."

In the final game of the season against Phoenix, North County could only field nine players, but this had a bigger consequence for Phoenix than for North

County because it deprived them of one bowling point which had the potential to be important the following season when points were being aggregated. At the end of the season, North County had won 3 games, lost 10, accumulated 99 points and finished second last in the league with only Merrion below them. Michael Murphy led the batting figures with 663 runs at an average of 36.8, but no other batsman had an average of over 20. John Mooney scored 257 (16.06), Christy Garry 295 (16.4) and Tommy Mooney 283 (17.7). Joe Murphy took 53 wickets, but injuries to Joey Mooney (12) and Liam Rooney (15) meant that they were well-down on their tallies for the previous season.

The 1992 season did not start well, and in the first game against Malahide, North County was bowled out for 46 runs, with Alan Hughes taking 6 wickets for 5 runs in 15.4 overs. To add insult to injury, 8 of the 46 runs were from no balls by Alan Brophy, and the report on the game referred to "embarrassing ineptitude" of the batsmen. Every cloud has a silver lining, and the 15-years old Paul Mooney made his debut and "displayed an impressive technique" by staying at the crease for over half-an-hour. By mid-June, North County had played 6 games, lost all 6, and was firmly at the foot of the table. The following week, North County managed to put its first points on the board by drawing with CYM at The Nevitt. Paul Martin (51*), Paul Mooney (28), and John Mooney (24*) were the main contributors to the score of 197 for 7. In reply, CYM scored 164 for 8, with wickets for Joe Murphy (6 for 53) and Tom Murphy (2 for 31). This game was noteworthy because Tom Murphy could lay claim to being the oldest ever senior cricketer in Leinster when at the age of 69, he bowled 5 overs and took 2 wickets. In August, North County recorded its only win of the season when it beat Phoenix by 70 runs. The main batsmen for North County were John Andrews (61), Joey Mooney (32) and Paul Martin (31), and the wickets were taken by Joe Murphy (3 for 28), Joey Mooney (2 for 36) and Liam Rooney (2 for 36).

At the end of the season, North County had 1 win, 1 draw, 11 losses, and finished last in the senior league. Michael Murphy continued to be the leading batsman for the club with 275 runs, but that was a significant reduction on previous years. The other batsmen with more than 200 runs were Paul Martin (257), Joey Mooney (253) and Paul Mooney (235). The leading wicket takers were Joe Murphy (31) and Joey Mooney (20). At the end of the 1992 season, North County was placed in the new Senior League B, along with Carlisle, Old Belvedere, The Hills, Railway Union, Merrion and Dublin University. Promotion and relegation were going to be based on one team being promoted, and one relegated.

In 1993, while there was a desire to bring silverware to The Nevitt, Joe Murphy was realistic in his appraisal of the playing strength, and the main aim for the season was to avoid relegation. There was no improvement in the performances during the 1993 season, and the team finished last in Section B, but this was totally irrelevant within the context of the sudden death on 5 August 1993 of John ("The Ranger) Mooney at 46 years old. He had given wonderful service to Balrothery for over 25 years and was one of the leading batsmen on North County's First XI. He was survived by his wife, Frances, his children, Jeanette, Pamela, Paul, John and Marguerite, his father, John, his brothers, Phil, Tommy, Joey and James, and his sister, Cathy.

It is only possible to provide a synopsis of North County's results between 1993 and 1999 because of the pressures imposed by the word budget, and it was never the intention to provide a year-by -year account of any club because that can be undertaken more appropriately by some of the clubs' members.

|  | Played | Won | Drew | Lost | Points | Place in League |
|---|---|---|---|---|---|---|
| 1993 | 12 | 1 | 3 | 8 | 115 | 7th in B League |
| 1994 | 12 | 3 | 4 | 5 | 205 | 4th in B League |
| 1995 | 12 | 3 | 2 | 7 | 124 | 6th in B League |
| 1996 | 12 | 1 | 8 | 3 | 102 | 7th in B League |
| 1997 | 12 | 3 | 2 (NR) | 7 | 125 | 5th in B League |
| 1998 | 12 | 5 | 1 (NR) | 7 | 100 | 5th in B League |
| 1999 | 12 | 5 | 1 (NR) | 6 | 125 | 5th in B League |

NR – No result due to rain; draws were abolished.

Between 1993 and 1999, North County entered a transitional phase where it struggled on the field, but during this period, there were positive aspects as well because many of the older players continued to play down the grades when they were no longer playing senior cricket, and they also provided coaching and advice for the younger players. Richard Beukes had been employed as the overseas player for two seasons (1997 and 1998), John Andrews re-joined the club in 1998, Conor and Dara Armstrong transferred from Malahide in 1999, Paul Mooney, at that stage a full international player, re-joined the club from The Hills in 2000, and David Ford, an Australian, played for North County during that season. With younger players such as John Mooney, Anthony and Thomas Rooney showing great promise, and the experienced players such as Paul and Paddy Martin, Joey Mooney, Michael, and Joe Murphy continuing to play a prominent part in the club, the structures were in place for North County to stage a resurgence and become the strongest club in Leinster and arguably the best club in Ireland between 2001 and 2010.

In 2000, North County played in Section B of the Senior League, and the other teams in the section were CYM, Malahide, Munster, Leinster, Old Belvedere, and Rush. North County, captained by John Andrews, won 8 games, lost 4, and finished top of the section, 32 points ahead of CYM. The Senior Cup final between North County and Clontarf was hosted by The Hills, and Clontarf won by 41 runs on scores of 228 for 8 to 187 all out. The top scorers for North County were C. Armstrong (31) and John Mooney 28); J Murphy took 2 wickets for 23 and John Mooney took 2 wickets for 40 runs. While the result on the day was disappointing, a conversation later in the evening was to produce a wonderful outcome for North County because André Botha, the Clontarf player, indicated his willingness to transfer to North County, and this transfer was one of the catalysts for the run of successes which followed during the next ten seasons. It was mentioned that many of the older players continued to play down the grades, and with the infusion of players to the First XI, every team in North County was strengthened with a combination of senior players and developing talent. In 2000, the Third XI won the Intermediate B League and the Fourth XI won the Minor Cup.

Success on the field of play was accompanied by a transformation off the field, and this was led by a dynamic Executive which included Derek Plant, Tom Armstrong, and Anthony Rooney. Development on a new ground at Inch had commenced in 1999 and planning permission for the first custom-built Centre of Excellence in Ireland was obtained in 2001. The first league match on the ground was between North County IV (198) and Pembroke V (150 for 7) on Saturday, 12 May 2001. North County's First XI played The Hills on the following day, but this game was abandoned due to rain. The Centre of Excellence was opened in 2003.

In 2001, North County finished top of Section B of the "Short League", beat Phoenix in the semi-final, and played Merrion in the final at the Phoenix Park. North County batted first, and with Botha scoring an undefeated 111 and John Mooney getting 75, its total was 240 for 4. The Merrion team which included Kade Beasley, Chris Torrisi, Brad Spanner, Damian Poder, Duncan Smythe, and Angus Fleming had a poor start, and only the 43 runs scored by Angus Fleming who was batting at No. 9 gave an element of respectability to

Merrion's score. This was North County's first trophy at senior level, and better was to follow later in that season.

North County and Cliftonville played in the final of the Irish Senior Cup at Waringstown on 31 August 2001. North County won the toss and after a nervous start during which 2 wickets were lost, Botha (66) and John Mooney (61) pressed the accelerator, and with valuable knocks from Paul Mooney (38) and John Andrews (22), posted a total of 272 for 7 wickets. North County then proceeded to bowl brilliantly, and there were wickets for Paul Mooney (3 for 34), André Botha (2 for 29), Joe Murphy (2 for 34) and Conor Armstrong (1 for 31). To cap a brilliant all-round performance, the North County fielding was superb. Paul Martin took a "stunning catch", Joe Murphy's catch was a "spectacular overhead effort", and Michael Murphy equalled this with a "blinder" to dismiss Kyle McCallan. The margin of victory was 74 runs, and North County became only the second team from Leinster to win the Irish Senior Cup in the twentieth final. The third trophy of the season to come to Inch was the Senior 2 League which was won by North County's Second XI.

After the successes of 2001, 2002 was a fallow year for North County in terms of winning trophies, with the Firsts finishing in mid-table in both the Senior A League and the Wiggins Teape League, but this was the calm before the storm because the 2003 season was the greatest one in the history of the club. In the final of the Leinster Senior Cup, North County played Clontarf at Malahide, and had another difficult start with 4 wickets falling for only 49 runs, but a partnership of 154 runs between Paul Mooney (68) and Dara Armstrong (50) with the assistance of 56 extras meant that North County ended with 220 runs for 7 wickets. Clontarf's reply started badly with Botha getting both openers for very few, and it was not until Cusack (46) and Spelman (48) who were batting at Nos. 8 and 9 that Clontarf dared to hope, but Duane Harper got rid of both, courtesy of two catches behind the wicket by Dara Armstrong. That was the end of Clontarf's resistance, and the margin of victory for North County was 49 runs.

North County also reached the final of the Irish Senior Cup and played Railway Union at Clontarf on 23 August 2003. The club now had Eoin Morgan in its ranks although he had not been available for all games due to his other commitments. Railway Union won the toss and decided to field. In what was now becoming commonplace, North County had a poor start, and lost 2 wickets for 37 runs. André Botha (40) and Eoin Morgan (70) compiled a partnership of 71 runs, and this was followed by another partnership between Morgan and Paul

Mooney (20) which brought the score to 194. North County's total for the innings was 217 for 7 wickets. Paul Mooney then took four of the first five Railway Union wickets, and at 5 for 25, the game was over as a contest. Conor Mullen (58), Kevin O'Brien (22) and Gary Black (20), kept the game going, but it was too little, too late, and North County won by 71 runs.

With the cup double completed, North County could focus on winning the league, and it had a tremendous battle with Phoenix right through the season. Phoenix's last game was against North County at Inch and ended in a controversial fashion. Phoenix had only bowled 48 overs at the end of its allotted time, and in that era, there was a two overs penalty for each over short. The required score for North County was based on Phoenix's score after 46 overs, and on that basis, North County was deemed to have won the game. North County had two further games to play; it won both and won the Senior League by 19 points from Phoenix. Other trophies which came to Inch that year were the Senior 3 League, and the Intermediate Cup. With the Centre of Excellence opening in that year and a crop of talented young players coming through the ranks, the auguries for many more years of success for North County were very positive.

When North County entered the Senior League in 1990, the team was reckoned to have decent bowling, but inadequate batting. This perception continued through the transitional years, but analysis of the batting figures for 2003 illustrates the extent to which a transformation had occurred, and at that stage, North County had become a team with very strong batting and competent bowling. That year, Conor Armstrong topped the batting figures with 713 runs at an average of 37.53, and he was closely followed by André Botha, 679 runs, average, 39.94. Paul Mooney scored 526 runs (40.46), Seán O'Connor had 397 runs (23.35), Dara Armstrong's figures were 320 runs (26.67), John Mooney had 375 runs (23.93), and Eoin Morgan who only played 7 games, scored 177 runs with an average of 35.40. At the end of the 1990 season, there were only two batsmen from North County with an average of 20 or more; in the season under review, there were seven batsmen with an average of greater than 20, and some of them had an appreciably higher average. That season, S. Grobler, the overseas player took 35 wickets, and the next best bowlers in order were John Mooney (23), Paul Mooney (22), André Botha (22), and Duane Harper (13).

In its defence of the Irish Senior Cup in 2004, North County was drawn against Donemana, and won by a margin of 131 runs. The main contributors on the day were Conor Armstrong (78), André Botha (125) and Eoin Morgan (23).

Botha also took 4 wickets for 23 runs, and for Donemana, Dwane McGerrigle batting at No. 8 scored 74 runs to bring Donemana up to 200. In the next round, North County played Instonians at Inch, and the Northern team scored 269 for 7 in 48 overs, with Andy White scoring an undefeated 177*. There was a rain-delay, and North County's target was 264 runs in 48 overs. Conor Armstrong scored 62, Botha got 76, Reinhardt Strydom scored 53, but North County was beaten by 5 runs in a great game.

This was the low point in a wonderful year for the club, in which all of its teams won trophies. The First XI won the Short League which had been rebranded as LHW League, and retained the Senior League A. The transformation from a good bowling team to a very good all-round team, with greater strength at that stage in the batting was reflected to an even greater extent in 2004. André Botha scored 1046 runs (69.73 average), Conor Armstrong scored 973 runs (57.2), Seán O'Connor had 362 runs (27.85), and the other batsmen with an average of 20 or greater were Paul Mooney, with 293 runs (29.3), John Mooney with 303 runs (20.00), Reinhardt Strydom with 262 runs (37.57) and Eoin Morgan with 208 runs in only 7 games (52.00). Again, it was an overseas player, Nathan Palmer, who topped the bowling figures by taking 49 wickets; the other wicket takers were Botha (33), Strydom (17) and Harper (17).

The Second XI beat Leinster in the Tillain Cup Final on a score of 116 for 7 to 107 for 5. Shane Plant (23*) and John Andrews (20) were the main contributors to the score, and P. Martin took 2 wickets for 15 runs. Other successes in that season were the Thirds winning the Middle B League, the Fourths winning the Junior A League, and the Fifths winning the Minor Cup.

The successes continued in 2005. In the Irish Senior Cup, North County played Railway Union in the final and won by 5 wickets in a low-scoring game. Railway scored 182 for 8. In reply, the required runs were scored for the loss of 5 wickets. Botha took 3 wickets for 43 runs, and John Mooney scored an undefeated 57. The Senior League was won for the third season year in a row, with a playing record of 10 wins, 1 no result and 1 defeat, and the team finished 68 points ahead of Malahide who took second place. The club's junior teams continued their run of successes with the Second XI winning the Senior 2 League and the Third XI won the Middle B League.

In 2006, the First XI won the Leinster Senior League for the fourth time in a row with a record of 10 wins and 2 defeats, and a total of 247 points with Rush a somewhat distant second on 165 points. The Second XI retained the

Senior 2 League, and there was an all-Fingal Senior Cup between North County and The Hills which The Hills won by 4 wickets.

The run of successive Senior League wins was ended in 2007 when Clontarf won the Senior League, but the Third XI won the Middle A League. There was some compensation for North County when it played in an all-Fingal All-Ireland final against The Hills. North County won comfortably by 105 runs, with A. Botha (84) and C. Armstrong (41), the main contributors with the bat, and R. Lawrence (5 for 38) and Botha (5 for 31) the main wicket-takers. The All-Ireland cup had been re-branded as the Bob Kerr Senior Cup in memory of Bob Kerr, the former Chairman and President of Cricket Ireland, who had died during the World Cup in 2007, and Dara Armstrong, Captain of North County, was presented with the cup by Mrs Hope Kerr. 2007 was also the year in which Ireland had performed so creditably at the World Cup in the West Indies, and North County had three players in the squad (André Botha, Paul and John Mooney), and numerous supporters in the stands.

In 2008, North County won the "Short League" which was then known as the Dublin Grass Machinery League by beating Pembroke by four wickets in the final at The Vineyard. The final of the Irish Senior Cup was played between North County and Donemana at Strabane. On a rain-affected day, North County managed to compile a score of 165 despite Botha, Lawrence and Strydom all failing to score. Conor Armstrong (68), Ciarán Garry (20), Dara Armstrong (30) and Denver D'Cruz (20) were the heroes with the bat; Eddie Richardson took 3 wickets for 25 runs, and Donemana finished on 112 runs with 10.2 overs not used.

In 2009, it was the junior teams which brought honours to Inch, with the Second XI winning the Tillain Cup, and the Fifths the Junior C League. Analysis of the runs scored by the batsmen on the First XI showed a significant decline from the heady days of 2007, and Conor Armstrong (435), John Mooney (352), Brian Shields (278) and Ciaran Garry (207) were the only batsmen to score above 200 runs. Paul Mooney had emigrated to New Zealand; Reinhardt Strydom had transferred to YMCA; André Botha had played nine games during the season, and Seán O'Connor had only played four games.

Cricket Leinster re-structured the leagues in 2010, and from that point onwards, the leagues were numbered from 1 to 13 instead of the somewhat confusing Junior, Middle, Intermediate names. North County won the newly titled OCD1 (Open Competitions Division 1) League with a tremendous all-round effort. Six players, Conor Armstrong (275), Ritchie Lawrence (289), Ciarán

Garry (256), John Mooney (234), André Botha (205), and Tomás Shiel (204) scored more than 200 runs, and the wickets were taken by Eddie Richardson (35), Jimmy Boyland (34) and Ritchie Lawrence (13). In addition to the Senior League, North County won the Alan Murray Cup by beating Railway Union in the final. Railway batted first, and there were wickets for John Mooney (3 for 12) and Jimmy Boyland (3 for 22). North County reached the target for the loss of 4 wickets, and the main contributors were John Mooney (35), Botha (31) and C. Garry (20*). The third trophy to come to Inch was the Tillain Cup which the Second XI retained.

In 2011, North County and Merrion reached the final of the Leinster Senior Cup, but North County's preparations for the game were disrupted by several of its first-choice players being unavailable due to a combination of injuries and illness. Merrion won the toss and opted to bat first, and there were significant innings from Kade Beasley (44), Dom Joyce (66), John Anderson (46) and Tyrone Kane (66) to leave Merrion with a total of 272 for 7, which some critics deemed to be about 30 below par. In reply, Tomás Shiel was out early, but Greg Hay (89) and Conor Armstrong (59) brought the score up to 153 for 2. When Armstrong was out, Mooney (15) and Hay steadied things down, but Hay, Mooney and Coghlan were out very quickly, and North County's score was 195 for 5. Josh Reeves (29) and Eddie Richardson (34) brought the score up to 247 for 5, but then there was a flurry of wickets, to leave North County on 249 for 8. With Terry Richardson and Eddie Richardson at the crease, North County needed 21 off 3 overs. 11 runs were scored off 2 overs, and North County needed 10 runs to win. Eddie scored two runs, then missed one, then scored one run; Terry hit a four, and then a single to leave Eddie facing with two required. Eddie was clean bowled by Dom Joyce with the last ball of the game to leave Merrion the winners by one run.

The run of narrow defeats did not end with the Cup because North County lost out by 4% to Railway Union in the OCD1. Both teams had won nine games, but North County had played 1 game more than Railway and ended up with 5 defeats whereas Railway had only lost 4 games. North County's Fourth XI was the only team to win a trophy when it beat Dundrum by 5 wickets in the final of the Whelan Cup. Dundrum scored 132 for 5, and North County won by 5 wickets. D. Bertram took 4 wickets for 31 runs, and B. Smith (64) and R. White (32*) were the main contributors to North County's score.

Between 2013 and 2018, the only North County team to win a league title was the Fourth XI which won OC9, but during that period, there have been some wonderful individual performances and several home-produced cricketers have been introduced to senior cricket. The standout local cricketer in Leinster has been Eddie Richardson who has contributed a significant number of runs and wickets each season, with his best season being 2013 when he scored 816 runs and took 35 wickets to win the Samuels Cup for being the best all-rounder in Leinster Cricket. He retained the title in 2014 and won it again in 2017. Among the young cricketers who have played consistently for North County's First XI are Adam Coughlan, Ciarán Garry, Jonathan Andrews, Andrew Sheridan, Jamie Grassi and Niall McGovern.

North County's development since the club was founded is a testament to what can be achieved through a combination of vision and action. From its initial phase as the top Senior 2 team in the late 1980s through to its being granted senior status somewhat begrudgingly in 1990, the club has evolved into one of the best cricket clubs in Ireland. In the early 1990s, its main ambition was to avoid relegation, but from 1999 onwards through a combination of a visionary Executive and wonderful recruitment, the club's aspirations become appreciably more ambitious. The achievements on the field of play were matched by the development of ancillary facilities which are the envy of most clubs in Ireland. The availability of the Centre of Excellence has ensured that constant practice and top-class coaching are embedded into the club's ethos, and as a result, the club has produced a succession of International players at youth and senior level. The players have been backed by an able Executive and by passionate and knowledgeable members who travel far and wide in support of the teams. North County remains a quintessential Fingal League club, ultra-competitive on the field and very hospitable at the end of the games.

## Derek Plant

## Anthony Rooney

## Tom Armstrong

## Inch

## Inch

## Early Days

Tommy Mooney, Derek Plant, Mo Gaffney, Tom Fanning
North County Cricket Club 1999

## Derek Plant and Joe Murphy

## Centre of Excellence

Joe Curtis © 2001

John Andrews

John, Kit, and Paul Mooney

Tommy Mooney and Anthony Rooney

Gillian Barnett

Deirdre Murphy

Angela Mooney

Paula Hickey

Irish Senior Cup Winners, 2001

Paul Mooney, André Botha, Reinhardt Strydom

© Joe Curtis 2005

Michael Baxter· Colm Connell·Dean Moore·Dominic(Kag) Richardson·Stevie Dwyer·Stuart Costello
Tommy(Chink) Mooney·Garry(Gazz) McNamee·Ciaran Murphy·Shane Plant· Ian Bertram·David O Connor

# Chapter 18: Miscellaneous

Note: For practical reasons, it has not been possible to put captions on the photographs

© Joe Curtis 2006

Photo: Joe Curtis ©

Photo © 2013 Joe Curtis

© Joe Curtis 2017

Joe Curtis © 2015

Joe Curtis © 2006

Joe Curtis © 2015

Joe Curtis © 2015

Joe Curtis © 2015

Photo: Joe Curtis ©

Photo: Joe Curtis ©

491

*Figure 22, Joe Curtis presenting Photographic Archive to Cricket Leinster, photo taken by Margaret Curtis*

Printed in Great Britain
by Amazon